Table of Contents

Mercury Retrograde 2022

	DATE	ET	PT			DATE	ET	PT
Mercury Retrograde	1/14	**6:41 am**	3:41 am	—	Mercury Direct	2/3	**11:13 pm**	8:13 pm
Mercury Retrograde	5/10	**7:47 am**	4:47 am	—	Mercury Direct	6/3	**4:00 am**	1:00 am
Mercury Retrograde	9/9	**11:38 pm**	8:38 pm	—	Mercury Direct	10/2	**5:07 am**	2:07 am
Mercury Retrograde	12/29	**4:32 am**	1:32 pm	—	Mercury Direct	1/18/23	**8:12 am**	5:12 am

Moon Void-of-Course 2022

Times are listed in Eastern Time in this table only. All other information in the *Pocket Planner* is listed in both Eastern time and Pacific time. Refer to "Time Zone Conversions" on page 8 for changing to other time zones. Note: All times are corrected for Daylight Saving Time.

JANUARY

Last Aspect Date	Time	Moon Enters New Sign Date	Sign	Time
1	3:16 am	1	♑	6:02 pm
3	11:21 am	3	♒	5:44 pm
4	7:45 pm	5	♓	7:17 pm
7	5:23 pm	8	♈	12:26 am
10	2:23 am	10	♉	9:47 am
12	2:39 pm	12	♊	10:08 pm
14	9:22 pm	15	♋	11:11 am
17	6:48 pm	17	♌	11:03 pm
20	3:15 am	20	♍	9:02 am
22	2:46 pm	22	♎	5:03 pm
24	5:10 pm	24	♏	10:57 pm
27	12:28 am	27	♐	2:34 am
28	2:00 pm	29	♑	4:09 am
30	11:44 pm	31	♒	4:43 am

FEBRUARY

Last Aspect Date	Time	Moon Enters New Sign Date	Sign	Time
1	6:01 am	2	♓	6:00 am
4	4:41 am	4	♈	9:57 am
6	12:21 pm	6	♉	5:52 pm
8	11:48 pm	9	♊	5:27 am
11	3:23 am	11	♋	6:27 pm
14	5:27 am	14	♌	6:17 am
16	11:56 am	16	♍	3:42 pm
18	6:20 pm	18	♎	10:51 pm
21	12:02 am	21	♏	4:19 am
23	4:24 am	23	♐	8:29 am
24	10:24 pm	25	♑	11:27 am
27	9:49 am	27	♒	1:36 am
28	9:01 pm	3/1	♓	3:53 pm

MARCH

Last Aspect Date	Time	Moon Enters New Sign Date	Sign	Time
2/28	9:01 pm	1	♓	3:53 pm
3	4:45 pm	3	♈	7:52 pm
5	11:02 pm	6	♉	3:00 am
8	9:35 am	8	♊	1:40 pm
10	11:43 am	11	♋	2:24 am
13	11:44 am	13	♌	3:32 pm
15	6:56 am	16	♍	12:59 am
18	4:11 am	18	♎	7:26 am
20	8:40 am	20	♏	11:45 am
22	12:01 pm	22	♐	2:59 pm
24	8:59 am	24	♑	5:54 pm
26	7:51 pm	28	♒	8:55 pm
28	10:11 am	29	♓	12:32 am
31	2:37 am	31	♈	5:30 am

Moon Void-of-Course 2022 (cont.)

APRIL

Last Aspect Date	Time	Moon Enters New Sign Date	Sign	Time
2	9:51 am	2	♉	12:50 pm
4	9:53 pm	4	♊	11:04 pm
6	11:15 pm	7	♋	11:30 am
9	9:01 pm	10	♌	12:00 am
12	6:16 am	12	♍	10:07 am
14	2:11 pm	14	♎	4:46 pm
16	5:57 pm	16	♏	8:23 pm
18	7:55 pm	18	♐	10:16 pm
20	4:56 pm	20	♑	11:52 pm
22	11:53 pm	23	♒	2:17 am
24	8:33 pm	25	♓	6:15 am
27	9:36 am	27	♈	12:10 pm
29	5:38 pm	29	♉	8:19 pm

MAY

Last Aspect Date	Time	Moon Enters New Sign Date	Sign	Time
2	6:13 am	2	♊	6:47 am
4	4:37 pm	4	♋	7:05 pm
7	6:26 am	7	♌	7:50 am
9	8:39 am	9	♍	6:53 pm
12	12:00 am	12	♎	2:34 am
14	4:07 am	14	♏	6:34 am
16	5:28 am	16	♐	7:50 am
17	11:59 pm	18	♑	8:02 am
20	8:00 am	20	♒	8:53 am
22	3:19 am	22	♓	11:49 am
24	5:33 pm	24	♈	5:39 pm
26	11:20 pm	27	♉	2:22 am
29	10:11 am	29	♊	1:23 pm
31	4:10 pm	6/1	♋	1:49 am

JUNE

Last Aspect Date	Time	Moon Enters New Sign Date	Sign	Time
5/31	4:10 pm	1	♋	1:49 am
3	11:15 am	3	♌	2:38 pm
5	7:12 pm	6	♍	2:22 am
8	8:09 am	8	♎	11:23 am
10	1:36 pm	10	♏	4:41 pm
12	5:40 pm	12	♐	6:31 pm
14	10:58 am	14	♑	6:14 pm
16	2:41 pm	16	♒	5:44 pm
18	2:50 pm	18	♓	7:01 pm
20	11:11 pm	20	♈	11:37 pm
23	4:02 am	23	♉	7:58 am
25	3:02 pm	25	♊	7:13 pm
27	10:38 pm	28	♋	7:53 am
30	4:14 pm	30	♌	8:40 pm

JULY

Last Aspect Date	Time	Moon Enters New Sign Date	Sign	Time
3	5:59 am	3	♍	8:31 am
5	2:04 pm	5	♎	6:25 pm
7	9:04 pm	8	♏	1:15 am
10	12:34 am	10	♐	4:34 am
11	9:42 pm	12	♑	5:01 am
14	12:17 am	14	♒	4:13 am
16	12:36 am	16	♓	4:18 am
18	2:43 am	18	♈	7:17 am
20	10:19 am	20	♉	2:23 pm
22	7:45 pm	23	♊	1:11 am
25	4:14 am	25	♋	1:54 pm
27	8:54 pm	28	♌	2:36 am
30	12:29 am	30	♍	2:11 pm

AUGUST

Last Aspect Date	Time	Moon Enters New Sign Date	Sign	Time
1	6:29 pm	2	♎	12:06 am
4	2:20 am	4	♏	7:47 am
6	7:24 am	6	♐	12:39 pm
8	6:30 am	8	♑	2:39 pm
10	12:39 pm	10	♒	2:45 pm
12	7:07 am	12	♓	2:44 pm
14	11:11 am	14	♈	4:43 pm
16	4:18 pm	16	♉	10:22 pm
19	7:06 am	19	♊	8:06 am
21	6:06 pm	21	♋	8:29 pm
24	5:40 am	24	♌	9:09 am
26	2:55 am	26	♍	8:25 pm
28	11:08 pm	29	♎	5:45 am
31	6:43 am	31	♏	1:11 pm

SEPTEMBER

Last Aspect Date	Time	Moon Enters New Sign Date	Sign	Time
2	1:22 pm	2	♐	6:39 pm
4	9:51 pm	4	♑	10:03 pm
6	5:43 pm	6	♒	11:41 pm
8	8:34 am	9	♓	12:42 am
10	8:29 pm	11	♈	2:47 am
13	12:53 am	13	♉	7:39 am
15	8:59 am	15	♊	4:16 pm
17	5:52 pm	18	♋	3:59 am
20	11:57 am	20	♌	4:38 pm
22	7:07 am	23	♍	3:53 am
25	8:49 am	25	♎	12:43 pm
27	12:21 pm	27	♏	7:15 pm
29	5:20 pm	30	♐	12:03 am

OCTOBER

Last Aspect Date	Time	Moon Enters New Sign Date	Sign	Time
1	5:46 pm	2	♑	3:38 am
3	11:49 pm	4	♒	6:20 am
5	6:46 pm	6	♓	8:47 am
8	7:10 am	8	♈	11:57 am
10	10:02 am	10	♉	5:04 pm
12	5:42 pm	13	♊	1:08 am
15	12:11 am	15	♋	12:11 pm
17	4:56 pm	18	♌	12:45 am
20	6:35 am	20	♍	12:25 pm
22	2:17 pm	22	♎	9:24 pm
24	8:36 pm	25	♏	3:18 am
27	12:27 am	27	♐	6:55 am
29	9:10 am	29	♑	9:21 am
31	11:14 am	31	♒	11:43 am

NOVEMBER

Last Aspect Date	Time	Moon Enters New Sign Date	Sign	Time
2	7:08 am	2	♓	2:46 am
4	6:05 pm	4	♈	7:07 pm
6	5:30 pm	7	♉	12:15 am
9	7:00 am	9	♊	8:37 am
11	5:28 pm	11	♋	7:22 pm
14	5:41 am	14	♌	7:48 am
16	6:55 pm	16	♍	8:04 pm
19	3:47 am	19	♎	5:58 am
21	6:14 am	21	♏	12:16 pm
23	1:16 pm	23	♐	3:16 pm
25	2:22 pm	25	♑	4:18 pm
27	3:11 pm	27	♒	5:07 pm
29	1:53 am	29	♓	7:15 pm

DECEMBER

Last Aspect Date	Time	Moon Enters New Sign Date	Sign	Time
1	9:44 am	1	♈	11:41 pm
4	12:46 am	4	♉	6:38 am
6	2:02 pm	6	♊	3:49 pm
9	1:13 am	9	♋	2:49 am
11	1:49 pm	11	♌	3:09 pm
13	10:52 am	14	♍	3:45 am
16	2:13 pm	16	♎	2:49 pm
18	5:35 pm	18	♏	10:31 pm
20	9:45 pm	21	♐	2:12 am
22	3:16 pm	23	♑	2:49 am
24	10:11 pm	25	♒	2:14 am
26	1:19 pm	27	♓	2:34 am
29	1:21 am	29	♈	5:36 am
31	7:44 am	31	♉	12:08 pm

LLEWELLYN'S

2·0·2·2 ASTROLOGICAL POCKET PLANNER

Daily Ephemeris & Aspectarian

2021–2023

ISBN-13: 978-0-7387-6041-4

Cover design by Shannon McKuhen
Edited by Hanna Grimson

A special thanks to Beth Rosato for astrological proofreading.

Astrological calculations compiled and programmed by Rique Pottenger based on the earlier work of Neil F. Michelsen. Reuse is prohibited.

Published by
LLEWELLYN WORLDWIDE LTD.
2143 Wooddale Drive
Woodbury, MN 55125-2989
www.llewellyn.com

Printed in the United States of America

How to Use the *Pocket Planner*

by Leslie Nielsen

This handy guide contains information that can be most valuable to you as you plan your daily activities. As you read through the first few pages, you can start to get a feel for how well organized this guide is.

Read the Symbol Key on the next page, which is rather like astrological shorthand. The characteristics of the planets can give you direction in planning your strategies. Much like traffic signs that signal "go," "stop," or even "caution," you can determine for yourself the most propitious time to get things done.

You'll find tables that show the dates when Mercury is retrograde (℞) or direct (**D**). Because Mercury deals with the exchange of information, a retrograde Mercury makes miscommunication more noticeable.

There's also a section dedicated to the times when the Moon is void-of-course (V/C). These are generally poor times to conduct business because activities begun during these times usually end badly or fail to get started. If you make an appointment during a void-of-course, you might save yourself a lot of aggravation by confirming the time and date later. The Moon is only void-of-course for 7 percent of the time when business is usually conducted during a normal workday (that is, 8:00 am to 5:00 pm). Sometimes, by waiting a matter of minutes or a few hours until the Moon has left the void-of-course phase, you have a much better chance to make action move more smoothly. Moon voids can also be used successfully to do routine activities or inner work, such as dream therapy or personal contemplation.

You'll find Moon phases, as well as each of the Moon's entries into a new sign. Times are expressed in Eastern time (in bold type) and Pacific time (in regular type). The New Moon time is generally best for beginning new activities, as the Moon is increasing in light and can offer the element of growth to our endeavors. When the Moon is Full, its illumination is greatest and we can see the results of our efforts. When it moves from the Full stage back to the New stage, it can best be used to reflect on our projects. If necessary, we can make corrections at the New Moon.

The section of "Planetary Stations" on page 9 will give you the times when the planets are changing signs or direction, thereby affording us opportunities for new starts.

The ephemeris in the back of your *Pocket Planner* can be very helpful to you. As you start to work with the ephemeris, you may notice that not all planets seem to be comfortable in every sign. Think of the planets as actors and the signs as the costumes they wear. Sometimes, costumes just itch. If you find this to be so for a certain time period, you may choose to delay your plans for a time or be more creative with the energies at hand.

As you turn to the daily pages, you'll find information about the Moon's sign, phase, and the time it changes phase. You'll find icons indicating the best days to plant and fish. Also, you will find times and dates when the planets and asteroids change signs and go either retrograde or direct, major holidays, a three-month calendar, and room to record your appointments.

This guide is a powerful tool. Make the most of it!

Symbol Key

Planets:	☉	Sun	⚳	Ceres	♄	Saturn
	☽	Moon	⚴	Pallas	⚷	Chiron
	☿	Mercury	⚵	Juno	♅	Uranus
	♀	Venus	⚶	Vesta	♆	Neptune
	♂	Mars	♃	Jupiter	♇	Pluto
Signs:	♈	Aries	♌	Leo	♐	Sagittarius
	♉	Taurus	♍	Virgo	♑	Capricorn
	♊	Gemini	♎	Libra	♒	Aquarius
	♋	Cancer	♏	Scorpio	♓	Pisces
Aspects:	☌	Conjunction (0°)	⚺	Semisextile (30°)	⚹	Sextile (60°)
	□	Square (90°)	△	Trine (120°)		
	⚻	Quincunx (150°)	☍	Opposition (180°)		
Motion:	℞	Retrograde	D	Direct		

Best Days for Planting: **Best Days for Fishing:**

World Map of Time Zones

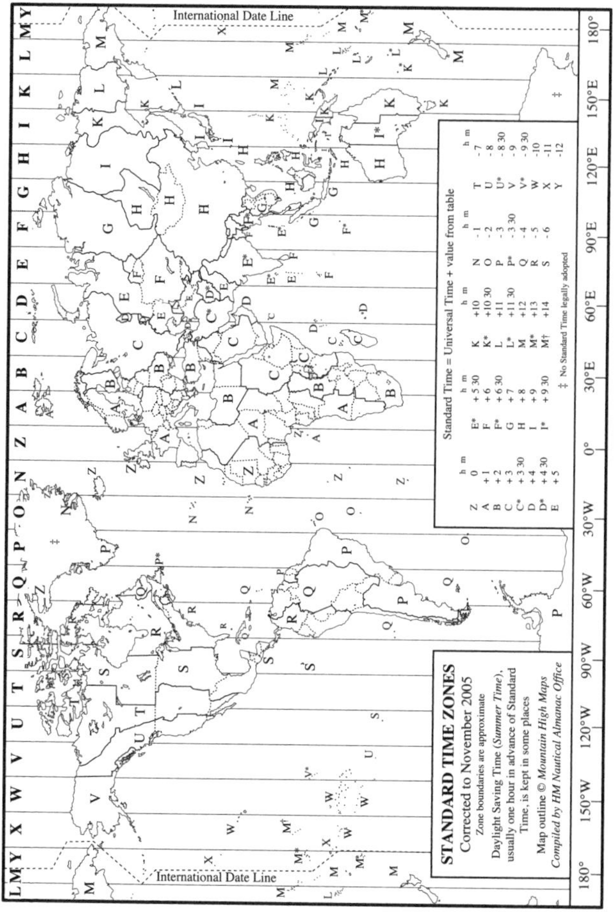

Time Zone Conversions

World Time Zones

Compared to Eastern Standard Time

( ) From Map
(S) CST/Subtract 1 hour
(R) EST
(Q) Add 1 hour
(P) Add 2 hours
(O) Add 3 hours
(N) Add 4 hours
(Z) Add 5 hours
(T) MST/Subtract 2 hours
(U) PST/Subtract 3 hours
(V) Subtract 4 hours
(W) Subtract 5 hours
(X) Subtract 6 hours
(Y) Subtract 7 hours
(A) Add 6 hours
(B) Add 7 hours
(C) Add 8 hours
(D) Add 9 hours
(E) Add 10 hours
(F) Add 11 hours
(G) Add 12 hours
(H) Add 13 hours
(I) Add 14 hours
(K) Add 15 hours
(L) Add 16 hours
(M) Add 17 hours
(C*) Add 8.5 hours
(D*) Add 9.5 hours
(E*) Add 10.5 hours
(F*) Add 11.5 hours
(I*) Add 14.5 hours
(K*) Add 15.5 hours
(L*) Add 16.5 hours
(M*) Add 18 hours
(P*) Add 2.5 hours
(U*) Subtract 3.5 hours
(V*) Subtract 4.5 hours

World Map of Time Zones is supplied by HM Nautical Almanac Office © Center for the Central Laboratory of the Research Councils. Note: This is not an official map. Countries change their time zones as they wish.

Planetary Stations for 2022

	JAN	FEB	MAR	APR	MAY	JUN	JUL	AUG	SEP	OCT	NOV	DEC
☿	1/14–2/3				5/10–6/3				9/9–10/2			12/29–
♀	–1/29											
♂											10/30–1/12/23	
♃									7/28–11/23			
♄								6/4–10/23				
♅	–1/18									8/19–1/18/22		
♆									6/28–12/3			
♇							4/29–10/8					
⚷									7/19–12/19			
⚳	–1/14											
⚴											11/30–2/16	
⚵									7/25–10/23			
⚶								7/7–10/5				

27 Monday

4th ♎

28 Tuesday

4th ♎

☽ v/c	**4:11 pm**	1:11 pm
☽ enters ♏	**4:16 pm**	1:16 pm
♃ enters ♓	**11:09 pm**	8:09 pm

29 Wednesday

4th ♏

30 Thursday

4th ♏

☽ v/c	**12:10 pm**	9:10 am
☽ enters ♐	**6:08 pm**	3:08 pm

Eastern time in bold type
Pacific time in medium type

31 Friday

4th ♐

New Year's Eve

1 Saturday

4th ♐

☽ v/c	**3:16 am**	12:16 am
☽ enters ♑	**6:02 pm**	3:02 pm
☿ enters ♒		11:10 pm

New Year's Day • Kwanzaa ends

2 Sunday

4th ♑

☿ enters ♒	**2:10 am**	
New Moon	**1:33 pm**	10:33 am

December 2021

S	M	T	W	T	F	S
			1	2	3	4
5	6	7	8	9	10	11
12	13	14	15	16	17	18
19	20	21	22	23	24	25
26	27	28	29	30	31	

January 2022

S	M	T	W	T	F	S
						1
2	3	4	5	6	7	8
9	10	11	12	13	14	15
16	17	18	19	20	21	22
23	24	25	26	27	28	29
30	31					

February 2022

S	M	T	W	T	F	S
		1	2	3	4	5
6	7	8	9	10	11	12
13	14	15	16	17	18	19
20	21	22	23	24	25	26
27	28					

Eastern time in bold type
Pacific time in medium type

3 Monday

1st ♑
☽ v/c **11:21 am** 8:21 am
☽ enters ♒ **5:44 pm** 2:44 pm

4 Tuesday

1st ♒
☽ v/c **7:45 pm** 4:45 pm

5 Wednesday

1st ♒
☽ enters ♓ **7:17 pm** 4:17 pm

6 Thursday

1st ♓

Eastern time in bold type
Pacific time in medium type

7 Friday

1st ♓

☽ v/c	**5:23 pm**	2:23 pm
☽ enters ♈		9:26 pm

8 Saturday

1st ♓

☽ enters ♈ **12:26 am**

9 Sunday

1st ♈

2nd Quarter	**1:11 pm**	10:11 am
☽ v/c		11:23 pm

December 2021

S	M	T	W	T	F	S
			1	2	3	4
5	6	7	8	9	10	11
12	13	14	15	16	17	18
19	20	21	22	23	24	25
26	27	28	29	30	31	

January 2022

S	M	T	W	T	F	S
						1
2	3	4	5	6	7	8
9	10	11	12	13	14	15
16	17	18	19	20	21	22
23	24	25	26	27	28	29
30	31					

February 2022

S	M	T	W	T	F	S
		1	2	3	4	5
6	7	8	9	10	11	12
13	14	15	16	17	18	19
20	21	22	23	24	25	26
27	28					

Eastern time in bold type
Pacific time in medium type

10 Monday

2nd ♈

☽ v/c	**2:23 am**	
☽ enters ♉	**9:47 am**	6:47 am
⚶ enters ♑		9:19 pm

11 Tuesday

2nd ♉

⚶ enters ♑ **12:19 am**

12 Wednesday

2nd ♉

☽ v/c	**2:39 pm**	11:39 am
☽ enters ♊	**10:08 pm**	7:08 pm

13 Thursday

2nd ♊

Eastern time in bold type
Pacific time in medium type

14 Friday

2nd ♊

☿ ℞	**6:41 am**	3:41 am
⚳ D	**4:20 pm**	1:20 pm
☽ v/c	**9:22 pm**	6:22 pm

Mercury retrograde until 2/3

15 Saturday

2nd ♊

☽ enters ♋	**11:11 am**	8:11 am

16 Sunday

2nd ♋

December 2021

S	M	T	W	T	F	S
			1	2	3	4
5	6	7	8	9	10	11
12	13	14	15	16	17	18
19	20	21	22	23	24	25
26	27	28	29	30	31	

January 2022

S	M	T	W	T	F	S
						1
2	3	4	5	6	7	8
9	10	11	12	13	14	15
16	17	18	19	20	21	22
23	24	25	26	27	28	29
30	31					

February 2022

S	M	T	W	T	F	S
		1	2	3	4	5
6	7	8	9	10	11	12
13	14	15	16	17	18	19
20	21	22	23	24	25	26
27	28					

Eastern time in bold type
Pacific time in medium type

17 Monday

2nd ♋

☽ v/c	**6:48 pm**	3:48 pm
Full Moon	**6:48 pm**	3:48 pm
☽ enters ♌	**11:03 pm**	8:03 pm

Martin Luther King Jr. Day

18 Tuesday

3rd ♌

♅ D	**10:27 am**	7:27 am

19 Wednesday

3rd ♌

☉ enters ♒	**9:39 pm**	6:39 pm

Sun enters Aquarius

20 Thursday

3rd ♌

☽ v/c	**3:15 am**	12:15 am
☽ enters ♍	**9:02 am**	6:02 am

Eastern time in bold type
Pacific time in medium type

21 Friday
3rd ♍

22 Saturday
3rd ♍
☽ v/c **2:46 pm** 11:46 am
☽ enters ♎ **5:03 pm** 2:03 pm

23 Sunday
3rd ♎

December 2021

S	M	T	W	T	F	S
			1	2	3	4
5	6	7	8	9	10	11
12	13	14	15	16	17	18
19	20	21	22	23	24	25
26	27	28	29	30	31	

January 2022

S	M	T	W	T	F	S
						1
2	3	4	5	6	7	8
9	10	11	12	13	14	15
16	17	18	19	20	21	22
23	24	25	26	27	28	29
30	31					

February 2022

S	M	T	W	T	F	S
		1	2	3	4	5
6	7	8	9	10	11	12
13	14	15	16	17	18	19
20	21	22	23	24	25	26
27	28					

24 Monday

3rd ♎

♂ enters ♑	**7:53 am**	4:53 am
☽ v/c	**5:10 pm**	2:10 pm
☽ enters ♏	**10:57 pm**	7:57 pm

25 Tuesday

3rd ♏

4th Quarter	**8:41 am**	5:41 am
☿ enters ♑	**10:05 pm**	7:05 pm

26 Wednesday

4th ♏

☽ v/c		9:28 pm
☽ enters ♐		11:34 pm

27 Thursday

4th ♏

☽ v/c	**12:28 am**
☽ enters ♐	**2:34 am**

Eastern time in bold type
Pacific time in medium type

28 Friday

4th ♐

☽ v/c **2:00 pm** 11:00 am

29 Saturday

4th ♐

♀ D **3:46 am** 12:46 am

☽ enters ♑ **4:09 am** 1:09 am

30 Sunday

4th ♑

☽ v/c **11:44 pm** 8:44 pm

December 2021

S	M	T	W	T	F	S
			1	2	3	4
5	6	7	8	9	10	11
12	13	14	15	16	17	18
19	20	21	22	23	24	25
26	27	28	29	30	31	

January 2022

S	M	T	W	T	F	S
						1
2	3	4	5	6	7	8
9	10	11	12	13	14	15
16	17	18	19	20	21	22
23	24	25	26	27	28	29
30	31					

February 2022

S	M	T	W	T	F	S
		1	2	3	4	5
6	7	8	9	10	11	12
13	14	15	16	17	18	19
20	21	22	23	24	25	26
27	28					

31 Monday

4th ♑
☽ enters ♒ **4:43 am** 1:43 am
New Moon 9:46 pm

1 Tuesday

4th ♒
New Moon **12:46 am**
☽ v/c **6:01 am** 3:01 am
⚵ enters ♒ **6:04 pm** 3:04 pm

Lunar New Year (Tiger)

2 Wednesday

1st ♒
☽ enters ♓ **6:00 am** 3:00 am

Imbolc • Groundhog Day

3 Thursday

1st ♓
☿ D **11:13 pm** 8:13 pm

Eastern time in bold type
Pacific time in medium type

4 Friday

1st ♓
☽ v/c **4:41 am** 1:41 am
☽ enters ♈ **9:57 am** 6:57 am

5 Saturday

1st ♈

6 Sunday

1st ♈
☽ v/c **12:21 pm** 9:21 am
☽ enters ♉ **5:52 pm** 2:52 pm

January 2022

S	M	T	W	T	F	S
						1
2	3	4	5	6	7	8
9	10	11	12	13	14	15
16	17	18	19	20	21	22
23	24	25	26	27	28	29
30	31					

February 2022

S	M	T	W	T	F	S
		1	2	3	4	5
6	7	8	9	10	11	12
13	14	15	16	17	18	19
20	21	22	23	24	25	26
27	28					

March 2022

S	M	T	W	T	F	S
		1	2	3	4	5
6	7	8	9	10	11	12
13	14	15	16	17	18	19
20	21	22	23	24	25	26
27	28	29	30	31		

Eastern time in bold type
Pacific time in medium type

7 Monday
1st ♉

8 Tuesday
1st ♉

2nd Quarter	**8:50 am**	5:50 am
⚳ enters ♊	**9:13 pm**	6:13 pm
☽ v/c	**11:48 pm**	8:48 pm

9 Wednesday
2nd ♉

☽ enters ♊	**5:27 am**	2:27 am

10 Thursday
2nd ♊

Eastern time in bold type
Pacific time in medium type

11 Friday

2nd ♊
☽ v/c **3:23 am** 12:23 am
☽ enters ♋ **6:27 pm** 3:27 pm

12 Saturday

2nd ♋

13 Sunday

2nd ♋
♀ enters ♈ 9:53 pm

January 2022

S	M	T	W	T	F	S
						1
2	3	4	5	6	7	8
9	10	11	12	13	14	15
16	17	18	19	20	21	22
23	24	25	26	27	28	29
30	31					

February 2022

S	M	T	W	T	F	S
		1	2	3	4	5
6	7	8	9	10	11	12
13	14	15	16	17	18	19
20	21	22	23	24	25	26
27	28					

March 2022

S	M	T	W	T	F	S
		1	2	3	4	5
6	7	8	9	10	11	12
13	14	15	16	17	18	19
20	21	22	23	24	25	26
27	28	29	30	31		

Eastern time in bold type
Pacific time in medium type

14 Monday

2nd ♋

⚴ enters ♈	**12:53 am**	
☽ v/c	**5:27 am**	2:27 am
☽ enters ♌	**6:17 am**	3:17 am
☿ enters ♒	**4:54 pm**	1:54 pm

Valentine's Day

15 Tuesday

2nd ♌

16 Wednesday

2nd ♌

☽ v/c	**11:56 am**	8:56 am
Full Moon	**11:56 am**	8:56 am
☽ enters ♍	**3:42 pm**	12:42 pm

17 Thursday

3rd ♍

Eastern time in bold type
Pacific time in medium type

18 Friday

3rd ♍

☉ enters ♓	**11:43 am**	8:43 am
☽ v/c	**6:20 pm**	3:20 pm
☽ enters ♎	**10:51 pm**	7:51 pm

Sun enters Pisces

19 Saturday

3rd ♎

20 Sunday

3rd ♎

☽ v/c		9:02 pm

January 2022

S	M	T	W	T	F	S
						1
2	3	4	5	6	7	8
9	10	11	12	13	14	15
16	17	18	19	20	21	22
23	24	25	26	27	28	29
30	31					

February 2022

S	M	T	W	T	F	S
		1	2	3	4	5
6	7	8	9	10	11	12
13	14	15	16	17	18	19
20	21	22	23	24	25	26
27	28					

March 2022

S	M	T	W	T	F	S
		1	2	3	4	5
6	7	8	9	10	11	12
13	14	15	16	17	18	19
20	21	22	23	24	25	26
27	28	29	30	31		

Eastern time in bold type
Pacific time in medium type

21 Monday

3rd ♎

☽ v/c **12:02 am**

☽ enters ♏ **4:19 am** 1:19 am

Presidents' Day

22 Tuesday

3rd ♏

23 Wednesday

3rd ♏

☽ v/c **4:24 am** 1:24 am

☽ enters ♐ **8:29 am** 5:29 am

4th Quarter **5:32 pm** 2:32 pm

24 Thursday

4th ♐

☽ v/c **10:24 pm** 7:24 pm

Eastern time in bold type
Pacific time in medium type

25 Friday

4th ♐

☽ enters ♑ **11:27 am** 8:27 am

26 Saturday

4th ♑

27 Sunday

4th ♑

☽ v/c **9:49 am** 6:49 am

☽ enters ♒ **1:36 pm** 10:36 am

January 2022

S	M	T	W	T	F	S
						1
2	3	4	5	6	7	8
9	10	11	12	13	14	15
16	17	18	19	20	21	22
23	24	25	26	27	28	29
30	31					

February 2022

S	M	T	W	T	F	S
		1	2	3	4	5
6	7	8	9	10	11	12
13	14	15	16	17	18	19
20	21	22	23	24	25	26
27	28					

March 2022

S	M	T	W	T	F	S
		1	2	3	4	5
6	7	8	9	10	11	12
13	14	15	16	17	18	19
20	21	22	23	24	25	26
27	28	29	30	31		

28 Monday

4th ♒
☽ v/c **9:01 pm** 6:01 pm

1 Tuesday

4th ♒
☽ enters ♓ **3:53 pm** 12:53 pm

Mardi Gras (Fat Tuesday)

2 Wednesday

4th ♓
New Moon **12:35 pm** 9:35 am

Ash Wednesday

3 Thursday

1st ♓
☽ v/c **4:45 pm** 1:45 pm
☽ enters ♈ **7:52 pm** 4:52 pm

Eastern time in bold type
Pacific time in medium type

4 Friday
1st ♈

5 Saturday
1st ♈

☽ v/c	**11:02 pm**	8:02 pm
♂ enters ♒		10:23 pm
♀ enters ♒		10:30 pm

6 Sunday
1st ♈

♂ enters ♒	**1:23 am**	
♀ enters ♒	**1:30 am**	
☽ enters ♉	**3:00 am**	12:00 am

February 2022

S	M	T	W	T	F	S
		1	2	3	4	5
6	7	8	9	10	11	12
13	14	15	16	17	18	19
20	21	22	23	24	25	26
27	28					

March 2022

S	M	T	W	T	F	S
		1	2	3	4	5
6	7	8	9	10	11	12
13	14	15	16	17	18	19
20	21	22	23	24	25	26
27	28	29	30	31		

April 2022

S	M	T	W	T	F	S
					1	2
3	4	5	6	7	8	9
10	11	12	13	14	15	16
17	18	19	20	21	22	23
24	25	26	27	28	29	30

Eastern time in bold type
Pacific time in medium type

7 Monday

1st ♉

8 Tuesday

1st ♉

☽ v/c **9:35 am** 6:35 am

☽ enters ♊ **1:40 pm** 10:40 am

9 Wednesday

1st ♊

☿ enters ♓ **8:32 pm** 5:32 pm

10 Thursday

1st ♊

2nd Quarter **5:45 am** 2:45 am

☽ v/c **11:43 am** 8:43 am

⚶ enters ♒ **1:22 pm** 10:22 am

☽ enters ♋ 11:24 pm

Eastern time in bold type
Pacific time in medium type

11 Friday
2nd ♊
☽ enters ♋ **2:24 am**

12 Saturday
2nd ♋

13 Sunday
2nd ♋
☽ v/c **11:44 am** 8:44 am
☽ enters ♌ **3:32 pm** 12:32 pm

Daylight Saving Time begins at 2 am

February 2022

S	M	T	W	T	F	S
		1	2	3	4	5
6	7	8	9	10	11	12
13	14	15	16	17	18	19
20	21	22	23	24	25	26
27	28					

March 2022

S	M	T	W	T	F	S
		1	2	3	4	5
6	7	8	9	10	11	12
13	14	15	16	17	18	19
20	21	22	23	24	25	26
27	28	29	30	31		

April 2022

S	M	T	W	T	F	S
					1	2
3	4	5	6	7	8	9
10	11	12	13	14	15	16
17	18	19	20	21	22	23
24	25	26	27	28	29	30

Eastern time in bold type
Pacific time in medium type

14 Monday

2nd ♌

15 Tuesday

2nd ♌

☽ v/c **6:56 am** 3:56 am

☽ enters ♍ 9:59 pm

16 Wednesday

2nd ♌

☽ enters ♍ **12:59 am**

Purim begins at sundown

17 Thursday

2nd ♍

St. Patrick's Day

Eastern time in bold type

Pacific time in medium type

18 Friday

2nd ♍

Full Moon	**3:18 am**	12:18 am
☽ v/c	**4:11 am**	1:11 am
☽ enters ♎	**7:26 am**	4:26 am

19 Saturday

3rd ♎

20 Sunday

3rd ♎

☽ v/c	**8:40 am**	5:40 am
☉ enters ♈	**11:33 am**	8:33 am
☽ enters ♏	**11:45 am**	8:45 am

Int'l Astrology Day

Sun enters Aries • Ostara • Spring Equinox • 11:33 am EDT/8:33 am PDT

February 2022

S	M	T	W	T	F	S
		1	2	3	4	5
6	7	8	9	10	11	12
13	14	15	16	17	18	19
20	21	22	23	24	25	26
27	28					

March 2022

S	M	T	W	T	F	S
		1	2	3	4	5
6	7	8	9	10	11	12
13	14	15	16	17	18	19
20	21	22	23	24	25	26
27	28	29	30	31		

April 2022

S	M	T	W	T	F	S
					1	2
3	4	5	6	7	8	9
10	11	12	13	14	15	16
17	18	19	20	21	22	23
24	25	26	27	28	29	30

21 Monday
3rd ♏

22 Tuesday
3rd ♏
☽ v/c **12:01 pm** 9:01 am
☽ enters ♐ **2:59 pm** 11:59 am

23 Wednesday
3rd ♐

24 Thursday
3rd ♐
☽ v/c **8:59 am** 5:59 am
☽ enters ♑ **5:54 pm** 2:54 pm
4th Quarter 10:37 pm

Eastern time in bold type
Pacific time in medium type

25 Friday

3rd ♑
4th Quarter **1:37 am**

26 Saturday

4th ♑
☽ v/c **7:51 pm** 4:51 pm
☽ enters ♒ **8:55 pm** 5:55 pm

27 Sunday

4th ♒
☿ enters ♈ **3:44 am** 12:44 am

February 2022

S	M	T	W	T	F	S
		1	2	3	4	5
6	7	8	9	10	11	12
13	14	15	16	17	18	19
20	21	22	23	24	25	26
27	28					

March 2022

S	M	T	W	T	F	S
		1	2	3	4	5
6	7	8	9	10	11	12
13	14	15	16	17	18	19
20	21	22	23	24	25	26
27	28	29	30	31		

April 2022

S	M	T	W	T	F	S
					1	2
3	4	5	6	7	8	9
10	11	12	13	14	15	16
17	18	19	20	21	22	23
24	25	26	27	28	29	30

Eastern time in bold type
Pacific time in medium type

28 Monday

4th ♒
☽ v/c **10:11 am** 7:11 am
☽ enters ♓ 9:32 pm

29 Tuesday

4th ♒
☽ enters ♓ **12:32 am**

30 Wednesday

4th ♓
☽ v/c 11:37 pm

31 Thursday

4th ♓
☽ v/c **2:37 am**
☽ enters ♈ **5:30 am** 2:30 am
New Moon 11:24 pm

Eastern time in bold type
Pacific time in medium type

1 Friday

4th ♈

New Moon **2:24 am**

April Fools' Day (All Fools' Day—Pagan)

2 Saturday

1st ♈

☽ v/c	**9:51 am**	6:51 am
☽ enters ♉	**12:50 pm**	9:50 am

Ramadan begins at sundown

3 Sunday

1st ♉

March 2022

S	M	T	W	T	F	S
		1	2	3	4	5
6	7	8	9	10	11	12
13	14	15	16	17	18	19
20	21	22	23	24	25	26
27	28	29	30	31		

April 2022

S	M	T	W	T	F	S
					1	2
3	4	5	6	7	8	9
10	11	12	13	14	15	16
17	18	19	20	21	22	23
24	25	26	27	28	29	30

May 2022

S	M	T	W	T	F	S
1	2	3	4	5	6	7
8	9	10	11	12	13	14
15	16	17	18	19	20	21
22	23	24	25	26	27	28
29	30	31				

4 Monday

1st ♉

☽ v/c **9:53 pm** 6:53 pm

☽ enters ♊ **11:04 pm** 8:04 pm

5 Tuesday

1st ♊

♀ enters ♓ **11:18 am** 8:18 am

6 Wednesday

1st ♊

☽ v/c **11:15 pm** 8:15 pm

7 Thursday

1st ♊

☽ enters ♋ **11:30 am** 8:30 am

Eastern time in bold type

Pacific time in medium type

8 Friday

1st ♋
2nd Quarter 11:48 pm

9 Saturday

1st ♋
2nd Quarter **2:48 am**
☽ v/c **9:01 pm** 6:01 pm
☽ enters ♌ 9:00 pm

10 Sunday

2nd ♌
☽ enters ♌ **12:00 am**
☿ enters ♉ **10:09 pm** 7:09 pm

Palm Sunday

March 2022

S	M	T	W	T	F	S
		1	2	3	4	5
6	7	8	9	10	11	12
13	14	15	16	17	18	19
20	21	22	23	24	25	26
27	28	29	30	31		

April 2022

S	M	T	W	T	F	S
					1	2
3	4	5	6	7	8	9
10	11	12	13	14	15	16
17	18	19	20	21	22	23
24	25	26	27	28	29	30

May 2022

S	M	T	W	T	F	S
1	2	3	4	5	6	7
8	9	10	11	12	13	14
15	16	17	18	19	20	21
22	23	24	25	26	27	28
29	30	31				

11 Monday

2nd ♌

12 Tuesday

2nd ♌

☽ v/c	**6:16 am**	3:16 am
☽ enters ♍	**10:07 am**	7:07 am

13 Wednesday

2nd ♍

14 Thursday

2nd ♍

☽ v/c	**2:11 pm**	11:11 am
☽ enters ♎	**4:46 pm**	1:46 pm
♂ enters ♓	**11:06 pm**	8:06 pm

Eastern time in bold type
Pacific time in medium type

15 Friday

2nd ♎

Good Friday • Passover begins at sundown

16 Saturday

2nd ♎

Full Moon	**2:55 pm**	11:55 am
☽ v/c	**5:57 pm**	2:57 pm
☽ enters ♏	**8:23 pm**	5:23 pm

17 Sunday

3rd ♏

Easter

March 2022

S	M	T	W	T	F	S
		1	2	3	4	5
6	7	8	9	10	11	12
13	14	15	16	17	18	19
20	21	22	23	24	25	26
27	28	29	30	31		

April 2022

S	M	T	W	T	F	S
					1	2
3	4	5	6	7	8	9
10	11	12	13	14	15	16
17	18	19	20	21	22	23
24	25	26	27	28	29	30

May 2022

S	M	T	W	T	F	S
1	2	3	4	5	6	7
8	9	10	11	12	13	14
15	16	17	18	19	20	21
22	23	24	25	26	27	28
29	30	31				

18 Monday

3rd ♏

☽ v/c **7:55 pm** 4:55 pm

☽ enters ♐ **10:16 pm** 7:16 pm

19 Tuesday

3rd ♐

☉ enters ♉ **10:24 pm** 7:24 pm

Sun enters Taurus

20 Wednesday

3rd ♐

⚵ enters ♓ **11:51 am** 8:51 am

☽ v/c **4:56 pm** 1:56 pm

☽ enters ♑ **11:52 pm** 8:52 pm

21 Thursday

3rd ♑

Eastern time in bold type
Pacific time in medium type

22 Friday

3rd ♑

☽ v/c	**11:53 pm**	8:53 pm
☽ enters ♒		11:17 pm

Earth Day • Orthodox Good Friday

23 Saturday

3rd ♑

☽ enters ♒	**2:17 am**	
4th Quarter	**7:56 am**	4:56 am

Passover ends

24 Sunday

4th ♒

☽ v/c	**8:33 pm**	5:33 pm

Orthodox Easter

March 2022

S	M	T	W	T	F	S
		1	2	3	4	5
6	7	8	9	10	11	12
13	14	15	16	17	18	19
20	21	22	23	24	25	26
27	28	29	30	31		

April 2022

S	M	T	W	T	F	S
					1	2
3	4	5	6	7	8	9
10	11	12	13	14	15	16
17	18	19	20	21	22	23
24	25	26	27	28	29	30

May 2022

S	M	T	W	T	F	S
1	2	3	4	5	6	7
8	9	10	11	12	13	14
15	16	17	18	19	20	21
22	23	24	25	26	27	28
29	30	31				

25 Monday

4th ♒
☽ enters ♓ **6:15 am** 3:15 am

26 Tuesday

4th ♓

27 Wednesday

4th ♓
☽ v/c **9:36 am** 6:36 am
☽ enters ♈ **12:10 pm** 9:10 am

28 Thursday

4th ♈

Eastern time in bold type
Pacific time in medium type

29 Friday

4th ♈

♇ ℞	**2:38 pm**	11:38 am
☽ v/c	**5:38 pm**	2:38 pm
☿ enters ♊	**6:23 pm**	3:23 pm
☽ enters ♉	**8:19 pm**	5:19 pm

30 Saturday

4th ♉

♀ enters ♉	**4:50 am**	1:50 am
New Moon	**4:28 pm**	1:28 pm

Solar Eclipse 10° ♉ 28'

1 Sunday

1st ♉

Beltane • Ramadan ends

April 2022

S	M	T	W	T	F	S
					1	2
3	4	5	6	7	8	9
10	11	12	13	14	15	16
17	18	19	20	21	22	23
24	25	26	27	28	29	30

May 2022

S	M	T	W	T	F	S
1	2	3	4	5	6	7
8	9	10	11	12	13	14
15	16	17	18	19	20	21
22	23	24	25	26	27	28
29	30	31				

June 2022

S	M	T	W	T	F	S
			1	2	3	4
5	6	7	8	9	10	11
12	13	14	15	16	17	18
19	20	21	22	23	2	25
26	27	28	29	30		

Eastern time in bold type
Pacific time in medium type

2 Monday

1st ♉

☽ v/c	**6:13 am**	3:13 am
☽ enters ♊	**6:47 am**	3:47 am
♀ enters ♈	**12:10 pm**	9:10 am

3 Tuesday

1st ♊

4 Wednesday

1st ♊

☽ v/c	**4:37 pm**	1:37 pm
☽ enters ♋	**7:05 pm**	4:05 pm

5 Thursday

1st ♋

Cinco de Mayo

Eastern time in bold type
Pacific time in medium type

6 Friday
1st ♋

7 Saturday
1st ♋

☽ v/c	**6:26 am**	3:26 am
☽ enters ♌	**7:50 am**	4:50 am

8 Sunday
1st ♌

2nd Quarter	**8:21 pm**	5:21 pm

Mother's Day

April 2022

S	M	T	W	T	F	S
					1	2
3	4	5	6	7	8	9
10	11	12	13	14	15	16
17	18	19	20	21	22	23
24	25	26	27	28	29	30

May 2022

S	M	T	W	T	F	S
1	2	3	4	5	6	7
8	9	10	11	12	13	14
15	16	17	18	19	20	21
22	23	24	25	26	27	28
29	30	31				

June 2022

S	M	T	W	T	F	S
			1	2	3	4
5	6	7	8	9	10	11
12	13	14	15	16	17	18
19	20	21	22	23	2	25
26	27	28	29	30		

Eastern time in bold type
Pacific time in medium type

9 Monday

2nd ♌

☽ v/c	**8:39 am**	5:39 am
☽ enters ♍	**6:53 pm**	3:53 pm

10 Tuesday

2nd ♍

☿ ℞	**7:47 am**	4:47 am
♃ enters ♈	**7:22 pm**	4:22 pm

Mercury retrograde until 6/3

11 Wednesday

2nd ♍

☽ v/c		9:00 pm
☽ enters ♎		11:34 pm

12 Thursday

2nd ♍

☽ v/c	**12:00 am**	
☽ enters ♎	**2:34 am**	

Eastern time in bold type
Pacific time in medium type

13 Friday
2nd ♎

14 Saturday
2nd ♎

☽ v/c	**4:07 am**	1:07 am
☽ enters ♏	**6:34 am**	3:34 am

15 Sunday
2nd ♏

⚳ enters ♋	**3:11 am**	12:11 am
Full Moon		9:14 pm

April 2022

S	M	T	W	T	F	S
					1	2
3	4	5	6	7	8	9
10	11	12	13	14	15	16
17	18	19	20	21	22	23
24	25	26	27	28	29	30

May 2022

S	M	T	W	T	F	S
1	2	3	4	5	6	7
8	9	10	11	12	13	14
15	16	17	18	19	20	21
22	23	24	25	26	27	28
29	30	31				

June 2022

S	M	T	W	T	F	S
			1	2	3	4
5	6	7	8	9	10	11
12	13	14	15	16	17	18
19	20	21	22	23	2	25
26	27	28	29	30		

16 Monday

2nd ♏

Full Moon	**12:14 am**	
☽ v/c	**5:28 am**	2:28 am
☽ enters ♐	**7:50 am**	4:50 am

Lunar Eclipse 25° ♏ 18'

17 Tuesday

3rd ♐

☽ v/c	**11:59 pm**	8:59 pm

18 Wednesday

3rd ♐

☽ enters ♑	**8:02 am**	5:02 am

19 Thursday

3rd ♑

Eastern time in bold type
Pacific time in medium type

20 Friday

3rd ♑

☽ v/c	**8:00 am**	5:00 am
☽ enters ♒	**8:53 am**	5:53 am
☉ enters ♊	**9:23 pm**	6:23 pm

Sun enters Gemini

21 Saturday

3rd ♒

22 Sunday

3rd ♒

☽ v/c	**3:19 am**	12:19 am
☽ enters ♓	**11:49 am**	8:49 am
4th Quarter	**2:43 pm**	11:43 am
☿ enters ♉	**9:15 pm**	6:15 pm

April 2022

S	M	T	W	T	F	S
					1	2
3	4	5	6	7	8	9
10	11	12	13	14	15	16
17	18	19	20	21	22	23
24	25	26	27	28	29	30

May 2022

S	M	T	W	T	F	S
1	2	3	4	5	6	7
8	9	10	11	12	13	14
15	16	17	18	19	20	21
22	23	24	25	26	27	28
29	30	31				

June 2022

S	M	T	W	T	F	S
			1	2	3	4
5	6	7	8	9	10	11
12	13	14	15	16	17	18
19	20	21	22	23	2	25
26	27	28	29	30		

23 Monday
4th ♓

24 Tuesday
4th ♓

⚶ enters ♓	**5:46 am**	2:46 am
☽ v/c	**5:33 pm**	2:33 pm
☽ enters ♈	**5:39 pm**	2:39 pm
♂ enters ♈	**7:17 pm**	4:17 pm

25 Wednesday
4th ♈

26 Thursday
4th ♈

☽ v/c	**11:20 pm**	8:20 pm
☽ enters ♉		11:22 pm

Eastern time in bold type
Pacific time in medium type

27 Friday

4th ♈
☽ enters ♉ **2:22 am**

28 Saturday

4th ♉
♀ enters ♉ **10:46 am** 7:46 am

29 Sunday

4th ♉
☽ v/c **10:11 am** 7:11 am
☽ enters ♊ **1:23 pm** 10:23 am

April 2022

S	M	T	W	T	F	S
					1	2
3	4	5	6	7	8	9
10	11	12	13	14	15	16
17	18	19	20	21	22	23
24	25	26	27	28	29	30

May 2022

S	M	T	W	T	F	S
1	2	3	4	5	6	7
8	9	10	11	12	13	14
15	16	17	18	19	20	21
22	23	24	25	26	27	28
29	30	31				

June 2022

S	M	T	W	T	F	S
			1	2	3	4
5	6	7	8	9	10	11
12	13	14	15	16	17	18
19	20	21	22	23	2	25
26	27	28	29	30		

Eastern time in bold type
Pacific time in medium type

30 Monday

4th ♊

New Moon **7:30 am** 4:30 am

Memorial Day

31 Tuesday

1st ♊

☽ v/c **4:10 pm** 1:10 pm

☽ enters ♋ 10:49 pm

1 Wednesday

1st ♊

☽ enters ♋ **1:49 am**

2 Thursday

1st ♋

Eastern time in bold type
Pacific time in medium type

3 Friday

1st ♋

☿ D	**4:00 am**	1:00 am
☽ v/c	**11:15 am**	8:15 am
☽ enters ♌	**2:38 pm**	11:38 am

4 Saturday

1st ♌

♄ ℞	**5:47 pm**	2:47 pm

Shavuot begins at sundown

5 Sunday

1st ♌

☽ v/c	**7:12 pm**	4:12 pm
☽ enters ♍		11:22 pm

May 2022

S	M	T	W	T	F	S
1	2	3	4	5	6	7
8	9	10	11	12	13	14
15	16	17	18	19	20	21
22	23	24	25	26	27	28
29	30	31				

June 2022

S	M	T	W	T	F	S
			1	2	3	4
5	6	7	8	9	10	11
12	13	14	15	16	17	18
19	20	21	22	23	2	25
26	27	28	29	30		

July 2022

S	M	T	W	T	F	S
					1	2
3	4	5	6	7	8	9
10	11	12	13	14	15	16
17	18	19	20	21	22	23
24	25	26	27	28	29	30
31						

Eastern time in bold type
Pacific time in medium type

6 Monday
1st ♌
☽ enters ♍ **2:22 am**

7 Tuesday
1st ♍
2nd Quarter **10:48 am** 7:48 am

8 Wednesday
2nd ♍
☽ v/c **8:09 am** 5:09 am
☽ enters ♎ **11:23 am** 8:23 am

9 Thursday
2nd ♎

Eastern time in bold type
Pacific time in medium type

10 Friday

2nd ♎

☽ v/c **1:36 pm** 10:36 am

☽ enters ♏ **4:41 pm** 1:41 pm

11 Saturday

2nd ♏

12 Sunday

2nd ♏

☽ v/c **5:40 pm** 2:40 pm

☽ enters ♐ **6:31 pm** 3:31 pm

May 2022

S	M	T	W	T	F	S
1	2	3	4	5	6	7
8	9	10	11	12	13	14
15	16	17	18	19	20	21
22	23	24	25	26	27	28
29	30	31				

June 2022

S	M	T	W	T	F	S
			1	2	3	4
5	6	7	8	9	10	11
12	13	14	15	16	17	18
19	20	21	22	23	2	25
26	27	28	29	30		

July 2022

S	M	T	W	T	F	S
					1	2
3	4	5	6	7	8	9
10	11	12	13	14	15	16
17	18	19	20	21	22	23
24	25	26	27	28	29	30
31						

13 Monday

2nd ♐

☿ enters ♊ **11:27 am** 8:27 am

14 Tuesday

2nd ♐

Full Moon **7:52 am** 4:52 am

☽ v/c **10:58 am** 7:58 am

☽ enters ♑ **6:14 pm** 3:14 pm

Flag Day

15 Wednesday

3rd ♑

16 Thursday

3rd ♑

☽ v/c **2:41 pm** 11:41 am

☽ enters ♒ **5:44 pm** 2:44 pm

Eastern time in bold type
Pacific time in medium type

17 Friday

3rd ♒

18 Saturday

3rd ♒

☽ v/c	**2:50 pm**	11:50 am
☽ enters ♓	**7:01 pm**	4:01 pm

19 Sunday

3rd ♓

Father's Day • Juneteenth

May 2022

S	M	T	W	T	F	S
1	2	3	4	5	6	7
8	9	10	11	12	13	14
15	16	17	18	19	20	21
22	23	24	25	26	27	28
29	30	31				

June 2022

S	M	T	W	T	F	S
			1	2	3	4
5	6	7	8	9	10	11
12	13	14	15	16	17	18
19	20	21	22	23	2	25
26	27	28	29	30		

July 2022

S	M	T	W	T	F	S
					1	2
3	4	5	6	7	8	9
10	11	12	13	14	15	16
17	18	19	20	21	22	23
24	25	26	27	28	29	30
31						

20 Monday

3rd ♓
☽ v/c **11:11 pm** 8:11 pm
4th Quarter **11:11 pm** 8:11 pm
☽ enters ♈ **11:37 pm** 8:37 pm

21 Tuesday

4th ♈
☉ enters ♋ **5:14 am** 2:14 am

Sun enters Cancer • Litha • Summer Solstice • 5:14 am EDT/2:14 am PDT

22 Wednesday

4th ♈
♀ enters ♊ **8:34 pm** 5:34 pm

23 Thursday

4th ♈
☽ v/c **4:02 am** 1:02 am
☽ enters ♉ **7:58 am** 4:58 am

24 Friday

4th ♉

25 Saturday

4th ♉

☽ v/c **3:02 pm** 12:02 pm

☽ enters ♊ **7:13 pm** 4:13 pm

26 Sunday

4th ♊

May 2022

S	M	T	W	T	F	S
1	2	3	4	5	6	7
8	9	10	11	12	13	14
15	16	17	18	19	20	21
22	23	24	25	26	27	28
29	30	31				

June 2022

S	M	T	W	T	F	S
			1	2	3	4
5	6	7	8	9	10	11
12	13	14	15	16	17	18
19	20	21	22	23	2	25
26	27	28	29	30		

July 2022

S	M	T	W	T	F	S
					1	2
3	4	5	6	7	8	9
10	11	12	13	14	15	16
17	18	19	20	21	22	23
24	25	26	27	28	29	30
31						

Eastern time in bold type
Pacific time in medium type

27 Monday

4th ♊

☽ v/c	**10:38 pm**	7:38 pm

28 Tuesday

4th ♊

♆ ℞	**3:55 am**	12:55 am
☽ enters ♋	**7:53 am**	4:53 am
New Moon	**10:52 pm**	7:52 pm

29 Wednesday

1st ♋

30 Thursday

1st ♋

☽ v/c	**4:14 pm**	1:14 pm
☽ enters ♌	**8:40 pm**	5:40 pm

Eastern time in bold type
Pacific time in medium type

1 Friday
1st ♌

2 Saturday
1st ♌

3 Sunday
1st ♌

☽ v/c	**5:59 am**	2:59 am
☽ enters ♍	**8:31 am**	5:31 am

June 2022

S	M	T	W	T	F	S
			1	2	3	4
5	6	7	8	9	10	11
12	13	14	15	16	17	18
19	20	21	22	23	2	25
26	27	28	29	30		

July 2022

S	M	T	W	T	F	S
					1	2
3	4	5	6	7	8	9
10	11	12	13	14	15	16
17	18	19	20	21	22	23
24	25	26	27	28	29	30
31						

August 2022

S	M	T	W	T	F	S
	1	2	3	4	5	6
7	8	9	10	11	12	13
14	15	16	17	18	19	20
21	22	23	24	25	26	27
28	29	30	31			

Eastern time in bold type
Pacific time in medium type

4 Monday

1st ♍
♀ enters ♊ **11:16 pm** 8:16 pm
♂ enters ♉ 11:04 pm
☿ enters ♋ 11:25 pm

Independence Day

5 Tuesday

1st ♍
♂ enters ♉ **2:04 am**
☿ enters ♋ **2:25 am**
☽ v/c **2:04 pm** 11:04 am
☽ enters ♎ **6:25 pm** 3:25 pm

6 Wednesday

1st ♎
2nd Quarter **10:14 pm** 7:14 pm

7 Thursday

2nd ♎
♆ ℞ **5:30 pm** 2:30 pm
☽ v/c **9:04 pm** 6:04 pm
☽ enters ♏ 10:15 pm

8 Friday

2nd ♎

☽ enters ♏ **1:15 am**

9 Saturday

2nd ♏

☽ v/c 9:34 pm

10 Sunday

2nd ♏

☽ v/c **12:34 am**

☽ enters ♐ **4:34 am** 1:34 am

June 2022

S	M	T	W	T	F	S
			1	2	3	4
5	6	7	8	9	10	11
12	13	14	15	16	17	18
19	20	21	22	23	2	25
26	27	28	29	30		

July 2022

S	M	T	W	T	F	S
					1	2
3	4	5	6	7	8	9
10	11	12	13	14	15	16
17	18	19	20	21	22	23
24	25	26	27	28	29	30
31						

August 2022

S	M	T	W	T	F	S
	1	2	3	4	5	6
7	8	9	10	11	12	13
14	15	16	17	18	19	20
21	22	23	24	25	26	27
28	29	30	31			

Eastern time in bold type
Pacific time in medium type

11 Monday

2nd ♐
☽ v/c **9:42 pm** 6:42 pm

12 Tuesday

2nd ♐
☽ enters ♑ **5:01 am** 2:01 am

13 Wednesday

2nd ♑
Full Moon **2:38 pm** 11:38 am
☽ v/c 9:17 pm

14 Thursday

3rd ♑
☽ v/c **12:17 am**
☽ enters ♒ **4:13 am** 1:13 am

Eastern time in bold type
Pacific time in medium type

15 Friday

3rd ♒

☽ v/c 9:36 pm

16 Saturday

3rd ♒

☽ v/c **12:36 am**

☽ enters ♓ **4:18 am** 1:18 am

17 Sunday

3rd ♓

♀ enters ♋ **9:32 pm** 6:32 pm

☽ v/c 11:43 pm

June 2022

S	M	T	W	T	F	S
			1	2	3	4
5	6	7	8	9	10	11
12	13	14	15	16	17	18
19	20	21	22	23	2	25
26	27	28	29	30		

July 2022

S	M	T	W	T	F	S
					1	2
3	4	5	6	7	8	9
10	11	12	13	14	15	16
17	18	19	20	21	22	23
24	25	26	27	28	29	30
31						

August 2022

S	M	T	W	T	F	S
	1	2	3	4	5	6
7	8	9	10	11	12	13
14	15	16	17	18	19	20
21	22	23	24	25	26	27
28	29	30	31			

Eastern time in bold type
Pacific time in medium type

18 Monday

3rd ♓

☽ v/c **2:43 am**

☽ enters ♈ **7:17 am** 4:17 am

19 Tuesday

3rd ♈

☿ enters ♌ **8:35 am** 5:35 am

⚷ ℞ **11:21 am** 8:21 am

20 Wednesday

3rd ♈

☽ v/c **10:19 am** 7:19 am

4th Quarter **10:19 am** 7:19 am

☽ enters ♉ **2:23 pm** 11:23 am

21 Thursday

4th ♉

Eastern time in bold type
Pacific time in medium type

22 Friday

4th ♉
☉ enters ♌ **4:07 pm** 1:07 pm
☽ v/c **7:45 pm** 4:45 pm
☽ enters ♊ 10:11 pm

Sun enters Leo

23 Saturday

4th ♉
☽ enters ♊ **1:11 am**
⚳ enters ♌ **1:29 pm** 10:29 am

24 Sunday

4th ♊
⚵ ℞ 11:48 pm

June 2022

S	M	T	W	T	F	S
			1	2	3	4
5	6	7	8	9	10	11
12	13	14	15	16	17	18
19	20	21	22	23	2	25
26	27	28	29	30		

July 2022

S	M	T	W	T	F	S
					1	2
3	4	5	6	7	8	9
10	11	12	13	14	15	16
17	18	19	20	21	22	23
24	25	26	27	28	29	30
31						

August 2022

S	M	T	W	T	F	S
	1	2	3	4	5	6
7	8	9	10	11	12	13
14	15	16	17	18	19	20
21	22	23	24	25	26	27
28	29	30	31			

Eastern time in bold type
Pacific time in medium type

25 Monday

4th ♊

⚵ ℞	**2:48 am**	
☽ v/c	**4:14 am**	1:14 am
☽ enters ♋	**1:54 pm**	10:54 am

26 Tuesday

4th ♋

27 Wednesday

4th ♋

☽ v/c	**8:54 pm**	5:54 pm
☽ enters ♌		11:36 pm

28 Thursday

4th ♋

☽ enters ♌	**2:36 am**	
New Moon	**1:55 pm**	10:55 am
♃ ℞	**4:37 pm**	1:37 pm

Eastern time in bold type
Pacific time in medium type

29 Friday

1st ♌
☽ v/c 9:29 pm

Islamic New Year begins at sundown

30 Saturday

1st ♌
☽ v/c **12:29 am**
☽ enters ♍ **2:11 pm** 11:11 am

31 Sunday

1st ♍

June 2022

S	M	T	W	T	F	S
			1	2	3	4
5	6	7	8	9	10	11
12	13	14	15	16	17	18
19	20	21	22	23	2	25
26	27	28	29	30		

July 2022

S	M	T	W	T	F	S
					1	2
3	4	5	6	7	8	9
10	11	12	13	14	15	16
17	18	19	20	21	22	23
24	25	26	27	28	29	30
31						

August 2022

S	M	T	W	T	F	S
	1	2	3	4	5	6
7	8	9	10	11	12	13
14	15	16	17	18	19	20
21	22	23	24	25	26	27
28	29	30	31			

1 Monday

1st ♍
☽ v/c **6:29 pm** 3:29 pm
☽ enters ♎ 9:06 pm

Lammas

2 Tuesday

1st ♍
☽ enters ♎ **12:06 am**

3 Wednesday

1st ♎
☽ v/c 11:20 pm
☿ enters ♍ 11:58 pm

4 Thursday

1st ♎
☽ v/c **2:20 am**
☿ enters ♍ **2:58 am**
☽ enters ♏ **7:47 am** 4:47 am

Eastern time in bold type
Pacific time in medium type

5 Friday

1st ♏

2nd Quarter **7:07 am** 4:07 am

6 Saturday

2nd ♏

☽ v/c **7:24 am** 4:24 am

☽ enters ♐ **12:39 pm** 9:39 am

7 Sunday

2nd ♐

July 2022

S	M	T	W	T	F	S
					1	2
3	4	5	6	7	8	9
10	11	12	13	14	15	16
17	18	19	20	21	22	23
24	25	26	27	28	29	30
31						

August 2022

S	M	T	W	T	F	S
	1	2	3	4	5	6
7	8	9	10	11	12	13
14	15	16	17	18	19	20
21	22	23	24	25	26	27
28	29	30	31			

September 2022

S	M	T	W	T	F	S
				1	2	3
4	5	6	7	8	9	10
11	12	13	14	15	16	17
18	19	20	21	22	23	24
25	26	27	28	29	30	

8 Monday

2nd ♐

☽ v/c	**6:30 am**	3:30 am
☽ enters ♑	**2:39 pm**	11:39 am

9 Tuesday

2nd ♑

10 Wednesday

2nd ♑

☽ v/c	**12:39 pm**	9:39 am
☽ enters ♒	**2:45 pm**	11:45 am

11 Thursday

2nd ♒

♀ enters ♌	**2:30 pm**	11:30 am
Full Moon	**9:36 pm**	6:36 pm

Eastern time in bold type
Pacific time in medium type

12 Friday

3rd ♒︎

☽ v/c	**7:07 am**	4:07 am
☽ enters ♓︎	**2:44 pm**	11:44 am

13 Saturday

3rd ♓︎

14 Sunday

3rd ♓︎

☽ v/c	**11:11 am**	8:11 am
☽ enters ♈︎	**4:43 pm**	1:43 pm

July 2022

S	M	T	W	T	F	S
					1	2
3	4	5	6	7	8	9
10	11	12	13	14	15	16
17	18	19	20	21	22	23
24	25	26	27	28	29	30
31						

August 2022

S	M	T	W	T	F	S
	1	2	3	4	5	6
7	8	9	10	11	12	13
14	15	16	17	18	19	20
21	22	23	24	25	26	27
28	29	30	31			

September 2022

S	M	T	W	T	F	S
				1	2	3
4	5	6	7	8	9	10
11	12	13	14	15	16	17
18	19	20	21	22	23	24
25	26	27	28	29	30	

15 Monday
3rd ♈

16 Tuesday
3rd ♈

☽ v/c	**4:18 pm**	1:18 pm
☽ enters ♉	**10:22 pm**	7:22 pm

17 Wednesday
3rd ♉

18 Thursday
3rd ♉

4th Quarter		9:36 pm

Eastern time in bold type
Pacific time in medium type

19 Friday

3rd ♉

4th Quarter	**12:36 am**	
☽ v/c	**7:06 am**	4:06 am
☽ enters ♊	**8:06 am**	5:06 am

20 Saturday

4th ♊

♂ enters ♊	**3:56 am**	12:56 am

21 Sunday

4th ♊

⚳ enters ♒	**6:33 am**	3:33 am
☽ v/c	**6:06 pm**	3:06 pm
☽ enters ♋	**8:29 pm**	5:29 pm

July 2022

S	M	T	W	T	F	S
					1	2
3	4	5	6	7	8	9
10	11	12	13	14	15	16
17	18	19	20	21	22	23
24	25	26	27	28	29	30
31						

August 2022

S	M	T	W	T	F	S
	1	2	3	4	5	6
7	8	9	10	11	12	13
14	15	16	17	18	19	20
21	22	23	24	25	26	27
28	29	30	31			

September 2022

S	M	T	W	T	F	S
				1	2	3
4	5	6	7	8	9	10
11	12	13	14	15	16	17
18	19	20	21	22	23	24
25	26	27	28	29	30	

22 Monday

4th ♋

☉ enters ♍ **11:16 pm** 8:16 pm

Sun enters Virgo

23 Tuesday

4th ♋

24 Wednesday

4th ♋

☽ v/c	**5:40 am**	2:40 am
☽ enters ♌	**9:09 am**	6:09 am
♅ ℞	**9:54 am**	6:54 am

25 Thursday

4th ♌

☿ enters ♎	**9:03 pm**	6:03 pm
☽ v/c		11:55 pm

Eastern time in bold type
Pacific time in medium type

26 Friday

4th ♌
☽ v/c **2:55 am**
☽ enters ♍ **8:25 pm** 5:25 pm

27 Saturday

4th ♍
New Moon **4:17 am** 1:17 am

28 Sunday

1st ♍
☽ v/c **11:08 pm** 8:08 pm

July 2022

S	M	T	W	T	F	S
					1	2
3	4	5	6	7	8	9
10	11	12	13	14	15	16
17	18	19	20	21	22	23
24	25	26	27	28	29	30
31						

August 2022

S	M	T	W	T	F	S
	1	2	3	4	5	6
7	8	9	10	11	12	13
14	15	16	17	18	19	20
21	22	23	24	25	26	27
28	29	30	31			

September 2022

S	M	T	W	T	F	S
				1	2	3
4	5	6	7	8	9	10
11	12	13	14	15	16	17
18	19	20	21	22	23	24
25	26	27	28	29	30	

Eastern time in bold type
Pacific time in medium type

29 Monday
1st ♍
☽ enters ♎ **5:45 am** 2:45 am

30 Tuesday
1st ♎

31 Wednesday
1st ♎
☽ v/c **6:43 am** 3:43 am
☽ enters ♏ **1:11 pm** 10:11 am

1 Thursday
1st ♏

Eastern time in bold type
Pacific time in medium type

2 Friday

1st ♏

☽ v/c	**1:22 pm**	10:22 am
☽ enters ♐	**6:39 pm**	3:39 pm

3 Saturday

1st ♐

2nd Quarter	**2:08 pm**	11:08 am

4 Sunday

2nd ♐

☽ v/c	**9:51 pm**	6:51 pm
☽ enters ♑	**10:03 pm**	7:03 pm
♀ enters ♍		9:05 pm

August 2022

S	M	T	W	T	F	S
	1	2	3	4	5	6
7	8	9	10	11	12	13
14	15	16	17	18	19	20
21	22	23	24	25	26	27
28	29	30	31			

September 2022

S	M	T	W	T	F	S
				1	2	3
4	5	6	7	8	9	10
11	12	13	14	15	16	17
18	19	20	21	22	23	24
25	26	27	28	29	30	

October 2022

S	M	T	W	T	F	S
						1
2	3	4	5	6	7	8
9	10	11	12	13	14	15
16	17	18	19	20	21	22
23	24	25	26	27	28	29
30	31					

Eastern time in bold type
Pacific time in medium type

5 Monday

2nd ♑
♀ enters ♍ **12:05 am**
☿ enters ♋ 10:04 pm

Labor Day

6 Tuesday

2nd ♑
☿ enters ♋ **1:04 am**
☽ v/c **5:43 pm** 2:43 pm
☽ enters ♒ **11:41 pm** 8:41 pm

7 Wednesday

2nd ♒

8 Thursday

2nd ♒
☽ v/c **8:34 am** 5:34 am
☽ enters ♓ 9:42 pm

9 Friday

2nd ♒
☽ enters ♓ **12:42 am**
☿ ℞ **11:38 pm** 8:38 pm

Mercury retrograde until 10/2

10 Saturday

2nd ♓
Full Moon **5:59 am** 2:59 am
☽ v/c **8:29 pm** 5:29 pm
☽ enters ♈ 11:47 pm

11 Sunday

3rd ♓
☽ enters ♈ **2:47 am**

August 2022

S	M	T	W	T	F	S
	1	2	3	4	5	6
7	8	9	10	11	12	13
14	15	16	17	18	19	20
21	22	23	24	25	26	27
28	29	30	31			

September 2022

S	M	T	W	T	F	S
				1	2	3
4	5	6	7	8	9	10
11	12	13	14	15	16	17
18	19	20	21	22	23	24
25	26	27	28	29	30	

October 2022

S	M	T	W	T	F	S
						1
2	3	4	5	6	7	8
9	10	11	12	13	14	15
16	17	18	19	20	21	22
23	24	25	26	27	28	29
30	31					

Eastern time in bold type
Pacific time in medium type

12 Monday

3rd ♈
☽ v/c 9:53 pm

13 Tuesday

3rd ♈
☽ v/c **12:53 am**
☽ enters ♉ **7:39 am** 4:39 am

14 Wednesday

3rd ♉

15 Thursday

3rd ♉
☽ v/c **8:59 am** 5:59 am
☽ enters ♊ **4:16 pm** 1:16 pm

Eastern time in bold type
Pacific time in medium type

16 Friday

3rd ♊

17 Saturday

3rd ♊

☽ v/c	**5:52 pm**	2:52 pm
4th Quarter	**5:52 pm**	2:52 pm

18 Sunday

4th ♊

☽ enters ♋	**3:59 am**	12:59 am

August 2022

S	M	T	W	T	F	S
	1	2	3	4	5	6
7	8	9	10	11	12	13
14	15	16	17	18	19	20
21	22	23	24	25	26	27
28	29	30	31			

September 2022

S	M	T	W	T	F	S
				1	2	3
4	5	6	7	8	9	10
11	12	13	14	15	16	17
18	19	20	21	22	23	24
25	26	27	28	29	30	

October 2022

S	M	T	W	T	F	S
						1
2	3	4	5	6	7	8
9	10	11	12	13	14	15
16	17	18	19	20	21	22
23	24	25	26	27	28	29
30	31					

Eastern time in bold type
Pacific time in medium type

19 Monday

4th ♋

20 Tuesday

4th ♋

☽ v/c	**11:57 am**	8:57 am
☽ enters ♌	**4:38 pm**	1:38 pm

21 Wednesday

4th ♌

UN International Day of Peace

22 Thursday

4th ♌

☽ v/c	**7:07 am**	4:07 am
☉ enters ♎	**9:04 pm**	6:04 pm

Sun enters Libra • Mabon • Fall Equinox • 9:04 pm EDT/6:04 pm PDT

23 Friday

4th ♌︎
☽ enters ♍︎ **3:53 am** 12:53 am
☿ enters ♍︎ **8:04 am** 5:04 am

24 Saturday

4th ♍︎

25 Sunday

4th ♍︎
☽ v/c **8:49 am** 5:49 am
☽ enters ♎︎ **12:43 pm** 9:43 am
New Moon **5:55 pm** 2:55 pm

Rosh Hashanah begins at sundown

August 2022

S	M	T	W	T	F	S
	1	2	3	4	5	6
7	8	9	10	11	12	13
14	15	16	17	18	19	20
21	22	23	24	25	26	27
28	29	30	31			

September 2022

S	M	T	W	T	F	S
				1	2	3
4	5	6	7	8	9	10
11	12	13	14	15	16	17
18	19	20	21	22	23	24
25	26	27	28	29	30	

October 2022

S	M	T	W	T	F	S
						1
2	3	4	5	6	7	8
9	10	11	12	13	14	15
16	17	18	19	20	21	22
23	24	25	26	27	28	29
30	31					

26 Monday

1st ♎

27 Tuesday

1st ♎

☽ v/c	**12:21 pm**	9:21 am
☽ enters ♏	**7:15 pm**	4:15 pm

28 Wednesday

1st ♏

29 Thursday

1st ♏

♀ enters ♎	**3:49 am**	12:49 am
⚳ enters ♍	**4:59 am**	1:59 am
☽ v/c	**5:20 pm**	2:20 pm
☽ enters ♐		9:03 pm

30 Friday

1st ♏
☽ enters ♐ **12:03 am**

1 Saturday

1st ♐
☽ v/c **5:46 pm** 2:46 pm

2 Sunday

1st ♐
☽ enters ♑ **3:38 am** 12:38 am
☿ D **5:07 am** 2:07 am
2nd Quarter **8:14 pm** 5:14 pm

September 2022

S	M	T	W	T	F	S
				1	2	3
4	5	6	7	8	9	10
11	12	13	14	15	16	17
18	19	20	21	22	23	24
25	26	27	28	29	30	

October 2022

S	M	T	W	T	F	S
						1
2	3	4	5	6	7	8
9	10	11	12	13	14	15
16	17	18	19	20	21	22
23	24	25	26	27	28	29
30	31					

November 2022

S	M	T	W	T	F	S
		1	2	3	4	5
6	7	8	9	10	11	12
13	14	15	16	17	18	19
20	21	22	23	24	25	26
27	28	29	30			

Eastern time in bold type
Pacific time in medium type

3 Monday

2nd ♑
☽ v/c **11:49 pm** 8:49 pm

4 Tuesday

2nd ♑
☽ enters ♒ **6:20 am** 3:20 am

Yom Kippur begins at sundown

5 Wednesday

2nd ♒
⚶ D **2:10 pm** 11:10 am
☽ v/c **6:46 pm** 3:46 pm

6 Thursday

2nd ♒
☽ enters ♓ **8:47 am** 5:47 am

Eastern time in bold type
Pacific time in medium type

7 Friday

2nd ♓

8 Saturday

2nd ♓

☽ v/c	**7:10 am**	4:10 am
☽ enters ♈	**11:57 am**	8:57 am
♇ D	**5:56 pm**	2:56 pm

9 Sunday

2nd ♈

Full Moon	**4:55 pm**	1:55 pm

Sukkot begins at sundown

September 2022

S	M	T	W	T	F	S
				1	2	3
4	5	6	7	8	9	10
11	12	13	14	15	16	17
18	19	20	21	22	23	24
25	26	27	28	29	30	

October 2022

S	M	T	W	T	F	S
						1
2	3	4	5	6	7	8
9	10	11	12	13	14	15
16	17	18	19	20	21	22
23	24	25	26	27	28	29
30	31					

November 2022

S	M	T	W	T	F	S
		1	2	3	4	5
6	7	8	9	10	11	12
13	14	15	16	17	18	19
20	21	22	23	24	25	26
27	28	29	30			

10 Monday

3rd ♈︎

☽ v/c **10:02 am** 7:02 am

☽ enters ♉︎ **5:04 pm** 2:04 pm

☿ enters ♎︎ **7:51 pm** 4:51 pm

Indigenous Peoples' Day

11 Tuesday

3rd ♉︎

12 Wednesday

3rd ♉︎

☽ v/c **5:42 pm** 2:42 pm

☽ enters ♊︎ 10:08 pm

13 Thursday

3rd ♉︎

☽ enters ♊︎ **1:08 am**

Eastern time in bold type

Pacific time in medium type

14 Friday

3rd ♊
☽ v/c 9:11 pm

15 Saturday

3rd ♊
☽ v/c **12:11 am**
☽ enters ♋ **12:11 pm** 9:11 am

16 Sunday

3rd ♋

Sukkot ends

September 2022

S	M	T	W	T	F	S
				1	2	3
4	5	6	7	8	9	10
11	12	13	14	15	16	17
18	19	20	21	22	23	24
25	26	27	28	29	30	

October 2022

S	M	T	W	T	F	S
						1
2	3	4	5	6	7	8
9	10	11	12	13	14	15
16	17	18	19	20	21	22
23	24	25	26	27	28	29
30	31					

November 2022

S	M	T	W	T	F	S
		1	2	3	4	5
6	7	8	9	10	11	12
13	14	15	16	17	18	19
20	21	22	23	24	25	26
27	28	29	30			

Eastern time in bold type
Pacific time in medium type

17 Monday

3rd ♋
4th Quarter **1:15 pm** 10:15 am
☽ v/c **4:56 pm** 1:56 pm
☽ enters ♌ 9:45 pm

18 Tuesday

4th ♋
☽ enters ♌ **12:45 am**

19 Wednesday

4th ♌

20 Thursday

4th ♌
☽ v/c **6:35 am** 3:35 am
☽ enters ♍ **12:25 pm** 9:25 am

Eastern time in bold type
Pacific time in medium type

21 Friday
4th ♍

22 Saturday
4th ♍

☽ v/c	**2:17 pm**	11:17 am
☽ enters ♎	**9:24 pm**	6:24 pm
♄ D		9:07 pm

23 Sunday
4th ♎

♄ D	**12:07 am**	
♀ enters ♏	**3:52 am**	12:52 am
☉ enters ♏	**6:36 am**	3:36 am
⚵ D	**9:05 am**	6:05 am

Sun enters Scorpio

September 2022

S	M	T	W	T	F	S
				1	2	3
4	5	6	7	8	9	10
11	12	13	14	15	16	17
18	19	20	21	22	23	24
25	26	27	28	29	30	

October 2022

S	M	T	W	T	F	S
						1
2	3	4	5	6	7	8
9	10	11	12	13	14	15
16	17	18	19	20	21	22
23	24	25	26	27	28	29
30	31					

November 2022

S	M	T	W	T	F	S
		1	2	3	4	5
6	7	8	9	10	11	12
13	14	15	16	17	18	19
20	21	22	23	24	25	26
27	28	29	30			

24 Monday

4th ♎

☽ v/c	**8:36 pm**	5:36 pm

25 Tuesday

4th ♎

☽ enters ♏	**3:18 am**	12:18 am
New Moon	**6:49 am**	3:49 am

Solar Eclipse 2° ♏ 00'

26 Wednesday

1st ♏

☽ v/c		9:27 pm

27 Thursday

1st ♏

☽ v/c	**12:27 am**	
☽ enters ♐	**6:55 am**	3:55 am
♃ enters ♓		10:10 pm

Eastern time in bold type
Pacific time in medium type

28 Friday

1st ♐
♃ enters ♓ **1:10 am**

29 Saturday

1st ♐

☽ v/c	**9:10 am**	6:10 am
☽ enters ♑	**9:21 am**	6:21 am
☿ enters ♏	**3:22 pm**	12:22 pm

30 Sunday

1st ♑

♂ ℞	**9:26 am**	6:26 am

Mars retrograde until 1/12/23

September 2022

S	M	T	W	T	F	S
				1	2	3
4	5	6	7	8	9	10
11	12	13	14	15	16	17
18	19	20	21	22	23	24
25	26	27	28	29	30	

October 2022

S	M	T	W	T	F	S
						1
2	3	4	5	6	7	8
9	10	11	12	13	14	15
16	17	18	19	20	21	22
23	24	25	26	27	28	29
30	31					

November 2022

S	M	T	W	T	F	S
		1	2	3	4	5
6	7	8	9	10	11	12
13	14	15	16	17	18	19
20	21	22	23	24	25	26
27	28	29	30			

31 Monday

1st ♑
☽ v/c **11:14 am** 8:14 am
☽ enters ♒ **11:43 am** 8:43 am
2nd Quarter 11:37 pm

Halloween • Samhain

1 Tuesday

1st ♒
2nd Quarter **2:37 am**

All Saints' Day

2 Wednesday

2nd ♒
☽ v/c **7:08 am** 4:08 am
☽ enters ♓ **2:46 pm** 11:46 am

3 Thursday

2nd ♓

Eastern time in bold type
Pacific time in medium type

4 Friday

2nd ♓

☽ v/c	**6:05 pm**	3:05 pm
☽ enters ♈	**7:07 pm**	4:07 pm

5 Saturday

2nd ♈

6 Sunday

2nd ♈

☽ v/c	**5:30 pm**	2:30 pm
☽ enters ♉		9:15 pm

Daylight Saving Time ends at 2 am

October 2022

S	M	T	W	T	F	S
						1
2	3	4	5	6	7	8
9	10	11	12	13	14	15
16	17	18	19	20	21	22
23	24	25	26	27	28	29
30	31					

November 2022

S	M	T	W	T	F	S
		1	2	3	4	5
6	7	8	9	10	11	12
13	14	15	16	17	18	19
20	21	22	23	24	25	26
27	28	29	30			

December 2022

S	M	T	W	T	F	S
				1	2	3
4	5	6	7	8	9	10
11	12	13	14	15	16	17
18	19	20	21	22	23	24
25	26	27	28	29	30	31

7 Monday

2nd ♈
☽ enters ♉ **12:15 am**

8 Tuesday

2nd ♉
Full Moon **6:02 am** 3:02 am

Election Day (general) • Lunar Eclipse 16° ♉ 01'

9 Wednesday

3rd ♉
☽ v/c **7:00 am** 4:00 am
☽ enters ♊ **8:37 am** 5:37 am

10 Thursday

3rd ♊

Eastern time in bold type
Pacific time in medium type

11 Friday

3rd ♊

☽ v/c	**5:28 pm**	2:28 pm
☽ enters ♋	**7:22 pm**	4:22 pm

Veterans Day

12 Saturday

3rd ♋

13 Sunday

3rd ♋

October 2022

S	M	T	W	T	F	S
						1
2	3	4	5	6	7	8
9	10	11	12	13	14	15
16	17	18	19	20	21	22
23	24	25	26	27	28	29
30	31					

November 2022

S	M	T	W	T	F	S
		1	2	3	4	5
6	7	8	9	10	11	12
13	14	15	16	17	18	19
20	21	22	23	24	25	26
27	28	29	30			

December 2022

S	M	T	W	T	F	S
				1	2	3
4	5	6	7	8	9	10
11	12	13	14	15	16	17
18	19	20	21	22	23	24
25	26	27	28	29	30	31

Eastern time in bold type
Pacific time in medium type

14 Monday

3rd ♋
☽ v/c **5:41 am** 2:41 am
☽ enters ♌ **7:48 am** 4:48 am

15 Tuesday

3rd ♌
♀ enters ♐ 10:09 pm

16 Wednesday

3rd ♌
♀ enters ♐ **1:09 am**
4th Quarter **8:27 am** 5:27 am
☽ v/c **6:55 pm** 3:55 pm
☽ enters ♍ **8:04 pm** 5:04 pm

17 Thursday

4th ♍
☿ enters ♐ **3:42 am** 12:42 am

Eastern time in bold type
Pacific time in medium type

18 Friday

4th ♍

19 Saturday

4th ♍

☽ v/c **3:47 am** 12:47 am

☽ enters ♎ **5:58 am** 2:58 am

20 Sunday

4th ♎

⚵ enters ♓ **4:25 pm** 1:25 pm

October 2022

S	M	T	W	T	F	S
						1
2	3	4	5	6	7	8
9	10	11	12	13	14	15
16	17	18	19	20	21	22
23	24	25	26	27	28	29
30	31					

November 2022

S	M	T	W	T	F	S
		1	2	3	4	5
6	7	8	9	10	11	12
13	14	15	16	17	18	19
20	21	22	23	24	25	26
27	28	29	30			

December 2022

S	M	T	W	T	F	S
				1	2	3
4	5	6	7	8	9	10
11	12	13	14	15	16	17
18	19	20	21	22	23	24
25	26	27	28	29	30	31

21 Monday

4th ♎

☽ v/c	**6:14 am**	3:14 am
☽ enters ♏	**12:16 pm**	9:16 am

22 Tuesday

4th ♏

☉ enters ♐	**3:20 am**	12:20 am

Sun enters Sagittarius

23 Wednesday

4th ♏

☽ v/c	**1:16 pm**	10:16 am
☽ enters ♐	**3:16 pm**	12:16 pm
New Moon	**5:57 pm**	2:57 pm
♃ D	**6:02 pm**	3:02 pm

24 Thursday

1st ♐

Thanksgiving Day

Eastern time in bold type
Pacific time in medium type

25 Friday

1st ♐

☽ v/c	**2:22 pm**	11:22 am
☽ enters ♑	**4:18 pm**	1:18 pm

26 Saturday

1st ♑

27 Sunday

1st ♑

☽ v/c	**3:11 pm**	12:11 pm
☽ enters ♒	**5:07 pm**	2:07 pm

October 2022

S	M	T	W	T	F	S
						1
2	3	4	5	6	7	8
9	10	11	12	13	14	15
16	17	18	19	20	21	22
23	24	25	26	27	28	29
30	31					

November 2022

S	M	T	W	T	F	S
		1	2	3	4	5
6	7	8	9	10	11	12
13	14	15	16	17	18	19
20	21	22	23	24	25	26
27	28	29	30			

December 2022

S	M	T	W	T	F	S
				1	2	3
4	5	6	7	8	9	10
11	12	13	14	15	16	17
18	19	20	21	22	23	24
25	26	27	28	29	30	31

Eastern time in bold type
Pacific time in medium type

28 Monday

1st ♒
☽ v/c 10:53 pm

29 Tuesday

1st ♒
☽ v/c **1:53 am**
☽ enters ♓ **7:15 pm** 4:15 pm

30 Wednesday

1st ♓
⚴ ℞ **3:33 am** 12:33 am
2nd Quarter **9:37 am** 6:37 am

1 Thursday

2nd ♓
☽ v/c **9:44 pm** 6:44 pm
☽ enters ♈ **11:41 pm** 8:41 pm

Eastern time in bold type
Pacific time in medium type

2 Friday
2nd ♈

3 Saturday
2nd ♈

♆ D	**7:15 pm**	4:15 pm
☽ v/c		9:46 pm

4 Sunday
2nd ♈

☽ v/c	**12:46 am**	
☽ enters ♉	**6:38 am**	3:38 am

November 2022

S	M	T	W	T	F	S
		1	2	3	4	5
6	7	8	9	10	11	12
13	14	15	16	17	18	19
20	21	22	23	24	25	26
27	28	29	30			

December 2022

S	M	T	W	T	F	S
				1	2	3
4	5	6	7	8	9	10
11	12	13	14	15	16	17
18	19	20	21	22	23	24
25	26	27	28	29	30	31

January 2023

S	M	T	W	T	F	S
1	2	3	4	5	6	7
8	9	10	11	12	13	14
15	16	17	18	19	20	21
22	23	24	25	26	27	28
29	30	31				

5 Monday

2nd ♉

6 Tuesday

2nd ♉

☽ v/c **2:02 pm** 11:02 am
☽ enters ♊ **3:49 pm** 12:49 pm
☿ enters ♑ **5:08 pm** 2:08 pm

7 Wednesday

2nd ♊

Full Moon **11:08 pm** 8:08 pm

8 Thursday

3rd ♊

☽ v/c 10:13 pm
☽ enters ♋ 11:49 pm

Eastern time in bold type
Pacific time in medium type

9 Friday

3rd ♊
☽ v/c **1:13 am**
☽ enters ♋ **2:49 am**
♀ enters ♑ **10:54 pm** 7:54 pm

10 Saturday

3rd ♋

11 Sunday

3rd ♋
☽ v/c **1:49 pm** 10:49 am
☽ enters ♌ **3:09 pm** 12:09 pm

November 2022

S	M	T	W	T	F	S
		1	2	3	4	5
6	7	8	9	10	11	12
13	14	15	16	17	18	19
20	21	22	23	24	25	26
27	28	29	30			

December 2022

S	M	T	W	T	F	S
				1	2	3
4	5	6	7	8	9	10
11	12	13	14	15	16	17
18	19	20	21	22	23	24
25	26	27	28	29	30	31

January 2023

S	M	T	W	T	F	S
1	2	3	4	5	6	7
8	9	10	11	12	13	14
15	16	17	18	19	20	21
22	23	24	25	26	27	28
29	30	31				

Eastern time in bold type
Pacific time in medium type

12 Monday

3rd ♌

13 Tuesday

3rd ♌

☽ v/c **10:52 am** 7:52 am

14 Wednesday

3rd ♌

☽ enters ♍ **3:45 am** 12:45 am

15 Thursday

3rd ♍

Eastern time in bold type

Pacific time in medium type

16 Friday

3rd ♍

4th Quarter	**3:56 am**	12:56 am
☽ v/c	**2:13 pm**	11:13 am
☽ enters ♎	**2:49 pm**	11:49 am

17 Saturday

4th ♎

18 Sunday

4th ♎

☽ v/c	**5:35 pm**	2:35 pm
⚳ enters ♎	**6:34 pm**	3:34 pm
☽ enters ♏	**10:31 pm**	7:31 pm

Hanukkah begins at sundown

November 2022

S	M	T	W	T	F	S
		1	2	3	4	5
6	7	8	9	10	11	12
13	14	15	16	17	18	19
20	21	22	23	24	25	26
27	28	29	30			

December 2022

S	M	T	W	T	F	S
				1	2	3
4	5	6	7	8	9	10
11	12	13	14	15	16	17
18	19	20	21	22	23	24
25	26	27	28	29	30	31

January 2023

S	M	T	W	T	F	S
1	2	3	4	5	6	7
8	9	10	11	12	13	14
15	16	17	18	19	20	21
22	23	24	25	26	27	28
29	30	31				

Eastern time in bold type
Pacific time in medium type

19 Monday

4th ♏

20 Tuesday

4th ♏

♃ enters ♈	**9:32 am**	6:32 am
☽ v/c	**9:45 pm**	6:45 pm
☽ enters ♐		11:12 pm

21 Wednesday

4th ♏

☽ enters ♐	**2:12 am**	
☉ enters ♑	**4:48 pm**	1:48 pm

Sun enters Capricorn • Yule • Winter Solstice • 4:48 pm EDT/1:48 pm PDT

22 Thursday

4th ♐

☽ v/c	**3:16 pm**	12:16 pm
☽ enters ♑		11:49 pm

Eastern time in bold type
Pacific time in medium type

23 Friday

4th ♐
☽ enters ♑ **2:49 am**
⚷ D **4:31 am** 1:31 am
New Moon **5:17 am** 2:17 am

24 Saturday

1st ♑
☽ v/c **10:11 pm** 7:11 pm
☽ enters ♒ 11:14 pm

Christmas Eve

25 Sunday

1st ♑
☽ enters ♒ **2:14 am**

Christmas Day

November 2022

S	M	T	W	T	F	S
		1	2	3	4	5
6	7	8	9	10	11	12
13	14	15	16	17	18	19
20	21	22	23	24	25	26
27	28	29	30			

December 2022

S	M	T	W	T	F	S
				1	2	3
4	5	6	7	8	9	10
11	12	13	14	15	16	17
18	19	20	21	22	23	24
25	26	27	28	29	30	31

January 2023

S	M	T	W	T	F	S
1	2	3	4	5	6	7
8	9	10	11	12	13	14
15	16	17	18	19	20	21
22	23	24	25	26	27	28
29	30	31				

26 Monday

1st ≈

☽ v/c	**1:19 pm**	10:19 am
☽ enters ♓		11:34 pm

Kwanzaa begins

27 Tuesday

1st ≈

☽ enters ♓	**2:34 am**	

28 Wednesday

1st ♓

☽ v/c		10:21 pm

29 Thursday

1st ♓

☽ v/c	**1:21 am**	
☿ ℞	**4:32 am**	1:32 am
☽ enters ♈	**5:36 am**	2:36 am
2nd Quarter	**8:21 pm**	5:21 pm

Eastern time in bold type
Pacific time in medium type

30 Friday

2nd ♈

31 Saturday

2nd ♈

☽ v/c **7:44 am** 4:44 am

☽ enters ♉ **12:08 pm** 9:08 am

New Year's Eve

1 Sunday

2nd ♉

Kwanzaa ends • New Year's Day

November 2022

S	M	T	W	T	F	S
		1	2	3	4	5
6	7	8	9	10	11	12
13	14	15	16	17	18	19
20	21	22	23	24	25	26
27	28	29	30			

December 2022

S	M	T	W	T	F	S
				1	2	3
4	5	6	7	8	9	10
11	12	13	14	15	16	17
18	19	20	21	22	23	24
25	26	27	28	29	30	31

January 2023

S	M	T	W	T	F	S
1	2	3	4	5	6	7
8	9	10	11	12	13	14
15	16	17	18	19	20	21
22	23	24	25	26	27	28
29	30	31				

The Year 2022

January

S	M	T	W	T	F	S
						1
2	3	4	5	6	7	8
9	10	11	12	13	14	15
16	17	18	19	20	21	22
23	24	25	26	27	28	29
30	31					

February

S	M	T	W	T	F	S
		1	2	3	4	5
6	7	8	9	10	11	12
13	14	15	16	17	18	19
20	21	22	23	24	25	26
27	28					

March

S	M	T	W	T	F	S
		1	2	3	4	5
6	7	8	9	10	11	12
13	14	15	16	17	18	19
20	21	22	23	24	25	26
27	28	29	30	31		

April

S	M	T	W	T	F	S
					1	2
3	4	5	6	7	8	9
10	11	12	13	14	15	16
17	18	19	20	21	22	23
24	25	26	27	28	29	30

May

S	M	T	W	T	F	S
1	2	3	4	5	6	7
8	9	10	11	12	13	14
15	16	17	18	19	20	21
22	23	24	25	26	27	28
29	30	31				

June

S	M	T	W	T	F	S
			1	2	3	4
5	6	7	8	9	10	11
12	13	14	15	16	17	18
19	20	21	22	23	24	25
26	27	28	29	30		

July

S	M	T	W	T	F	S
					1	2
3	4	5	6	7	8	9
10	11	12	13	14	15	16
17	18	19	20	21	22	23
24	25	26	27	28	29	30
31						

August

S	M	T	W	T	F	S
	1	2	3	4	5	6
7	8	9	10	11	12	13
14	15	16	17	18	19	20
21	22	23	24	25	26	27
28	29	30	31			

September

S	M	T	W	T	F	S
				1	2	3
4	5	6	7	8	9	10
11	12	13	14	15	16	17
18	19	20	21	22	23	24
25	26	27	28	29	30	

October

S	M	T	W	T	F	S
						1
2	3	4	5	6	7	8
9	10	11	12	13	14	15
16	17	18	19	20	21	22
23	24	25	26	27	28	29
30	31					

November

S	M	T	W	T	F	S
		1	2	3	4	5
6	7	8	9	10	11	12
13	14	15	16	17	18	19
20	21	22	23	24	25	26
27	28	29	30			

December

S	M	T	W	T	F	S
				1	2	3
4	5	6	7	8	9	10
11	12	13	14	15	16	17
18	19	20	21	22	23	24
25	26	27	28	29	30	31

The Year 2023

January

S	M	T	W	T	F	S
1	2	3	4	5	6	7
8	9	10	11	12	13	14
15	16	17	18	19	20	21
22	23	24	25	26	27	28
29	30	31				

February

S	M	T	W	T	F	S
			1	2	3	4
5	6	7	8	9	10	11
12	13	14	15	16	17	18
19	20	21	22	23	24	25
26	27	28				

March

S	M	T	W	T	F	S
			1	2	3	4
5	6	7	8	9	10	11
12	13	14	15	16	17	18
19	20	21	22	23	24	25
26	27	28	29	30	31	

April

S	M	T	W	T	F	S
						1
2	3	4	5	6	7	8
9	10	11	12	13	14	15
16	17	18	19	20	21	22
23	24	25	26	27	28	29
30						

May

S	M	T	W	T	F	S
	1	2	3	4	5	6
7	8	9	10	11	12	13
14	15	16	17	18	19	20
21	22	23	24	25	26	27
28	29	30	31			

June

S	M	T	W	T	F	S
				1	2	3
4	5	6	7	8	9	10
11	12	13	14	15	16	17
18	19	20	21	22	23	24
25	26	27	28	29	30	

July

S	M	T	W	T	F	S
						1
2	3	4	5	6	7	8
9	10	11	12	13	14	15
16	17	18	19	20	21	22
23	24	25	26	27	28	29
30	31					

August

S	M	T	W	T	F	S
		1	2	3	4	5
6	7	8	9	10	11	12
13	14	15	16	17	18	19
20	21	22	23	24	25	26
27	28	29	30	31		

September

S	M	T	W	T	F	S
					1	2
3	4	5	6	7	8	9
10	11	12	13	14	15	16
17	18	19	20	21	22	23
24	25	26	27	28	29	30

October

S	M	T	W	T	F	S
1	2	3	4	5	6	7
8	9	10	11	12	13	14
15	16	17	18	19	20	21
22	23	24	25	26	27	28
29	30	31				

November

S	M	T	W	T	F	S
			1	2	3	4
5	6	7	8	9	10	11
12	13	14	15	16	17	18
19	20	21	22	23	24	25
26	27	28	29	30		

December

S	M	T	W	T	F	S
					1	2
3	4	5	6	7	8	9
10	11	12	13	14	15	16
17	18	19	20	21	22	23
24	25	26	27	28	29	30
31						

☽ Last Aspect day	ET / hr:mn / PT		asp	☽ Ingress sign day	ET / hr:mn / PT	
2	**5:00 pm**	2:00 pm	△♂	♍ 2	**8:13 pm**	5:13 pm
4	**4:34 pm**	1:34 pm	□♀	♎ 4		9:42 pm
4	**4:34 pm**	1:34 pm	□♀	♎ 5	**12:42 am**	
6		9:55 pm	⚹♀	♏ 7	**3:53 am**	12:53 am
7	**12:55 am**		⚹♀	♏ 7	**3:53 am**	12:53 am
8	**8:59 pm**	5:59 pm	⚹♇	♐ 9	**6:15 am**	3:15 am
10	**1:29 pm**	10:29 am	□♆	♑ 11	**8:30 am**	5:30 am
12		11:22 pm	☌♇	♒ 13	**11:44 am**	8:44 am
13	**2:22 am**		☌♇	♒ 13	**11:44 am**	8:44 am
14	**4:28 am**	1:28 am	☌☿	♓ 15	**5:17 pm**	2:17 pm

☽ Last Aspect day	ET / hr:mn / PT		asp	☽ Ingress sign day	ET / hr:mn / PT	
17	**10:44 pm**	7:44 pm	⚹☉	♈ 17		11:07 pm
17	**10:44 pm**	7:44 pm	⚹☉	♈ 18	**2:07 am**	
20	**3:29 am**	12:29 am	□♇	♉ 20	**1:56 pm**	10:56 am
22	**4:28 pm**	1:28 pm	△♇	♊ 22		11:43 pm
22	**4:28 pm**	1:28 pm	△♇	♊ 23	**2:43 am**	
24		11:17 pm	△☿	♋ 25	**1:52 pm**	10:52 am
25	**2:17 am**		△☿	♋ 25	**1:52 pm**	10:52 am
27	**12:55 pm**	9:55 am	☍♇	♌ 27	**9:54 pm**	6:54 pm
29	**8:53 pm**	5:53 pm	☍☿	♍ 30	**3:02 am**	12:02 am

☽ Phases & Eclipses phase	day	ET / hr:mn / PT	
4th Quarter	6	**4:37 am**	1:37 am
New Moon	12		9:00 pm
New Moon	13	**12:00 am**	
2nd Quarter	20	**4:02 pm**	1:02 pm
Full Moon	28	**2:16 pm**	11:16 am

Planet Ingress	day	ET / hr:mn / PT	
♂ ♉	6	**5:27 pm**	2:27 pm
☿ ♒	8	**7:00 am**	4:00 am
♀ ♑	8	**10:41 am**	7:41 am
☉ ♒	19	**3:40 pm**	12:40 pm

Planetary Motion		day	ET / hr:mn / PT	
♅	D	14	**3:36 am**	12:36 am
⚵	℞	19	**3:54 am**	12:54 am
☿	℞	30	**10:52 am**	7:52 am

1 FRIDAY
☽ □ ♅ **2:26 am**
☿ ⚹ ♆ **6:18 am** 3:18 am
☽ ⚻ ☉ **10:55 am** 7:55 am
☽ ⚻ ♆ **11:39 pm** 8:39 pm
☽ ⚻ ☿ 11:02 pm

2 SATURDAY
☽ ⚻ ☿ **2:02 am**
☽ △ ♀ **6:24 am** 3:24 am
☽ ⚻ ♇ **9:57 am** 6:57 am
☽ △ ♂ **5:00 pm** 2:00 pm
☽ ⚻ ♄ **11:32 pm** 8:32 pm
☽ ⚻ ♃ 11:05 pm

3 SUNDAY
☽ ⚻ ♃ **2:05 am**
☽ △ ♅ **8:12 am** 5:12 am
☽ △ ☉ **8:44 pm** 5:44 pm
♀ ⚺ ♇ **9:19 pm** 6:19 pm

4 MONDAY
☽ ☍ ♆ **4:50 am** 1:50 am
☽ △ ☿ **2:11 pm** 11:11 am
☽ △ ♇ **2:52 pm** 11:52 am
☽ □ ♀ **4:34 pm** 1:34 pm
☿ ☌ ♇ **7:58 pm** 4:58 pm
☽ ⚻ ♂ **11:19 pm** 8:19 pm

5 TUESDAY
☽ △ ♄ **4:22 am** 1:22 am
☽ △ ♃ **7:17 am** 4:17 am
☽ ⚻ ♅ **12:19 pm** 9:19 am

Eastern time in bold type
Pacific time in medium type

6 WEDNESDAY
☽ □ ☉ **4:37 am** 1:37 am
☽ ⚻ ♆ **8:32 am** 5:32 am
☽ □ ♇ **6:23 pm** 3:23 pm
☽ □ ☿ 9:21 pm
☽ ⚹ ♀ 9:55 pm

7 THURSDAY
☽ □ ☿ **12:21 am**
☽ ⚹ ♀ **12:55 am**
☽ ☍ ♂ **4:14 am** 1:14 am
☽ □ ♄ **7:54 am** 4:54 am
☽ □ ♃ **11:11 am** 8:11 am
☽ ☍ ♅ **3:16 pm** 12:16 pm
☿ ⚺ ♀ **7:04 pm** 4:04 pm

8 FRIDAY
☽ ⚹ ☉ **11:11 am** 8:11 am
☽ △ ♆ **11:14 am** 8:14 am
☉ ⚹ ♆ **11:53 am** 8:53 am
☽ ⚹ ♇ **8:59 pm** 5:59 pm
☿ □ ♂ **9:44 pm** 6:44 pm

9 SATURDAY
☽ ⚺ ♀ **8:07 am** 5:07 am
☽ ⚻ ♂ **8:17 am** 5:17 am
☽ ⚹ ☿ **9:15 am** 6:15 am
☽ ⚹ ♄ **10:38 am** 7:38 am
♀ △ ♂ **10:53 am** 7:53 am
☽ ⚹ ♃ **2:18 pm** 11:18 am
☽ ⚻ ♅ **5:30 pm** 2:30 pm
☿ ☌ ♄ **10:17 pm** 7:17 pm

10 SUNDAY
☽ □ ♆ **1:29 pm** 10:29 am
♀ ⚺ ♄ **3:39 pm** 12:39 pm
☽ ⚺ ☉ **5:12 pm** 2:12 pm
☽ ⚺ ♇ **11:17 pm** 8:17 pm

11 MONDAY
☽ △ ♂ **12:16 pm** 9:16 am
☿ ☌ ♃ **12:19 pm** 9:19 am
☽ ⚺ ♄ **1:20 pm** 10:20 am
☽ ☌ ♀ **3:14 pm** 12:14 pm
☽ ⚺ ♃ **5:28 pm** 2:28 pm
☽ ⚺ ☿ **6:02 pm** 3:02 pm
☽ △ ♅ **7:51 pm** 4:51 pm

12 TUESDAY
☿ □ ♅ **10:00 am** 7:00 am
☽ ⚹ ♆ **4:17 pm** 1:17 pm
♀ ⚺ ♃ **9:40 pm** 6:40 pm
☽ ☌ ☉ 9:00 pm
☽ ☌ ♇ 11:22 pm

13 WEDNESDAY
☽ ☌ ☉ **12:00 am**
☽ ☌ ♇ **2:22 am**
♂ □ ♄ **6:02 am** 3:02 am
☽ ☌ ♄ **5:11 pm** 2:11 pm
☽ □ ♂ **5:30 pm** 2:30 pm
♀ △ ♅ **7:22 pm** 4:22 pm
☽ ☌ ♃ **9:55 pm** 6:55 pm
☽ □ ♅ **11:29 pm** 8:29 pm
☽ ⚺ ♀ **11:54 pm** 8:54 pm

14 THURSDAY
☽ ☌ ☿ **4:28 am** 1:28 am
☉ ☌ ♇ **9:19 am** 6:19 am
☽ ⚺ ♆ **8:55 pm** 5:55 pm

15 FRIDAY
☽ ⚺ ♇ **7:33 am** 4:33 am
☽ ⚺ ☉ **9:21 am** 6:21 am
☽ ⚺ ♄ **11:33 pm** 8:33 pm
☽ ⚹ ♂ 10:29 pm

16 SATURDAY
☽ ⚹ ♂ **1:29 am**
☽ ⚺ ♃ **5:03 am** 2:03 am
☽ ⚹ ♅ **5:43 am** 2:43 am
☽ ⚹ ♀ **12:02 pm** 9:02 am
☽ ⚺ ☿ **6:33 pm** 3:33 pm

17 SUNDAY
☽ ☌ ♆ **4:35 am** 1:35 am
☽ ⚹ ♇ **3:55 pm** 12:55 pm
♃ □ ♅ **5:50 pm** 2:50 pm
☽ ⚹ ☉ **10:44 pm** 7:44 pm

18 MONDAY
☽ ⚹ ♄ **9:20 am** 6:20 am
☽ ⚺ ♂ **1:16 pm** 10:16 am
☽ ⚺ ♅ **3:20 pm** 12:20 pm
☽ ⚹ ♃ **3:45 pm** 12:45 pm

19 TUESDAY
☽ □ ♀ **4:43 am** 1:43 am
☽ ⚹ ☿ **12:54 pm** 9:54 am
☽ ⚺ ♆ **3:34 pm** 12:34 pm

20 WEDNESDAY
☽ □ ♇ **3:29 am** 12:29 am
☿ ⚺ ♆ **1:04 pm** 10:04 am
♂ ☌ ♅ **3:38 pm** 12:38 pm
☽ □ ☉ **4:02 pm** 1:02 pm
☽ □ ♄ **10:00 pm** 7:00 pm

21 THURSDAY
☽ ☌ ♅ **3:37 am** 12:37 am
☽ ☌ ♂ **4:08 am** 1:08 am
☽ □ ♃ **5:15 am** 2:15 am
☽ △ ♀ 9:28 pm

22 FRIDAY
☽ △ ♀ **12:28 am**
☽ ⚹ ♆ **4:27 am** 1:27 am
☽ □ ☿ **8:59 am** 5:59 am
☽ △ ♇ **4:28 pm** 1:28 pm
♂ □ ♃ 11:49 pm

23 SATURDAY
♂ □ ♃ **2:49 am**
☽ △ ☉ **10:27 am** 7:27 am
☽ △ ♄ **11:19 am** 8:19 am
♀ ⚹ ♆ **2:49 pm** 11:49 am
☽ ⚺ ♅ **4:16 pm** 1:16 pm
☽ △ ♃ **7:04 pm** 4:04 pm
☽ ⚺ ♂ **7:27 pm** 4:27 pm
☉ ☌ ♄ **10:01 pm** 7:01 pm

24 SUNDAY
☽ □ ♆ **4:36 pm** 1:36 pm
☽ ⚻ ♀ **7:28 pm** 4:28 pm
☽ △ ☿ 11:17 pm

25 MONDAY
☽ △ ☿ **2:17 am**
☽ ⚻ ♇ **4:12 am** 1:12 am
☽ ⚻ ♄ **10:38 pm** 7:38 pm
☽ ⚻ ☉ 11:23 pm
☽ ⚹ ♅ 11:49 pm

26 TUESDAY
☽ ⚻ ☉ **2:23 am**
☽ ⚹ ♅ **2:49 am**
☽ ⚻ ♃ **6:32 am** 3:32 am
☉ □ ♅ **7:48 am** 4:48 am
☽ ⚹ ♂ **8:17 am** 5:17 am
☿ ⚺ ♇ **9:35 am** 6:35 am
☽ △ ♆ 10:57 pm

27 WEDNESDAY
☽ △ ♆ **1:57 am**
☽ ☍ ♀ **10:37 am** 7:37 am
☽ ☍ ♇ **12:55 pm** 9:55 am
☽ ⚻ ☿ **2:09 pm** 11:09 am

28 THURSDAY
☽ ☍ ♄ **6:41 am** 3:41 am
☽ □ ♅ **10:11 am** 7:11 am
♀ ☌ ♇ **11:18 am** 8:18 am
☽ ☍ ☉ **2:16 pm** 11:16 am
☽ ☍ ♃ **2:39 pm** 11:39 am
☽ □ ♂ **5:32 pm** 2:32 pm
☉ ☌ ♃ **8:40 pm** 5:40 pm

29 FRIDAY
☽ ⚻ ♆ **8:10 am** 5:10 am
☿ ⚺ ♀ **12:19 pm** 9:19 am
☽ ⚻ ♇ **6:36 pm** 3:36 pm
☽ ☍ ☿ **8:53 pm** 5:53 pm
☽ ⚻ ♀ **9:39 pm** 6:39 pm

30 SATURDAY
☽ ⚻ ♄ **11:54 am** 8:54 am
☽ △ ♅ **2:52 pm** 11:52 am
☽ ⚻ ♃ **8:01 pm** 5:01 pm
☽ ⚻ ☉ **10:51 pm** 7:51 pm
☽ △ ♂ **11:57 pm** 8:57 pm

31 SUNDAY
☽ ☍ ♆ **12:09 pm** 9:09 am
☽ △ ♇ **10:17 pm** 7:17 pm
☽ ⚻ ☿ 9:05 pm

JANUARY 2021

DATE	SID.TIME	SUN	MOON	NODE	MERCURY	VENUS	MARS	JUPITER	SATURN	URANUS	NEPTUNE	PLUTO	CERES	PALLAS	JUNO	VESTA	CHIRON
1 F	6 43 27	10♑46 47	2♌44	19♊53℞	17♑43	20♐25	27♈21	2♒47	1♒37	6♉48℞	18♓28	24♑11	12♓00	7♒51	4♐15	20♍09	5♈04
2 Sa	6 47 24	11 47 56	15 55	19 49	19 21	21 40	27 48	3 01	1 44	6 47	18 30	24 13	12 18	8 11	4 34	20 16	5 04
3 Su	6 51 21	12 49 04	29 19	19 46	20 59	22 55	28 14	3 14	1 51	6 47	18 31	24 15	12 37	8 31	4 52	20 24	5 05
4 M	6 55 17	13 50 13	12♍55	19 43	22 37	24 10	28 40	3 28	1 58	6 46	18 32	24 17	12 56	8 51	5 11	20 30	5 06
5 T	6 59 14	14 51 22	26 42	19 40	24 15	25 25	29 07	3 42	2 05	6 46	18 33	24 19	13 15	9 11	5 30	20 37	5 08
6 W	7 3 10	15 52 31	10♎39	19 39D	25 54	26 40	29 34	3 56	2 12	6 45	18 34	24 21	13 34	9 31	5 48	20 43	5 09
7 Th	7 7 7	16 53 40	24 45	19 39	27 32	27 56	0♉02	4 10	2 19	6 45	18 36	24 23	13 53	9 51	6 07	20 49	5 10
8 F	7 11 3	17 54 50	8♏58	19 40	29 11	29 11	0 29	4 24	2 26	6 44	18 37	24 25	14 13	10 11	6 25	20 54	5 11
9 Sa	7 15 0	18 56 00	23 16	19 42	0♒49	0♑26	0 57	4 38	2 33	6 44	18 38	24 27	14 32	10 31	6 43	20 59	5 12
10 Su	7 18 56	19 57 09	7♐38	19 43℞	2 27	1 41	1 25	4 52	2 40	6 44	18 40	24 29	14 52	10 51	7 01	21 04	5 14
11 M	7 22 53	20 58 19	21 58	19 44	4 05	2 56	1 54	5 06	2 47	6 44	18 41	24 31	15 11	11 11	7 19	21 08	5 15
12 T	7 26 50	21 59 29	6♑13	19 43	5 43	4 12	2 22	5 20	2 54	6 43	18 42	24 33	15 31	11 31	7 37	21 11	5 16
13 W	7 30 46	23 00 39	20 19	19 40	7 20	5 27	2 51	5 34	3 01	6 43	18 44	24 35	15 51	11 51	7 55	21 14	5 18
14 Th	7 34 43	24 01 48	4♒10	19 35	8 56	6 42	3 20	5 48	3 08	6 43D	18 45	24 37	16 11	12 12	8 13	21 17	5 19
15 F	7 38 39	25 02 57	17 43	19 30	10 30	7 57	3 49	6 02	3 15	6 43	18 47	24 39	16 31	12 32	8 31	21 19	5 21
16 Sa	7 42 36	26 04 05	0♓56	19 23	12 04	9 13	4 19	6 16	3 22	6 43	18 48	24 41	16 52	12 52	8 49	21 21	5 23
17 Su	7 46 32	27 05 12	13 48	19 17	13 35	10 28	4 48	6 30	3 30	6 43	18 50	24 43	17 12	13 12	9 06	21 22	5 24
18 M	7 50 29	28 06 19	26 20	19 11	15 05	11 43	5 18	6 44	3 37	6 44	18 52	24 45	17 32	13 33	9 24	21 23	5 26
19 T	7 54 25	29 07 24	8♈35	19 07	16 32	12 58	5 48	6 59	3 44	6 44	18 53	24 47	17 53	13 53	9 41	21 24℞	5 28
20 W	7 58 22	0♒08 29	20 37	19 05D	17 55	14 13	6 18	7 13	3 51	6 44	18 55	24 49	18 14	14 13	9 58	21 24	5 30
21 Th	8 2 19	1 09 34	2♉30	19 04	19 15	15 29	6 49	7 27	3 58	6 44	18 56	24 51	18 34	14 34	10 15	21 23	5 31
22 F	8 6 15	2 10 37	14 19	19 05	20 31	16 44	7 19	7 41	4 05	6 45	18 58	24 53	18 55	14 54	10 32	21 22	5 33
23 Sa	8 10 12	3 11 39	26 10	19 07	21 42	17 59	7 50	7 55	4 12	6 45	19 00	24 55	19 16	15 14	10 49	21 21	5 35
24 Su	8 14 8	4 12 40	8♊08	19 08℞	22 47	19 14	8 21	8 10	4 19	6 46	19 02	24 57	19 37	15 34	11 06	21 19	5 37
25 M	8 18 5	5 13 41	20 17	19 09	23 45	20 30	8 52	8 24	4 27	6 46	19 03	24 59	19 58	15 55	11 23	21 16	5 39
26 T	8 22 1	6 14 40	2♋41	19 07	24 35	21 45	9 23	8 38	4 34	6 47	19 05	25 01	20 19	16 15	11 39	21 13	5 41
27 W	8 25 58	7 15 39	15 23	19 04	25 18	23 00	9 54	8 52	4 41	6 48	19 07	25 03	20 41	16 36	11 56	21 10	5 44
28 Th	8 29 54	8 16 36	28 24	18 59	25 51	24 15	10 26	9 07	4 48	6 48	19 09	25 05	21 02	16 56	12 12	21 06	5 46
29 F	8 33 51	9 17 33	11♌45	18 51	26 14	25 30	10 57	9 21	4 55	6 49	19 10	25 07	21 23	17 16	12 29	21 02	5 48
30 Sa	8 37 48	10 18 28	25 23	18 42	26 27℞	26 45	11 29	9 35	5 02	6 50	19 12	25 09	21 45	17 37	12 45	20 57	5 50
31 Su	8 41 44	11 19 23	9♍15	18 33	26 29	28 01	12 01	9 49	5 09	6 51	19 14	25 11	22 07	17 57	13 01	20 52	5 53

EPHEMERIS CALCULATED FOR 12 MIDNIGHT GREENWICH MEAN TIME. ALL OTHER DATA AND FACING ASPECTARIAN PAGE IN **EASTERN TIME (BOLD)** AND PACIFIC TIME (REGULAR).

FEBRUARY 2021

☽ Last Aspect day	ET / hr:mn / PT		asp	☽ Ingress sign	day	ET / hr:mn / PT	
1	**6:10 am**	3:10 am	△♀	♎	1	**6:25 am**	3:25 am
2		10:15 pm	△☿	♏	3	**9:15 am**	6:15 am
3	**1:15 am**		△☿	♏	3	**9:15 am**	6:15 am
5	**4:20 am**	1:20 am	✶♇	♐	5	**12:16 pm**	9:16 am
6		10:16 pm	✶☿	♑	7	**3:52 pm**	12:52 pm
7	**1:16 am**		✶☿	♑	7	**3:52 pm**	12:52 pm
9	**12:22 pm**	9:22 am	☌♇	♒	9	**8:20 pm**	5:20 pm
11	**2:06 pm**	11:06 am	☌☉	♓	11		11:23 pm
11	**2:06 pm**	11:06 am	☌☉	♓	12	**2:23 am**	
13		11:29 pm	✶♇	♈	14	**10:54 am**	7:54 am

☽ Last Aspect day	ET / hr:mn / PT		asp	☽ Ingress sign	day	ET / hr:mn / PT	
14	**2:29 am**		✶♇	♈	14	**10:54 am**	7:54 am
16	**7:17 pm**	4:17 pm	✶☉	♉	16	**10:12 pm**	7:12 pm
18		11:28 pm	△♇	♊	19	**11:04 am**	8:04 am
19	**2:28 am**		△♇	♊	19	**11:04 am**	8:04 am
21	**1:39 pm**	10:39 am	△♀	♋	21	**10:53 pm**	7:53 pm
23	**11:54 pm**	8:54 pm	☍♇	♌	24	**7:23 am**	4:23 am
26	**6:32 am**	3:32 am	□♂	♍	26	**12:07 pm**	9:07 am
28	**10:58 am**	7:58 am	△♂	♎	28	**2:17 pm**	11:17 am

☽ Phases & Eclipses phase	day	ET / hr:mn / PT	
4th Quarter	4	**12:37 pm**	9:37 am
New Moon	11	**2:06 pm**	11:06 am
2nd Quarter	19	**1:47 pm**	10:47 am
Full Moon	27	**3:17 am**	12:17 am

Planet Ingress		day	ET / hr:mn / PT	
♀	♒	1	**9:05 am**	6:05 am
☉	♓	18	**5:44 am**	2:44 am
⚳	♈	20		9:23 pm
⚳	♈	21	**12:23 am**	
♀	♓	25	**8:11 am**	5:11 am

Planetary Motion		day	ET / hr:mn / PT	
☿	D	20	**7:52 pm**	4:52 pm

1 MONDAY
☽ ⚻ ☿ **12:05 am**
☉ □ ♂ **5:34 am** 2:34 am
☽ △ ♀ **6:10 am** 3:10 am
☽ △ ♄ **3:32 pm** 12:32 pm
☽ ⚻ ♅ **6:05 pm** 3:05 pm
☽ △ ♃ **11:58 pm** 8:58 pm

2 TUESDAY
☽ ⚻ ♂ **4:59 am** 1:59 am
☽ △ ☉ **5:50 am** 2:50 am
☽ ⚻ ♆ **3:10 pm** 12:10 pm
☽ □ ♇ 10:15 pm
☽ △ ☿ 10:15 pm
☿ ⚺ ♇ 10:22 pm

3 WEDNESDAY
☽ □ ♇ **1:15 am**
☽ △ ☿ **1:15 am**
☿ ⚺ ♇ **1:22 am**
☽ □ ♀ **1:55 pm** 10:55 am
☽ □ ♄ **6:47 pm** 3:47 pm
☽ ☍ ♅ **8:57 pm** 5:57 pm

4 THURSDAY
☽ □ ♃ **3:40 am** 12:40 am
☽ ☍ ♂ **9:51 am** 6:51 am
☽ □ ☉ **12:37 pm** 9:37 am
☽ △ ♆ **6:11 pm** 3:11 pm
☽ □ ☿ 10:27 pm

5 FRIDAY
☽ □ ☿ **1:27 am**
☽ ✶ ♇ **4:20 am** 1:20 am
☽ ✶ ♀ **10:00 pm** 7:00 pm
☽ ✶ ♄ **10:20 pm** 7:20 pm
☽ ⚻ ♅ 9:10 pm
♀ ☌ ♄ 11:07 pm

6 SATURDAY
☽ ⚻ ♅ **12:10 am**
♀ ☌ ♄ **2:07 am**
☽ ✶ ♃ **7:45 am** 4:45 am
☽ ⚻ ♂ **3:12 pm** 12:12 pm
☽ ✶ ☉ **7:56 pm** 4:56 pm
☽ □ ♆ **9:40 pm** 6:40 pm
♀ □ ♅ **10:33 pm** 7:33 pm
☽ ✶ ☿ 10:16 pm

7 SUNDAY
☽ ✶ ☿ **1:16 am**
☽ ⚺ ♇ **7:56 am** 4:56 am
☉ ⚺ ♆ **8:32 pm** 5:32 pm
☽ ⚺ ♄ 11:31 pm

8 MONDAY
☽ ⚺ ♄ **2:31 am**
☽ △ ♅ **4:00 am** 1:00 am
☽ ⚺ ♀ **6:53 am** 3:53 am
☉ ☌ ☿ **8:48 am** 5:48 am
☽ ⚺ ♃ **12:32 pm** 9:32 am
☿ ⚺ ♆ **6:35 pm** 3:35 pm
☽ △ ♂ **9:21 pm** 6:21 pm
☽ ⚺ ☿ 10:18 pm
☽ ✶ ♆ 10:55 pm

9 TUESDAY
☽ ⚺ ☿ **1:18 am**
☽ ✶ ♆ **1:55 am**
☽ ⚺ ☉ **4:11 am** 1:11 am
☽ ☌ ♇ **12:22 pm** 9:22 am

10 WEDNESDAY
☿ □ ♂ **7:16 am** 4:16 am
☽ ☌ ♄ **7:42 am** 4:42 am
☽ □ ♅ **8:51 am** 5:51 am
☽ ☌ ♀ **5:11 pm** 2:11 pm
☽ ☌ ♃ **6:29 pm** 3:29 pm
☽ ☌ ☿ 11:22 pm

11 THURSDAY
☽ ☌ ☿ **2:22 am**
☽ □ ♂ **4:55 am** 1:55 am
☽ ⚺ ♆ **7:27 am** 4:27 am
♀ ☌ ♃ **10:00 am** 7:00 am
☽ ☌ ☉ **2:06 pm** 11:06 am
☽ ⚺ ♇ **6:14 pm** 3:14 pm

12 FRIDAY
☽ ⚺ ♄ **2:42 pm** 11:42 am
☽ ✶ ♅ **3:30 pm** 12:30 pm
☽ ⚺ ♃ 11:29 pm
☿ ☌ ♀ 11:48 pm

13 SATURDAY
☽ ⚺ ♃ **2:29 am**
☿ ☌ ♀ **2:48 am**
☽ ⚺ ☿ **5:32 am** 2:32 am
☽ ⚺ ♀ **6:03 am** 3:03 am
☽ ✶ ♂ **2:55 pm** 11:55 am
☽ ☌ ♆ **3:11 pm** 12:11 pm
♂ ✶ ♆ **9:13 pm** 6:13 pm
☉ ⚺ ♇ **9:34 pm** 6:34 pm
☽ ✶ ♇ 11:29 pm
☽ ⚺ ☉ 11:54 pm

14 SUNDAY
☽ ✶ ♇ **2:29 am**
☽ ⚺ ☉ **2:54 am**
☿ ☌ ♃ **4:40 pm** 1:40 pm
☽ ✶ ♄ 9:23 pm
☽ ⚺ ♅ 9:49 pm

15 MONDAY
☽ ✶ ♄ **12:23 am**
☽ ⚺ ♅ **12:49 am**
☽ ✶ ☿ **11:50 am** 8:50 am
☽ ✶ ♃ **1:22 pm** 10:22 am
☽ ✶ ♀ **10:40 pm** 7:40 pm
☽ ⚺ ♆ 10:44 pm

16 TUESDAY
☽ ⚺ ♆ **1:44 am**
☽ ⚺ ♂ **4:08 am** 1:08 am
☽ □ ♇ **1:32 pm** 10:32 am
☽ ✶ ☉ **7:17 pm** 4:17 pm

17 WEDNESDAY
♀ ⚺ ♆ **5:00 am** 2:00 am
☽ □ ♄ **12:48 pm** 9:48 am
☽ ☌ ♅ **12:48 pm** 9:48 am
♄ □ ♅ **2:08 pm** 11:08 am
☽ □ ☿ **9:32 pm** 6:32 pm
☽ □ ♃ 11:51 pm

18 THURSDAY
☽ □ ♃ **2:51 am**
☽ ✶ ♆ **2:30 pm** 11:30 am
☽ □ ♀ **6:21 pm** 3:21 pm
☽ ☌ ♂ **7:48 pm** 4:48 pm
☽ △ ♇ 11:28 pm

19 FRIDAY
☽ △ ♇ **2:28 am**
☽ □ ☉ **1:47 pm** 10:47 am
♀ □ ♂ **6:04 pm** 3:04 pm
☽ ⚺ ♅ 10:50 pm
☽ △ ♄ 11:15 pm

20 SATURDAY
☽ ⚺ ♅ **1:50 am**
☽ △ ♄ **2:15 am**
☽ △ ☿ **9:20 am** 6:20 am
☽ △ ♃ **4:46 pm** 1:46 pm

21 SUNDAY
☽ □ ♆ **3:10 am** 12:10 am
☽ ⚺ ♂ **11:06 am** 8:06 am
☽ △ ♀ **1:39 pm** 10:39 am
☽ ⚻ ♇ **2:45 pm** 11:45 am
♀ ⚺ ♇ 9:31 pm

22 MONDAY
♀ ⚺ ♇ **12:31 am**
☽ △ ☉ **6:47 am** 3:47 am
☽ ✶ ♅ **1:09 pm** 10:09 am
☽ ⚻ ♄ **1:55 pm** 10:55 am
☽ ⚻ ☿ **8:31 pm** 5:31 pm

23 TUESDAY
☽ ⚻ ♃ **4:14 am** 1:14 am
☽ △ ♆ **1:06 pm** 10:06 am
☽ ✶ ♂ **10:59 pm** 7:59 pm
☽ ☍ ♇ **11:54 pm** 8:54 pm

24 WEDNESDAY
☽ ⚻ ♀ **4:47 am** 1:47 am
☽ ⚻ ☉ **7:18 pm** 4:18 pm
☽ □ ♅ **8:49 pm** 5:49 pm
♂ △ ♇ **8:52 pm** 5:52 pm
☽ ☍ ♄ **9:52 pm** 6:52 pm

25 THURSDAY
☽ ☍ ☿ **4:56 am** 1:56 am
☽ ☍ ♃ **11:40 am** 8:40 am
☉ ✶ ♅ **4:13 pm** 1:13 pm
☽ ⚻ ♆ **7:09 pm** 4:09 pm

26 FRIDAY
☽ ⚻ ♇ **5:12 am** 2:12 am
☽ □ ♂ **6:32 am** 3:32 am
☉ ⚺ ♄ **9:25 am** 6:25 am
☽ ☍ ♀ **2:50 pm** 11:50 am
☽ △ ♅ 9:54 pm
☽ ⚻ ♄ 11:09 pm

27 SATURDAY
☽ △ ♅ **12:54 am**
☽ ⚻ ♄ **2:09 am**
☽ ☍ ☉ **3:17 am** 12:17 am
☽ ⚻ ☿ **10:25 am** 7:25 am
☽ ⚻ ♃ **3:40 pm** 12:40 pm
☽ ☍ ♆ **10:06 pm** 7:06 pm

28 SUNDAY
☽ △ ♇ **7:42 am** 4:42 am
☽ △ ♂ **10:58 am** 7:58 am
☽ ⚻ ♀ **9:36 pm** 6:36 pm
☽ ⚻ ♅ 11:49 pm

Eastern time in bold type
Pacific time in medium type

FEBRUARY 2021

DATE	SID.TIME	SUN	MOON	NODE	MERCURY	VENUS	MARS	JUPITER	SATURN	URANUS	NEPTUNE	PLUTO	CERES	PALLAS	JUNO	VESTA	CHIRON
1 M	8 45 41	12♒20 16	23♍17	18♊25℞	26♒19℞	29♑16	12♉33	10♒04	5♒17	6♉51	19♓16	25♑13	22♓28	18♒17	13♐17	20♍46℞	5♈55
2 T	8 49 37	13 21 09	7♎25	18 18	25 59	0♒31	13 05	10 18	5 24	6 52	19 18	25 15	22 50	18 38	13 33	20 40	5 57
3 W	8 53 34	14 22 01	21 36	18 13	25 27	1 46	13 37	10 32	5 31	6 53	19 20	25 16	23 12	18 58	13 48	20 33	6 00
4 Th	8 57 30	15 22 52	5♏45	18 11D	24 45	3 01	14 10	10 46	5 38	6 54	19 22	25 18	23 34	19 19	14 04	20 26	6 02
5 F	9 1 27	16 23 43	19 52	18 10	23 54	4 17	14 42	11 00	5 45	6 56	19 24	25 20	23 56	19 39	14 19	20 18	6 05
6 Sa	9 5 23	17 24 32	3♐56	18 11	22 56	5 32	15 15	11 15	5 52	6 57	19 26	25 22	24 18	19 59	14 34	20 10	6 07
7 Su	9 9 20	18 25 21	17 55	18 12℞	21 51	6 47	15 47	11 29	5 59	6 58	19 28	25 24	24 40	20 20	14 50	20 02	6 10
8 M	9 13 17	19 26 09	1♑49	18 11	20 42	8 02	16 20	11 43	6 06	6 59	19 30	25 26	25 02	20 40	15 05	19 53	6 12
9 T	9 17 13	20 26 56	15 36	18 08	19 31	9 17	16 53	11 57	6 13	7 00	19 32	25 28	25 24	21 00	15 19	19 43	6 15
10 W	9 21 10	21 27 42	29 15	18 02	18 19	10 32	17 26	12 12	6 20	7 02	19 34	25 30	25 46	21 21	15 34	19 33	6 18
11 Th	9 25 6	22 28 26	12♒43	17 53	17 09	11 48	17 59	12 26	6 27	7 03	19 36	25 31	26 09	21 41	15 49	19 23	6 20
12 F	9 29 3	23 29 09	25 58	17 42	16 03	13 03	18 33	12 40	6 34	7 05	19 38	25 33	26 31	22 01	16 03	19 12	6 23
13 Sa	9 32 59	24 29 51	8♓58	17 30	15 01	14 18	19 06	12 54	6 41	7 06	19 40	25 35	26 53	22 22	16 17	19 01	6 26
14 Su	9 36 56	25 30 31	21 43	17 18	14 05	15 33	19 39	13 08	6 48	7 08	19 42	25 37	27 16	22 42	16 31	18 50	6 29
15 M	9 40 52	26 31 10	4♈11	17 06	13 16	16 48	20 13	13 22	6 55	7 09	19 44	25 39	27 38	23 02	16 45	18 38	6 32
16 T	9 44 49	27 31 47	16 24	16 57	12 35	18 03	20 47	13 36	7 02	7 11	19 47	25 40	28 01	23 22	16 59	18 26	6 35
17 W	9 48 46	28 32 22	28 25	16 50	12 01	19 18	21 20	13 50	7 08	7 13	19 49	25 42	28 24	23 43	17 13	18 13	6 37
18 Th	9 52 42	29 32 56	10♉17	16 46	11 35	20 33	21 54	14 04	7 15	7 14	19 51	25 44	28 46	24 03	17 26	18 00	6 40
19 F	9 56 39	0♓33 28	22 06	16 44D	11 16	21 49	22 28	14 18	7 22	7 16	19 53	25 46	29 09	24 23	17 39	17 47	6 43
20 Sa	10 0 35	1 33 58	3♊55	16 44	11 05	23 04	23 02	14 32	7 29	7 18	19 55	25 47	29 32	24 43	17 52	17 34	6 46
21 Su	10 4 32	2 34 26	15 52	16 44℞	11 01D	24 19	23 36	14 46	7 36	7 20	19 57	25 49	29 55	25 03	18 05	17 20	6 49
22 M	10 8 28	3 34 52	28 01	16 44	11 05	25 34	24 10	15 00	7 42	7 22	20 00	25 51	0♈18	25 24	18 18	17 06	6 52
23 T	10 12 25	4 35 17	10♋27	16 41	11 14	26 49	24 44	15 14	7 49	7 23	20 02	25 52	0 41	25 44	18 31	16 52	6 55
24 W	10 16 21	5 35 40	23 15	16 37	11 30	28 04	25 19	15 28	7 55	7 25	20 04	25 54	1 04	26 04	18 43	16 37	6 59
25 Th	10 20 18	6 36 00	6♌27	16 29	11 51	29 19	25 53	15 42	8 02	7 28	20 06	25 55	1 27	26 24	18 55	16 22	7 02
26 F	10 24 15	7 36 19	20 03	16 20	12 18	0♓34	26 27	15 56	8 09	7 30	20 09	25 57	1 50	26 44	19 07	16 07	7 05
27 Sa	10 28 11	8 36 36	4♍03	16 08	12 50	1 49	27 02	16 09	8 15	7 32	20 11	25 59	2 13	27 04	19 19	15 52	7 08
28 Su	10 32 8	9 36 52	18 21	15 56	13 26	3 04	27 36	16 23	8 22	7 34	20 13	26 00	2 36	27 24	19 31	15 37	7 11

EPHEMERIS CALCULATED FOR 12 MIDNIGHT GREENWICH MEAN TIME. ALL OTHER DATA AND FACING ASPECTARIAN PAGE IN **EASTERN TIME (BOLD)** AND PACIFIC TIME (REGULAR).

MARCH 2021

☽ Last Aspect day	ET / hr:mn / PT	asp	☽ Ingress sign day	ET / hr:mn / PT
2	**9:09 am** 6:09 am	□♇	♏ 2	**3:38 pm** 12:38 pm
4	**11:10 am** 8:10 am	✶♇	♐ 4	**5:43 pm** 2:43 pm
6	**4:44 am** 1:44 am	□♆	♑ 6	**9:20 pm** 6:20 pm
8	**7:52 pm** 4:52 pm	☌♇	♒ 8	11:41 pm
8	**7:52 pm** 4:52 pm	☌♇	♒ 9	**2:41 am**
10	**10:32 pm** 7:32 pm	☌☿	♓ 11	**9:44 am** 6:44 am
13	**11:38 am** 8:38 am	✶♇	♈ 13	**6:44 pm** 3:44 pm
15	**11:40 pm** 8:40 pm	□♇	♉ 16	**6:56 am** 3:56 am
18	**4:40 pm** 1:40 pm	✶☉	♊ 18	**7:47 pm** 4:47 pm
21	**8:04 am** 5:04 am	□♀	♋ 21	**8:18 am** 5:18 am
23	**11:26 am** 8:26 am	☍♇	♌ 23	**5:56 pm** 2:56 pm
25	**9:27 am** 6:27 am	☍♃	♍ 25	**11:25 pm** 8:25 pm
27	**7:48 pm** 4:48 pm	△♇	♎ 27	10:22 pm
27	**7:48 pm** 4:48 pm	△♇	♎ 28	**1:22 am**
29	**8:08 pm** 5:08 pm	□♇	♏ 29	10:33 pm
29	**8:08 pm** 5:08 pm	□♇	♏ 30	**1:33 am**
31	**8:29 pm** 5:29 pm	✶♇	♐ 31	10:59 pm
31	**8:29 pm** 5:29 pm	✶♇	♐ 4/1	**1:59 am**

☽ Phases & Eclipses phase	day	ET / hr:mn / PT
4th Quarter	5	**8:30 pm** 5:30 pm
New Moon	13	**5:21 am** 2:21 am
2nd Quarter	21	**10:40 am** 7:40 am
Full Moon	28	**2:48 pm** 11:48 am

Planet Ingress	day	ET / hr:mn / PT
♂ ♊	3	**10:30 pm** 7:30 pm
♀ ♓	7	**4:06 pm** 1:06 pm
☿ ♓	15	**6:26 pm** 3:26 pm
☉ ♈	20	**5:37 am** 2:37 am
♀ ♈	21	**10:16 am** 7:16 am

Planetary Motion	day	ET / hr:mn / PT

1 MONDAY
☽ ⚻ ♅ **2:49 am**
☽ △ ♄ **4:17 am** 1:17 am
☽ ⚻ ☉ **8:42 am** 5:42 am
☽ △ ☿ **2:27 pm** 11:27 am
☽ △ ♃ **5:57 pm** 2:57 pm
☽ ⚻ ♆ **11:40 pm** 8:40 pm

2 TUESDAY
☽ □ ♇ **9:09 am** 6:09 am
☽ ⚻ ♂ **2:22 pm** 11:22 am

3 WEDNESDAY
☽ △ ♀ **3:39 am** 12:39 am
☽ ☍ ♅ **4:22 am** 1:22 am
☽ □ ♄ **6:05 am** 3:05 am
♀ ✶ ♅ **12:09 pm** 9:09 am
☽ △ ☉ **1:52 pm** 10:52 am
☽ □ ☿ **7:01 pm** 4:01 pm
☽ □ ♃ **8:22 pm** 5:22 pm
☽ △ ♆ 10:30 pm

4 THURSDAY
☽ △ ♆ **1:30 am**
♀ ⚺ ♄ **10:14 am** 7:14 am
☽ ✶ ♇ **11:10 am** 8:10 am
☽ ☍ ♂ **6:32 pm** 3:32 pm
☿ ☌ ♃ **10:27 pm** 7:27 pm

5 FRIDAY
☽ ⚻ ♅ **6:55 am** 3:55 am
☽ ✶ ♄ **8:56 am** 5:56 am
☽ □ ♀ **10:58 am** 7:58 am
☽ □ ☉ **8:30 pm** 5:30 pm
☽ ✶ ♃ 9:07 pm
☽ ✶ ☿ 10:36 pm

6 SATURDAY
☽ ✶ ♃ **12:07 am**
☽ ✶ ☿ **1:36 am**
☽ □ ♆ **4:44 am** 1:44 am
☽ ⚺ ♇ **2:39 pm** 11:39 am
☽ ⚻ ♂ 9:29 pm

7 SUNDAY
☽ ⚻ ♂ **12:29 am**
☽ △ ♅ **11:09 am** 8:09 am
☽ ⚺ ♄ **1:28 pm** 10:28 am
☽ ✶ ♀ **8:29 pm** 5:29 pm
☿ ⚺ ♆ **9:12 pm** 6:12 pm

8 MONDAY
☽ ✶ ☉ **5:15 am** 2:15 am
☽ ⚺ ♃ **5:39 am** 2:39 am
☽ ✶ ♆ **9:41 am** 6:41 am
☽ ⚺ ☿ **10:44 am** 7:44 am
☉ ⚺ ♃ **12:04 pm** 9:04 am
☽ ☌ ♇ **7:52 pm** 4:52 pm

9 TUESDAY
☽ △ ♂ **8:23 am** 5:23 am
☽ □ ♅ **5:06 pm** 2:06 pm
☽ ☌ ♄ **7:45 pm** 4:45 pm

10 WEDNESDAY
☽ ⚺ ♀ **8:16 am** 5:16 am
☽ ☌ ♃ **12:58 pm** 9:58 am
☽ ⚺ ☉ **4:08 pm** 1:08 pm
☽ ⚺ ♆ **4:21 pm** 1:21 pm
☉ ☌ ♆ **7:01 pm** 4:01 pm
☽ ☌ ☿ **10:32 pm** 7:32 pm
☽ ⚺ ♇ 11:48 pm

11 THURSDAY
☽ ⚺ ♇ **2:48 am**
☽ □ ♂ **6:16 pm** 3:16 pm
☽ ✶ ♅ 9:50 pm

12 FRIDAY
☽ ✶ ♅ **12:50 am**
☽ ⚺ ♄ **3:49 am** 12:49 am
♀ ⚺ ♃ **6:53 pm** 3:53 pm
☿ ⚺ ♇ **8:41 pm** 5:41 pm
☽ ⚺ ♃ **10:11 pm** 7:11 pm
☽ ☌ ♀ **10:29 pm** 7:29 pm
☽ ☌ ♆ 9:52 pm

13 SATURDAY
☽ ☌ ♆ **12:52 am**
☽ ☌ ☉ **5:21 am** 2:21 am
☽ ✶ ♇ **11:38 am** 8:38 am
☽ ⚺ ☿ **1:17 pm** 10:17 am
♀ ☌ ♆ **11:08 pm** 8:08 pm

14 SUNDAY
☽ ✶ ♂ **7:28 am** 4:28 am
☽ ⚺ ♅ **11:37 am** 8:37 am
☽ ✶ ♄ **2:58 pm** 11:58 am

15 MONDAY
☽ ✶ ♃ **10:40 am** 7:40 am
☽ ⚺ ♆ **12:35 pm** 9:35 am
☽ ⚺ ♀ **4:39 pm** 1:39 pm
☽ ⚺ ☉ **10:22 pm** 7:22 pm
☽ □ ♇ **11:40 pm** 8:40 pm

16 TUESDAY
☽ ✶ ☿ **8:31 am** 5:31 am
☉ ✶ ♇ **2:26 pm** 11:26 am
☽ ⚺ ♂ **10:12 pm** 7:12 pm
☽ ☌ ♅ **11:37 pm** 8:37 pm

17 WEDNESDAY
☽ □ ♄ **3:20 am** 12:20 am
☽ □ ♃ 9:14 pm
☽ ✶ ♆ 10:16 pm

18 THURSDAY
☽ □ ♃ **12:14 am**
☽ ✶ ♆ **1:16 am**
♂ ⚺ ♅ **4:48 am** 1:48 am
☽ ✶ ♀ **12:24 pm** 9:24 am
☽ △ ♇ **12:30 pm** 9:30 am
♀ ✶ ♇ **1:20 pm** 10:20 am
☽ ✶ ☉ **4:40 pm** 1:40 pm

19 FRIDAY
☽ □ ☿ **5:28 am** 2:28 am
☽ ⚺ ♅ **12:52 pm** 9:52 am
☽ ☌ ♂ **2:25 pm** 11:25 am
☽ △ ♄ **4:50 pm** 1:50 pm

20 SATURDAY
☽ △ ♃ **2:14 pm** 11:14 am
☽ □ ♆ **2:20 pm** 11:20 am
♃ ⚺ ♆ **9:51 pm** 6:51 pm
☽ ⚻ ♇ 10:17 pm

21 SUNDAY
☽ ⚻ ♇ **1:17 am**
☽ □ ♀ **8:04 am** 5:04 am
☽ □ ☉ **10:40 am** 7:40 am
☿ ✶ ♅ **7:35 pm** 4:35 pm
♂ △ ♄ **10:35 pm** 7:35 pm
☽ ✶ ♅ 10:02 pm
☽ △ ☿ 10:46 pm

22 MONDAY
☽ ✶ ♅ **1:02 am**
☽ △ ☿ **1:46 am**
☽ ⚻ ♄ **5:02 am** 2:02 am
☽ ⚺ ♂ **5:19 am** 2:19 am
☽ △ ♆ 10:14 pm
☽ ⚻ ♃ 10:56 pm

23 TUESDAY
☽ △ ♆ **1:14 am**
☽ ⚻ ♃ **1:56 am**
☿ ⚺ ♄ **6:12 am** 3:12 am
☽ ☍ ♇ **11:26 am** 8:26 am
☿ □ ♂ **11:26 pm** 8:26 pm
☽ △ ♀ **11:50 pm** 8:50 pm
☽ △ ☉ 9:54 pm

24 WEDNESDAY
☽ △ ☉ **12:54 am**
☽ □ ♅ **9:45 am** 6:45 am
☽ ☍ ♄ **1:38 pm** 10:38 am
☽ ✶ ♂ **4:08 pm** 1:08 pm
☽ ⚻ ☿ **5:28 pm** 2:28 pm

25 THURSDAY
☽ ⚻ ♆ **8:07 am** 5:07 am
☽ ☍ ♃ **9:27 am** 6:27 am
☽ ⚻ ♇ **5:28 pm** 2:28 pm
☉ ☌ ♀ 11:58 pm

26 FRIDAY
☉ ☌ ♀ **2:58 am**
☽ ⚻ ☉ **9:52 am** 6:52 am
☽ ⚻ ♀ **10:00 am** 7:00 am
☽ △ ♅ **2:17 pm** 11:17 am
☽ ⚻ ♄ **6:00 pm** 3:00 pm
☽ □ ♂ **10:16 pm** 7:16 pm

27 SATURDAY
☽ ☍ ☿ **3:37 am** 12:37 am
☽ ☍ ♆ **11:05 am** 8:05 am
☽ ⚻ ♃ **12:55 pm** 9:55 am
☽ △ ♇ **7:48 pm** 4:48 pm

28 SUNDAY
♀ ⚺ ♅ **12:53 pm** 9:53 am
☽ ☍ ☉ **2:48 pm** 11:48 am
☽ ⚻ ♅ **3:40 pm** 12:40 pm
☽ ☍ ♀ **3:55 pm** 12:55 pm
☽ △ ♄ **7:21 pm** 4:21 pm
☽ △ ♂ 10:12 pm

29 MONDAY
☽ △ ♂ **1:12 am**
☉ ⚺ ♅ **4:34 am** 1:34 am
☽ ⚻ ☿ **10:16 am** 7:16 am
☽ ⚻ ♆ **11:42 am** 8:42 am
☽ △ ♃ **2:01 pm** 11:01 am
☽ □ ♇ **8:08 pm** 5:08 pm
☿ ☌ ♆ **11:24 pm** 8:24 pm

30 TUESDAY
♀ ✶ ♄ **11:47 am** 8:47 am
☽ ☍ ♅ **3:54 pm** 12:54 pm
☽ ⚻ ☉ **6:16 pm** 3:16 pm
☽ □ ♄ **7:39 pm** 4:39 pm
☽ ⚻ ♀ **8:20 pm** 5:20 pm
☿ ⚺ ♃ **11:54 pm** 8:54 pm

31 WEDNESDAY
☽ ⚻ ♂ **3:17 am** 12:17 am
☽ △ ♆ **11:59 am** 8:59 am
☽ □ ♃ **2:52 pm** 11:52 am
☽ △ ☿ **4:35 pm** 1:35 pm
☉ ✶ ♄ **5:04 pm** 2:04 pm
☽ ✶ ♇ **8:29 pm** 5:29 pm

Eastern time in bold type
Pacific time in medium type

MARCH 2021

DATE	SID.TIME	SUN	MOON	NODE	MERCURY	VENUS	MARS	JUPITER	SATURN	URANUS	NEPTUNE	PLUTO	CERES	PALLAS	JUNO	VESTA	CHIRON
1 M	10 36 4	10♓37 05	2♎52	15♊44℞	14♒06	4♓19	28♉11	16♒37	8♒28	7♉36	20♓15	26♑02	2♈59	27♒44	19♐42	15♍22℞	7♈14
2 T	10 40 1	11 37 17	17 28	15 34	14 51	5 34	28 46	16 50	8 34	7 38	20 17	26 03	3 22	28 04	19 53	15 06	7 18
3 W	10 43 57	12 37 27	2♏02	15 27	15 39	6 49	29 20	17 04	8 41	7 41	20 20	26 05	3 46	28 23	20 04	14 50	7 21
4 Th	10 47 54	13 37 36	16 29	15 23	16 30	8 04	29 55	17 17	8 47	7 43	20 22	26 06	4 09	28 43	20 15	14 35	7 24
5 F	10 51 50	14 37 44	0♐46	15 22	17 25	9 18	0♊30	17 31	8 53	7 45	20 24	26 08	4 32	29 03	20 26	14 19	7 27
6 Sa	10 55 47	15 37 49	14 49	15 21	18 22	10 33	1 05	17 44	9 00	7 48	20 27	26 09	4 56	29 23	20 36	14 03	7 31
7 Su	10 59 44	16 37 54	28 40	15 21	19 23	11 48	1 40	17 58	9 06	7 50	20 29	26 11	5 19	29 43	20 46	13 48	7 34
8 M	11 3 40	17 37 57	12♑18	15 20	20 25	13 03	2 14	18 11	9 12	7 52	20 31	26 12	5 42	0♓02	20 56	13 32	7 37
9 T	11 7 37	18 37 58	25 44	15 16	21 31	14 18	2 50	18 24	9 18	7 55	20 33	26 13	6 06	0 22	21 06	13 16	7 41
10 W	11 11 33	19 37 57	9♒00	15 09	22 38	15 33	3 25	18 38	9 24	7 57	20 36	26 15	6 29	0 42	21 16	13 00	7 44
11 Th	11 15 30	20 37 55	22 04	14 59	23 48	16 48	4 00	18 51	9 30	8 00	20 38	26 16	6 53	1 01	21 25	12 45	7 48
12 F	11 19 26	21 37 51	4♓57	14 47	25 00	18 03	4 35	19 04	9 36	8 03	20 40	26 17	7 16	1 21	21 34	12 29	7 51
13 Sa	11 23 23	22 37 45	17 39	14 33	26 13	19 17	5 10	19 17	9 42	8 05	20 43	26 19	7 40	1 40	21 43	12 14	7 54
14 Su	11 27 19	23 37 37	0♈08	14 19	27 29	20 32	5 45	19 30	9 48	8 08	20 45	26 20	8 04	2 00	21 51	11 59	7 58
15 M	11 31 16	24 37 27	12 26	14 07	28 46	21 47	6 21	19 43	9 53	8 11	20 47	26 21	8 27	2 19	22 00	11 44	8 01
16 T	11 35 13	25 37 15	24 32	13 56	0♓05	23 02	6 56	19 56	9 59	8 13	20 49	26 22	8 51	2 39	22 08	11 29	8 05
17 W	11 39 9	26 37 01	6♉29	13 47	1 26	24 17	7 31	20 09	10 05	8 16	20 52	26 23	9 14	2 58	22 16	11 14	8 08
18 Th	11 43 6	27 36 44	18 19	13 42	2 48	25 31	8 07	20 22	10 10	8 19	20 54	26 25	9 38	3 17	22 23	11 00	8 12
19 F	11 47 2	28 36 26	0♊06	13 39	4 12	26 46	8 42	20 35	10 16	8 22	20 56	26 26	10 02	3 36	22 30	10 46	8 15
20 Sa	11 50 59	29 36 05	11 55	13 38D	5 37	28 01	9 18	20 47	10 21	8 25	20 58	26 27	10 25	3 56	22 38	10 32	8 19
21 Su	11 54 55	0♈35 42	23 50	13 39℞	7 04	29 16	9 53	21 00	10 27	8 27	21 01	26 28	10 49	4 15	22 44	10 18	8 22
22 M	11 58 52	1 35 17	5♋56	13 39	8 32	0♈30	10 29	21 12	10 32	8 30	21 03	26 29	11 13	4 34	22 51	10 05	8 26
23 T	12 2 48	2 34 50	18 20	13 37	10 01	1 45	11 05	21 25	10 38	8 33	21 05	26 30	11 37	4 53	22 57	9 52	8 29
24 W	12 6 45	3 34 20	1♌07	13 34	11 32	3 00	11 40	21 37	10 43	8 36	21 07	26 31	12 00	5 12	23 03	9 40	8 33
25 Th	12 10 42	4 33 48	14 20	13 29	13 05	4 14	12 16	21 50	10 48	8 39	21 10	26 32	12 24	5 31	23 09	9 27	8 36
26 F	12 14 38	5 33 14	28 01	13 21	14 38	5 29	12 52	22 02	10 53	8 42	21 12	26 33	12 48	5 49	23 14	9 16	8 40
27 Sa	12 18 35	6 32 37	12♍09	13 11	16 13	6 43	13 27	22 14	10 58	8 45	21 14	26 34	13 12	6 08	23 20	9 04	8 43
28 Su	12 22 31	7 31 58	26 42	13 01	17 50	7 58	14 03	22 26	11 03	8 48	21 16	26 35	13 36	6 27	23 24	8 53	8 47
29 M	12 26 28	8 31 17	11♎32	12 51	19 28	9 13	14 39	22 38	11 08	8 51	21 18	26 36	13 59	6 45	23 29	8 42	8 50
30 T	12 30 24	9 30 34	26 32	12 43	21 07	10 27	15 15	22 50	11 13	8 54	21 21	26 36	14 23	7 04	23 33	8 32	8 54
31 W	12 34 21	10 29 50	11♏30	12 37	22 47	11 42	15 51	23 02	11 18	8 58	21 23	26 37	14 47	7 23	23 37	8 22	8 57

EPHEMERIS CALCULATED FOR 12 MIDNIGHT GREENWICH MEAN TIME. ALL OTHER DATA AND FACING ASPECTARIAN PAGE IN **EASTERN TIME (BOLD)** AND PACIFIC TIME (REGULAR).

APRIL 2021

☽ Last Aspect day	ET / hr:mn / PT		asp	☽ Ingress sign	day	ET / hr:mn / PT	
3/31	**8:29 pm**	5:29 pm	⚹♇	♐	1	**1:59 am**	
2		10:24 pm	□☿	♑	3	**4:13 am**	1:13 am
3	**1:24 am**		□☿	♑	3	**4:13 am**	1:13 am
5	**3:05 am**	12:05 am	☌♇	♒	5	**9:04 am**	6:04 am
7	**6:05 am**	3:05 am	☌♃	♓	7	**4:30 pm**	1:30 pm
9	**7:48 pm**	4:48 pm	⚹♇	♈	9		11:11 pm
9	**7:48 pm**	4:48 pm	⚹♇	♈	10	**2:11 am**	
12	**8:06 am**	5:06 am	☌♀	♉	12	**1:44 pm**	10:44 am
14	**8:00 pm**	5:00 pm	△♇	♊	14		11:35 pm
14	**8:00 pm**	5:00 pm	△♇	♊	15	**2:35 am**	
17	**11:03 am**	8:03 am	⚹☉	♋	17	**3:25 pm**	12:25 pm
19	**8:03 pm**	5:03 pm	☍♇	♌	19		11:11 pm
19	**8:03 pm**	5:03 pm	☍♇	♌	20	**2:11 am**	
22	**8:05 am**	5:05 am	⚹♂	♍	22	**9:08 am**	6:08 am
24	**6:50 am**	3:50 am	△♇	♎	24	**12:06 pm**	9:06 am
26	**8:40 am**	5:40 am	△♃	♏	26	**12:18 pm**	9:18 am
28	**8:31 am**	5:31 am	□♃	♐	28	**11:42 am**	8:42 am
30	**9:27 am**	6:27 am	⚹♃	♑	30	**12:16 pm**	9:16 am

☽ Phases & Eclipses phase	day	ET / hr:mn / PT	
4th Quarter	4	**6:02 am**	3:02 am
New Moon	11	**10:31 pm**	7:31 pm
2nd Quarter	19		11:59 pm
2nd Quarter	20	**2:59 pm**	
Full Moon	26	**11:32 pm**	8:32 pm

Planet Ingress		day	ET / hr:mn / PT	
☿	♈	3	**11:41 pm**	8:41 pm
♀	♉	14	**2:22 pm**	11:22 am
☿	♉	19	**6:29 am**	3:29 am
☉	♉	19	**4:33 pm**	1:33 pm
♂	♋	23	**7:49 am**	4:49 am

Planetary Motion		day	ET / hr:mn / PT	
⚵	℞	12	**6:13 am**	3:13 am
⚶	D	20	**3:06 am**	12:06 am
♇	℞	27	**4:04 pm**	1:04 pm

1 THURSDAY
☽ ⚻ ♅ **4:54 pm** 1:54 pm
☽ ⚹ ♄ **8:53 pm** 5:53 pm
☽ △ ☉ **10:46 pm** 7:46 pm
☽ △ ♀ 10:56 pm
☿ ⚹ ♇ 11:04 pm

2 FRIDAY
☽ △ ♀ **1:56 am**
☿ ⚹ ♇ **2:04 am**
☽ ☍ ♂ **6:40 am** 3:40 am
☽ □ ♆ **1:42 pm** 10:42 am
☽ ⚹ ♃ **5:17 pm** 2:17 pm
☽ ⚺ ♇ **10:30 pm** 7:30 pm
☽ □ ☿ 10:24 pm

3 SATURDAY
☽ □ ☿ **1:24 am**
☽ △ ♅ **8:05 pm** 5:05 pm
☽ ⚺ ♄ 9:21 pm

4 SUNDAY
☽ ⚺ ♄ **12:21 am**
☽ □ ☉ **6:02 am** 3:02 am
☽ □ ♀ **10:33 am** 7:33 am
☽ ⚻ ♂ **12:46 pm** 9:46 am
☽ ⚹ ♆ **5:55 pm** 2:55 pm
☽ ⚺ ♃ **10:18 pm** 7:18 pm

5 MONDAY
☽ ☌ ♇ **3:05 am** 12:05 am
☽ ⚹ ☿ **2:19 pm** 11:19 am
☽ □ ♅ 10:58 pm

6 TUESDAY
☽ □ ♅ **1:58 am**
☽ ☌ ♄ **6:32 am** 3:32 am
♀ ⚹ ♂ **7:18 am** 4:18 am
☽ ⚹ ☉ **4:40 pm** 1:40 pm
☽ △ ♂ **9:55 pm** 6:55 pm
☽ ⚹ ♀ **10:44 pm** 7:44 pm
☽ ⚺ ♆ 9:49 pm

7 WEDNESDAY
☽ ⚺ ♆ **12:49 am**
☽ ☌ ♃ **6:05 am** 3:05 am
☽ ⚺ ♇ **10:18 am** 7:18 am
♀ ⚺ ♆ **8:55 pm** 5:55 pm

8 THURSDAY
☽ ⚺ ☿ **7:36 am** 4:36 am
☽ ⚹ ♅ **10:24 am** 7:24 am
☽ ⚺ ♄ **3:13 pm** 12:13 pm
☿ ⚺ ♅ 11:37 pm

9 FRIDAY
☿ ⚺ ♅ **2:37 am**
☽ ⚺ ☉ **6:19 am** 3:19 am
☽ □ ♂ **9:49 am** 6:49 am
☽ ☌ ♆ **10:04 am** 7:04 am
☽ ⚺ ♀ **2:05 pm** 11:05 am
♂ □ ♆ **3:18 pm** 12:18 pm
☽ ⚺ ♃ **4:15 pm** 1:15 pm
☽ ⚹ ♇ **7:48 pm** 4:48 pm

10 SATURDAY
☿ ⚹ ♄ **11:09 am** 8:09 am
♀ ⚹ ♃ **2:53 pm** 11:53 am
☽ ⚺ ♅ **8:58 pm** 5:58 pm
☽ ⚹ ♄ 11:01 pm

11 SUNDAY
☽ ⚹ ♄ **2:01 am**
☽ ☌ ☿ **4:46 am** 1:46 am
☉ ⚺ ♆ **7:10 am** 4:10 am
☽ ⚺ ♆ **9:18 pm** 6:18 pm
☽ ☌ ☉ **10:31 pm** 7:31 pm
♀ □ ♇ **11:20 pm** 8:20 pm
☽ ⚹ ♂ 9:00 pm

12 MONDAY
☽ ⚹ ♂ **12:00 am**
☽ ⚹ ♃ **4:24 am** 1:24 am
☽ □ ♇ **7:12 am** 4:12 am
☽ ☌ ♀ **8:06 am** 5:06 am

13 TUESDAY
☽ ☌ ♅ **9:18 am** 6:18 am
☽ □ ♄ **2:30 pm** 11:30 am
☉ ⚹ ♂ **7:09 pm** 4:09 pm

14 WEDNESDAY
☽ ⚺ ☿ **5:14 am** 2:14 am
☽ ⚹ ♆ **10:03 am** 7:03 am
☽ ⚺ ♂ **3:54 pm** 12:54 pm
☽ ⚺ ☉ **4:37 pm** 1:37 pm
☽ □ ♃ **6:02 pm** 3:02 pm
☽ △ ♇ **8:00 pm** 5:00 pm

15 THURSDAY
☽ ⚺ ♀ **4:01 am** 1:01 am
☿ ⚺ ♆ **9:32 am** 6:32 am
☉ ⚹ ♃ **12:59 pm** 9:59 am
☽ ⚺ ♅ **10:38 pm** 7:38 pm

16 FRIDAY
☽ △ ♄ **3:53 am** 12:53 am
☉ □ ♇ **9:27 am** 6:27 am
☽ □ ♆ **11:15 pm** 8:15 pm
♂ △ ♃ 10:14 pm

17 SATURDAY
♂ △ ♃ **1:14 am**
☽ ⚹ ☿ **7:05 am** 4:05 am
☽ △ ♃ **7:53 am** 4:53 am
☽ ☌ ♂ **8:08 am** 5:08 am
☽ ⚻ ♇ **8:58 am** 5:58 am
☽ ⚹ ☉ **11:03 am** 8:03 am
☿ ⚹ ♃ **12:00 pm** 9:00 am
☿ ⚹ ♂ **3:09 pm** 12:09 pm
☿ □ ♇ **5:49 pm** 2:49 pm
☽ ⚹ ♀ **11:49 pm** 8:49 pm
♂ ⚻ ♇ 9:26 pm

18 SUNDAY
♂ ⚻ ♇ **12:26 am**
☽ ⚹ ♅ **11:19 am** 8:19 am
☽ ⚻ ♄ **4:24 pm** 1:24 pm
☉ ☌ ☿ **9:50 pm** 6:50 pm

19 MONDAY
☽ △ ♆ **10:56 am** 7:56 am
☽ ⚻ ♃ **7:49 pm** 4:49 pm
☽ ☍ ♇ **8:03 pm** 5:03 pm
☽ ⚺ ♂ **10:15 pm** 7:15 pm
☽ □ ☉ 11:59 pm

20 TUESDAY
☽ □ ☉ **2:59 am**
☽ □ ☿ **6:08 am** 3:08 am
♃ ⚺ ♇ **3:09 pm** 12:09 pm
☽ □ ♀ **4:21 pm** 1:21 pm
☽ □ ♅ **9:11 pm** 6:11 pm
☽ ☍ ♄ 10:56 pm

21 WEDNESDAY
☽ ☍ ♄ **1:56 am**
☽ ⚻ ♆ **7:07 pm** 4:07 pm

22 THURSDAY
☽ ⚻ ♇ **3:29 am** 12:29 am
☽ ☍ ♃ **3:54 am** 12:54 am
☽ ⚹ ♂ **8:05 am** 5:05 am
☽ △ ☉ **2:06 pm** 11:06 am
♀ ☌ ♅ **9:01 pm** 6:01 pm
☽ △ ☿ **10:47 pm** 7:47 pm
☽ △ ♅ 11:57 pm

23 FRIDAY
☽ △ ♅ **2:57 am**
☽ △ ♀ **3:30 am** 12:30 am
☽ ⚻ ♄ **7:19 am** 4:19 am
☽ ☍ ♆ **11:10 pm** 8:10 pm
☿ ☌ ♅ 11:42 pm

24 SATURDAY
☿ ☌ ♅ **2:42 am**
☽ △ ♇ **6:50 am** 3:50 am
☽ ⚻ ♃ **7:47 am** 4:47 am
☽ □ ♂ **1:19 pm** 10:19 am
☽ ⚻ ☉ **8:19 pm** 5:19 pm
♀ □ ♄ 9:22 pm

25 SUNDAY
♀ □ ♄ **12:22 am**
☽ ⚻ ♅ **4:58 am** 1:58 am
☿ □ ♄ **7:58 am** 4:58 am
☽ △ ♄ **9:02 am** 6:02 am
☽ ⚻ ☿ **9:13 am** 6:13 am
☽ ⚻ ♀ **9:48 am** 6:48 am
☿ ☌ ♀ **6:19 pm** 3:19 pm
☽ ⚻ ♆ 9:01 pm

26 MONDAY
☽ ⚻ ♆ **12:01 am**
☽ □ ♇ **7:15 am** 4:15 am
☽ △ ♃ **8:40 am** 5:40 am
☽ △ ♂ **3:29 pm** 12:29 pm
☽ ☍ ☉ **11:32 pm** 8:32 pm

27 TUESDAY
☽ ☍ ♅ **4:51 am** 1:51 am
☽ □ ♄ **8:47 am** 5:47 am
☽ ☍ ♀ **1:35 pm** 10:35 am
☽ ☍ ☿ **4:24 pm** 1:24 pm
☽ △ ♆ **11:31 pm** 8:31 pm

28 WEDNESDAY
☽ ⚹ ♇ **6:38 am** 3:38 am
☽ □ ♃ **8:31 am** 5:31 am
☽ ⚻ ♂ **4:54 pm** 1:54 pm
☽ ⚻ ☉ 11:20 pm

29 THURSDAY
☽ ⚻ ☉ **2:20 am**
☽ ⚻ ♅ **4:38 am** 1:38 am
☽ ⚹ ♄ **8:36 am** 5:36 am
☽ ⚻ ♀ **5:44 pm** 2:44 pm
☿ ⚹ ♆ **10:27 pm** 7:27 pm
☽ □ ♆ **11:42 pm** 8:42 pm
☽ ⚻ ☿ **11:54 pm** 8:54 pm

30 FRIDAY
☽ ⚺ ♇ **7:00 am** 4:00 am
☽ ⚹ ♃ **9:27 am** 6:27 am
☉ ☌ ♅ **3:54 pm** 12:54 pm
☽ ☍ ♂ **7:51 pm** 4:51 pm

Eastern time in bold type
Pacific time in medium type

APRIL 2021

DATE	SID.TIME	SUN	MOON	NODE	MERCURY	VENUS	MARS	JUPITER	SATURN	URANUS	NEPTUNE	PLUTO	CERES	PALLAS	JUNO	VESTA	CHIRON
1 Th	12 38 17	11♈29 03	26♏20	12♊33℞	24♓29	12♈56	16♊27	23♒14	11♒22	9♉01	21♓25	26♑38	15♈11	7♓41	23♐41	8♍12℞	9♈01
2 F	12 42 14	12 28 14	10♐55	12 32D	26 13	14 11	17 03	23 25	11 27	9 04	21 27	26 39	15 35	7 59	23 45	8 03	9 04
3 Sa	12 46 10	13 27 24	25 12	12 33	27 57	15 25	17 38	23 37	11 32	9 07	21 29	26 40	15 59	8 18	23 48	7 55	9 08
4 Su	12 50 7	14 26 32	9♑07	12 33℞	29 44	16 40	18 14	23 49	11 36	9 10	21 31	26 40	16 22	8 36	23 51	7 47	9 11
5 M	12 54 4	15 25 39	22 44	12 33	1♈31	17 54	18 50	24 00	11 41	9 13	21 34	26 41	16 46	8 54	23 53	7 39	9 15
6 T	12 58 0	16 24 43	6♒02	12 31	3 20	19 08	19 26	24 11	11 45	9 17	21 36	26 42	17 10	9 12	23 55	7 32	9 18
7 W	13 1 57	17 23 46	19 03	12 27	5 11	20 23	20 02	24 23	11 49	9 20	21 38	26 42	17 34	9 30	23 57	7 25	9 22
8 Th	13 5 53	18 22 47	1♓51	12 21	7 03	21 37	20 39	24 34	11 53	9 23	21 40	26 43	17 58	9 48	23 59	7 19	9 25
9 F	13 9 50	19 21 46	14 26	12 12	8 56	22 52	21 15	24 45	11 57	9 27	21 42	26 43	18 22	10 06	24 00	7 13	9 29
10 Sa	13 13 46	20 20 43	26 50	12 03	10 51	24 06	21 51	24 56	12 01	9 30	21 44	26 44	18 46	10 24	24 01	7 08	9 32
11 Su	13 17 43	21 19 39	9♈04	11 53	12 47	25 20	22 27	25 07	12 05	9 33	21 46	26 44	19 10	10 42	24 02	7 03	9 36
12 M	13 21 39	22 18 32	21 09	11 44	14 45	26 35	23 03	25 17	12 09	9 36	21 48	26 45	19 34	10 59	24 02℞	6 58	9 39
13 T	13 25 36	23 17 23	3♉07	11 36	16 44	27 49	23 39	25 28	12 13	9 40	21 50	26 45	19 57	11 17	24 02	6 55	9 43
14 W	13 29 33	24 16 13	14 58	11 31	18 44	29 03	24 15	25 39	12 17	9 43	21 52	26 46	20 21	11 34	24 02	6 51	9 46
15 Th	13 33 29	25 15 00	26 46	11 27	20 46	0♉17	24 52	25 49	12 20	9 47	21 54	26 46	20 45	11 52	24 01	6 48	9 50
16 F	13 37 26	26 13 45	8♊33	11 26D	22 49	1 32	25 28	26 00	12 24	9 50	21 56	26 46	21 09	12 09	24 00	6 46	9 53
17 Sa	13 41 22	27 12 28	20 22	11 26	24 53	2 46	26 04	26 10	12 27	9 53	21 58	26 47	21 33	12 26	23 59	6 44	9 56
18 Su	13 45 19	28 11 09	2♋17	11 28	26 58	4 00	26 40	26 20	12 31	9 57	22 00	26 47	21 57	12 43	23 57	6 43	10 00
19 M	13 49 15	29 09 48	14 24	11 29	29 05	5 14	27 17	26 30	12 34	10 00	22 02	26 47	22 21	13 00	23 55	6 42	10 03
20 T	13 53 12	0♉08 24	26 46	11 30℞	1♉12	6 28	27 53	26 40	12 37	10 04	22 04	26 48	22 44	13 17	23 53	6 42D	10 07
21 W	13 57 8	1 06 59	9♌29	11 30	3 19	7 43	28 29	26 50	12 40	10 07	22 06	26 48	23 08	13 34	23 50	6 42	10 10
22 Th	14 1 5	2 05 31	22 37	11 28	5 27	8 57	29 06	26 59	12 43	10 10	22 08	26 48	23 32	13 51	23 47	6 42	10 13
23 F	14 5 2	3 04 01	6♍13	11 24	7 35	10 11	29 42	27 09	12 46	10 14	22 09	26 48	23 56	14 07	23 44	6 43	10 16
24 Sa	14 8 58	4 02 28	20 18	11 19	9 43	11 25	0♋18	27 18	12 49	10 17	22 11	26 48	24 20	14 24	23 40	6 45	10 20
25 Su	14 12 55	5 00 54	4♎50	11 14	11 50	12 39	0 55	27 28	12 52	10 21	22 13	26 48	24 43	14 40	23 36	6 47	10 23
26 M	14 16 51	5 59 17	19 44	11 09	13 57	13 53	1 31	27 37	12 55	10 24	22 15	26 48	25 07	14 57	23 32	6 49	10 26
27 T	14 20 48	6 57 39	4♏52	11 04	16 02	15 07	2 08	27 46	12 57	10 28	22 17	26 48℞	25 31	15 13	23 27	6 52	10 30
28 W	14 24 44	7 55 59	20 05	11 02	18 06	16 21	2 44	27 55	13 00	10 31	22 18	26 48	25 55	15 29	23 22	6 56	10 33
29 Th	14 28 41	8 54 17	5♐12	11 00D	20 09	17 35	3 21	28 04	13 02	10 35	22 20	26 48	26 18	15 45	23 17	7 00	10 36
30 F	14 32 37	9 52 34	20 06	11 00	22 10	18 49	3 57	28 13	13 04	10 38	22 22	26 48	26 42	16 01	23 11	7 04	10 39

EPHEMERIS CALCULATED FOR 12 MIDNIGHT GREENWICH MEAN TIME. ALL OTHER DATA AND FACING ASPECTARIAN PAGE IN **EASTERN TIME (BOLD)** AND PACIFIC TIME (REGULAR).

MAY 2021

☽ Last Aspect day	ET / hr:mn / PT	asp	☽ Ingress sign	day	ET / hr:mn / PT
2	**10:38 am** 7:38 am	△ ☿	♒	2	**3:31 pm** 12:31 pm
4	**8:05 pm** 5:05 pm	☌ ♃	♓	4	**10:09 pm** 7:09 pm
7	**3:36 am** 12:36 am	✶ ♀	♈	7	**7:52 am** 4:52 am
9	**6:50 pm** 3:50 pm	✶ ♃	♉	9	**7:46 pm** 4:46 pm
12	**8:23 am** 5:23 am	□ ♃	♊	12	**8:43 am** 5:43 am
14	**6:51 am** 3:51 am	□ ♆	♋	14	**9:30 pm** 6:30 pm
16	11:23 pm	☍ ♇	♌	17	**8:44 am** 5:44 am
17	**2:23 am**	☍ ♇	♌	17	**8:44 am** 5:44 am
19	**3:13 pm** 12:13 pm	□ ☉	♍	19	**4:59 pm** 1:59 pm
21	**3:56 pm** 12:56 pm	△ ♇	♎	21	**9:35 pm** 6:35 pm

☽ Last Aspect day	ET / hr:mn / PT	asp	☽ Ingress sign	day	ET / hr:mn / PT
23	**5:36 pm** 2:36 pm	□ ♇	♏	23	**11:00 pm** 8:00 pm
25	**5:20 pm** 2:20 pm	✶ ♇	♐	25	**10:39 pm** 7:39 pm
27	**1:35 pm** 10:35 am	☍ ☿	♑	27	**10:23 pm** 7:23 pm
29	**6:15 pm** 3:15 pm	☌ ♇	♒	29	9:04 pm
29	**6:15 pm** 3:15 pm	☌ ♇	♒	30	**12:04 am**
31	11:14 pm	△ ♀	♓	6/1	**5:07 am** 2:07 am
6/1	**2:14 am**	△ ♀	♓	6/1	**5:07 am** 2:07 am

☽ Phases & Eclipses phase	day	ET / hr:mn / PT
4th Quarter	3	**3:50 pm** 12:50 pm
New Moon	11	**3:00 pm** 12:00 pm
2nd Quarter	19	**3:13 pm** 12:13 pm
Full Moon	26	**7:14 am** 4:14 am
●	26	5° ♐ 26'

Planet Ingress		day	ET / hr:mn / PT
☿	♊	3	**10:49 pm** 7:49 pm
⚳	♉	8	**4:54 am** 1:54 am
♀	♊	8	**10:01 pm** 7:01 pm
♃	♓	13	**6:36 pm** 3:36 pm
☉	♊	20	**3:37 pm** 12:37 pm

Planetary Motion		day	ET / hr:mn / PT
♄	℞	23	**5:21 am** 2:21 am
☿	℞	29	**6:34 pm** 3:34 pm

1 SATURDAY
- ☽ △ ♅ **6:13 am** 3:13 am
- ☽ △ ☉ **7:12 am** 4:12 am
- ☽ ⚺ ♄ **10:18 am** 7:18 am
- ☽ △ ♀ 9:42 pm
- ☽ ✶ ♆ 11:16 pm

2 SUNDAY
- ☽ △ ♀ **12:42 am**
- ☽ ✶ ♆ **2:16 am**
- ☿ △ ♇ **5:19 am** 2:19 am
- ☽ ☌ ♇ **9:54 am** 6:54 am
- ☽ △ ☿ **10:38 am** 7:38 am
- ☽ ⚺ ♃ **1:02 pm** 10:02 am
- ♀ ✶ ♆ **6:38 pm** 3:38 pm
- ☽ ⚻ ♂ 11:02 pm

3 MONDAY
- ☽ ⚻ ♂ **2:02 am**
- ☿ □ ♃ **5:33 am** 2:33 am
- ☉ □ ♄ **6:02 am** 3:02 am
- ☽ □ ♅ **10:52 am** 7:52 am
- ☽ ☌ ♄ **3:08 pm** 12:08 pm
- ☽ □ ☉ **3:50 pm** 12:50 pm

4 TUESDAY
- ☽ ⚺ ♆ **8:08 am** 5:08 am
- ☽ □ ♀ **12:00 pm** 9:00 am
- ☽ ⚺ ♇ **4:09 pm** 1:09 pm
- ☽ ☌ ♃ **8:05 pm** 5:05 pm
- ☽ □ ☿ 10:54 pm

5 WEDNESDAY
- ☽ □ ☿ **1:54 am**
- ☽ △ ♂ **12:07 pm** 9:07 am
- ☽ ✶ ♅ **6:57 pm** 3:57 pm
- ☽ ⚺ ♄ **11:21 pm** 8:21 pm

6 THURSDAY
- ☽ ✶ ☉ **4:41 am** 1:41 am
- ♀ △ ♇ **7:25 am** 4:25 am
- ☽ ☌ ♆ **5:17 pm** 2:17 pm
- ☽ ✶ ♇ 10:34 pm

7 FRIDAY
- ☽ ✶ ♇ **1:34 am**
- ☽ ✶ ♀ **3:36 am** 12:36 am
- ☽ ⚺ ♃ **6:21 am** 3:21 am
- ☽ ✶ ☿ **9:01 pm** 6:01 pm
- ☽ □ ♂ 10:35 pm

8 SATURDAY
- ☽ □ ♂ **1:35 am**
- ☽ ⚺ ♅ **5:53 am** 2:53 am
- ♀ □ ♃ **9:38 am** 6:38 am
- ☽ ✶ ♄ **10:18 am** 7:18 am
- ☽ ⚺ ☉ **8:54 pm** 5:54 pm

9 SUNDAY
- ☽ ⚺ ♆ **4:52 am** 1:52 am
- ☽ □ ♇ **1:16 pm** 10:16 am
- ☽ ✶ ♃ **6:50 pm** 3:50 pm
- ☽ ⚺ ♀ **10:17 pm** 7:17 pm

10 MONDAY
- ☿ ⚺ ♂ **7:48 am** 4:48 am
- ☽ ✶ ♂ **5:12 pm** 2:12 pm
- ☽ ⚺ ☿ **5:55 pm** 2:55 pm
- ☽ ☌ ♅ **6:35 pm** 3:35 pm
- ☽ □ ♄ **10:55 pm** 7:55 pm
- ☿ ⚺ ♅ **11:48 pm** 8:48 pm

11 TUESDAY
- ☽ ☌ ☉ **3:00 pm** 12:00 pm
- ☽ ✶ ♆ **5:47 pm** 2:47 pm
- ♂ ✶ ♅ **10:48 pm** 7:48 pm
- ☽ △ ♇ 11:07 pm

12 WEDNESDAY
- ☽ △ ♇ **2:07 am**
- ☽ □ ♃ **8:23 am** 5:23 am
- ☿ △ ♄ **2:34 pm** 11:34 am
- ☽ ☌ ♀ **6:20 pm** 3:20 pm
- ☉ ✶ ♆ 10:45 pm

13 THURSDAY
- ☉ ✶ ♆ **1:45 am**
- ☽ ⚺ ♅ **7:55 am** 4:55 am
- ☽ ⚺ ♂ **9:33 am** 6:33 am
- ☽ △ ♄ **12:03 pm** 9:03 am
- ☽ ☌ ☿ **2:32 pm** 11:32 am

14 FRIDAY
- ☽ □ ♆ **6:51 am** 3:51 am
- ☽ ⚺ ☉ **9:22 am** 6:22 am
- ☽ ⚻ ♇ **2:57 pm** 11:57 am
- ☽ △ ♃ **9:45 pm** 6:45 pm

15 SATURDAY
- ♂ ⚻ ♄ **10:49 am** 7:49 am
- ☽ ⚺ ♀ **1:53 pm** 10:53 am
- ☽ ✶ ♅ **8:35 pm** 5:35 pm
- ☽ ⚻ ♄ 9:24 pm
- ☽ ☌ ♂ 10:06 pm

16 SUNDAY
- ☽ ⚻ ♄ **12:24 am**
- ☽ ☌ ♂ **1:06 am**
- ☽ ⚺ ☿ **8:51 am** 5:51 am
- ☽ △ ♆ **6:42 pm** 3:42 pm
- ☽ ✶ ☉ 11:05 pm
- ☽ ☍ ♇ 11:23 pm

17 MONDAY
- ☽ ✶ ☉ **2:05 am**
- ☽ ☍ ♇ **2:23 am**
- ☉ △ ♇ **5:49 am** 2:49 am
- ☽ ⚻ ♃ **9:29 am** 6:29 am

18 TUESDAY
- ☽ ✶ ♀ **6:43 am** 3:43 am
- ☽ □ ♅ **7:04 am** 4:04 am
- ☽ ☍ ♄ **10:29 am** 7:29 am
- ♀ ⚺ ♅ **10:31 am** 7:31 am
- ☽ ⚺ ♂ **2:01 pm** 11:01 am
- ☽ ✶ ☿ **10:55 pm** 7:55 pm

19 WEDNESDAY
- ☽ ⚻ ♆ **3:51 am** 12:51 am
- ☽ ⚻ ♇ **10:58 am** 7:58 am
- ☽ □ ☉ **3:13 pm** 12:13 pm
- ☽ ☍ ♃ **6:07 pm** 3:07 pm
- ♀ △ ♄ **9:58 pm** 6:58 pm

20 THURSDAY
- ☽ △ ♅ **2:09 pm** 11:09 am
- ☽ ⚻ ♄ **5:08 pm** 2:08 pm
- ☽ □ ♀ **7:01 pm** 4:01 pm
- ☽ ✶ ♂ **10:57 pm** 7:57 pm

21 FRIDAY
- ☽ □ ☿ **7:47 am** 4:47 am
- ☽ ☍ ♆ **9:24 am** 6:24 am
- ☉ □ ♃ **11:03 am** 8:03 am
- ☽ △ ♇ **3:56 pm** 12:56 pm
- ☽ ⚻ ♃ **10:59 pm** 7:59 pm
- ☽ △ ☉ **11:46 pm** 8:46 pm

22 SATURDAY
- ☽ ⚻ ♅ **5:34 pm** 2:34 pm
- ☽ △ ♄ **8:11 pm** 5:11 pm
- ☿ □ ♆ **10:43 pm** 7:43 pm
- ☽ △ ♀ 11:36 pm

23 SUNDAY
- ☽ △ ♀ **2:36 am**
- ☽ □ ♂ **3:51 am** 12:51 am
- ☽ ⚻ ♆ **11:33 am** 8:33 am
- ☽ △ ☿ **11:59 am** 8:59 am
- ☽ □ ♇ **5:36 pm** 2:36 pm
- ☽ △ ♃ 9:37 pm

24 MONDAY
- ☽ △ ♃ **12:37 am**
- ☽ ⚻ ☉ **4:28 am** 1:28 am
- ♀ ⚺ ♂ **7:15 am** 4:15 am
- ☽ ☍ ♅ **6:15 pm** 3:15 pm
- ☽ □ ♄ **8:35 pm** 5:35 pm

25 TUESDAY
- ☽ △ ♂ **6:01 am** 3:01 am
- ☽ ⚻ ♀ **7:01 am** 4:01 am
- ☽ △ ♆ **11:30 am** 8:30 am
- ☽ ⚻ ☿ **1:13 pm** 10:13 am
- ☽ ✶ ♇ **5:20 pm** 2:20 pm
- ☽ □ ♃ 9:30 pm

26 WEDNESDAY
- ☽ □ ♃ **12:30 am**
- ☽ ☍ ☉ **7:14 am** 4:14 am
- ☽ ⚻ ♅ **5:52 pm** 2:52 pm
- ☽ ✶ ♄ **8:01 pm** 5:01 pm

27 THURSDAY
- ☽ ⚻ ♂ **7:31 am** 4:31 am
- ☽ ☍ ♀ **10:43 am** 7:43 am
- ☽ □ ♆ **11:06 am** 8:06 am
- ☽ ☍ ☿ **1:35 pm** 10:35 am
- ♀ □ ♆ **3:25 pm** 12:25 pm
- ☽ ⚺ ♇ **4:55 pm** 1:55 pm
- ☽ ✶ ♃ 9:31 pm

28 FRIDAY
- ☽ ✶ ♃ **12:31 am**
- ☽ ⚻ ☉ **10:32 am** 7:32 am
- ☽ △ ♅ **6:22 pm** 3:22 pm
- ☽ ⚺ ♄ **8:23 pm** 5:23 pm
- ☿ ☌ ♀ 10:13 pm

29 SATURDAY
- ☿ ☌ ♀ **1:13 am**
- ☽ ☍ ♂ **10:36 am** 7:36 am
- ☽ ✶ ♆ **12:13 pm** 9:13 am
- ☽ ⚻ ☿ **3:07 pm** 12:07 pm
- ☽ ⚻ ♀ **4:23 pm** 1:23 pm
- ☽ ☌ ♇ **6:15 pm** 3:15 pm
- ☽ ⚺ ♃ 11:34 pm

30 SUNDAY
- ☽ ⚺ ♃ **2:34 am**
- ♀ ⚻ ♇ **1:47 pm** 10:47 am
- ☽ △ ☉ **4:43 pm** 1:43 pm
- ☽ □ ♅ **9:30 pm** 6:30 pm
- ☽ ☌ ♄ **11:25 pm** 8:25 pm
- ♂ △ ♆ 10:15 pm

31 MONDAY
- ♂ △ ♆ **1:15 am**
- ☽ ⚺ ♆ **4:27 pm** 1:27 pm
- ☽ ⚻ ♂ **5:11 pm** 2:11 pm
- ☽ △ ☿ **7:13 pm** 4:13 pm
- ☽ ⚺ ♇ **10:48 pm** 7:48 pm
- ☽ △ ♀ 11:14 pm

Eastern time in bold type
Pacific time in medium type

MAY 2021

DATE	SID.TIME	SUN	MOON	NODE	MERCURY	VENUS	MARS	JUPITER	SATURN	URANUS	NEPTUNE	PLUTO	CERES	PALLAS	JUNO	VESTA	CHIRON
1 Sa	14 36 34	10♉50 49	4♑39	11♊01	24♉08	20♉03	4♋33	28♒21	13♒07	10♉41	22♓23	26♑48℞	27♈06	16♓17	23♐05℞	7♍09	10♈42
2 Su	14 40 31	11 49 02	18 48	11 03	26 04	21 17	5 10	28 30	13 09	10 45	22 25	26 48	27 30	16 32	22 59	7 14	10 45
3 M	14 44 27	12 47 14	2♒32	11 04℞	27 57	22 31	5 46	28 38	13 11	10 48	22 27	26 48	27 53	16 48	22 52	7 19	10 49
4 T	14 48 24	13 45 25	15 53	11 04	29 47	23 45	6 23	28 46	13 13	10 52	22 28	26 48	28 17	17 03	22 45	7 25	10 52
5 W	14 52 20	14 43 34	28 51	11 04	1♊34	24 58	6 59	28 54	13 14	10 55	22 30	26 48	28 40	17 19	22 38	7 32	10 55
6 Th	14 56 17	15 41 41	11♓32	11 02	3 18	26 12	7 36	29 02	13 16	10 59	22 31	26 48	29 04	17 34	22 30	7 39	10 58
7 F	15 0 13	16 39 47	23 56	10 59	4 58	27 26	8 13	29 10	13 18	11 02	22 33	26 47	29 28	17 49	22 22	7 46	11 01
8 Sa	15 4 10	17 37 52	6♈09	10 55	6 35	28 40	8 49	29 18	13 19	11 06	22 34	26 47	29 51	18 04	22 14	7 54	11 04
9 Su	15 8 6	18 35 55	18 11	10 51	8 08	29 54	9 26	29 25	13 21	11 09	22 36	26 47	0♉15	18 19	22 06	8 02	11 07
10 M	15 12 3	19 33 57	0♉07	10 48	9 38	1♊08	10 02	29 32	13 22	11 13	22 37	26 46	0 38	18 34	21 57	8 10	11 10
11 T	15 16 0	20 31 57	11 57	10 45	11 03	2 21	10 39	29 40	13 24	11 16	22 39	26 46	1 02	18 48	21 48	8 19	11 12
12 W	15 19 56	21 29 56	23 45	10 43	12 25	3 35	11 15	29 47	13 25	11 19	22 40	26 46	1 25	19 03	21 38	8 29	11 15
13 Th	15 23 53	22 27 53	5♊33	10 42D	13 43	4 49	11 52	29 54	13 26	11 23	22 41	26 45	1 49	19 17	21 29	8 38	11 18
14 F	15 27 49	23 25 49	17 22	10 42	14 57	6 03	12 29	0♓00	13 27	11 26	22 43	26 45	2 12	19 31	21 19	8 49	11 21
15 Sa	15 31 46	24 23 43	29 15	10 43	16 06	7 16	13 05	0 07	13 28	11 30	22 44	26 44	2 36	19 45	21 09	8 59	11 24
16 Su	15 35 42	25 21 35	11♋16	10 44	17 12	8 30	13 42	0 13	13 28	11 33	22 45	26 44	2 59	19 59	20 58	9 10	11 27
17 M	15 39 39	26 19 26	23 27	10 46	18 13	9 44	14 19	0 20	13 29	11 36	22 47	26 43	3 22	20 13	20 48	9 21	11 29
18 T	15 43 35	27 17 15	5♌52	10 47	19 10	10 57	14 55	0 26	13 30	11 40	22 48	26 43	3 46	20 26	20 37	9 33	11 32
19 W	15 47 32	28 15 03	18 35	10 47℞	20 03	12 11	15 32	0 32	13 30	11 43	22 49	26 42	4 09	20 40	20 25	9 44	11 35
20 Th	15 51 29	29 12 48	1♍40	10 48	20 52	13 24	16 09	0 38	13 30	11 46	22 50	26 42	4 32	20 53	20 14	9 57	11 37
21 F	15 55 25	0♊10 32	15 09	10 47	21 36	14 38	16 46	0 43	13 31	11 50	22 51	26 41	4 55	21 06	20 02	10 09	11 40
22 Sa	15 59 22	1 08 15	29 04	10 47	22 15	15 52	17 22	0 49	13 31	11 53	22 53	26 40	5 18	21 19	19 51	10 22	11 42
23 Su	16 3 18	2 05 55	13♎24	10 46	22 50	17 05	17 59	0 54	13 31℞	11 56	22 54	26 40	5 42	21 32	19 39	10 36	11 45
24 M	16 7 15	3 03 35	28 08	10 45	23 20	18 19	18 36	0 59	13 31	12 00	22 55	26 39	6 05	21 44	19 27	10 49	11 47
25 T	16 11 11	4 01 12	13♏09	10 44	23 46	19 32	19 13	1 04	13 31	12 03	22 56	26 38	6 28	21 57	19 14	11 03	11 50
26 W	16 15 8	4 58 49	28 19	10 44D	24 07	20 46	19 49	1 09	13 31	12 06	22 57	26 37	6 51	22 09	19 02	11 17	11 52
27 Th	16 19 4	5 56 24	13♐30	10 43	24 23	21 59	20 26	1 14	13 30	12 09	22 58	26 37	7 14	22 21	18 49	11 32	11 54
28 F	16 23 1	6 53 58	28 31	10 44	24 34	23 12	21 03	1 18	13 30	12 13	22 59	26 36	7 37	22 33	18 36	11 47	11 57
29 Sa	16 26 58	7 51 31	13♑15	10 44	24 41℞	24 26	21 40	1 22	13 30	12 16	23 00	26 35	8 00	22 45	18 23	12 02	11 59
30 Su	16 30 54	8 49 04	27 36	10 44	24 43	25 39	22 17	1 27	13 29	12 19	23 00	26 34	8 23	22 57	18 10	12 17	12 01
31 M	16 34 51	9 46 35	11♒31	10 44	24 40	26 53	22 53	1 31	13 28	12 22	23 01	26 33	8 45	23 08	17 57	12 33	12 04

EPHEMERIS CALCULATED FOR 12 MIDNIGHT GREENWICH MEAN TIME. ALL OTHER DATA AND FACING ASPECTARIAN PAGE IN **EASTERN TIME (BOLD)** AND PACIFIC TIME (REGULAR).

JUNE 2021

☽ Last Aspect day	ET / hr:mn / PT	asp	☽ Ingress sign	day	ET / hr:mn / PT
1	**2:14 am**	△♀	♓	1	**5:07 am** 2:07 am
3	**7:10 am** 4:10 am	⚹♇	♈	3	**1:59 pm** 10:59 am
5	**6:47 pm** 3:47 pm	□♂	♉	5	10:46 pm
5	**6:47 pm** 3:47 pm	□♂	♉	6	**1:46 am**
8	**11:07 am** 8:07 am	⚹♂	♊	8	**2:47 pm** 11:47 am
10	**1:38 pm** 10:38 am	□♆	♋	11	**3:23 am** 12:23 am
13	**7:16 am** 4:16 am	☍♇	♌	13	**2:22 pm** 11:22 am
15	**1:27 pm** 10:27 am	⚹☉	♍	15	**11:02 pm** 8:02 pm
17	**11:54 pm** 8:54 pm	□☉	♎	18	**4:54 am** 1:54 am
20	**6:52 am** 3:52 am	△☉	♏	20	**7:58 am** 4:58 am
21	11:43 pm	⚹♇	♐	22	**8:55 am** 5:55 am
22	**2:43 am**	⚹♇	♐	22	**8:55 am** 5:55 am
23	**10:09 pm** 7:09 pm	□♆	♑	24	**9:05 am** 6:05 am
26	**8:49 am** 5:49 am	☍♀	♒	26	**10:09 am** 7:09 am
27	**3:08 pm** 12:08 pm	△☿	♓	28	**1:51 pm** 10:51 am
30	**1:40 pm** 10:40 am	⚹♇	♈	30	**9:21 pm** 6:21 pm

☽ Phases & Eclipses phase	day	ET / hr:mn / PT
4th Quarter	2	**3:24 am** 12:24 am
New Moon	10	**6:53 am** 3:53 am
●	10	19° ♊ 47'
2nd Quarter	17	**11:54 pm** 8:54 pm
Full Moon	24	**2:40 pm** 11:40 am

Planet Ingress	day	ET / hr:mn / PT
♀ ♋	2	**9:19 am** 6:19 am
♂ ♌	11	**9:34 am** 6:34 am
☉ ♋	20	**11:32 pm** 8:32 pm
♀ ♌	26	9:27 pm
♀ ♌	27	**12:27 am**

Planetary Motion	day	ET / hr:mn / PT
♃ ℞	20	**11:06 am** 8:06 am
☿ D	22	**6:00 pm** 3:00 pm
♆ ℞	25	**3:21 pm** 12:21 pm

1 TUESDAY
☽ △ ♀ **2:14 am**
☽ ☌ ♃ **8:04 am** 5:04 am

2 WEDNESDAY
☿ ⚺ ♂ **3:14 am** 12:14 am
☽ □ ☉ **3:24 am** 12:24 am
☽ ⚹ ♅ **4:22 am** 1:22 am
☽ ⚺ ♄ **6:08 am** 3:08 am
☉ ⚺ ♅ **4:43 pm** 1:43 pm
☽ ☌ ♆ 9:31 pm
☽ □ ☿ 11:24 pm

3 THURSDAY
☽ ☌ ♆ **12:31 am**
☽ □ ☿ **2:24 am**
☽ △ ♂ **4:08 am** 1:08 am
☽ ⚹ ♇ **7:10 am** 4:10 am
☉ △ ♄ **3:05 pm** 12:05 pm
☽ □ ♀ **5:09 pm** 2:09 pm
☽ ⚺ ♃ **5:23 pm** 2:23 pm
♀ △ ♃ **7:33 pm** 4:33 pm

4 FRIDAY
☽ ⚺ ♅ **2:52 pm** 11:52 am
☽ ⚹ ♄ **4:24 pm** 1:24 pm
☽ ⚹ ☉ **6:38 pm** 3:38 pm

5 SATURDAY
☽ ⚺ ♆ **11:49 am** 8:49 am
☽ ⚹ ☿ **11:56 am** 8:56 am
☿ □ ♆ **3:05 pm** 12:05 pm
♂ ☍ ♇ **3:45 pm** 12:45 pm

☽ □ ♇ **6:37 pm** 3:37 pm
☽ □ ♂ **6:47 pm** 3:47 pm

6 SUNDAY
☽ ⚹ ♃ **5:32 am** 2:32 am
☽ ⚹ ♀ **11:57 am** 8:57 am

7 MONDAY
☽ ☌ ♅ **3:39 am** 12:39 am
☽ □ ♄ **4:51 am** 1:51 am
☽ ⚺ ☉ **12:36 pm** 9:36 am
☽ ⚺ ☿ **10:27 pm** 7:27 pm
☽ ⚹ ♆ 9:47 pm

8 TUESDAY
☽ ⚹ ♆ **12:47 am**
☽ △ ♇ **7:30 am** 4:30 am
☽ ⚹ ♂ **11:07 am** 8:07 am
☽ □ ♃ **6:47 pm** 3:47 pm

9 WEDNESDAY
☽ ⚺ ♀ **8:01 am** 5:01 am
☽ ⚺ ♅ **4:55 pm** 1:55 pm
☽ △ ♄ **5:44 pm** 2:44 pm

10 THURSDAY
☽ ☌ ☉ **6:53 am** 3:53 am
☽ ☌ ☿ **8:37 am** 5:37 am
☽ □ ♆ **1:38 pm** 10:38 am
☽ ⚻ ♇ **8:07 pm** 5:07 pm
☉ ☌ ☿ **9:13 pm** 6:13 pm

11 FRIDAY
☽ ⚺ ♂ **3:02 am** 12:02 am
☽ △ ♃ **7:28 am** 4:28 am
☽ ☌ ♀ 11:59 pm

12 SATURDAY
☽ ☌ ♀ **2:59 am**
☽ ⚹ ♅ **5:11 am** 2:11 am
☽ ⚻ ♄ **5:35 am** 2:35 am
☽ ⚺ ☿ **5:38 pm** 2:38 pm
☽ ⚺ ☉ **11:33 pm** 8:33 pm
☽ △ ♆ 10:06 pm
♀ ⚹ ♅ 10:38 pm

13 SUNDAY
☽ △ ♆ **1:06 am**
♀ ⚹ ♅ **1:38 am**
♀ ⚻ ♄ **4:15 am** 1:15 am
☽ ☍ ♇ **7:16 am** 4:16 am
☽ ☌ ♂ **5:08 pm** 2:08 pm
☽ ⚻ ♃ **6:27 pm** 3:27 pm
☉ □ ♆ **7:40 pm** 4:40 pm

14 MONDAY
☽ □ ♅ **3:27 pm** 12:27 pm
☽ ☍ ♄ **3:28 pm** 12:28 pm
♄ □ ♅ **6:01 pm** 3:01 pm
☽ ⚺ ♀ **7:19 pm** 4:19 pm
♂ ⚻ ♃ **8:39 pm** 5:39 pm
☽ ⚹ ☿ 9:58 pm

15 TUESDAY
☽ ⚹ ☿ **12:58 am**
☽ ⚻ ♆ **10:22 am** 7:22 am

☽ ⚹ ☉ **1:27 pm** 10:27 am
☽ ⚻ ♇ **4:10 pm** 1:10 pm

16 WEDNESDAY
☽ ☍ ♃ **3:00 am** 12:00 am
☽ ⚺ ♂ **4:28 am** 1:28 am
☿ ⚺ ♀ **4:11 pm** 1:11 pm
☽ ⚻ ♄ **10:47 pm** 7:47 pm
☽ △ ♅ **11:07 pm** 8:07 pm
☉ ⚻ ♇ 10:24 pm

17 THURSDAY
☉ ⚻ ♇ **1:24 am**
☽ □ ☿ **6:16 am** 3:16 am
☽ ⚹ ♀ **8:07 am** 5:07 am
☽ ☍ ♆ **4:55 pm** 1:55 pm
☽ △ ♇ **10:18 pm** 7:18 pm
☽ □ ☉ **11:54 pm** 8:54 pm

18 FRIDAY
☽ ⚻ ♃ **8:41 am** 5:41 am
☽ ⚹ ♂ **12:32 pm** 9:32 am

19 SATURDAY
☽ △ ♄ **3:15 am** 12:15 am
☽ ⚻ ♅ **3:53 am** 12:53 am
☽ △ ☿ **9:22 am** 6:22 am
☽ □ ♀ **5:07 pm** 2:07 pm
☽ ⚻ ♆ **8:36 pm** 5:36 pm
☽ □ ♇ 10:37 pm

20 SUNDAY
☽ □ ♇ **1:37 am**
☽ △ ☉ **6:52 am** 3:52 am

☽ △ ♃ **11:35 am** 8:35 am
☽ □ ♂ **5:29 pm** 2:29 pm

21 MONDAY
☽ □ ♄ **5:09 am** 2:09 am
☽ ☍ ♅ **6:02 am** 3:02 am
♀ △ ♆ **9:57 am** 6:57 am
☽ ⚻ ☿ **10:35 am** 7:35 am
☽ △ ♆ **9:57 pm** 6:57 pm
☽ △ ♀ **11:01 pm** 8:01 pm
☽ ⚹ ♇ 11:43 pm

22 TUESDAY
☽ ⚹ ♇ **2:43 am**
☽ ⚻ ☉ **11:12 am** 8:12 am
☽ □ ♃ **12:26 pm** 9:26 am
☽ △ ♂ **8:17 pm** 5:17 pm

23 WEDNESDAY
☽ ⚹ ♄ **5:25 am** 2:25 am
☉ △ ♃ **6:11 am** 3:11 am
☽ ⚻ ♅ **6:35 am** 3:35 am
☽ ☍ ☿ **10:50 am** 7:50 am
♀ ☍ ♇ **7:39 pm** 4:39 pm
☽ □ ♆ **10:09 pm** 7:09 pm
☽ ⚺ ♇ 11:49 pm

24 THURSDAY
☽ ⚺ ♇ **2:49 am**
☽ ⚻ ♀ **3:28 am** 12:28 am
☽ ⚹ ♃ **12:33 pm** 9:33 am
☽ ☍ ☉ **2:40 pm** 11:40 am
☽ ⚻ ♂ **10:35 pm** 7:35 pm

25 FRIDAY
☽ ⚺ ♄ **5:35 am** 2:35 am
☽ △ ♅ **7:04 am** 4:04 am
☽ ⚻ ☿ **11:42 am** 8:42 am
☽ ⚹ ♆ **10:51 pm** 7:51 pm

26 SATURDAY
☽ ☌ ♇ **3:36 am** 12:36 am
☽ ☍ ♀ **8:49 am** 5:49 am
☽ ⚺ ♃ **1:42 pm** 10:42 am
☽ ⚻ ☉ **7:29 pm** 4:29 pm
☽ ☍ ♂ 11:30 pm

27 SUNDAY
☽ ☍ ♂ **2:30 am**
☽ ☌ ♄ **7:23 am** 4:23 am
☽ □ ♅ **9:16 am** 6:16 am
☽ △ ☿ **3:08 pm** 12:08 pm
☽ ⚺ ♆ 10:49 pm

28 MONDAY
☽ ⚺ ♆ **1:49 am**
☽ ⚺ ♇ **6:47 am** 3:47 am
♀ ⚻ ♃ **5:31 pm** 2:31 pm
☽ ☌ ♃ **5:33 pm** 2:33 pm
☽ ⚻ ♀ **5:34 pm** 2:34 pm

29 TUESDAY
☽ △ ☉ **3:54 am** 12:54 am
☽ ⚻ ♂ **9:58 am** 6:58 am
☽ ⚺ ♄ **12:24 pm** 9:24 am
☽ ⚹ ♅ **2:47 pm** 11:47 am
☽ □ ☿ **11:00 pm** 8:00 pm

30 WEDNESDAY
☽ ☌ ♆ **8:25 am** 5:25 am
☽ ⚹ ♇ **1:40 pm** 10:40 am
☽ ⚺ ♃ 10:12 pm

Eastern time in bold type
Pacific time in medium type

JUNE 2021

DATE	SID.TIME	SUN	MOON	NODE	MERCURY	VENUS	MARS	JUPITER	SATURN	URANUS	NEPTUNE	PLUTO	CERES	PALLAS	JUNO	VESTA	CHIRON
1 T	16 38 47	10♊44 05	25♒00	10♊44℞	24♊34℞	28♊06	23♋30	1♓34	13♒27℞	12♉25	23♓02	26♑33℞	9♉08	23♓19	17♐44℞	12♍49	12♈06
2 W	16 42 44	11 41 35	8♓02	10 44D	24 22	29 19	24 07	1 38	13 27	12 29	23 03	26 32	9 31	23 30	17 30	13 05	12 08
3 Th	16 46 40	12 39 04	20 43	10 44	24 07	0♋33	24 44	1 41	13 26	12 32	23 04	26 31	9 54	23 41	17 17	13 22	12 10
4 F	16 50 37	13 36 32	3♈05	10 44	23 48	1 46	25 21	1 45	13 25	12 35	23 04	26 30	10 16	23 52	17 03	13 38	12 12
5 Sa	16 54 33	14 33 59	15 12	10 45	23 26	2 59	25 58	1 48	13 23	12 38	23 05	26 29	10 39	24 02	16 50	13 55	12 14
6 Su	16 58 30	15 31 26	27 09	10 45	23 00	4 13	26 34	1 51	13 22	12 41	23 06	26 28	11 02	24 13	16 36	14 13	12 16
7 M	17 2 27	16 28 52	8♉59	10 46	22 32	5 26	27 11	1 53	13 21	12 44	23 06	26 27	11 24	24 23	16 23	14 30	12 18
8 T	17 6 23	17 26 17	20 46	10 46	22 02	6 39	27 48	1 56	13 19	12 47	23 07	26 26	11 47	24 33	16 09	14 48	12 20
9 W	17 10 20	18 23 42	2♊34	10 47℞	21 30	7 52	28 25	1 58	13 18	12 50	23 07	26 25	12 09	24 42	15 55	15 06	12 22
10 Th	17 14 16	19 21 06	14 24	10 47	20 57	9 05	29 02	2 00	13 16	12 53	23 08	26 24	12 31	24 52	15 42	15 25	12 23
11 F	17 18 13	20 18 29	26 19	10 46	20 23	10 19	29 39	2 02	13 14	12 56	23 08	26 23	12 54	25 01	15 28	15 43	12 25
12 Sa	17 22 9	21 15 51	8♋21	10 46	19 50	11 32	0♌16	2 04	13 13	12 59	23 09	26 21	13 16	25 10	15 15	16 02	12 27
13 Su	17 26 6	22 13 13	20 33	10 44	19 17	12 45	0 53	2 05	13 11	13 01	23 09	26 20	13 38	25 19	15 01	16 21	12 28
14 M	17 30 2	23 10 33	2♌55	10 43	18 45	13 58	1 30	2 07	13 09	13 04	23 10	26 19	14 00	25 27	14 48	16 40	12 30
15 T	17 33 59	24 07 53	15 31	10 41	18 15	15 11	2 07	2 08	13 07	13 07	23 10	26 18	14 22	25 36	14 34	17 00	12 32
16 W	17 37 56	25 05 12	28 21	10 39	17 47	16 24	2 44	2 09	13 05	13 10	23 10	26 17	14 44	25 44	14 21	17 20	12 33
17 Th	17 41 52	26 02 30	11♍29	10 38	17 22	17 37	3 21	2 10	13 02	13 13	23 11	26 16	15 06	25 52	14 08	17 40	12 35
18 F	17 45 49	26 59 47	24 56	10 38D	17 00	18 50	3 58	2 10	13 00	13 15	23 11	26 14	15 28	25 59	13 55	18 00	12 36
19 Sa	17 49 45	27 57 04	8♎43	10 38	16 41	20 03	4 35	2 11	12 58	13 18	23 11	26 13	15 50	26 07	13 42	18 20	12 37
20 Su	17 53 42	28 54 19	22 50	10 39	16 27	21 16	5 12	2 11℞	12 55	13 21	23 11	26 12	16 12	26 14	13 29	18 41	12 39
21 M	17 57 38	29 51 34	7♏17	10 40	16 16	22 29	5 49	2 11	12 53	13 23	23 12	26 11	16 34	26 21	13 16	19 01	12 40
22 T	18 1 35	0♋48 48	22 00	10 41	16 10D	23 42	6 26	2 11	12 50	13 26	23 12	26 09	16 55	26 27	13 04	19 22	12 41
23 W	18 5 32	1 46 02	6♐53	10 42℞	16 08	24 55	7 03	2 11	12 47	13 29	23 12	26 08	17 17	26 34	12 52	19 44	12 42
24 Th	18 9 28	2 43 15	21 52	10 41	16 10	26 08	7 40	2 10	12 44	13 31	23 12	26 07	17 38	26 40	12 39	20 05	12 44
25 F	18 13 25	3 40 28	6♑46	10 40	16 18	27 21	8 18	2 09	12 41	13 34	23 12℞	26 06	18 00	26 46	12 28	20 26	12 45
26 Sa	18 17 21	4 37 40	21 28	10 38	16 30	28 34	8 55	2 08	12 39	13 36	23 12	26 04	18 21	26 52	12 16	20 48	12 46
27 Su	18 21 18	5 34 52	5♒52	10 34	16 47	29 47	9 32	2 07	12 35	13 38	23 12	26 03	18 43	26 57	12 04	21 10	12 47
28 M	18 25 14	6 32 04	19 52	10 31	17 09	0♌59	10 09	2 06	12 32	13 41	23 12	26 02	19 04	27 02	11 53	21 32	12 48
29 T	18 29 11	7 29 16	3♓26	10 27	17 35	2 12	10 46	2 04	12 29	13 43	23 12	26 00	19 25	27 07	11 42	21 54	12 49
30 W	18 33 7	8 26 28	16 34	10 25	18 06	3 25	11 23	2 03	12 26	13 46	23 12	25 59	19 46	27 11	11 31	22 17	12 49

EPHEMERIS CALCULATED FOR 12 MIDNIGHT GREENWICH MEAN TIME. ALL OTHER DATA AND FACING ASPECTARIAN PAGE IN **EASTERN TIME (BOLD)** AND PACIFIC TIME (REGULAR).

JULY 2021

☽ Last Aspect day	ET / hr:mn / PT	asp	☽ Ingress sign	day	ET / hr:mn / PT
2	9:15 pm	□♇	♉	3	**8:28 am** 5:28 am
3	**12:15 am**	□♇	♉	3	**8:28 am** 5:28 am
5	**12:57 pm** 9:57 am	△♇	♊	5	**9:24 pm** 6:24 pm
7	9:20 pm	☌☿	♋	8	**9:51 am** 6:51 am
8	**12:20 am**	☌☿	♋	8	**9:51 am** 6:51 am
10	**12:10 pm** 9:10 am	☍♇	♌	10	**8:21 pm** 5:21 pm
12	**8:29 am** 5:29 am	☌♂	♍	13	**4:30 am** 1:30 am
14	11:46 pm	△♇	♎	15	**10:32 am** 7:32 am
15	**2:46 am**	△♇	♎	15	**10:32 am** 7:32 am
17	**7:03 am** 4:03 am	□♇	♏	17	**2:38 pm** 11:38 am
19	**12:30 pm** 9:30 am	△☉	♐	19	**5:08 pm** 2:08 pm
21	**6:26 pm** 3:26 pm	△♀	♑	21	**6:36 pm** 3:36 pm
23	**12:34 pm** 9:34 am	☌♇	♒	23	**8:12 pm** 5:12 pm
25	**7:14 pm** 4:14 pm	☍♂	♓	25	**11:30 pm** 8:30 pm
27	**9:13 pm** 6:13 pm	✶♇	♈	28	**5:58 am** 2:58 am
30	**3:38 pm** 12:38 pm	✶♃	♉	30	**4:08 pm** 1:08 pm

☽ Phases & Eclipses

phase	day	ET / hr:mn / PT
4th Quarter	1	**5:11 pm** 2:11 pm
New Moon	9	**9:17 pm** 6:17 pm
2nd Quarter	17	**6:11 am** 3:11 am
Full Moon	23	**10:37 pm** 7:37 pm
4th Quarter	31	**9:16 am** 6:16 am

Planet Ingress

	day	ET / hr:mn / PT
☿ ♋	11	**4:35 pm** 1:35 pm
⚶ ♎	18	11:31 pm
⚶ ♎	19	**2:31 am**
♀ ♍	21	**8:37 pm** 5:37 pm
☉ ♌	22	**10:26 am** 7:26 am
☿ ♌	27	**9:12 pm** 6:12 pm
♃ ♒	28	**8:43 am** 5:43 am
♂ ♍	29	**4:32 pm** 1:32 pm
⚳ ♊	31	**4:13 am** 1:13 am

Planetary Motion

	day	ET / hr:mn / PT
♆ ℞	14	**3:40 am** 12:40 am
⚷ ℞	15	**12:41 pm** 9:41 am

1 THURSDAY
☽ ⊻ ♃ **1:12 am**
☽ △ ♀ **7:22 am** 4:22 am
♂ ☍ ♄ **9:08 am** 6:08 am
☽ □ ☉ **5:11 pm** 2:11 pm
☽ ✶ ♄ **9:16 pm** 6:16 pm
☽ △ ♂ **9:58 pm** 6:58 pm
☽ ⊻ ♅ 9:15 pm

2 FRIDAY
☽ ⊻ ♅ **12:15 am**
☽ ✶ ☿ **12:12 pm** 9:12 am
☽ ⊻ ♆ **6:48 pm** 3:48 pm
☽ □ ♇ 9:15 pm

3 SATURDAY
☽ □ ♇ **12:15 am**
☽ ✶ ♃ **12:19 pm** 9:19 am
☉ ⊼ ♄ **6:51 pm** 3:51 pm
♂ □ ♅ **9:40 pm** 6:40 pm
☽ □ ♀ 10:44 pm

4 SUNDAY
☽ □ ♀ **1:44 am**
☽ □ ♄ **9:06 am** 6:06 am
☽ ✶ ☉ **10:26 am** 7:26 am
☽ ☌ ♅ **12:41 pm** 9:41 am
☽ □ ♂ **1:28 pm** 10:28 am

5 MONDAY
☽ ⊻ ☿ **5:36 am** 2:36 am
☽ ✶ ♆ **7:30 am** 4:30 am
☽ △ ♇ **12:57 pm** 9:57 am

☉ ✶ ♅ **3:14 pm** 12:14 pm
☽ □ ♃ 10:03 pm

6 TUESDAY
☽ □ ♃ **1:03 am**
☿ □ ♆ **3:39 am** 12:39 am
☽ ✶ ♀ **9:41 pm** 6:41 pm
☽ △ ♄ **9:47 pm** 6:47 pm
♀ ☍ ♄ **10:36 pm** 7:36 pm
☽ ⊻ ♅ 10:50 pm

7 WEDNESDAY
☽ ⊻ ♅ **1:50 am**
☽ ⊻ ☉ **4:44 am** 1:44 am
☽ ✶ ♂ **5:47 am** 2:47 am
☽ □ ♆ **8:12 pm** 5:12 pm
☽ ☌ ☿ 9:20 pm
☽ ⊼ ♇ 10:28 pm

8 THURSDAY
☽ ☌ ☿ **12:20 am**
☽ ⊼ ♇ **1:28 am**
☿ ⊼ ♇ **11:36 am** 8:36 am
☽ △ ♃ **1:09 pm** 10:09 am
♀ □ ♅ **3:25 pm** 12:25 pm
☉ ⊻ ♂ **4:29 pm** 1:29 pm

9 FRIDAY
☽ ⊼ ♄ **9:15 am** 6:15 am
☽ ✶ ♅ **1:38 pm** 10:38 am
☽ ⊻ ♀ **3:59 pm** 12:59 pm
☽ ⊻ ♂ **8:28 pm** 5:28 pm
☽ ☌ ☉ **9:17 pm** 6:17 pm

10 SATURDAY
☽ △ ♆ **7:11 am** 4:11 am
☽ ☍ ♇ **12:10 pm** 9:10 am
☽ ⊻ ☿ **5:49 pm** 2:49 pm
☽ ⊼ ♃ **11:14 pm** 8:14 pm

11 SUNDAY
☽ ☍ ♄ **6:32 pm** 3:32 pm
☽ □ ♅ **11:11 pm** 8:11 pm

12 MONDAY
☽ ☌ ♀ **7:14 am** 4:14 am
☽ ☌ ♂ **8:29 am** 5:29 am
☽ ⊻ ☉ **10:56 am** 7:56 am
☿ △ ♃ **3:45 pm** 12:45 pm
☽ ⊼ ♆ **3:50 pm** 12:50 pm
☽ ⊼ ♇ **8:33 pm** 5:33 pm

13 TUESDAY
☽ ☍ ♃ **7:00 am** 4:00 am
☽ ✶ ☿ **9:05 am** 6:05 am
♀ ☌ ♂ **9:33 am** 6:33 am
☽ ⊼ ♄ 10:33 pm

14 WEDNESDAY
☽ ⊼ ♄ **1:33 am**
☽ △ ♅ **6:25 am** 3:25 am
☽ ⊻ ♂ **5:55 pm** 2:55 pm
☽ ⊻ ♀ **7:28 pm** 4:28 pm
☽ ✶ ☉ **9:46 pm** 6:46 pm
☽ ☍ ♆ **10:17 pm** 7:17 pm
☽ △ ♇ 11:46 pm

15 THURSDAY
☽ △ ♇ **2:46 am**
☉ △ ♆ **4:49 am** 1:49 am
☽ ⊼ ♃ **12:38 pm** 9:38 am
☽ □ ☿ **10:09 pm** 7:09 pm
♀ ⊼ ♆ 11:41 pm

16 FRIDAY
♀ ⊼ ♆ **2:41 am**
☽ △ ♄ **6:33 am** 3:33 am
☽ ⊼ ♅ **11:37 am** 8:37 am
☽ ✶ ♂ 10:04 pm
☽ ⊼ ♆ 11:46 pm

17 SATURDAY
☽ ✶ ♂ **1:04 am**
☽ ⊼ ♆ **2:46 am**
☽ ✶ ♀ **5:04 am** 2:04 am
☽ □ ☉ **6:11 am** 3:11 am
☽ □ ♇ **7:03 am** 4:03 am
☽ △ ♃ **4:23 pm** 1:23 pm
☉ ☍ ♇ **6:46 pm** 3:46 pm

18 SUNDAY
♀ ⊼ ♇ **3:48 am** 12:48 am
☽ △ ☿ **9:13 am** 6:13 am
☽ □ ♄ **9:45 am** 6:45 am
☿ ⊼ ♄ **1:13 pm** 10:13 am
♂ ⊼ ♆ **2:22 pm** 11:22 am
☽ ☍ ♅ **3:00 pm** 12:00 pm

19 MONDAY
☽ △ ♆ **5:33 am** 2:33 am
☽ □ ♂ **6:15 am** 3:15 am
☽ ✶ ♇ **9:40 am** 6:40 am
☽ □ ♀ **12:27 pm** 9:27 am
☽ △ ☉ **12:30 pm** 9:30 am
☉ ⊻ ♀ **3:17 pm** 12:17 pm
☽ □ ♃ **6:32 pm** 3:32 pm

20 TUESDAY
☿ ✶ ♅ **5:38 am** 2:38 am
☽ ✶ ♄ **11:31 am** 8:31 am
☽ ⊼ ♅ **4:59 pm** 1:59 pm
☽ ⊼ ☿ **6:42 pm** 3:42 pm

21 WEDNESDAY
☽ □ ♆ **7:08 am** 4:08 am
☽ △ ♂ **10:06 am** 7:06 am
☽ ⊻ ♇ **11:10 am** 8:10 am
☽ ⊼ ☉ **5:30 pm** 2:30 pm
☽ △ ♀ **6:26 pm** 3:26 pm
☽ ✶ ♃ **7:41 pm** 4:41 pm

22 THURSDAY
♀ ☍ ♃ **8:45 am** 5:45 am
♂ ⊼ ♇ **10:09 am** 7:09 am
☽ ⊻ ♄ **12:38 pm** 9:38 am
☽ △ ♅ **6:25 pm** 3:25 pm
☉ ⊼ ♃ 9:10 pm

23 FRIDAY
☉ ⊼ ♃ **12:10 am**
☽ ☍ ☿ **3:53 am** 12:53 am
☽ ✶ ♆ **8:32 am** 5:32 am
☽ ☌ ♇ **12:34 pm** 9:34 am
☽ ⊼ ♂ **1:49 pm** 10:49 am
☽ ⊻ ♃ **8:59 pm** 5:59 pm
☽ ☍ ☉ **10:37 pm** 7:37 pm
☽ ⊼ ♀ 9:34 pm

24 SATURDAY
☽ ⊼ ♀ **12:34 am**
☿ △ ♆ **12:35 pm** 9:35 am
☽ ☌ ♄ **2:25 pm** 11:25 am
☽ □ ♅ **8:43 pm** 5:43 pm

25 SUNDAY
☽ ⊻ ♆ **11:14 am** 8:14 am
☽ ⊼ ☿ **3:15 pm** 12:15 pm
☽ ⊻ ♇ **3:25 pm** 12:25 pm
☿ ☍ ♇ **4:15 pm** 1:15 pm
☽ ☍ ♂ **7:14 pm** 4:14 pm
☽ ☌ ♃ **11:56 pm** 8:56 pm

26 MONDAY
☽ ⊼ ☉ **5:55 am** 2:55 am
☽ ☍ ♀ **9:04 am** 6:04 am
☽ ⊻ ♄ **6:25 pm** 3:25 pm
☽ ✶ ♅ 10:28 pm
☿ ⊻ ♂ 11:48 pm

27 TUESDAY
☽ ✶ ♅ **1:28 am**
☿ ⊻ ♂ **2:48 am**
☽ ☌ ♆ **4:47 pm** 1:47 pm
☽ ✶ ♇ **9:13 pm** 6:13 pm
☿ ⊼ ♃ **9:45 pm** 6:45 pm

28 WEDNESDAY
☽ ⊼ ♂ **4:11 am** 1:11 am
☽ ⊻ ♃ **5:59 am** 2:59 am
☽ △ ☿ **7:42 am** 4:42 am
☽ △ ☉ **5:19 pm** 2:19 pm
☽ ⊼ ♀ **10:00 pm** 7:00 pm
☽ ✶ ♄ 10:53 pm

29 THURSDAY
☽ ✶ ♄ **1:53 am**
☽ ⊻ ♅ **9:51 am** 6:51 am
♂ ☍ ♃ **11:50 am** 8:50 am
☽ ⊻ ♆ 11:03 pm

30 FRIDAY
☽ ⊻ ♆ **2:03 am**
☽ □ ♇ **6:44 am** 3:44 am
♀ ⊼ ♄ **12:27 pm** 9:27 am
☽ ✶ ♃ **3:38 pm** 12:38 pm
☽ △ ♂ **5:26 pm** 2:26 pm

31 SATURDAY
☽ □ ☿ **6:24 am** 3:24 am
☽ □ ☉ **9:16 am** 6:16 am
☽ □ ♄ **12:48 pm** 9:48 am
☽ △ ♀ **3:41 pm** 12:41 pm
☽ ☌ ♅ **9:34 pm** 6:34 pm

Eastern time in bold type
Pacific time in medium type

JULY 2021

DATE	SID.TIME	SUN	MOON	NODE	MERCURY	VENUS	MARS	JUPITER	SATURN	URANUS	NEPTUNE	PLUTO	CERES	PALLAS	JUNO	VESTA	CHIRON
1 Th	18 37 4	9♋23 40	29♓18	10♊23D	18♊42	4♌37	12♌00	2♓01℞	12♒23℞	13♉48	23♓12℞	25♑58℞	20♉07	27♓16	11♐20℞	22♍40	12♈50
2 F	18 41 1	10 20 52	11♈41	10 23	19 23	5 50	12 38	1 59	12 19	13 50	23 11	25 56	20 28	27 20	11 10	23 02	12 51
3 Sa	18 44 57	11 18 05	23 47	10 23	20 08	7 03	13 15	1 56	12 16	13 52	23 11	25 55	20 49	27 23	11 00	23 25	12 52
4 Su	18 48 54	12 15 17	5♉43	10 25	20 58	8 15	13 52	1 54	12 12	13 55	23 11	25 53	21 10	27 27	10 50	23 48	12 52
5 M	18 52 50	13 12 30	17 32	10 26	21 52	9 28	14 29	1 51	12 09	13 57	23 11	25 52	21 30	27 30	10 40	24 12	12 53
6 T	18 56 47	14 09 43	29 19	10 28℞	22 51	10 41	15 07	1 48	12 05	13 59	23 10	25 51	21 51	27 33	10 31	24 35	12 53
7 W	19 0 43	15 06 56	11♊08	10 28	23 54	11 53	15 44	1 45	12 02	14 01	23 10	25 49	22 12	27 35	10 22	24 59	12 54
8 Th	19 4 40	16 04 10	23 04	10 28	25 01	13 06	16 21	1 42	11 58	14 03	23 10	25 48	22 32	27 37	10 13	25 22	12 54
9 F	19 8 36	17 01 23	5♋07	10 25	26 12	14 18	16 58	1 39	11 54	14 05	23 09	25 46	22 52	27 39	10 05	25 46	12 55
10 Sa	19 12 33	17 58 37	17 22	10 21	27 28	15 31	17 36	1 35	11 50	14 07	23 09	25 45	23 13	27 41	9 57	26 10	12 55
11 Su	19 16 30	18 55 52	29 49	10 15	28 48	16 43	18 13	1 32	11 46	14 09	23 08	25 44	23 33	27 42	9 49	26 35	12 55
12 M	19 20 26	19 53 06	12♌29	10 09	0♋12	17 56	18 50	1 28	11 42	14 11	23 08	25 42	23 53	27 43	9 42	26 59	12 55
13 T	19 24 23	20 50 20	25 23	10 02	1 40	19 08	19 28	1 24	11 38	14 12	23 07	25 41	24 13	27 43	9 34	27 23	12 56
14 W	19 28 19	21 47 34	8♍29	9 56	3 12	20 20	20 05	1 19	11 34	14 14	23 07	25 39	24 33	27 44℞	9 28	27 48	12 56
15 Th	19 32 16	22 44 49	21 49	9 50	4 48	21 33	20 43	1 15	11 30	14 16	23 06	25 38	24 53	27 44	9 21	28 13	12 56℞
16 F	19 36 12	23 42 03	5♎23	9 47	6 27	22 45	21 20	1 10	11 26	14 18	23 05	25 36	25 12	27 43	9 15	28 38	12 56
17 Sa	19 40 9	24 39 18	19 09	9 46D	8 10	23 57	21 57	1 06	11 22	14 19	23 05	25 35	25 32	27 43	9 09	29 03	12 56
18 Su	19 44 5	25 36 32	3♏09	9 46	9 56	25 10	22 35	1 01	11 18	14 21	23 04	25 34	25 51	27 41	9 03	29 28	12 56
19 M	19 48 2	26 33 47	17 21	9 47	11 46	26 22	23 12	0 56	11 14	14 22	23 03	25 32	26 11	27 40	8 58	29 53	12 56
20 T	19 51 59	27 31 02	1♐44	9 48℞	13 39	27 34	23 50	0 50	11 09	14 24	23 03	25 31	26 30	27 38	8 53	0♎19	12 55
21 W	19 55 55	28 28 17	16 15	9 48	15 34	28 46	24 27	0 45	11 05	14 25	23 02	25 29	26 49	27 36	8 49	0 44	12 55
22 Th	19 59 52	29 25 33	0♑51	9 46	17 32	29 58	25 05	0 39	11 01	14 27	23 01	25 28	27 08	27 34	8 45	1 10	12 55
23 F	20 3 48	0♌22 49	15 25	9 42	19 32	1♍10	25 42	0 34	10 56	14 28	23 00	25 26	27 27	27 31	8 41	1 35	12 54
24 Sa	20 7 45	1 20 05	29 53	9 36	21 34	2 22	26 20	0 28	10 52	14 30	22 59	25 25	27 46	27 28	8 37	2 01	12 54
25 Su	20 11 41	2 17 22	14♒06	9 29	23 37	3 34	26 57	0 22	10 48	14 31	22 59	25 23	28 04	27 25	8 34	2 27	12 54
26 M	20 15 38	3 14 40	28 00	9 20	25 42	4 46	27 35	0 16	10 43	14 32	22 58	25 22	28 23	27 21	8 31	2 54	12 53
27 T	20 19 34	4 11 58	11♓32	9 11	27 47	5 58	28 13	0 10	10 39	14 33	22 57	25 21	28 41	27 17	8 29	3 20	12 53
28 W	20 23 31	5 09 17	24 40	9 04	29 54	7 10	28 50	0 03	10 34	14 34	22 56	25 19	29 00	27 12	8 26	3 46	12 52
29 Th	20 27 28	6 06 37	7♈25	8 58	2♌00	8 22	29 28	29♒57	10 30	14 36	22 55	25 18	29 18	27 07	8 25	4 13	12 51
30 F	20 31 24	7 03 58	19 49	8 55	4 07	9 33	0♍05	29 50	10 26	14 37	22 54	25 16	29 36	27 02	8 23	4 39	12 51
31 Sa	20 35 21	8 01 21	1♉56	8 53D	6 13	10 45	0 43	29 44	10 21	14 38	22 53	25 15	29 54	26 57	8 22	5 06	12 50

EPHEMERIS CALCULATED FOR 12 MIDNIGHT GREENWICH MEAN TIME. ALL OTHER DATA AND FACING ASPECTARIAN PAGE IN **EASTERN TIME (BOLD)** AND PACIFIC TIME (REGULAR).

AUGUST 2021

☽ Last Aspect day	ET / hr:mn / PT	asp	☽ Ingress sign	day	ET / hr:mn / PT
2	**3:41 am** 12:41 am	□♃	♊	2	**4:46 am** 1:46 am
4	**3:38 pm** 12:38 pm	△♃	♋	4	**5:17 pm** 2:17 pm
6	**6:12 pm** 3:12 pm	☍♇	♌	7	**3:31 am** 12:31 am
9	**8:23 am** 5:23 am	☍♃	♍	9	**10:56 am** 7:56 am
11	**7:22 am** 4:22 am	△♇	♎	11	**4:08 pm** 1:08 pm
13	**4:39 pm** 1:39 pm	△♃	♏	13	**8:01 pm** 5:01 pm
15	**11:05 pm** 8:05 pm	⚹♀	♐	15	**11:12 pm** 8:12 pm
17	**9:43 pm** 6:43 pm	⚹♃	♑	17	10:58 pm
17	**9:43 pm** 6:43 pm	⚹♃	♑	18	**1:58 am**
19	**7:59 pm** 4:59 pm	☌♇	♒	20	**4:49 am** 1:49 am
22	**8:02 am** 5:02 am	☍☉	♓	22	**8:43 am** 5:43 am
24	**5:12 am** 2:12 am	⚹♇	♈	24	**2:57 pm** 11:57 am
26	**5:14 pm** 2:14 pm	⚹♃	♉	26	9:27 pm
26	**5:14 pm** 2:14 pm	⚹♃	♉	27	**12:27 am**
29	**10:59 am** 7:59 am	△☿	♊	29	**12:42 pm** 9:42 am
31	**4:48 pm** 1:48 pm	△♃	♋	31	10:26 pm

☽ Phases & Eclipses phase	day	ET / hr:mn / PT
New Moon	8	**9:50 am** 6:50 am
2nd Quarter	15	**11:20 am** 8:20 am
Full Moon	22	**8:02 am** 5:02 am
4th Quarter	30	**3:13 am** 12:13 am

Planet Ingress		day	ET / hr:mn / PT
☿	♍	11	**5:57 pm** 2:57 pm
♀	♎	15	9:27 pm
♀	♎	16	**12:27 am**
☉	♍	22	**5:35 pm** 2:35 pm
☿	♎	29	10:10 pm
☿	♎	30	1:10 am

Planetary Motion		day	ET / hr:mn / PT
⚳	D	2	**7:43 pm** 4:43 pm
♅	℞	19	**9:40 pm** 6:40 pm

1 SUNDAY
☉☌☿ **10:08 am** 7:08 am
☽⚹♆ **2:13 pm** 11:13 am
☿☍♄ **5:50 pm** 2:50 pm
☽△♇ **7:01 pm** 4:01 pm
☉☍♄ 11:14 pm

2 MONDAY
☉☍♄ **2:14 am**
☽□♃ **3:41 am** 12:41 am
☽□♂ **9:30 am** 6:30 am
☽△♄ 10:19 pm
♀△♅ 11:53 pm

3 TUESDAY
☽△♄ **1:19 am**
♀△♅ **2:53 am**
☽⚹☉ **3:30 am** 12:30 am
☽⚹☿ **8:12 am** 5:12 am
☽⚺♅ **10:34 am** 7:34 am
☽□♀ **11:25 am** 8:25 am
☿□♅ **9:57 pm** 6:57 pm
☽□♆ 11:55 pm

4 WEDNESDAY
☽□♆ **2:55 am**
☽⚻♇ **7:37 am** 4:37 am
☽△♃ **3:38 pm** 12:38 pm
☿⚺♀ 9:43 pm
☽⚹♂ 10:12 pm

5 THURSDAY
☿⚺♀ **12:43 am**
☽⚹♂ **1:12 am**
☽⚻♄ **12:52 pm** 9:52 am
☽⚺☉ **8:24 pm** 5:24 pm
☽⚹♅ **10:12 pm** 7:12 pm

6 FRIDAY
☽⚹♀ **5:17 am** 2:17 am
☽⚺☿ **7:31 am** 4:31 am
☽△♆ **1:43 pm** 10:43 am
☽☍♇ **6:12 pm** 3:12 pm
☉□♅ **7:57 pm** 4:57 pm
☽⚻♃ 10:23 pm

7 SATURDAY
☽⚻♃ **1:23 am**
☽⚺♂ **2:04 pm** 11:04 am
☽☍♄ **9:50 pm** 6:50 pm
☿⚻♆ **10:24 pm** 7:24 pm

8 SUNDAY
☽□♅ **7:04 am** 4:04 am
☽☌☉ **9:50 am** 6:50 am
☽⚺♀ **7:24 pm** 4:24 pm
☽⚻♆ **9:42 pm** 6:42 pm
☽☌☿ 10:45 pm
☽⚻♇ 10:57 pm

9 MONDAY
☽☌☿ **1:45 am**
☽⚻♇ **1:57 am**
☿⚻♇ **3:03 am** 12:03 am

☽☍♃ **8:23 am** 5:23 am
♀☍♆ **8:20 pm** 5:20 pm
☽☌♂ **11:42 pm** 8:42 pm

10 TUESDAY
☽⚻♄ **4:07 am** 1:07 am
☽△♅ **1:19 pm** 10:19 am
☽⚺☉ **8:03 pm** 5:03 pm
☿☍♃ **9:20 pm** 6:20 pm

11 WEDNESDAY
☽☍♆ **3:16 am** 12:16 am
☽☌♀ **6:15 am** 3:15 am
☽△♇ **7:22 am** 4:22 am
☽⚻♃ **1:10 pm** 10:10 am
☽⚺☿ **3:51 pm** 12:51 pm
♀△♇ **6:46 pm** 3:46 pm

12 THURSDAY
☽⚺♂ **7:03 am** 4:03 am
☽△♄ **8:32 am** 5:32 am
☽⚻♅ **5:48 pm** 2:48 pm

13 FRIDAY
☽⚹☉ **4:13 am** 1:13 am
☽⚻♆ **7:19 am** 4:19 am
☽□♇ **11:20 am** 8:20 am
♂⚻♄ **12:27 pm** 9:27 am
☽⚺♀ **3:10 pm** 12:10 pm
☽△♃ **4:39 pm** 1:39 pm

14 SATURDAY
☽⚹☿ **3:33 am** 12:33 am
♀⚻♃ **6:58 am** 3:58 am
☽□♄ **11:54 am** 8:54 am

☽⚹♂ **1:08 pm** 10:08 am
☽☍♅ **9:18 pm** 6:18 pm
☉⚻♆ 9:14 pm

15 SUNDAY
☉⚻♆ **12:14 am**
☽△♆ **10:33 am** 7:33 am
☽□☉ **11:20 am** 8:20 am
☽⚹♇ **2:32 pm** 11:32 am
☽□♃ **7:23 pm** 4:23 pm
☽⚹♀ **11:05 pm** 8:05 pm

16 MONDAY
☽□☿ **1:57 pm** 10:57 am
☽⚹♄ **2:40 pm** 11:40 am
☽□♂ **6:31 pm** 3:31 pm
☿⚻♄ **7:35 pm** 4:35 pm
☽⚻♅ 9:15 pm

17 TUESDAY
☽⚻♅ **12:15 am**
☉⚻♇ **9:31 am** 6:31 am
☽□♆ **1:19 pm** 10:19 am
☽⚺♇ **5:17 pm** 2:17 pm
☽△☉ **5:51 pm** 2:51 pm
☽⚹♃ **9:43 pm** 6:43 pm

18 WEDNESDAY
☽□♀ **6:27 am** 3:27 am
☽⚺♄ **5:08 pm** 2:08 pm
☿☌♂ **11:28 pm** 8:28 pm
☽△♂ **11:37 pm** 8:37 pm
☽△☿ **11:38 pm** 8:38 pm
☽△♅ 11:59 pm

19 THURSDAY
☽△♅ **2:59 am**
☽⚹♆ **3:59 pm** 12:59 pm
☽☌♇ **7:59 pm** 4:59 pm
☉☍♃ **8:29 pm** 5:29 pm
☽⚺♃ 9:03 pm
☽⚻☉ 9:21 pm

20 FRIDAY
☽⚺♃ **12:03 am**
☽⚻☉ **12:21 am**
☿△♅ **4:06 am** 1:06 am
☽△♀ **2:01 pm** 11:01 am
☽☌♄ **7:55 pm** 4:55 pm

21 SATURDAY
☽⚻♂ **5:13 am** 2:13 am
☽□♅ **6:12 am** 3:12 am
☽⚻☿ **9:41 am** 6:41 am
☽⚺♆ **7:24 pm** 4:24 pm
☽⚺♇ **11:32 pm** 8:32 pm
♂△♅ 11:38 pm

22 SUNDAY
♂△♅ **2:38 am**
☽☌♃ **3:19 am** 12:19 am
☽☍☉ **8:02 am** 5:02 am
☽⚻♀ **11:14 pm** 8:14 pm
☽⚺♄ 9:07 pm

23 MONDAY
☽⚺♄ **12:07 am**
♀△♄ **8:48 am** 5:48 am
☽⚹♅ **11:04 am** 8:04 am
☽☍♂ **12:43 pm** 9:43 am

☽☍☿ **10:03 pm** 7:03 pm
☽☌♆ 9:50 pm

24 TUESDAY
☽☌♆ **12:50 am**
☽⚹♇ **5:12 am** 2:12 am
☽⚺♃ **8:43 am** 5:43 am
☽⚻☉ **6:37 pm** 3:37 pm
☿☍♆ **9:14 pm** 6:14 pm

25 WEDNESDAY
☽⚹♄ **6:58 am** 3:58 am
☽☍♀ **11:57 am** 8:57 am
☽⚺♅ **6:51 pm** 3:51 pm
☽⚻♂ **11:37 pm** 8:37 pm

26 THURSDAY
☽⚺♆ **9:22 am** 6:22 am
☿△♇ **10:23 am** 7:23 am
☽□♇ **2:02 pm** 11:02 am
☽⚻☿ **2:33 pm** 11:33 am
☽⚹♃ **5:14 pm** 2:14 pm

27 FRIDAY
☽△☉ **9:19 am** 6:19 am
☿⚻♃ **11:05 am** 8:05 am
☽□♄ **5:04 pm** 2:04 pm

28 SATURDAY
☽⚻♀ **5:00 am** 2:00 am
☽☌♅ **5:52 am** 2:52 am
♀⚻♅ **1:43 pm** 10:43 am
☽△♂ **2:14 pm** 11:14 am
☽⚹♆ **8:56 pm** 5:56 pm
☽△♇ 10:50 pm

29 SUNDAY
☽△♇ **1:50 am**
☽□♃ **4:36 am** 1:36 am
☽△☿ **10:59 am** 7:59 am

30 MONDAY
☽□☉ **3:13 am** 12:13 am
☽△♄ **5:26 am** 2:26 am
☽⚺♅ **6:40 pm** 3:40 pm
☽△♀ 9:30 pm

31 TUESDAY
☽△♀ **12:30 am**
☉⚻♄ **4:46 am** 1:46 am
☽□♂ **6:36 am** 3:36 am
☽□♆ **9:41 am** 6:41 am
☽⚻♇ **2:37 pm** 11:37 am
☽△♃ **4:48 pm** 1:48 pm

Eastern time in bold type
Pacific time in medium type

AUGUST 2021

DATE	SID. TIME	SUN	MOON	NODE	MERCURY	VENUS	MARS	JUPITER	SATURN	URANUS	NEPTUNE	PLUTO	CERES	PALLAS	JUNO	VESTA	CHIRON
1 Su	20 39 17	8♌58 44	13♉52	8♊53	8♌19	11♍57	1♍21	29♒37℞	10♒17℞	14♉39	22♓52℞	25♑14℞	0♊12	26♓51℞	8♐21℞	5♎33	12♈49℞
2 M	20 43 14	9 56 08	25 41	8 54	10 24	13 08	1 58	29 30	10 12	14 40	22 51	25 12	0 29	26 44	8 21D	5 59	12 48
3 T	20 47 10	10 53 34	7♊29	8 54℞	12 28	14 20	2 36	29 23	10 08	14 40	22 49	25 11	0 47	26 38	8 20	6 26	12 47
4 W	20 51 7	11 51 01	19 22	8 53	14 31	15 32	3 14	29 16	10 03	14 41	22 48	25 09	1 04	26 31	8 21	6 54	12 46
5 Th	20 55 3	12 48 29	1♋22	8 51	16 33	16 43	3 52	29 09	9 59	14 42	22 47	25 08	1 21	26 24	8 21	7 21	12 45
6 F	20 59 0	13 45 58	13 35	8 46	18 34	17 55	4 29	29 01	9 54	14 43	22 46	25 07	1 39	26 16	8 22	7 48	12 44
7 Sa	21 2 57	14 43 28	26 02	8 39	20 34	19 06	5 07	28 54	9 50	14 43	22 45	25 05	1 55	26 08	8 23	8 15	12 43
8 Su	21 6 53	15 40 59	8♌46	8 29	22 32	20 17	5 45	28 47	9 46	14 44	22 44	25 04	2 12	25 59	8 25	8 43	12 42
9 M	21 10 50	16 38 32	21 47	8 18	24 28	21 29	6 23	28 39	9 41	14 45	22 42	25 03	2 29	25 51	8 26	9 10	12 41
10 T	21 14 46	17 36 05	5♍03	8 07	26 24	22 40	7 01	28 32	9 37	14 45	22 41	25 01	2 45	25 42	8 29	9 38	12 40
11 W	21 18 43	18 33 39	18 32	7 56	28 17	23 51	7 39	28 24	9 32	14 46	22 40	25 00	3 02	25 32	8 31	10 06	12 38
12 Th	21 22 39	19 31 15	2♎13	7 47	0♍10	25 03	8 17	28 16	9 28	14 46	22 39	24 59	3 18	25 23	8 34	10 34	12 37
13 F	21 26 36	20 28 51	16 03	7 41	2 00	26 14	8 55	28 09	9 24	14 46	22 37	24 58	3 34	25 13	8 37	11 02	12 36
14 Sa	21 30 32	21 26 28	29 59	7 37	3 50	27 25	9 33	28 01	9 19	14 47	22 36	24 56	3 49	25 02	8 40	11 30	12 34
15 Su	21 34 29	22 24 06	14♏01	7 36D	5 37	28 36	10 11	27 53	9 15	14 47	22 34	24 55	4 05	24 52	8 44	11 58	12 33
16 M	21 38 26	23 21 45	28 07	7 35℞	7 24	29 47	10 49	27 45	9 11	14 47	22 33	24 54	4 20	24 41	8 48	12 26	12 31
17 T	21 42 22	24 19 25	12♐17	7 35	9 08	0♎58	11 27	27 37	9 06	14 47	22 32	24 53	4 36	24 29	8 52	12 54	12 30
18 W	21 46 19	25 17 07	26 28	7 34	10 52	2 09	12 05	27 30	9 02	14 47	22 30	24 51	4 51	24 18	8 57	13 23	12 28
19 Th	21 50 15	26 14 49	10♑40	7 31	12 34	3 19	12 43	27 22	8 58	14 48	22 29	24 50	5 06	24 06	9 02	13 51	12 26
20 F	21 54 12	27 12 32	24 49	7 25	14 14	4 30	13 21	27 14	8 54	14 48℞	22 27	24 49	5 20	23 54	9 07	14 20	12 25
21 Sa	21 58 8	28 10 17	8♒53	7 17	15 53	5 41	13 59	27 06	8 50	14 48	22 26	24 48	5 35	23 41	9 13	14 48	12 23
22 Su	22 2 5	29 08 02	22 45	7 06	17 31	6 52	14 37	26 58	8 46	14 47	22 25	24 47	5 49	23 29	9 18	15 17	12 21
23 M	22 6 1	0♍05 49	6♓23	6 54	19 07	8 02	15 15	26 50	8 42	14 47	22 23	24 46	6 03	23 16	9 24	15 46	12 19
24 T	22 9 58	1 03 38	19 43	6 42	20 42	9 13	15 53	26 42	8 38	14 47	22 22	24 45	6 17	23 03	9 31	16 15	12 18
25 W	22 13 55	2 01 28	2♈43	6 31	22 15	10 23	16 31	26 35	8 34	14 47	22 20	24 43	6 31	22 49	9 37	16 44	12 16
26 Th	22 17 51	2 59 19	15 23	6 22	23 47	11 33	17 10	26 27	8 30	14 47	22 18	24 42	6 44	22 36	9 44	17 13	12 14
27 F	22 21 48	3 57 13	27 44	6 15	25 18	12 44	17 48	26 19	8 26	14 46	22 17	24 41	6 58	22 22	9 51	17 42	12 12
28 Sa	22 25 44	4 55 08	9♉51	6 11	26 47	13 54	18 26	26 11	8 23	14 46	22 15	24 40	7 11	22 08	9 59	18 11	12 10
29 Su	22 29 41	5 53 05	21 46	6 10	28 15	15 04	19 04	26 04	8 19	14 46	22 14	24 39	7 23	21 53	10 07	18 40	12 08
30 M	22 33 37	6 51 03	3♊36	6 09	29 42	16 14	19 43	25 56	8 15	14 45	22 12	24 38	7 36	21 39	10 15	19 09	12 06
31 T	22 37 34	7 49 04	15 24	6 09	1♎07	17 24	20 21	25 48	8 12	14 45	22 11	24 37	7 48	21 24	10 23	19 38	12 04

EPHEMERIS CALCULATED FOR 12 MIDNIGHT GREENWICH MEAN TIME. ALL OTHER DATA AND FACING ASPECTARIAN PAGE IN **EASTERN TIME (BOLD)** AND PACIFIC TIME (REGULAR).

SEPTEMBER 2021

☽ Last Aspect day	ET / hr:mn / PT	asp	☽ Ingress sign	day	ET / hr:mn / PT
8/31	**4:48 pm** 1:48 pm	△♃	♋	1	**1:26 am**
2	10:37 pm	☍♇	♌	3	**11:58 am** 8:58 am
3	**1:37 am**	☍♇	♌	3	**11:58 am** 8:58 am
5	**10:22 am** 7:22 am	☍♃	♍	5	**7:06 pm** 4:06 pm
7	**3:24 pm** 12:24 pm	☌♂	♎	7	**11:20 pm** 8:20 pm
9	9:48 pm	☌♀	♏	9	11:05 pm
10	**12:48 am**	☌♀	♏	10	**2:05 am**
11	10:33 pm	✶♂	♐	12	**4:34 am** 1:34 am
12	**1:33 am**	✶♂	♐	12	**4:34 am** 1:34 am
14	**6:57 am** 3:57 am	☐♂	♑	14	**7:34 am** 4:34 am
15	10:40 pm	☌♇	♒	16	**11:23 am** 8:23 am
16	**1:40 am**	☌♇	♒	16	**11:23 am** 8:23 am
18	**5:14 am** 2:14 am	☌♃	♓	18	**4:22 pm** 1:22 pm
20	**7:55 pm** 4:55 pm	☍☉	♈	20	**11:13 pm** 8:13 pm
22	**10:05 pm** 7:05 pm	☍☿	♉	23	**8:38 am** 5:38 am
25	**9:09 am** 6:09 am	△♇	♊	25	**8:36 pm** 5:36 pm
27	9:18 pm	△☿	♋	28	**9:34 am** 6:34 am
28	**12:18 pm**	△☿	♋	28	**9:34 am** 6:34 am
30	**10:49 am** 7:49 am	☐☿	♌	30	**8:53 pm** 5:53 pm

☽ Phases & Eclipses phase	day	ET / hr:mn / PT
New Moon	6	**8:52 pm** 5:52 pm
2nd Quarter	13	**4:39 pm** 1:39 pm
Full Moon	20	**7:55 pm** 4:55 pm
4th Quarter	28	**9:57 pm** 6:57 pm

Planet Ingress	day	ET / hr:mn / PT
♀ ♏	10	**4:39 pm** 1:39 pm
♂ ♎	14	**8:14 pm** 5:14 pm
⚵ ♏	20	**12:57 pm** 9:57 am
☉ ♎	22	**3:21 pm** 12:21 pm

Planetary Motion	day	ET / hr:mn / PT
☿ ℞	26	10:10 pm
☿ ℞	27	**1:10 am**

1 WEDNESDAY
☽☐☿ **7:46 am** 4:46 am
☽⚻♄ **5:30 pm** 2:30 pm
☽✶☉ **8:52 pm** 5:52 pm

2 THURSDAY
☽✶♅ **6:33 am** 3:33 am
♂☍♆ **1:43 pm** 10:43 am
☽☐♀ **6:24 pm** 3:24 pm
☽△♆ **8:52 pm** 5:52 pm
☽✶♂ **9:16 pm** 6:16 pm
☽☍♇ 10:37 pm

3 FRIDAY
☽☍♇ **1:37 am**
☽⚻♃ **3:12 am** 12:12 am
♀⚻♆ **8:13 pm** 5:13 pm
☽✶☿ 9:45 pm
☽☍♄ 11:55 pm

4 SATURDAY
☽✶☿ **12:45 am**
☽☍♄ **2:55 am**
☽⚺☉ **10:58 am** 7:58 am
☽☐♅ **3:23 pm** 12:23 pm
☿△♄ **9:30 pm** 6:30 pm

5 SUNDAY
☽⚻♆ **4:47 am** 1:47 am
☽✶♀ **7:58 am** 4:58 am
☽⚺♂ **8:07 am** 5:07 am
☽⚻♇ **9:18 am** 6:18 am
☽☍♃ **10:22 am** 7:22 am

♀⚺♂ **11:26 am** 8:26 am
♀☐♇ **11:07 pm** 8:07 pm

6 MONDAY
♂△♇ **8:20 am** 5:20 am
☽⚻♄ **8:57 am** 5:57 am
♀△♃ **9:05 am** 6:05 am
☽⚺☿ **12:41 pm** 9:41 am
☽☌☉ **8:52 pm** 5:52 pm
☽△♅ **8:54 pm** 5:54 pm
☉△♅ **9:29 pm** 6:29 pm
♂⚻♃ **11:50 pm** 8:50 pm

7 TUESDAY
☽☍♆ **9:34 am** 6:34 am
☽△♇ **1:56 pm** 10:56 am
☽⚻♃ **2:33 pm** 11:33 am
☽☌♂ **3:24 pm** 12:24 pm
☽⚺♀ **5:29 pm** 2:29 pm

8 WEDNESDAY
☽△♄ **12:29 pm** 9:29 am
☽☌☿ **9:01 pm** 6:01 pm
☽⚻♅ 9:11 pm

9 THURSDAY
☽⚻♅ **12:11 am**
☽⚺☉ **3:58 am** 12:58 am
☽⚻♆ **12:28 pm** 9:28 am
☽☐♇ **4:48 pm** 1:48 pm
☽△♃ **5:03 pm** 2:03 pm
☽⚺♂ **8:40 pm** 5:40 pm
☽☌♀ 9:48 pm

10 FRIDAY
☽☌♀ **12:48 am**
☿⚻♅ **12:17 pm** 9:17 am
☽☐♄ **2:53 pm** 11:53 am
☽☍♅ 11:37 pm

11 SATURDAY
☽☍♅ **2:37 am**
☽⚺☿ **3:49 am** 12:49 am
♃⚺♇ **6:06 am** 3:06 am
☽✶☉ **10:08 am** 7:08 am
☽△♆ **2:50 pm** 11:50 am
☽☐♃ **7:08 pm** 4:08 pm
☽✶♇ **7:13 pm** 4:13 pm
☽✶♂ 10:33 pm

12 SUNDAY
☽✶♂ **1:33 am**
☽⚺♀ **7:45 am** 4:45 am
☽✶♄ **5:18 pm** 2:18 pm

13 MONDAY
☽⚻♅ **5:13 am** 2:13 am
☽✶☿ **10:31 am** 7:31 am
☽☐☉ **4:39 pm** 1:39 pm
☽☐♆ **5:33 pm** 2:33 pm
☽✶♃ **9:38 pm** 6:38 pm
☽⚺♇ **10:03 pm** 7:03 pm

14 TUESDAY
☉☍♆ **5:21 am** 2:21 am
☽☐♂ **6:57 am** 3:57 am
☽✶♀ **3:21 pm** 12:21 pm
☽⚺♄ **8:19 pm** 5:19 pm

15 WEDNESDAY
☽△♅ **8:31 am** 5:31 am
☽☐☿ **5:41 pm** 2:41 pm
☽✶♆ **9:01 pm** 6:01 pm
☽△☉ 9:07 pm
☽⚺♃ 9:54 pm
☽☌♇ 10:40 pm

16 THURSDAY
☽△☉ **12:07 am**
☽⚺♃ **12:54 am**
☽☌♇ **1:40 am**
☉⚻♃ **10:18 am** 7:18 am
☽△♂ **1:19 pm** 10:19 am
☉△♇ **9:53 pm** 6:53 pm
☽☐♀ 9:03 pm
☽☌♄ 9:14 pm
♀☐♄ 11:15 pm

17 FRIDAY
☽☐♀ **12:03 am**
☽☌♄ **12:14 am**
♀☐♄ **2:15 am**
☽☐♅ **12:45 pm** 9:45 am
☿⚻♆ 9:18 pm
☽⚺♆ 10:32 pm
☽△☿ 10:36 pm

18 SATURDAY
☿⚻♆ **12:18 am**
☽⚺♆ **1:32 am**
☽△☿ **1:36 am**
☽☌♃ **5:14 am** 2:14 am
☽⚺♇ **6:21 am** 3:21 am

☽⚻☉ **8:55 am** 5:55 am
☽⚻♂ **9:04 pm** 6:04 pm

19 SUNDAY
☽⚺♄ **5:27 am** 2:27 am
☽△♀ **10:26 am** 7:26 am
☽✶♅ **6:26 pm** 3:26 pm

20 MONDAY
☽☌♆ **7:39 am** 4:39 am
☽⚻☿ **10:50 am** 7:50 am
☽⚺♃ **11:15 am** 8:15 am
☽✶♇ **12:45 pm** 9:45 am
☿△♃ **6:53 pm** 3:53 pm
☽☍☉ **7:55 pm** 4:55 pm

21 TUESDAY
☽☍♂ **7:03 am** 4:03 am
☽✶♄ **12:43 pm** 9:43 am
☽⚻♀ **11:34 pm** 8:34 pm
☽⚺♅ 11:20 pm

22 WEDNESDAY
☽⚺♅ **2:20 am**
☿☐♇ **9:12 am** 6:12 am
☽⚺♆ **4:11 pm** 1:11 pm
☽✶♃ **7:42 pm** 4:42 pm
☽☐♇ **9:37 pm** 6:37 pm
☽☍☿ **10:05 pm** 7:05 pm

23 THURSDAY
♀☍♅ **5:41 am** 2:41 am
☽⚻☉ **10:08 am** 7:08 am
☽⚻♂ **8:07 pm** 5:07 pm
☽☐♄ **10:40 pm** 7:40 pm

24 FRIDAY
☽☌♅ **12:56 pm** 9:56 am
☽☍♀ **4:16 pm** 1:16 pm

25 SATURDAY
☽✶♆ **3:23 am** 12:23 am
☽☐♃ **6:49 am** 3:49 am
☽△♇ **9:09 am** 6:09 am
☽⚻☿ **11:10 am** 8:10 am
♂△♄ **5:50 pm** 2:50 pm

26 SUNDAY
☽△☉ **3:35 am** 12:35 am
☽△♄ **10:57 am** 7:57 am
☽△♂ **11:59 am** 8:59 am
☽⚺♅ 10:32 pm

27 MONDAY
☽⚺♅ **1:32 am**
☽⚻♀ **11:28 am** 8:28 am
☽☐♆ **4:11 pm** 1:11 pm
☽△♃ **7:25 pm** 4:25 pm
☽⚻♇ **10:06 pm** 7:06 pm
☽△☿ 9:18 pm

28 TUESDAY
☽△☿ **12:18 am**
☽☐☉ **9:57 pm** 6:57 pm
☽⚻♄ **11:39 pm** 8:39 pm

29 WEDNESDAY
☽☐♂ **4:17 am** 1:17 am
♀△♆ **12:14 pm** 9:14 am
☽✶♅ **1:54 pm** 10:54 am
☉△♄ **6:19 pm** 3:19 pm

30 THURSDAY
☽△♆ **4:06 am** 1:06 am
☽△♀ **5:44 am** 2:44 am
☽⚻♃ **7:02 am** 4:02 am
☽☍♇ **9:54 am** 6:54 am
☽☐☿ **10:49 am** 7:49 am
♀☐♃ **7:31 pm** 4:31 pm

Eastern time in bold type
Pacific time in medium type

SEPTEMBER 2021

DATE	SID.TIME	SUN	MOON	NODE	MERCURY	VENUS	MARS	JUPITER	SATURN	URANUS	NEPTUNE	PLUTO	CERES	PALLAS	JUNO	VESTA	CHIRON
1 W	22 41 30	8♍47 07	27♊17	6♊08R	2♎30	18♎34	20♍59	25♒41R	8♒08R	14♉44R	22♓09R	24♑36R	8♊01	21♓09R	10♐31	20♎08	12♈01R
2 Th	22 45 27	9 45 11	9♋21	6 06	3 52	19 44	21 38	25 34	8 05	14 43	22 07	24 35	8 12	20 54	10 40	20 37	11 59
3 F	22 49 24	10 43 17	21 39	6 01	5 13	20 54	22 16	25 26	8 01	14 43	22 06	24 35	8 24	20 39	10 49	21 07	11 57
4 Sa	22 53 20	11 41 26	4♌15	5 53	6 32	22 04	22 55	25 19	7 58	14 42	22 04	24 34	8 36	20 24	10 58	21 37	11 55
5 Su	22 57 17	12 39 36	17 12	5 43	7 50	23 13	23 33	25 12	7 55	14 41	22 03	24 33	8 47	20 09	11 08	22 06	11 53
6 M	23 1 13	13 37 47	0♍31	5 31	9 05	24 23	24 12	25 05	7 51	14 41	22 01	24 32	8 58	19 53	11 18	22 36	11 50
7 T	23 5 10	14 36 01	14 08	5 19	10 20	25 32	24 50	24 58	7 48	14 40	21 59	24 31	9 08	19 38	11 27	23 06	11 48
8 W	23 9 6	15 34 16	28 03	5 07	11 32	26 42	25 29	24 51	7 45	14 39	21 58	24 30	9 19	19 22	11 38	23 36	11 46
9 Th	23 13 3	16 32 33	12♎09	4 58	12 42	27 51	26 07	24 44	7 42	14 38	21 56	24 30	9 29	19 06	11 48	24 06	11 43
10 F	23 16 59	17 30 52	26 23	4 50	13 51	29 00	26 46	24 37	7 39	14 37	21 54	24 29	9 39	18 51	11 59	24 35	11 41
11 Sa	23 20 56	18 29 12	10♏40	4 46	14 57	0♏10	27 25	24 31	7 36	14 36	21 53	24 28	9 48	18 35	12 10	25 06	11 38
12 Su	23 24 53	19 27 34	24 55	4 44D	16 02	1 19	28 03	24 24	7 34	14 35	21 51	24 27	9 58	18 19	12 21	25 36	11 36
13 M	23 28 49	20 25 58	9♐07	4 44R	17 03	2 28	28 42	24 18	7 31	14 34	21 49	24 27	10 07	18 03	12 32	26 06	11 34
14 T	23 32 46	21 24 23	23 14	4 44	18 03	3 37	29 21	24 12	7 28	14 32	21 48	24 26	10 15	17 47	12 44	26 36	11 31
15 W	23 36 42	22 22 49	7♑15	4 43	19 00	4 45	0♎00	24 06	7 26	14 31	21 46	24 26	10 24	17 32	12 56	27 06	11 29
16 Th	23 40 39	23 21 17	21 09	4 41	19 54	5 54	0 38	24 00	7 24	14 30	21 44	24 25	10 32	17 16	13 08	27 37	11 26
17 F	23 44 35	24 19 47	4♒56	4 35	20 45	7 03	1 17	23 54	7 21	14 29	21 43	24 24	10 40	17 00	13 20	28 07	11 23
18 Sa	23 48 32	25 18 19	18 34	4 27	21 33	8 11	1 56	23 48	7 19	14 27	21 41	24 24	10 47	16 45	13 32	28 37	11 21
19 Su	23 52 28	26 16 52	2♓01	4 17	22 17	9 20	2 35	23 43	7 17	14 26	21 40	24 23	10 55	16 29	13 45	29 08	11 18
20 M	23 56 25	27 15 26	15 16	4 06	22 58	10 28	3 14	23 37	7 15	14 25	21 38	24 23	11 01	16 14	13 58	29 38	11 16
21 T	0 0 22	28 14 03	28 17	3 55	23 34	11 36	3 53	23 32	7 13	14 23	21 36	24 22	11 08	15 58	14 11	0♏09	11 13
22 W	0 4 18	29 12 42	11♈02	3 44	24 06	12 44	4 32	23 27	7 11	14 22	21 35	24 22	11 14	15 43	14 24	0 40	11 10
23 Th	0 8 15	0♎11 22	23 31	3 36	24 33	13 52	5 11	23 22	7 09	14 20	21 33	24 22	11 20	15 28	14 37	1 10	11 08
24 F	0 12 11	1 10 05	5♉46	3 30	24 56	15 00	5 50	23 18	7 07	14 18	21 31	24 21	11 26	15 13	14 51	1 41	11 05
25 Sa	0 16 8	2 08 50	17 49	3 26	25 13	16 07	6 29	23 13	7 06	14 17	21 30	24 21	11 31	14 59	15 05	2 12	11 03
26 Su	0 20 4	3 07 37	29 42	3 25D	25 24	17 15	7 08	23 09	7 04	14 15	21 28	24 21	11 36	14 44	15 19	2 43	11 00
27 M	0 24 1	4 06 26	11♊30	3 25	25 28R	18 22	7 47	23 04	7 03	14 13	21 26	24 20	11 41	14 30	15 33	3 13	10 57
28 T	0 27 57	5 05 18	23 18	3 26	25 26	19 30	8 26	23 00	7 01	14 12	21 25	24 20	11 45	14 16	15 47	3 44	10 54
29 W	0 31 54	6 04 11	5♋11	3 26R	25 17	20 37	9 05	22 57	7 00	14 10	21 23	24 20	11 49	14 02	16 01	4 15	10 52
30 Th	0 35 51	7 03 07	17 14	3 26	25 01	21 44	9 44	22 53	6 59	14 08	21 22	24 20	11 53	13 48	16 16	4 46	10 49

EPHEMERIS CALCULATED FOR 12 MIDNIGHT GREENWICH MEAN TIME. ALL OTHER DATA AND FACING ASPECTARIAN PAGE IN **EASTERN TIME (BOLD)** AND PACIFIC TIME (REGULAR).

OCTOBER 2021

☽ Last Aspect day	ET / hr:mn / PT		asp	☽ Ingress sign	day	ET / hr:mn / PT	
2	**7:43 pm**	4:43 pm	□♀	♍	3	**4:38 am**	1:38 am
5	**4:46 am**	1:46 am	⚹♀	♎	5	**8:41 am**	5:41 am
6		10:03 pm	□♇	♏	7	**10:22 am**	7:22 am
7	**1:03 am**		□♇	♏	7	**10:22 am**	7:22 am
8		11:05 pm	⚹♇	♐	9	**11:24 am**	8:24 am
9	**2:05 am**		⚹♇	♐	9	**11:24 am**	8:24 am
10		9:30 pm	⚹♃	♑	11	**1:15 pm**	10:15 am
11	**12:30 am**		⚹♃	♑	11	**1:15 pm**	10:15 am
13	**6:53 am**	3:53 am	☌♇	♒	13	**4:47 pm**	1:47 pm
15	**8:33 am**	5:33 am	△☉	♓	15	**10:22 pm**	7:22 pm
17	**7:24 pm**	4:24 pm	⚹♇	♈	18	**6:04 am**	3:04 am
20	**10:57 am**	7:57 am	☍☉	♉	20	**3:59 pm**	12:59 pm
22	**4:35 pm**	1:35 pm	△♇	♊	23	**3:57 am**	12:57 am
25	**10:11 am**	7:11 am	△♂	♋	25	**5:00 pm**	2:00 pm
27		11:02 pm	□♂	♌	28	**5:07 am**	2:07 am
28	**2:02 am**		□♂	♌	28	**5:07 am**	2:07 am
30	**3:05 am**	12:05 am	△♀	♍	30	**2:09 pm**	11:09 am

☽ Phases & Eclipses phase	day	ET / hr:mn / PT	
New Moon	6	**7:05 am**	4:05 am
2nd Quarter	12	**11:25 pm**	8:25 pm
Full Moon	20	**10:57 am**	7:57 am
4th Quarter	28	**4:05 pm**	1:05 pm

Planet Ingress	day	ET / hr:mn / PT	
♀ ♐	7	**7:21 am**	4:21 am
☉ ♏	22		9:51 pm
☉ ♏	23	**12:51 am**	
♂ ♏	30	**10:21 am**	7:21 am

Planetary Motion		day	ET / hr:mn / PT	
♇	D	6	**2:29 pm**	11:29 am
⚳	R	8	**9:31 pm**	6:31 pm
♄	D	10	**10:17 pm**	7:17 pm
♃	D	17		10:30 pm
♃	D	18	**1:30 am**	
☿	D	18	**11:17 am**	8:17 am

1 FRIDAY
☽ ☍ ♄ **10:10 am** 7:10 am
☿ □ ♇ **10:26 am** 7:26 am
☽ ⚹ ☉ **1:34 pm** 10:34 am
☽ ⚹ ♂ **5:46 pm** 2:46 pm
☿ ⚺ ♀ **9:56 pm** 6:56 pm
☽ □ ♅ **11:32 pm** 8:32 pm

2 SATURDAY
♀ ⚹ ♇ **3:48 am** 12:48 am
☽ ⚻ ♆ **12:51 pm** 9:51 am
☽ ☍ ♃ **3:29 pm** 12:29 pm
☽ ⚹ ☿ **4:57 pm** 1:57 pm
☽ ⚻ ♇ **6:22 pm** 3:22 pm
☽ □ ♀ **7:43 pm** 4:43 pm

3 SUNDAY
☽ ⚻ ♄ **4:56 pm** 1:56 pm
☿ △ ♃ **8:05 pm** 5:05 pm
☽ ⚺ ☉ 9:23 pm
☽ ⚺ ♂ 11:47 pm

4 MONDAY
☽ ⚺ ☉ **12:23 am**
☽ ⚺ ♂ **2:47 am**
☽ △ ♅ **5:19 am** 2:19 am
☽ ☍ ♆ **5:48 pm** 2:48 pm
☽ ⚺ ☿ **6:48 pm** 3:48 pm
☽ ⚻ ♃ **8:10 pm** 5:10 pm
☽ △ ♇ **11:03 pm** 8:03 pm

5 TUESDAY
☽ ⚹ ♀ **4:46 am** 1:46 am
☿ ⚻ ♆ **9:53 am** 6:53 am
☽ △ ♄ **8:16 pm** 5:16 pm

6 WEDNESDAY
♂ ⚻ ♅ **5:27 am** 2:27 am
☽ ☌ ☉ **7:05 am** 4:05 am
☽ ⚻ ♅ **7:56 am** 4:56 am
☽ ☌ ♂ **8:04 am** 5:04 am
☽ ☌ ☿ **5:40 pm** 2:40 pm
☉ ⚻ ♅ **7:11 pm** 4:11 pm
☽ ⚻ ♆ **7:54 pm** 4:54 pm
☽ △ ♃ **10:08 pm** 7:08 pm
☽ □ ♇ 10:03 pm

7 THURSDAY
☽ □ ♇ **1:03 am**
☽ ⚺ ♀ **10:37 am** 7:37 am
☽ □ ♄ **9:37 pm** 6:37 pm
☉ ☌ ♂ 9:01 pm

8 FRIDAY
☉ ☌ ♂ **12:01 am**
☽ ☍ ♅ **9:00 am** 6:00 am
☽ ⚺ ♂ **11:32 am** 8:32 am
☽ ⚺ ☉ **11:49 am** 8:49 am
☽ ⚺ ☿ **3:10 pm** 12:10 pm
☽ △ ♆ **8:53 pm** 5:53 pm
☽ □ ♃ **11:04 pm** 8:04 pm
☽ ⚹ ♇ 11:05 pm

9 SATURDAY
☽ ⚹ ♇ **2:05 am**
☉ ☌ ☿ **12:18 pm** 9:18 am
☽ ☌ ♀ **3:37 pm** 12:37 pm
☿ ☌ ♂ **6:48 pm** 3:48 pm
☽ ⚹ ♄ **10:43 pm** 7:43 pm

10 SUNDAY
☽ ⚻ ♅ **10:08 am** 7:08 am
☽ ⚹ ☿ **12:49 pm** 9:49 am
☽ ⚹ ♂ **3:12 pm** 12:12 pm
☽ ⚹ ☉ **4:45 pm** 1:45 pm
☽ □ ♆ **10:17 pm** 7:17 pm
☽ ⚹ ♃ 9:30 pm

11 MONDAY
☽ ⚹ ♃ **12:30 am**
☽ ⚺ ♇ **3:42 am** 12:42 am
☽ ⚺ ♀ **9:43 pm** 6:43 pm
☽ ⚺ ♄ 9:54 pm
☿ ⚻ ♅ 10:29 pm

12 TUESDAY
☽ ⚺ ♄ **12:54 am**
☿ ⚻ ♅ **1:29 am**
☽ □ ☿ **11:51 am** 8:51 am
☽ △ ♅ **12:34 pm** 9:34 am
☽ □ ♂ **8:27 pm** 5:27 pm
☽ □ ☉ **11:25 pm** 8:25 pm
☽ ⚹ ♆ 10:11 pm

13 WEDNESDAY
☽ ⚹ ♆ **1:11 am**
☽ ⚺ ♃ **3:30 am** 12:30 am
☽ ☌ ♇ **6:53 am** 3:53 am
♀ ⚹ ♄ **3:26 pm** 12:26 pm
☉ ⚻ ♆ **11:32 pm** 8:32 pm

14 THURSDAY
☽ ☌ ♄ **4:54 am** 1:54 am
☽ ⚹ ♀ **6:03 am** 3:03 am
☽ △ ☿ **1:09 pm** 10:09 am
☽ □ ♅ **4:52 pm** 1:52 pm

15 FRIDAY
☽ △ ♂ **3:58 am** 12:58 am
☽ ⚺ ♆ **6:02 am** 3:02 am
☉ △ ♃ **7:46 am** 4:46 am
☽ ☌ ♃ **8:29 am** 5:29 am
☽ △ ☉ **8:33 am** 5:33 am
☽ ⚺ ♇ **12:05 pm** 9:05 am

16 SATURDAY
☽ ⚺ ♄ **10:59 am** 7:59 am
☽ □ ♀ **4:59 pm** 1:59 pm
☽ ⚻ ☿ **5:27 pm** 2:27 pm
♂ ⚻ ♆ **8:32 pm** 5:32 pm
☿ ⚹ ♀ **9:24 pm** 6:24 pm
☽ ⚹ ♅ **11:14 pm** 8:14 pm

17 SUNDAY
☉ □ ♇ **8:12 am** 5:12 am
☽ ☌ ♆ **1:00 pm** 10:00 am
☽ ⚻ ♂ **1:56 pm** 10:56 am
☽ ⚺ ♃ **3:37 pm** 12:37 pm
☽ ⚹ ♇ **7:24 pm** 4:24 pm
☽ ⚻ ☉ **8:20 pm** 5:20 pm

18 MONDAY
☽ ⚹ ♄ **7:15 pm** 4:15 pm
♂ △ ♃ **10:36 pm** 7:36 pm
☽ ☍ ☿ 10:26 pm

19 TUESDAY
☽ ☍ ☿ **1:26 am**
☽ △ ♀ **6:40 am** 3:40 am
☽ ⚺ ♅ **7:46 am** 4:46 am
♀ ⚻ ♅ **7:15 pm** 4:15 pm
☽ ⚺ ♆ **10:09 pm** 7:09 pm
☽ ⚹ ♃ 9:59 pm
☽ ☍ ♂ 11:28 pm

20 WEDNESDAY
☽ ⚹ ♃ **12:59 am**
☽ ☍ ♂ **2:28 am**
☽ □ ♇ **4:56 am** 1:56 am
☽ ☍ ☉ **10:57 am** 7:57 am

21 THURSDAY
☽ □ ♄ **5:45 am** 2:45 am
☽ ⚻ ☿ **1:44 pm** 10:44 am
☽ ☌ ♅ **6:28 pm** 3:28 pm
☽ ⚻ ♀ **11:08 pm** 8:08 pm
♂ □ ♇ 9:20 pm

22 FRIDAY
♂ □ ♇ **12:20 am**
☽ ⚹ ♆ **9:26 am** 6:26 am
☽ □ ♃ **12:32 pm** 9:32 am
☽ △ ♇ **4:35 pm** 1:35 pm
☽ ⚻ ♂ **5:33 pm** 2:33 pm

23 SATURDAY
☽ ⚻ ☉ **4:14 am** 1:14 am
☽ △ ♄ **6:12 pm** 3:12 pm

24 SUNDAY
☽ △ ☿ **6:17 am** 3:17 am
☽ ⚺ ♅ **6:54 am** 3:54 am
☿ ⚻ ♅ **1:45 pm** 10:45 am
☽ ☍ ♀ **5:42 pm** 2:42 pm
☽ □ ♆ **10:14 pm** 7:14 pm
☽ △ ♃ 10:33 pm

25 MONDAY
☽ △ ♃ **1:33 am**
☽ ⚻ ♇ **5:36 am** 2:36 am
☽ △ ♂ **10:11 am** 7:11 am
☽ △ ☉ **10:54 pm** 7:54 pm

26 TUESDAY
☽ ⚻ ♄ **7:21 am** 4:21 am
☽ ⚹ ♅ **7:37 pm** 4:37 pm
♀ □ ♆ **9:06 pm** 6:06 pm
☽ □ ☿ 10:10 pm

27 WEDNESDAY
☽ □ ☿ **1:10 am**
☽ △ ♆ **10:48 am** 7:48 am
☽ ⚻ ♀ **12:04 pm** 9:04 am
☽ ⚻ ♃ **2:16 pm** 11:16 am
☽ ☍ ♇ **6:08 pm** 3:08 pm
☽ □ ♂ 11:02 pm

28 THURSDAY
☽ □ ♂ **2:02 am**
♀ ⚹ ♃ **3:15 pm** 12:15 pm
☽ □ ☉ **4:05 pm** 1:05 pm
☽ ☍ ♄ **7:03 pm** 4:03 pm

29 FRIDAY
☽ □ ♅ **6:25 am** 3:25 am
☽ ⚹ ☿ **6:32 pm** 3:32 pm
☽ ⚻ ♆ **8:53 pm** 5:53 pm
☽ ☍ ♃ 9:24 pm

30 SATURDAY
☽ ☍ ♃ **12:24 am**
☽ △ ♀ **3:05 am** 12:05 am
☽ ⚻ ♇ **3:54 am** 12:54 am
☉ □ ♄ **5:53 am** 2:53 am
♀ ⚺ ♇ **1:54 pm** 10:54 am
☽ ⚹ ♂ **2:22 pm** 11:22 am
☿ ⚻ ♆ **3:40 pm** 12:40 pm

31 SUNDAY
☽ ⚻ ♄ **3:17 am** 12:17 am
☽ ⚹ ☉ **4:58 am** 1:58 am
☽ △ ♅ **1:33 pm** 10:33 am
☿ △ ♃ 9:18 pm

Eastern time in bold type
Pacific time in medium type

OCTOBER 2021

DATE	SID.TIME	SUN	MOON	NODE	MERCURY	VENUS	MARS	JUPITER	SATURN	URANUS	NEPTUNE	PLUTO	CERES	PALLAS	JUNO	VESTA	CHIRON
1 F	0 39 47	8♎02 06	29♋32	3♊23℞	24♎37℞	22♏51	10♎24	22♒49℞	6♒58℞	14♉06℞	21♓20℞	24♑19℞	11♊56	13♓34℞	16♐31	5♏17	10♈46℞
2 Sa	0 43 44	9 01 06	12♌11	3 19	24 06	23 58	11 03	22 46	6 57	14 04	21 19	24 19	11 59	13 21	16 46	5 48	10 44
3 Su	0 47 40	10 00 09	25 13	3 12	23 27	25 04	11 42	22 43	6 56	14 03	21 17	24 19	12 01	13 08	17 01	6 20	10 41
4 M	0 51 37	10 59 14	8♍40	3 04	22 40	26 11	12 22	22 40	6 55	14 01	21 15	24 19	12 03	12 55	17 17	6 51	10 38
5 T	0 55 33	11 58 22	22 32	2 55	21 47	27 17	13 01	22 37	6 55	13 59	21 14	24 19	12 05	12 43	17 32	7 22	10 36
6 W	0 59 30	12 57 31	6♎45	2 47	20 47	28 23	13 40	22 35	6 54	13 57	21 12	24 19D	12 06	12 31	17 48	7 53	10 33
7 Th	1 3 26	13 56 42	21 14	2 40	19 43	29 29	14 20	22 32	6 54	13 55	21 11	24 19	12 07	12 19	18 04	8 25	10 30
8 F	1 7 23	14 55 56	5♏54	2 35	18 34	0♐35	14 59	22 30	6 53	13 53	21 09	24 19	12 08	12 07	18 20	8 56	10 27
9 Sa	1 11 19	15 55 11	20 36	2 33D	17 24	1 40	15 39	22 28	6 53	13 50	21 08	24 19	12 08℞	11 56	18 36	9 27	10 25
10 Su	1 15 16	16 54 28	5♐14	2 32	16 13	2 46	16 18	22 27	6 53	13 48	21 07	24 19	12 08	11 45	18 52	9 59	10 22
11 M	1 19 13	17 53 48	19 43	2 33	15 04	3 51	16 58	22 25	6 53D	13 46	21 05	24 19	12 08	11 34	19 08	10 30	10 19
12 T	1 23 9	18 53 08	4♑00	2 34	13 58	4 56	17 37	22 24	6 53	13 44	21 04	24 19	12 07	11 24	19 25	11 02	10 17
13 W	1 27 6	19 52 31	18 02	2 35℞	12 58	6 01	18 17	22 23	6 53	13 42	21 02	24 19	12 05	11 14	19 42	11 33	10 14
14 Th	1 31 2	20 51 56	1♒50	2 35	12 05	7 05	18 57	22 22	6 53	13 40	21 01	24 20	12 04	11 04	19 59	12 05	10 11
15 F	1 34 59	21 51 22	15 23	2 32	11 21	8 10	19 36	22 21	6 53	13 37	20 59	24 20	12 01	10 55	20 16	12 36	10 09
16 Sa	1 38 55	22 50 49	28 42	2 28	10 46	9 14	20 16	22 20	6 54	13 35	20 58	24 20	11 59	10 46	20 33	13 08	10 06
17 Su	1 42 52	23 50 19	11♓48	2 22	10 23	10 18	20 56	22 20	6 54	13 33	20 57	24 20	11 56	10 38	20 50	13 40	10 03
18 M	1 46 48	24 49 50	24 40	2 16	10 10D	11 21	21 36	22 20D	6 55	13 31	20 55	24 21	11 53	10 29	21 08	14 11	10 01
19 T	1 50 45	25 49 23	7♈19	2 09	10 08	12 25	22 16	22 20	6 56	13 28	20 54	24 21	11 49	10 22	21 25	14 43	9 58
20 W	1 54 42	26 48 58	19 47	2 03	10 18	13 28	22 55	22 20	6 57	13 26	20 53	24 21	11 45	10 14	21 43	15 15	9 56
21 Th	1 58 38	27 48 35	2♉02	1 58	10 38	14 31	23 35	22 21	6 58	13 24	20 52	24 22	11 40	10 07	22 01	15 46	9 53
22 F	2 2 35	28 48 14	14 08	1 55	11 08	15 33	24 15	22 21	6 59	13 21	20 50	24 22	11 36	10 00	22 19	16 18	9 51
23 Sa	2 6 31	29 47 56	26 04	1 54D	11 47	16 36	24 55	22 22	7 00	13 19	20 49	24 23	11 30	9 54	22 37	16 50	9 48
24 Su	2 10 28	0♏47 39	7♊54	1 54	12 35	17 38	25 35	22 23	7 01	13 16	20 48	24 23	11 25	9 48	22 55	17 22	9 46
25 M	2 14 24	1 47 25	19 41	1 55	13 30	18 39	26 15	22 24	7 02	13 14	20 47	24 24	11 19	9 42	23 13	17 54	9 43
26 T	2 18 21	2 47 12	1♋29	1 57	14 32	19 41	26 55	22 26	7 04	13 12	20 46	24 24	11 12	9 37	23 32	18 26	9 41
27 W	2 22 17	3 47 02	13 21	1 58	15 40	20 42	27 35	22 27	7 05	13 09	20 45	24 25	11 05	9 32	23 50	18 58	9 38
28 Th	2 26 14	4 46 54	25 22	2 00℞	16 53	21 43	28 16	22 29	7 07	13 07	20 44	24 26	10 58	9 28	24 09	19 30	9 36
29 F	2 30 11	5 46 48	7♌38	2 00	18 10	22 43	28 56	22 31	7 09	13 04	20 43	24 26	10 51	9 24	24 28	20 02	9 33
30 Sa	2 34 7	6 46 45	20 13	1 59	19 32	23 43	29 36	22 34	7 11	13 02	20 41	24 27	10 43	9 20	24 47	20 34	9 31
31 Su	2 38 4	7 46 43	3♍12	1 57	20 56	24 42	0♏16	22 36	7 13	12 59	20 40	24 28	10 35	9 17	25 06	21 06	9 29

EPHEMERIS CALCULATED FOR 12 MIDNIGHT GREENWICH MEAN TIME. ALL OTHER DATA AND FACING ASPECTARIAN PAGE IN **EASTERN TIME (BOLD)** AND PACIFIC TIME (REGULAR).

NOVEMBER 2021

☽ Last Aspect day	ET / hr:mn / PT	asp	☽ Ingress sign	day	ET / hr:mn / PT
1	**1:00 pm** 10:00 am	□ ♀	♎	1	**7:11 pm** 4:11 pm
3	**6:32 pm** 3:32 pm	⚹ ♀	♏	3	**8:52 pm** 5:52 pm
5	**12:10 pm** 9:10 am	⚹ ♇	♐	5	**8:52 pm** 5:52 pm
7	**8:44 am** 5:44 am	⚹ ♃	♑	7	**8:03 pm** 5:03 pm
9	**12:51 pm** 9:51 am	☌ ♇	♒	9	**10:03 pm** 7:03 pm
11	**2:52 pm** 11:52 am	☌ ♃	♓	11	11:54 pm
11	**2:52 pm** 11:52 am	☌ ♃	♓	12	**2:54 am**
13	9:40 pm	⚹ ♇	♈	14	**10:48 am** 7:48 am
14	**12:40 am**	⚹ ♇	♈	14	**10:48 am** 7:48 am
16	**10:51 am** 7:51 am	□ ♇	♉	16	**9:18 pm** 6:18 pm
19	**3:57 am** 12:57 am	☍ ☉	♊	19	**9:33 am** 6:33 am
21	**10:52 am** 7:52 am	△ ♃	♋	21	**10:33 pm** 7:33 pm
23	9:46 pm	☍ ♇	♌	24	**10:59 am** 7:59 am
24	**12:46 am**	☍ ♇	♌	24	**10:59 am** 7:59 am
26	**11:24 am** 8:24 am	☍ ♃	♍	26	**9:12 pm** 6:12 pm
28	**7:02 pm** 4:02 pm	△ ♇	♎	29	**3:55 am** 12:55 am
30	**11:20 pm** 8:20 pm	△ ♃	♏	12/1	**6:55 am** 3:55 am

☽ Phases & Eclipses phase	day	ET / hr:mn / PT
New Moon	4	**5:15 pm** 2:15 pm
2nd Quarter	11	**7:46 am** 4:46 am
Full Moon	19	**3:57 am** 12:57 am
(eclipse)	19	27° ♉ 14′
4th Quarter	27	**7:28 am** 4:28 am

Planet Ingress		day	ET / hr:mn / PT
♀	♑	5	**6:44 am** 3:44 am
⚵	♑	14	**3:23 pm** 12:23 pm
⚶	♐	16	**9:07 am** 6:07 am
☉	♐	21	**9:34 pm** 6:34 pm
☿	♐	24	**10:36 am** 7:36 am

Planetary Motion		day	ET / hr:mn / PT
♀	D	8	**4:23 am** 1:23 am

1 MONDAY
☿ △ ♃ **12:18 am**
☽ ☍ ♆ **3:05 am** 12:05 am
☽ ⊼ ♃ **6:35 am** 3:35 am
☽ ⊻ ☿ **7:18 am** 4:18 am
☽ △ ♇ **9:43 am** 6:43 am
☽ □ ♀ **1:00 pm** 10:00 am
☽ ⊻ ♂ **10:01 pm** 7:01 pm

2 TUESDAY
☿ □ ♇ **5:39 am** 2:39 am
☽ △ ♄ **7:31 am** 4:31 am
☽ ⊻ ☉ **12:51 pm** 9:51 am
☽ ⊼ ♅ **4:50 pm** 1:50 pm

3 WEDNESDAY
☽ ⊼ ♆ **5:36 am** 2:36 am
☽ △ ♃ **9:08 am** 6:08 am
☽ □ ♇ **11:57 am** 8:57 am
☽ ☌ ☿ **3:27 pm** 12:27 pm
☽ ⚹ ♀ **6:32 pm** 3:32 pm
☽ ☌ ♂ 10:55 pm

4 THURSDAY
☽ ☌ ♂ **1:55 am**
☽ □ ♄ **8:46 am** 5:46 am
☽ ☌ ☉ **5:15 pm** 2:15 pm
☽ ☍ ♅ **5:26 pm** 2:26 pm
☉ ☍ ♅ **7:58 pm** 4:58 pm

5 FRIDAY
☽ △ ♆ **5:53 am** 2:53 am
☽ □ ♃ **9:33 am** 6:33 am
☽ ⚹ ♇ **12:10 pm** 9:10 am
☽ ⊻ ☿ **9:09 pm** 6:09 pm
☽ ⊻ ♀ **9:49 pm** 6:49 pm

6 SATURDAY
☽ ⊻ ♂ **4:06 am** 1:06 am
☽ ⚹ ♄ **8:46 am** 5:46 am
☿ ⚹ ♀ **11:59 am** 8:59 am
☽ ⊼ ♅ **5:09 pm** 2:09 pm
☽ ⊻ ☉ **8:32 pm** 5:32 pm

7 SUNDAY
☽ □ ♆ **4:47 am** 1:47 am
☽ ⚹ ♃ **8:44 am** 5:44 am
☽ ⊻ ♇ **11:14 am** 8:14 am
☽ ☌ ♀ 9:19 pm
☽ ⚹ ☿ 11:13 pm

8 MONDAY
☽ ☌ ♀ **12:19 am**
☽ ⚹ ☿ **2:13 am**
☽ ⚹ ♂ **5:49 am** 2:49 am
☽ ⊻ ♄ **8:25 am** 5:25 am
☽ △ ♅ **4:48 pm** 1:48 pm
☽ ⚹ ☉ 9:06 pm

9 TUESDAY
☽ ⚹ ☉ **12:06 am**
☽ ⚹ ♆ **6:01 am** 3:01 am
☽ ⊻ ♃ **10:26 am** 7:26 am
☽ ☌ ♇ **12:51 pm** 9:51 am

10 WEDNESDAY
☽ ⊻ ♀ **6:04 am** 3:04 am
☿ ☌ ♂ **7:57 am** 4:57 am
☽ □ ♂ **10:55 am** 7:55 am
☽ □ ☿ **11:08 am** 8:08 am
☽ ☌ ♄ **11:15 am** 8:15 am
☿ □ ♄ **12:04 pm** 9:04 am
♂ □ ♄ **6:14 pm** 3:14 pm
☽ □ ♅ **7:45 pm** 4:45 pm

11 THURSDAY
☽ □ ☉ **7:46 am** 4:46 am
☽ ⊻ ♆ **9:51 am** 6:51 am
☽ ☌ ♃ **2:52 pm** 11:52 am
☽ ⊻ ♇ **5:13 pm** 2:13 pm

12 FRIDAY
☉ △ ♆ **11:24 am** 8:24 am
☽ ⚹ ♀ **3:18 pm** 12:18 pm
☽ ⊻ ♄ **5:05 pm** 2:05 pm
☽ △ ♂ **7:28 pm** 4:28 pm
☽ △ ☿ 9:23 pm
☽ ⚹ ♅ 10:44 pm

13 SATURDAY
☽ △ ☿ **12:23 am**
☽ ⚹ ♅ **1:44 am**
☿ ☍ ♅ **10:57 am** 7:57 am
☽ ☌ ♆ **4:46 pm** 1:46 pm
☽ △ ☉ **7:19 pm** 4:19 pm
♀ ⊻ ♄ **7:43 pm** 4:43 pm
☽ ⊻ ♃ **10:29 pm** 7:29 pm
☽ ⚹ ♇ 9:40 pm

14 SUNDAY
☽ ⚹ ♇ **12:40 am**
☽ ⚹ ♄ 10:59 pm

15 MONDAY
☽ ⚹ ♄ **1:59 am**
☽ □ ♀ **4:06 am** 1:06 am
☽ ⊼ ♂ **7:32 am** 4:32 am
☽ ⊻ ♅ **10:36 am** 7:36 am
☉ □ ♃ **2:58 pm** 11:58 am
☽ ⊼ ☿ **5:58 pm** 2:58 pm
☽ ⊻ ♆ 11:29 pm

16 TUESDAY
☽ ⊻ ♆ **2:29 am**
☽ ⚹ ♃ **8:55 am** 5:55 am
☽ ⊼ ☉ **10:23 am** 7:23 am
☽ □ ♇ **10:51 am** 7:51 am
☉ ⚹ ♇ **4:01 pm** 1:01 pm

17 WEDNESDAY
♂ ☍ ♅ **12:23 pm** 9:23 am
☽ □ ♄ **1:19 pm** 10:19 am
☽ △ ♀ **7:39 pm** 4:39 pm
☽ ☌ ♅ **9:44 pm** 6:44 pm
☽ ☍ ♂ **10:20 pm** 7:20 pm

18 THURSDAY
☿ △ ♆ **10:38 am** 7:38 am
☽ ⚹ ♆ **2:14 pm** 11:14 am
☽ ☍ ☿ **2:48 pm** 11:48 am
☽ □ ♃ **9:23 pm** 6:23 pm
☽ △ ♇ **10:57 pm** 7:57 pm
♀ △ ♅ 10:08 pm

19 FRIDAY
♀ △ ♅ **1:08 am**
☽ ☍ ☉ **3:57 am** 12:57 am
☽ △ ♄ 11:12 pm

20 SATURDAY
☽ △ ♄ **2:12 am**
☽ ⊻ ♅ **10:14 am** 7:14 am
☽ ⊼ ♀ **12:43 pm** 9:43 am
☽ ⊼ ♂ **2:46 pm** 11:46 am
☿ □ ♃ **6:43 pm** 3:43 pm

21 SUNDAY
☽ □ ♆ **3:05 am** 12:05 am
☿ ⚹ ♇ **4:14 am** 1:14 am
☽ △ ♃ **10:52 am** 7:52 am
☽ ⊼ ♇ **12:01 pm** 9:01 am
☽ ⊼ ☿ **1:13 pm** 10:13 am
☽ ⊼ ☉ **10:38 pm** 7:38 pm

22 MONDAY
☽ ⊼ ♄ **3:32 pm** 12:32 pm
☽ ⚹ ♅ **10:59 pm** 7:59 pm

23 TUESDAY
☽ ☍ ♀ **5:49 am** 2:49 am
☽ △ ♂ **7:24 am** 4:24 am
☽ △ ♆ **3:50 pm** 12:50 pm
☽ ⊼ ♃ 9:06 pm
☽ ☍ ♇ 9:46 pm

24 WEDNESDAY
☽ ⊼ ♃ **12:06 am**
☽ ☍ ♇ **12:46 am**
☽ △ ☿ **11:02 am** 8:02 am
☽ △ ☉ **4:34 pm** 1:34 pm

25 THURSDAY
☽ ☍ ♄ **3:52 am** 12:52 am
☽ □ ♅ **10:32 am** 7:32 am
☽ ⊼ ♀ **8:57 pm** 5:57 pm
☽ □ ♂ **10:19 pm** 7:19 pm
☽ ⊼ ♆ 11:55 pm

26 FRIDAY
☽ ⊼ ♆ **2:55 am**
☽ ☍ ♃ **11:24 am** 8:24 am
☽ ⊼ ♇ **11:35 am** 8:35 am

27 SATURDAY
☽ □ ☿ **5:27 am** 2:27 am
☽ □ ☉ **7:28 am** 4:28 am
♃ ⊻ ♇ **11:16 am** 8:16 am
☽ ⊼ ♄ **1:30 pm** 10:30 am
☽ △ ♅ **7:18 pm** 4:18 pm

28 SUNDAY
☽ △ ♀ **8:15 am** 5:15 am
☽ ⚹ ♂ **9:37 am** 6:37 am
☽ ☍ ♆ **10:50 am** 7:50 am
☽ △ ♇ **7:02 pm** 4:02 pm
☽ ⊼ ♃ **7:17 pm** 4:17 pm
☉ ☌ ☿ **11:39 pm** 8:39 pm

29 MONDAY
♂ △ ♆ **9:10 am** 6:10 am
☽ ⚹ ☉ **5:44 pm** 2:44 pm
☽ ⚹ ☿ **6:33 pm** 3:33 pm
☽ △ ♄ **7:24 pm** 4:24 pm
☽ ⊼ ♅ 9:22 pm
☿ ⚹ ♄ 11:19 pm

30 TUESDAY
☽ ⊼ ♅ **12:22 am**
☿ ⚹ ♄ **2:19 am**
☽ □ ♀ **2:56 pm** 11:56 am
☽ ⊼ ♆ **2:58 pm** 11:58 am
♀ ⚹ ♆ **3:46 pm** 12:46 pm
☽ ⊻ ♂ **4:29 pm** 1:29 pm
☉ ⚹ ♄ **6:14 pm** 3:14 pm
☽ □ ♇ **10:43 pm** 7:43 pm
☽ △ ♃ **11:20 pm** 8:20 pm

Eastern time in bold type
Pacific time in medium type

NOVEMBER 2021

DATE	SID.TIME	SUN	MOON	NODE	MERCURY	VENUS	MARS	JUPITER	SATURN	URANUS	NEPTUNE	PLUTO	CERES	PALLAS	JUNO	VESTA	CHIRON
1 M	2 42 0	8♏46 44	16♍37	1♊55℞	22♎23	25♐42	0♏56	22♒39	7♒15	12♉57℞	20♓39℞	24♑28	10♊26℞	9♓14℞	25♐25	21♏38	9♈27℞
2 T	2 45 57	9 46 47	0♎29	1 51	23 53	26 41	1 37	22 42	7 17	12 54	20 39	24 29	10 17	9 11	25 44	22 10	9 24
3 W	2 49 53	10 46 52	14 47	1 48	25 24	27 39	2 17	22 45	7 19	12 52	20 38	24 30	10 08	9 09	26 03	22 42	9 22
4 Th	2 53 50	11 46 58	29 28	1 46	26 57	28 37	2 58	22 48	7 21	12 50	20 37	24 31	9 58	9 07	26 23	23 14	9 20
5 F	2 57 46	12 47 07	14♏24	1 44	28 31	29 34	3 38	22 51	7 24	12 47	20 36	24 31	9 48	9 06	26 42	23 46	9 18
6 Sa	3 1 43	13 47 18	29 27	1 43D	0♏06	0♑31	4 19	22 55	7 26	12 45	20 35	24 32	9 38	9 04	27 02	24 18	9 16
7 Su	3 5 40	14 47 30	14♐29	1 44	1 41	1 28	4 59	22 59	7 29	12 42	20 34	24 33	9 27	9 04	27 22	24 51	9 13
8 M	3 9 36	15 47 45	29 21	1 45	3 17	2 24	5 40	23 03	7 32	12 40	20 33	24 34	9 16	9 03D	27 41	25 23	9 11
9 T	3 13 33	16 48 00	13♑57	1 46	4 54	3 20	6 20	23 07	7 34	12 37	20 33	24 35	9 05	9 03	28 01	25 55	9 09
10 W	3 17 29	17 48 17	28 13	1 47	6 31	4 15	7 01	23 11	7 37	12 35	20 32	24 36	8 53	9 04	28 21	26 27	9 07
11 Th	3 21 26	18 48 36	12♒06	1 48℞	8 07	5 09	7 42	23 16	7 40	12 32	20 31	24 37	8 42	9 05	28 42	26 59	9 05
12 F	3 25 22	19 48 56	25 38	1 48	9 44	6 03	8 22	23 21	7 43	12 30	20 31	24 38	8 30	9 06	29 02	27 32	9 04
13 Sa	3 29 19	20 49 17	8♓48	1 47	11 21	6 56	9 03	23 25	7 47	12 27	20 30	24 39	8 17	9 07	29 22	28 04	9 02
14 Su	3 33 15	21 49 39	21 41	1 46	12 58	7 48	9 44	23 31	7 50	12 25	20 29	24 40	8 05	9 09	29 43	28 36	9 00
15 M	3 37 12	22 50 03	4♈17	1 45	14 35	8 40	10 25	23 36	7 53	12 22	20 29	24 41	7 52	9 11	0♑03	29 09	8 58
16 T	3 41 9	23 50 28	16 39	1 44	16 12	9 31	11 05	23 41	7 57	12 20	20 28	24 42	7 39	9 14	0 24	29 41	8 56
17 W	3 45 5	24 50 55	28 51	1 43	17 48	10 22	11 46	23 47	8 00	12 18	20 28	24 44	7 26	9 17	0 44	0♐13	8 55
18 Th	3 49 2	25 51 23	10♉53	1 42	19 24	11 11	12 27	23 53	8 04	12 15	20 27	24 45	7 13	9 20	1 05	0 46	8 53
19 F	3 52 58	26 51 53	22 49	1 42D	21 00	12 00	13 08	23 59	8 07	12 13	20 27	24 46	7 00	9 24	1 26	1 18	8 51
20 Sa	3 56 55	27 52 25	4♊40	1 41	22 36	12 48	13 49	24 05	8 11	12 10	20 26	24 47	6 46	9 27	1 47	1 50	8 50
21 Su	4 0 51	28 52 57	16 28	1 42	24 12	13 35	14 30	24 11	8 15	12 08	20 26	24 48	6 32	9 32	2 08	2 23	8 48
22 M	4 4 48	29 53 32	28 15	1 42	25 48	14 21	15 11	24 18	8 19	12 06	20 26	24 50	6 19	9 36	2 29	2 55	8 47
23 T	4 8 44	0♐54 08	10♋05	1 42℞	27 23	15 06	15 52	24 24	8 23	12 03	20 25	24 51	6 05	9 41	2 50	3 28	8 45
24 W	4 12 41	1 54 46	22 00	1 42	28 58	15 50	16 33	24 31	8 27	12 01	20 25	24 52	5 51	9 46	3 11	4 00	8 44
25 Th	4 16 38	2 55 25	4♌03	1 42	0♐33	16 34	17 15	24 38	8 31	11 59	20 25	24 54	5 37	9 52	3 33	4 32	8 43
26 F	4 20 34	3 56 06	16 19	1 42	2 08	17 16	17 56	24 45	8 36	11 57	20 25	24 55	5 23	9 58	3 54	5 05	8 41
27 Sa	4 24 31	4 56 48	28 50	1 42D	3 43	17 57	18 37	24 52	8 40	11 54	20 25	24 56	5 09	10 04	4 15	5 37	8 40
28 Su	4 28 27	5 57 32	11♍42	1 42	5 17	18 37	19 18	25 00	8 44	11 52	20 24	24 58	4 55	10 10	4 37	6 10	8 39
29 M	4 32 24	6 58 18	24 58	1 42	6 52	19 15	20 00	25 07	8 49	11 50	20 24	24 59	4 40	10 17	4 58	6 42	8 38
30 T	4 36 20	7 59 05	8♎40	1 42	8 26	19 53	20 41	25 15	8 53	11 48	20 24	25 01	4 26	10 24	5 20	7 15	8 37

EPHEMERIS CALCULATED FOR 12 MIDNIGHT GREENWICH MEAN TIME. ALL OTHER DATA AND FACING ASPECTARIAN PAGE IN **EASTERN TIME (BOLD)** AND PACIFIC TIME (REGULAR).

DECEMBER 2021

☽ Last Aspect day	ET / hr:mn / PT	asp	☽ Ingress sign	day	ET / hr:mn / PT
11/30	**11:20 pm** 8:20 pm	△ ♃	♏	1	**6:55 am** 3:55 am
2	9:22 pm	□ ♃	♐	3	**7:13 am** 4:13 am
3	**12:22 am**	□ ♃	♐	3	**7:13 am** 4:13 am
4	9:08 pm	⚹ ♃	♑	5	**6:31 am** 3:31 am
5	**12:08 am**	⚹ ♃	♑	5	**6:31 am** 3:31 am
6	**11:42 pm** 8:42 pm	⚹ ♂	♒	7	**6:49 am** 3:49 am
9	**5:00 am** 2:00 am	□ ♂	♓	9	**9:53 am** 6:53 am
11	**2:40 pm** 11:40 am	△ ♂	♈	11	**4:46 pm** 1:46 pm
13	**9:52 pm** 6:52 pm	⚹ ♃	♉	14	**3:11 am** 12:11 am
16	**11:08 am** 8:08 am	□ ♃	♊	16	**3:43 pm** 12:43 pm
18	10:02 pm	△ ♃	♋	19	**4:42 am** 1:42 am
19	**1:02 am**	△ ♃	♋	19	**4:42 am** 1:42 am
21	**9:44 am** 6:44 am	☍ ♀	♌	21	**4:54 pm** 1:54 pm
23	10:39 pm	☍ ♃	♍	24	**3:24 am** 12:24 am
24	**1:39 am**	☍ ♃	♍	24	**3:24 am** 12:24 am
26	**3:39 am** 12:39 am	△ ♇	♎	26	**11:24 am** 8:24 am
28	**4:11 pm** 1:11 pm	△ ♃	♏	28	**4:16 pm** 1:16 pm
30	**12:10 pm** 9:10 am	⚹ ☿	♐	30	**6:08 pm** 3:08 pm

☽ Phases & Eclipses phase	day	ET / hr:mn / PT
New Moon	3	11:43 pm
New Moon	4	**2:43 am**
●	3/4	12° ♐ 22'
2nd Quarter	10	**8:36 pm** 5:36 pm
Full Moon	18	**11:36 pm** 8:36 pm
4th Quarter	26	**9:24 pm** 6:24 pm

Planet Ingress		day	ET / hr:mn / PT
♂	♐	13	**4:53 am** 1:53 am
☿	♑	13	**12:52 pm** 9:52 am
⚳	♉	21	**5:38 am** 2:38 am
☉	♑	21	**10:59 am** 7:59 am
♃	♓	28	**11:09 pm** 8:09 pm

Planetary Motion		day	ET / hr:mn / PT
♆	D	1	**8:22 am** 5:22 am
♀	℞	19	**5:36 am** 2:36 am
⚷	D	19	**11:33 am** 8:33 am

1 WEDNESDAY
☿ ⚻ ♅ **9:15 pm** 6:15 pm
☽ □ ♄ **9:43 pm** 6:43 pm
☽ ⚺ ☉ **11:35 pm** 8:35 pm
☽ ☍ ♅ 11:01 pm
☽ ⚺ ☿ 11:36 pm

2 THURSDAY
☽ ☍ ♅ **2:01 am**
☽ ⚺ ☿ **2:36 am**
☽ △ ♆ **3:58 pm** 12:58 pm
☽ ⚹ ♀ **5:52 pm** 2:52 pm
☽ ☌ ♂ **7:45 pm** 4:45 pm
☽ ⚹ ♇ **11:26 pm** 8:26 pm
☽ □ ♃ 9:22 pm

3 FRIDAY
☽ □ ♃ **12:22 am**
☉ ⚻ ♅ **10:14 am** 7:14 am
☽ ⚹ ♄ **9:46 pm** 6:46 pm
☽ ⚻ ♅ 10:35 pm
☽ ☌ ☉ 11:43 pm

4 SATURDAY
☽ ⚻ ♅ **1:35 am**
☽ ☌ ☉ **2:43 am**
☽ ☌ ☿ **7:43 am** 4:43 am
☽ □ ♆ **3:22 pm** 12:22 pm
☽ ⚺ ♀ **6:55 pm** 3:55 pm
☽ ⚺ ♂ **9:22 pm** 6:22 pm
☽ ⚺ ♇ **10:50 pm** 7:50 pm
☽ ⚹ ♃ 9:08 pm

5 SUNDAY
☽ ⚹ ♃ **12:08 am**
☽ ⚺ ♄ **9:25 pm** 6:25 pm
☽ △ ♅ 9:56 pm

6 MONDAY
☽ △ ♅ **12:56 am**
☽ ⚺ ☉ **5:39 am** 2:39 am
♂ ⚹ ♇ **6:41 am** 3:41 am
☽ ⚺ ☿ **12:53 pm** 9:53 am
☽ ⚹ ♆ **3:09 pm** 12:09 pm
☽ ☌ ♀ **8:21 pm** 5:21 pm
☽ ☌ ♇ **10:56 pm** 7:56 pm
☽ ⚹ ♂ **11:42 pm** 8:42 pm
☽ ⚺ ♃ 9:40 pm

7 TUESDAY
☽ ⚺ ♃ **12:40 am**
☿ □ ♆ **10:16 am** 7:16 am
☽ ☌ ♄ **10:43 pm** 7:43 pm
♂ □ ♃ 10:21 pm
☽ □ ♅ 11:01 pm

8 WEDNESDAY
♂ □ ♃ **1:21 am**
☽ □ ♅ **2:01 am**
☽ ⚹ ☉ **10:57 am** 7:57 am
☽ ⚺ ♆ **5:11 pm** 2:11 pm
☽ ⚹ ☿ **9:07 pm** 6:07 pm
☽ ⚺ ♀ 9:15 pm
☽ ⚺ ♇ 10:34 pm

9 THURSDAY
☽ ⚺ ♀ **12:15 am**
☽ ⚺ ♇ **1:34 am**
☽ ☌ ♃ **3:53 am** 12:53 am
☽ □ ♂ **5:00 am** 2:00 am

10 FRIDAY
☽ ⚺ ♄ **3:18 am** 12:18 am
☽ ⚹ ♅ **6:22 am** 3:22 am
☿ ⚺ ♀ **7:50 am** 4:50 am
☿ ⚺ ♇ **12:56 pm** 9:56 am
☽ □ ☉ **8:36 pm** 5:36 pm
☽ ☌ ♆ **10:50 pm** 7:50 pm

11 SATURDAY
☽ ⚹ ♀ **7:52 am** 4:52 am
☽ ⚹ ♇ **7:56 am** 4:56 am
☽ □ ☿ **10:33 am** 7:33 am
☽ ⚺ ♃ **10:59 am** 7:59 am
♀ ☌ ♇ **11:29 am** 8:29 am
☿ ⚹ ♃ **2:24 pm** 11:24 am
☽ △ ♂ **2:40 pm** 11:40 am
☉ □ ♆ 10:21 pm

12 SUNDAY
☉ □ ♆ **1:21 am**
☽ ⚹ ♄ **11:50 am** 8:50 am
☽ ⚺ ♅ **2:34 pm** 11:34 am

13 MONDAY
☽ ⚺ ♆ **8:16 am** 5:16 am
☽ △ ☉ **11:03 am** 8:03 am
☽ □ ♇ **6:01 pm** 3:01 pm
☽ □ ♀ **7:02 pm** 4:02 pm
☿ ⚺ ♂ **7:16 pm** 4:16 pm
☽ ⚹ ♃ **9:52 pm** 6:52 pm

14 TUESDAY
☽ ⚻ ♂ **4:33 am** 1:33 am
☽ △ ☿ **5:20 am** 2:20 am
☽ □ ♄ **11:36 pm** 8:36 pm
☽ ☌ ♅ 10:51 pm

15 WEDNESDAY
☽ ☌ ♅ **1:51 am**
☽ ⚹ ♆ **8:21 pm** 5:21 pm

16 THURSDAY
☽ ⚻ ☉ **4:50 am** 1:50 am
☽ △ ♇ **6:29 am** 3:29 am
☽ △ ♀ **8:14 am** 5:14 am
☽ □ ♃ **11:08 am** 8:08 am
☽ ☍ ♂ **8:56 pm** 5:56 pm
☉ ⚺ ♇ 9:21 pm

17 FRIDAY
☉ ⚺ ♇ **12:21 am**
☽ ⚻ ☿ **3:14 am** 12:14 am
☽ △ ♄ **12:57 pm** 9:57 am
☽ ⚺ ♅ **2:36 pm** 11:36 am
☉ ⚺ ♀ **11:28 pm** 8:28 pm

18 SATURDAY
☽ □ ♆ **9:24 am** 6:24 am
☽ ⚻ ♇ **7:38 pm** 4:38 pm
☽ ⚻ ♀ **9:35 pm** 6:35 pm
☽ ☍ ☉ **11:36 pm** 8:36 pm
☽ △ ♃ 10:02 pm

19 SUNDAY
☽ △ ♃ **1:02 am**
☽ ⚻ ♂ **1:43 pm** 10:43 am
☉ ⚹ ♃ **7:32 pm** 4:32 pm
☽ ☍ ☿ 10:25 pm
☽ ⚻ ♄ 11:17 pm

20 MONDAY
☽ ☍ ☿ **1:25 am**
☽ ⚻ ♄ **2:17 am**
☽ ⚹ ♅ **3:17 am** 12:17 am
☿ ⚺ ♄ **8:22 am** 5:22 am
☿ △ ♅ **3:18 pm** 12:18 pm
☽ △ ♆ **10:00 pm** 7:00 pm

21 TUESDAY
☽ ☍ ♇ **8:10 am** 5:10 am
☽ ☍ ♀ **9:44 am** 6:44 am
☽ ⚻ ♃ **2:12 pm** 11:12 am
☽ ⚻ ☉ **5:26 pm** 2:26 pm

22 WEDNESDAY
☽ △ ♂ **5:24 am** 2:24 am
☽ ☍ ♄ **2:28 pm** 11:28 am
☽ □ ♅ **2:50 pm** 11:50 am
☽ ⚻ ☿ **9:54 pm** 6:54 pm

23 THURSDAY
☽ ⚻ ♆ **9:12 am** 6:12 am
☽ ⚻ ♇ **7:07 pm** 4:07 pm
☽ ⚻ ♀ **7:50 pm** 4:50 pm
☽ ☍ ♃ 10:39 pm
♄ □ ♅ 11:17 pm

24 FRIDAY
☽ ☍ ♃ **1:39 am**
♄ □ ♅ **2:17 am**
☽ △ ☉ **9:05 am** 6:05 am
☽ □ ♂ **6:52 pm** 3:52 pm
☽ △ ♅ 9:24 pm
☽ ⚻ ♄ 9:37 pm

25 SATURDAY
☽ △ ♅ **12:24 am**
☽ ⚻ ♄ **12:37 am**
♀ ☌ ♇ **7:02 am** 4:02 am
☽ △ ☿ **3:08 pm** 12:08 pm
☽ ☍ ♆ **6:07 pm** 3:07 pm

26 SUNDAY
☽ △ ♀ **3:12 am** 12:12 am
☽ △ ♇ **3:39 am** 12:39 am
☽ ⚻ ♃ **10:32 am** 7:32 am
☿ ⚹ ♆ **4:29 pm** 1:29 pm
☽ □ ☉ **9:24 pm** 6:24 pm

27 MONDAY
☽ ⚹ ♂ **5:07 am** 2:07 am
☽ ⚻ ♅ **7:13 am** 4:13 am
☽ △ ♄ **7:55 am** 4:55 am
☽ ⚻ ♆ 9:04 pm

28 TUESDAY
☽ ⚻ ♆ **12:04 am**
☽ □ ☿ **3:57 am** 12:57 am
☽ □ ♀ **7:19 am** 4:19 am
☽ □ ♇ **9:06 am** 6:06 am
☽ △ ♃ **4:11 pm** 1:11 pm
♂ ⚻ ♅ **8:04 pm** 5:04 pm

29 WEDNESDAY
☿ ☌ ♀ **5:27 am** 2:27 am
☽ ⚹ ☉ **5:43 am** 2:43 am
☽ ☍ ♅ **10:51 am** 7:51 am
☽ ⚺ ♂ **11:38 am** 8:38 am
☽ □ ♄ **11:58 am** 8:58 am
♂ ⚹ ♄ **7:22 pm** 4:22 pm
☽ △ ♆ 11:51 pm

30 THURSDAY
☽ △ ♆ **2:51 am**
☿ ☌ ♇ **4:54 am** 1:54 am
☽ ⚹ ♀ **8:19 am** 5:19 am
☽ ⚹ ♇ **11:27 am** 8:27 am
☽ ⚹ ☿ **12:10 pm** 9:10 am
☽ □ ♃ **6:42 pm** 3:42 pm

31 FRIDAY
☽ ⚺ ☉ **10:31 am** 7:31 am
☽ ⚻ ♅ **11:47 am** 8:47 am
☽ ⚹ ♄ **1:15 pm** 10:15 am
☽ ☌ ♂ **3:01 pm** 12:01 pm

Eastern time in bold type
Pacific time in medium type

DECEMBER 2021

DATE	SID.TIME	SUN	MOON	NODE	MERCURY	VENUS	MARS	JUPITER	SATURN	URANUS	NEPTUNE	PLUTO	CERES	PALLAS	JUNO	VESTA	CHIRON
1 W	4 40 17	8♐59 53	22♎49	1♊43	10♐00	20♑29	21♏23	25♒23	8♒58	11♉46℞	20♓24D	25♑02	4♊12℞	10♓31	5♑42	7♐47	8♈36℞
2 Th	4 44 13	10 00 43	7♏23	1 44	11 35	21 04	22 04	25 31	9 03	11 44	20 24	25 04	3 58	10 39	6 04	8 20	8 35
3 F	4 48 10	11 01 35	22 18	1 44℞	13 09	21 37	22 46	25 39	9 08	11 42	20 24	25 05	3 44	10 47	6 26	8 52	8 34
4 Sa	4 52 7	12 02 27	7♐28	1 44	14 43	22 09	23 27	25 48	9 13	11 39	20 24	25 07	3 31	10 55	6 47	9 25	8 33
5 Su	4 56 3	13 03 21	22 43	1 44	16 17	22 40	24 09	25 56	9 17	11 37	20 24	25 08	3 17	11 04	7 09	9 57	8 32
6 M	5 0 0	14 04 16	7♑52	1 43	17 51	23 08	24 50	26 05	9 23	11 35	20 25	25 10	3 03	11 13	7 32	10 29	8 31
7 T	5 3 56	15 05 12	22 47	1 41	19 25	23 36	25 32	26 13	9 28	11 34	20 25	25 11	2 50	11 22	7 54	11 02	8 31
8 W	5 7 53	16 06 09	7♒21	1 39	20 59	24 01	26 14	26 22	9 33	11 32	20 25	25 13	2 36	11 31	8 16	11 34	8 30
9 Th	5 11 49	17 07 06	21 28	1 37	22 33	24 25	26 55	26 31	9 38	11 30	20 25	25 15	2 23	11 41	8 38	12 07	8 29
10 F	5 15 46	18 08 04	5♓08	1 36	24 07	24 47	27 37	26 41	9 43	11 28	20 25	25 16	2 10	11 50	9 00	12 39	8 29
11 Sa	5 19 43	19 09 03	18 21	1 36D	25 41	25 07	28 19	26 50	9 49	11 26	20 26	25 18	1 58	12 01	9 23	13 12	8 28
12 Su	5 23 39	20 10 02	1♈11	1 36	27 16	25 25	29 01	26 59	9 54	11 24	20 26	25 20	1 45	12 11	9 45	13 44	8 28
13 M	5 27 36	21 11 01	13 40	1 37	28 50	25 40	29 43	27 09	10 00	11 23	20 26	25 21	1 33	12 22	10 08	14 17	8 27
14 T	5 31 32	22 12 01	25 53	1 39	0♑24	25 54	0♐25	27 19	10 05	11 21	20 27	25 23	1 21	12 33	10 30	14 49	8 27
15 W	5 35 29	23 13 02	7♉54	1 41	1 58	26 06	1 07	27 28	10 11	11 19	20 27	25 25	1 09	12 44	10 53	15 22	8 27
16 Th	5 39 25	24 14 03	19 48	1 42	3 33	26 15	1 49	27 38	10 16	11 17	20 28	25 27	0 57	12 55	11 15	15 54	8 27
17 F	5 43 22	25 15 05	1♊37	1 42℞	5 07	26 22	2 31	27 48	10 22	11 16	20 28	25 28	0 46	13 07	11 38	16 26	8 26
18 Sa	5 47 18	26 16 08	13 25	1 42	6 42	26 27	3 13	27 59	10 28	11 14	20 29	25 30	0 35	13 19	12 01	16 59	8 26
19 Su	5 51 15	27 17 11	25 13	1 40	8 16	26 29℞	3 55	28 09	10 34	11 13	20 29	25 32	0 25	13 31	12 23	17 31	8 26D
20 M	5 55 12	28 18 14	7♋05	1 37	9 50	26 29	4 37	28 19	10 40	11 11	20 30	25 34	0 14	13 43	12 46	18 04	8 26
21 T	5 59 8	29 19 19	19 01	1 32	11 25	26 26	5 19	28 30	10 46	11 10	20 31	25 35	0 04	13 56	13 09	18 36	8 26
22 W	6 3 5	0♑20 24	1♌04	1 27	12 59	26 21	6 01	28 41	10 52	11 09	20 31	25 37	29♉55	14 08	13 32	19 08	8 26
23 Th	6 7 1	1 21 29	13 15	1 21	14 33	26 14	6 44	28 51	10 58	11 07	20 32	25 39	29 45	14 21	13 55	19 41	8 26
24 F	6 10 58	2 22 35	25 37	1 16	16 06	26 04	7 26	29 02	11 04	11 06	20 33	25 41	29 36	14 34	14 18	20 13	8 27
25 Sa	6 14 54	3 23 42	8♍12	1 13	17 40	25 51	8 08	29 13	11 10	11 05	20 34	25 43	29 28	14 48	14 41	20 46	8 27
26 Su	6 18 51	4 24 49	21 03	1 10	19 13	25 36	8 51	29 24	11 16	11 03	20 35	25 45	29 19	15 02	15 04	21 18	8 27
27 M	6 22 47	5 25 57	4♎12	1 09D	20 45	25 18	9 33	29 35	11 22	11 02	20 35	25 47	29 12	15 15	15 27	21 50	8 28
28 T	6 26 44	6 27 05	17 43	1 10	22 16	24 59	10 16	29 47	11 29	11 01	20 36	25 48	29 04	15 29	15 50	22 22	8 28
29 W	6 30 41	7 28 14	1♏36	1 11	23 47	24 37	10 58	29 58	11 35	11 00	20 37	25 50	28 57	15 44	16 13	22 55	8 29
30 Th	6 34 37	8 29 24	15 53	1 12	25 17	24 12	11 41	0♓09	11 41	10 59	20 38	25 52	28 50	15 58	16 36	23 27	8 29
31 F	6 38 34	9 30 34	0♐32	1 13℞	26 45	23 46	12 23	0 21	11 48	10 58	20 39	25 54	28 44	16 13	17 00	23 59	8 30

EPHEMERIS CALCULATED FOR 12 MIDNIGHT GREENWICH MEAN TIME. ALL OTHER DATA AND FACING ASPECTARIAN PAGE IN **EASTERN TIME (BOLD)** AND PACIFIC TIME (REGULAR).

JANUARY 2022

☽ Last Aspect day	ET / hr:mn / PT	asp	☽ Ingress sign	day	ET / hr:mn / PT
1	**3:16 am** 12:16 am	□♆	♑	1	**6:02 pm** 3:02 pm
3	**11:21 am** 8:21 am	☌♇	♒	3	**5:44 pm** 2:44 pm
4	**7:45 pm** 4:45 pm	⚹♂	♓	5	**7:17 pm** 4:17 pm
7	**5:23 pm** 2:23 pm	⚹♇	♈	7	9:26 pm
7	**5:23 pm** 2:23 pm	⚹♇	♈	8	**12:26 am**
9	11:23 pm	□♇	♉	10	**9:47 am** 6:47 am
10	**2:23 am**	□♇	♉	10	**9:47 am** 6:47 am
12	**2:39 pm** 11:39 am	△♇	♊	12	**10:08 pm** 7:08 pm
14	**9:22 pm** 6:22 pm	☍♂	♋	15	**11:11 am** 8:11 am
17	**6:48 pm** 3:48 pm	☍☉	♌	17	**11:03 pm** 8:03 pm
20	**3:15 am** 12:15 am	△♂	♍	20	**9:02 am** 6:02 am
22	**2:46 pm** 11:46 am	□♂	♎	22	**5:03 pm** 2:03 pm
24	**5:10 pm** 2:10 pm	□♇	♏	24	**10:57 pm** 7:57 pm
26	9:28 pm	⚹☿	♐	26	11:34 pm
27	**12:28 am**	⚹☿	♐	27	**2:34 am**
28	**2:00 pm** 11:00 am	□♆	♑	29	**4:09 am** 1:09 am
30	**11:44 pm** 8:44 pm	☌♇	♒	31	**4:43 am** 1:43 am

☽ Phases & Eclipses phase	day	ET / hr:mn / PT
New Moon	2	**1:33 pm** 10:33 am
2nd Quarter	9	**1:11 pm** 10:11 am
Full Moon	17	**6:48 pm** 3:48 pm
4th Quarter	25	**8:41 am** 5:41 am
New Moon	31	9:46 pm
New Moon	2/1	**12:46 am**

Planet Ingress		day	ET / hr:mn / PT
☿	♒	1	11:10 pm
☿	♒	2	**2:10 am**
⚵	♑	10	9:19 pm
⚵	♑	11	**12:19 am**
☉	♒	19	**9:39 pm** 6:39 pm
♂	♑	24	**7:53 am** 4:53 am
☿	♑	25	**10:05 pm** 7:05 pm

Planetary Motion		day	ET / hr:mn / PT
☿	℞	14	**6:41 am** 3:41 am
⚳	D	14	**4:20 pm** 1:20 pm
♅	D	18	**10:27 am** 7:27 am
♀	D	29	**3:46 am** 12:46 am

1 SATURDAY
☽□♆ **3:16 am** 12:16 am
☉△♅ **4:50 am** 1:50 am
☽⚺♀ **7:02 am** 4:02 am
☽⚺♇ **11:38 am** 8:38 am
☽⚺☿ **5:13 pm** 2:13 pm
☽⚹♃ **7:13 pm** 4:13 pm

2 SUNDAY
☉⚺♄ **7:12 am** 4:12 am
☽△♅ **11:20 am** 8:20 am
☽⚺♄ **1:10 pm** 10:10 am
☽☌☉ **1:33 pm** 10:33 am
☽⚺♂ **4:56 pm** 1:56 pm
☿⚺♃ **6:44 pm** 3:44 pm
☽⚹♆ 11:52 pm

3 MONDAY
☽⚹♆ **2:52 am**
☽☌♀ **4:59 am** 1:59 am
☽☌♇ **11:21 am** 8:21 am
☽⚺♃ **7:34 pm** 4:34 pm
☽☌☿ **9:37 pm** 6:37 pm

4 TUESDAY
☽□♅ **11:25 am** 8:25 am
☽☌♄ **1:44 pm** 10:44 am
☽⚺☉ **5:23 pm** 2:23 pm
☽⚹♂ **7:45 pm** 4:45 pm

5 WEDNESDAY
☽⚺♆ **3:41 am** 12:41 am
☽⚺♀ **3:59 am** 12:59 am
♀⚹♆ **11:03 am** 8:03 am
☽⚺♇ **12:39 pm** 9:39 am
☽☌♃ **9:57 pm** 6:57 pm

6 THURSDAY
☽⚺☿ **4:07 am** 1:07 am
☽⚹♅ **2:04 pm** 11:04 am
☽⚺♄ **5:01 pm** 2:01 pm
☽⚹☉ 9:41 pm
☽□♂ 10:55 pm

7 FRIDAY
☽⚹☉ **12:41 am**
☽□♂ **1:55 am**
☽⚹♀ **5:41 am** 2:41 am
☽☌♆ **7:40 am** 4:40 am
☽⚹♇ **5:23 pm** 2:23 pm

8 SATURDAY
☽⚺♃ **4:11 am** 1:11 am
☽⚹☿ **2:37 pm** 11:37 am
♀⚺♂ **5:48 pm** 2:48 pm
☉☌♀ **7:48 pm** 4:48 pm
☽⚺♅ **8:44 pm** 5:44 pm
☽⚹♄ 9:27 pm

9 SUNDAY
☽⚹♄ **12:27 am**
☉⚺♂ **4:32 am** 1:32 am
☽□♀ **11:01 am** 8:01 am

☽△♂ **12:58 pm** 9:58 am
☽□☉ **1:11 pm** 10:11 am
☽⚺♆ **3:52 pm** 12:52 pm
☽□♇ 11:23 pm

10 MONDAY
☽□♇ **2:23 am**
☽⚹♃ **2:48 pm** 11:48 am
☉⚹♆ **10:28 pm** 7:28 pm

11 TUESDAY
☽□☿ **4:38 am** 1:38 am
☽☌♅ **7:21 am** 4:21 am
☽□♄ **11:53 am** 8:53 am
♂□♆ **4:43 pm** 1:43 pm
☽△♀ **7:34 pm** 4:34 pm

12 WEDNESDAY
☽⚹♆ **3:38 am** 12:38 am
☽⚻♂ **4:19 am** 1:19 am
☽△☉ **6:20 am** 3:20 am
☽△♇ **2:39 pm** 11:39 am

13 THURSDAY
☽□♃ **4:24 am** 1:24 am
☽△☿ **7:10 pm** 4:10 pm
☽⚺♅ **8:12 pm** 5:12 pm
☽△♄ 10:26 pm

14 FRIDAY
☽△♄ **1:26 am**
☽⚻♀ **5:46 am** 2:46 am
☽□♆ **4:50 pm** 1:50 pm
☽☍♂ **9:22 pm** 6:22 pm
☽⚻☉ 10:10 pm

15 SATURDAY
☽⚻☉ **1:10 am**
☽⚻♇ **3:54 am** 12:54 am
☽△♃ **6:31 pm** 3:31 pm

16 SUNDAY
☽⚻☿ **7:12 am** 4:12 am
☽⚹♅ **8:58 am** 5:58 am
☉☌♇ **9:51 am** 6:51 am
☽⚻♄ **2:42 pm** 11:42 am
☽☍♀ **3:50 pm** 12:50 pm

17 MONDAY
☽△♆ **5:19 am** 2:19 am
☽⚻♂ **1:24 pm** 10:24 am
♀⚺♄ **2:44 pm** 11:44 am
☽☍♇ **4:08 pm** 1:08 pm
☽☍☉ **6:48 pm** 3:48 pm

18 TUESDAY
☽⚻♃ **7:15 am** 4:15 am
☽☍☿ **3:39 pm** 12:39 pm
☽□♅ **8:11 pm** 5:11 pm
☽⚻♀ 9:47 pm
☽☍♄ 11:19 pm

19 WEDNESDAY
☽⚻♀ **12:47 am**
☽☍♄ **2:19 am**
♂⚺♇ **1:30 pm** 10:30 am
☽⚻♆ **4:00 pm** 1:00 pm
☽⚻♇ 11:30 pm

20 THURSDAY
☽⚻♇ **2:30 am**
☽△♂ **3:15 am** 12:15 am
☽⚻☉ **10:02 am** 7:02 am
☽☍♃ **5:58 pm** 2:58 pm
☽⚻☿ **8:55 pm** 5:55 pm

21 FRIDAY
☽△♅ **5:28 am** 2:28 am
☽△♀ **8:19 am** 5:19 am
☽⚻♄ **11:54 am** 8:54 am
☿⚺♃ **11:00 pm** 8:00 pm
☽☍♆ 9:43 pm

22 SATURDAY
☽☍♆ **12:43 am**
☽△♇ **10:53 am** 7:53 am
☽□♂ **2:46 pm** 11:46 am
☽△☉ **10:43 pm** 7:43 pm
☽△☿ **11:47 pm** 8:47 pm
☽⚻♃ 11:37 pm

23 SUNDAY
☽⚻♃ **2:37 am**
☉☌☿ **5:28 am** 2:28 am
☽⚻♅ **12:45 pm** 9:45 am
☽□♀ **2:22 pm** 11:22 am
☽△♄ **7:26 pm** 4:26 pm

24 MONDAY
☽⚻♆ **7:23 am** 4:23 am
☽□♇ **5:10 pm** 2:10 pm
☽⚹♂ **11:48 pm** 8:48 pm
☽□☿ 9:51 pm

25 TUESDAY
☽□☿ **12:51 am**
☿⚺♂ **7:46 am** 4:46 am
☽□☉ **8:41 am** 5:41 am
☽△♃ **9:01 am** 6:01 am
☉⚺♃ **2:32 pm** 11:32 am
☽☍♅ **5:52 pm** 2:52 pm
☽⚹♀ **6:41 pm** 3:41 pm
☽□♄ 9:42 pm

26 WEDNESDAY
☽□♄ **12:42 am**
☽△♆ **11:47 am** 8:47 am
☽⚹♇ **9:10 pm** 6:10 pm
☽⚹☿ 9:28 pm

27 THURSDAY
☽⚹☿ **12:28 am**
☽⚺♂ **6:09 am** 3:09 am
☽□♃ **1:02 pm** 10:02 am
☽⚹☉ **3:47 pm** 12:47 pm
☽⚻♅ **8:43 pm** 5:43 pm
☽⚺♀ **9:08 pm** 6:08 pm

28 FRIDAY
☽⚹♄ **3:39 am** 12:39 am
☽□♆ **2:00 pm** 11:00 am
☽⚺♇ **11:02 pm** 8:02 pm
☽⚺☿ **11:03 pm** 8:03 pm
☿☌♇ **11:16 pm** 8:16 pm

29 SATURDAY
☽☌♂ **10:10 am** 7:10 am
☽⚹♃ **3:03 pm** 12:03 pm

☽⚺☉ **8:34 pm** 5:34 pm
☽△♅ **9:47 pm** 6:47 pm
☽☌♀ **10:08 pm** 7:08 pm

30 SUNDAY
☽⚺♄ **4:56 am** 1:56 am
☉□♅ **2:32 pm** 11:32 am
☽⚹♆ **2:48 pm** 11:48 am
☉⚺♀ **8:29 pm** 5:29 pm
☽☌☿ **9:26 pm** 6:26 pm
☽☌♇ **11:44 pm** 8:44 pm

31 MONDAY
☽⚺♂ **1:14 pm** 10:14 am
☽⚺♃ **4:22 pm** 1:22 pm
☽□♅ **10:25 pm** 7:25 pm
☽⚺♀ **10:58 pm** 7:58 pm
☽☌☉ 9:46 pm

Eastern time in bold type
Pacific time in medium type

JANUARY 2022

DATE	SID.TIME	SUN	MOON	NODE	MERCURY	VENUS	MARS	JUPITER	SATURN	URANUS	NEPTUNE	PLUTO	CERES	PALLAS	JUNO	VESTA	CHIRON
1 Sa	6 42 30	10♑31 44	15♐29	1♊12℞	28♑11	23♑18℞	13♐06	0♓33	11♒54	10♉57℞	20♓40	25♑56	28♉38℞	16♓28	17♑23	24♐32	8♈30
2 Su	6 46 27	11 32 55	0♑37	1 10	29 35	22 48	13 49	0 45	12 01	10 56	20 41	25 58	28 32	16 43	17 46	25 04	8 31
3 M	6 50 23	12 34 06	15 46	1 05	0♒57	22 16	14 31	0 56	12 07	10 55	20 42	26 00	28 27	16 58	18 10	25 36	8 32
4 T	6 54 20	13 35 17	0♒47	0 59	2 16	21 43	15 14	1 08	12 14	10 55	20 43	26 02	28 22	17 13	18 33	26 08	8 33
5 W	6 58 17	14 36 28	15 31	0 51	3 32	21 09	15 57	1 20	12 20	10 54	20 45	26 04	28 18	17 29	18 56	26 40	8 34
6 Th	7 2 13	15 37 38	29 50	0 44	4 43	20 34	16 40	1 33	12 27	10 53	20 46	26 06	28 14	17 45	19 20	27 13	8 34
7 F	7 6 10	16 38 48	13♓41	0 38	5 50	19 58	17 23	1 45	12 34	10 53	20 47	26 08	28 11	18 01	19 43	27 45	8 35
8 Sa	7 10 6	17 39 58	27 03	0 34	6 52	19 21	18 05	1 57	12 41	10 52	20 48	26 10	28 08	18 17	20 07	28 17	8 36
9 Su	7 14 3	18 41 07	9♈57	0 32D	7 47	18 44	18 48	2 09	12 47	10 52	20 49	26 12	28 05	18 33	20 30	28 49	8 38
10 M	7 17 59	19 42 16	22 27	0 32	8 35	18 08	19 31	2 22	12 54	10 51	20 51	26 14	28 03	18 49	20 54	29 21	8 39
11 T	7 21 56	20 43 24	4♉39	0 32	9 15	17 31	20 14	2 34	13 01	10 51	20 52	26 16	28 01	19 06	21 18	29 53	8 40
12 W	7 25 52	21 44 32	16 38	0 34	9 46	16 55	20 57	2 47	13 08	10 50	20 53	26 18	28 00	19 23	21 41	0♑25	8 41
13 Th	7 29 49	22 45 40	28 28	0 34℞	10 08	16 20	21 40	3 00	13 15	10 50	20 55	26 20	27 59	19 40	22 05	0 57	8 42
14 F	7 33 45	23 46 46	10♊14	0 34	10 19℞	15 46	22 24	3 12	13 22	10 50	20 56	26 22	27 58D	19 57	22 28	1 29	8 44
15 Sa	7 37 42	24 47 53	22 01	0 31	10 19	15 13	23 07	3 25	13 28	10 49	20 58	26 24	27 58	20 14	22 52	2 01	8 45
16 Su	7 41 39	25 48 58	3♋52	0 26	10 07	14 41	23 50	3 38	13 35	10 49	20 59	26 26	27 58	20 32	23 16	2 33	8 47
17 M	7 45 35	26 50 03	15 50	0 18	9 43	14 11	24 33	3 51	13 42	10 49	21 01	26 28	27 59	20 49	23 40	3 04	8 48
18 T	7 49 32	27 51 08	27 57	0 09	9 08	13 43	25 16	4 04	13 49	10 49D	21 02	26 29	28 00	21 07	24 03	3 36	8 50
19 W	7 53 28	28 52 12	10♌12	29♉57	8 22	13 17	26 00	4 17	13 56	10 49	21 04	26 31	28 01	21 25	24 27	4 08	8 51
20 Th	7 57 25	29 53 15	22 39	29 46	7 26	12 53	26 43	4 30	14 03	10 49	21 05	26 33	28 03	21 43	24 51	4 40	8 53
21 F	8 1 21	0♒54 18	5♍16	29 34	6 22	12 31	27 26	4 44	14 11	10 49	21 07	26 35	28 05	22 01	25 15	5 12	8 54
22 Sa	8 5 18	1 55 21	18 04	29 25	5 11	12 12	28 10	4 57	14 18	10 49	21 08	26 37	28 08	22 19	25 38	5 43	[illegible] 56
23 Su	8 9 15	2 56 22	1♎04	29 18	3 56	11 55	28 53	5 10	14 25	10 50	21 10	26 39	28 11	22 38	26 02	6 15	8 58
24 M	8 13 11	3 57 24	14 17	29 14	2 40	11 40	29 37	5 24	14 32	10 50	21 12	26 41	28 14	22 56	26 26	6 47	9 00
25 T	8 17 8	4 58 25	27 45	29 12D	1 23	11 28	0♑20	5 37	14 39	10 50	21 13	26 43	28 18	23 15	26 50	7 18	9 02
26 W	8 21 4	5 59 25	11♏30	29 12	0 09	11 19	1 04	5 51	14 46	10 51	21 15	26 45	28 22	23 34	27 14	7 50	9 04
27 Th	8 25 1	7 00 25	25 31	29 12℞	29♑00	11 12	1 47	6 04	14 53	10 51	21 17	26 47	28 27	23 53	27 38	8 21	9 06
28 F	8 28 57	8 01 25	9♐49	29 12	27 57	11 07	2 31	6 18	15 00	10 51	21 19	26 49	28 32	24 12	28 01	8 53	9 08
29 Sa	8 32 54	9 02 24	24 23	29 10	27 01	11 05D	3 15	6 31	15 08	10 52	21 20	26 51	28 37	24 31	28 25	9 24	9 10
30 Su	8 36 50	10 03 23	9♑09	29 05	26 13	11 05	3 58	6 45	15 15	10 52	21 22	26 53	28 43	24 50	28 49	9 55	9 12
31 M	8 40 47	11 04 20	24 00	28 57	25 34	11 08	4 42	6 59	15 22	10 53	21 24	26 55	28 49	25 10	29 13	10 27	9 14

EPHEMERIS CALCULATED FOR 12 MIDNIGHT GREENWICH MEAN TIME. ALL OTHER DATA AND FACING ASPECTARIAN PAGE IN **EASTERN TIME (BOLD)** AND PACIFIC TIME (REGULAR).

FEBRUARY 2022

☽ Last Aspect day	ET / hr:mn / PT		asp	☽ Ingress sign day	ET / hr:mn / PT	
1	**6:01 am**	3:01 am	☌ ♄	♓ 2	**6:00 am**	3:00 am
4	**4:41 am**	1:41 am	⚹ ♇	♈ 4	**9:57 am**	6:57 am
6	**12:21 pm**	9:21 am	□ ♇	♉ 6	**5:52 pm**	2:52 pm
8	**11:48 pm**	8:48 pm	△ ♇	♊ 9	**5:27 am**	2:27 am
11	**3:23 am**	12:23 am	△ ☉	♋ 11	**6:27 pm**	3:27 pm
14	**5:27 am**	2:27 am	☍ ☿	♌ 14	**6:17 am**	3:17 am
16	**11:56 am**	8:56 am	☍ ☉	♍ 16	**3:42 pm**	12:42 pm
18	**6:20 pm**	3:20 pm	△ ♇	♎ 18	**10:51 pm**	7:51 pm
20		9:02 pm	□ ♇	♏ 21	**4:19 am**	1:19 am
21	**12:02 am**		□ ♇	♏ 21	**4:19 am**	1:19 am

☽ Last Aspect day	ET / hr:mn / PT		asp	☽ Ingress sign day	ET / hr:mn / PT	
23	**4:24 am**	1:24 am	⚹ ♇	♐ 23	**8:29 am**	5:29 am
24	**10:24 pm**	7:24 pm	□ ♆	♑ 25	**11:27 am**	8:27 am
27	**9:49 am**	6:49 am	☌ ♇	♒ 27	**1:36 pm**	10:36 am
28	**9:01 pm**	6:01 pm	☌ ♄	♓ 3/1	**3:53 pm**	12:53 pm

☽ Phases & Eclipses phase	day	ET / hr:mn / PT	
New Moon	1/31		9:46 pm
New Moon	1	**12:46 am**	
2nd Quarter	8	**8:50 am**	5:50 am
Full Moon	16	**11:56 am**	8:56 am
4th Quarter	23	**5:32 pm**	2:32 pm

Planet Ingress	day	ET / hr:mn / PT	
⚵ ♒	1	**6:04 pm**	3:04 pm
⚳ ♊	8	**9:13 pm**	6:13 pm
♀ ♈	13		9:53 pm
♀ ♈	14	**12:53 am**	
☿ ♒	14	**4:54 pm**	1:54 pm
☉ ♓	18	**11:43 am**	8:43 am

Planetary Motion	day	ET / hr:mn / PT	
☿ D	3	**11:13 pm**	8:13 pm

1 TUESDAY
- ☽ ☌ ☉ **12:46 am**
- ☽ ☌ ♄ **6:01 am** 3:01 am
- ☽ ⚺ ♆ **3:46 pm** 12:46 pm
- ☽ ⚺ ☿ **9:05 pm** 6:05 pm
- ☽ ⚺ ♇ 9:57 pm

2 WEDNESDAY
- ☽ ⚺ ♇ **12:57 am**
- ☽ ⚹ ♂ **5:33 pm** 2:33 pm
- ☽ ☌ ♃ **6:57 pm** 3:57 pm
- ☽ ⚹ ♅ 9:30 pm
- ☽ ⚹ ♀ 10:35 pm

3 THURSDAY
- ☽ ⚹ ♅ **12:30 am**
- ☽ ⚹ ♀ **1:35 am**
- ☽ ⚺ ☉ **6:52 am** 3:52 am
- ☽ ⚺ ♄ **8:54 am** 5:54 am
- ☽ ☌ ♆ **6:54 pm** 3:54 pm
- ☽ ⚹ ☿ **11:55 pm** 8:55 pm

4 FRIDAY
- ☽ ⚹ ♇ **4:41 am** 1:41 am
- ♂ ⚹ ♃ **8:38 am** 5:38 am
- ☉ ☌ ♄ **2:05 pm** 11:05 am
- ☽ ⚺ ♃ 9:48 pm
- ☽ □ ♂ 10:27 pm

5 SATURDAY
- ☽ ⚺ ♃ **12:48 am**
- ☽ □ ♂ **1:27 am**
- ☽ ⚺ ♅ **5:53 am** 2:53 am
- ☽ □ ♀ **7:56 am** 4:56 am
- ☽ ⚹ ♄ **3:22 pm** 12:22 pm
- ☽ ⚹ ☉ **5:17 pm** 2:17 pm
- ☽ ⚺ ♆ 10:47 pm

6 SUNDAY
- ☽ ⚺ ♆ **1:47 am**
- ☽ □ ☿ **7:42 am** 4:42 am
- ☽ □ ♇ **12:21 pm** 9:21 am

7 MONDAY
- ☽ ⚹ ♃ **10:58 am** 7:58 am
- ☽ △ ♂ **2:12 pm** 11:12 am
- ☽ ☌ ♅ **3:22 pm** 12:22 pm
- ☽ △ ♀ **7:00 pm** 4:00 pm
- ☽ □ ♄ 11:01 pm

8 TUESDAY
- ☽ □ ♄ **2:01 am**
- ☽ □ ☉ **8:50 am** 5:50 am
- ♂ △ ♅ **9:57 am** 6:57 am
- ☽ ⚹ ♆ **12:40 pm** 9:40 am
- ☽ △ ☿ **8:48 pm** 5:48 pm
- ☽ △ ♇ **11:48 pm** 8:48 pm

9 WEDNESDAY
- ☽ □ ♃ 9:28 pm

10 THURSDAY
- ☽ □ ♃ **12:28 am**
- ☽ ⚺ ♅ **3:53 am** 12:53 am
- ☽ ⚻ ♂ **6:36 am** 3:36 am
- ☉ ⚺ ♆ **7:29 am** 4:29 am
- ☽ ⚻ ♀ **9:35 am** 6:35 am
- ☽ △ ♄ **3:20 pm** 12:20 pm
- ☽ □ ♆ 10:43 pm

11 FRIDAY
- ☽ □ ♆ **1:43 am**
- ☽ △ ☉ **3:23 am** 12:23 am
- ☿ ☌ ♇ **9:04 am** 6:04 am
- ☽ ⚻ ♇ **12:56 pm** 9:56 am
- ☽ ⚻ ☿ **1:11 pm** 10:11 am

12 SATURDAY
- ☽ △ ♃ **2:35 pm** 11:35 am
- ☽ ⚹ ♅ **4:49 pm** 1:49 pm
- ☽ ☍ ♂ **11:21 pm** 8:21 pm
- ☽ ☍ ♀ 9:45 pm

13 SUNDAY
- ☽ ☍ ♀ **12:45 am**
- ☽ ⚻ ♄ **4:33 am** 1:33 am
- ☽ △ ♆ **2:15 pm** 11:15 am
- ☽ ⚻ ☉ **9:09 pm** 6:09 pm
- ☽ ☍ ♇ 10:07 pm

14 MONDAY
- ☽ ☍ ♇ **1:07 am**
- ☽ ☍ ☿ **5:27 am** 2:27 am
- ☽ ⚻ ♃ 11:49 pm

15 TUESDAY
- ☽ ⚻ ♃ **2:49 am**
- ☽ □ ♅ **3:56 am** 12:56 am
- ☽ ⚻ ♂ **1:45 pm** 10:45 am
- ☽ ⚻ ♀ **2:02 pm** 11:02 am
- ☽ ☍ ♄ **3:38 pm** 12:38 pm
- ☉ ⚺ ♇ **10:17 pm** 7:17 pm
- ☽ ⚻ ♆ 9:31 pm

16 WEDNESDAY
- ☽ ⚻ ♆ **12:31 am**
- ♀ ☌ ♂ **9:29 am** 6:29 am
- ☽ ⚻ ♇ **10:53 am** 7:53 am
- ☽ ☍ ☉ **11:56 am** 8:56 am
- ☽ ⚻ ☿ **7:31 pm** 4:31 pm

17 THURSDAY
- ♂ ⚺ ♄ **3:34 am** 12:34 am
- ♀ ⚺ ♄ **9:09 am** 6:09 am
- ☽ ☍ ♃ **12:26 pm** 9:26 am
- ☽ △ ♅ **12:33 pm** 9:33 am
- ♃ ⚹ ♅ **7:13 pm** 4:13 pm
- ☽ ⚻ ♄ 9:11 pm
- ☽ △ ♀ 9:47 pm
- ☽ △ ♂ 10:13 pm

18 FRIDAY
- ☽ ⚻ ♄ **12:11 am**
- ☽ △ ♀ **12:47 am**
- ☽ △ ♂ **1:13 am**
- ☽ ☍ ♆ **8:22 am** 5:22 am
- ☽ △ ♇ **6:20 pm** 3:20 pm
- ☽ ⚻ ☉ **11:46 pm** 8:46 pm

19 SATURDAY
- ☽ △ ☿ **7:18 am** 4:18 am
- ☽ ⚻ ♅ **7:06 pm** 4:06 pm
- ☽ ⚻ ♃ **7:53 pm** 4:53 pm

20 SUNDAY
- ☽ △ ♄ **6:46 am** 3:46 am
- ☽ □ ♀ **9:33 am** 6:33 am
- ☽ □ ♂ **10:25 am** 7:25 am
- ☽ ⚻ ♆ **2:22 pm** 11:22 am
- ☽ □ ♇ 9:02 pm

21 MONDAY
- ☽ □ ♇ **12:02 am**
- ☽ △ ☉ **9:28 am** 6:28 am
- ☽ □ ☿ **5:28 pm** 2:28 pm
- ☽ ☍ ♅ 9:10 pm
- ☽ △ ♃ 10:45 pm

22 TUESDAY
- ☽ ☍ ♅ **12:10 am**
- ☽ △ ♃ **1:45 am**
- ☽ □ ♄ **11:53 am** 8:53 am
- ☽ ⚹ ♀ **4:55 pm** 1:55 pm
- ☽ ⚹ ♂ **5:58 pm** 2:58 pm
- ☽ △ ♆ **7:00 pm** 4:00 pm

23 WEDNESDAY
- ☽ ⚹ ♇ **4:24 am** 1:24 am
- ♂ ⚹ ♆ **2:12 pm** 11:12 am
- ☽ □ ☉ **5:32 pm** 2:32 pm
- ☽ ⚹ ☿ 11:17 pm

24 THURSDAY
- ☽ ⚹ ☿ **2:17 am**
- ☽ ⚻ ♅ **3:59 am** 12:59 am
- ☽ □ ♃ **6:19 am** 3:19 am
- ♀ ⚹ ♆ **11:04 am** 8:04 am
- ☽ ⚹ ♄ **3:45 pm** 12:45 pm
- ☿ □ ♅ **9:22 pm** 6:22 pm
- ☽ □ ♆ **10:24 pm** 7:24 pm
- ☽ ⚺ ♀ **11:00 pm** 8:00 pm
- ☽ ⚺ ♂ 9:06 pm

25 FRIDAY
- ☽ ⚺ ♂ **12:06 am**
- ☽ ⚺ ♇ **7:33 am** 4:33 am
- ☽ ⚹ ☉ 9:10 pm

26 SATURDAY
- ☽ ⚹ ☉ **12:10 am**
- ☽ △ ♅ **6:40 am** 3:40 am
- ☿ ⚺ ♃ **7:16 am** 4:16 am
- ☽ ⚹ ♃ **9:43 am** 6:43 am
- ☽ ⚺ ☿ **9:55 am** 6:55 am
- ☽ ⚺ ♄ **6:32 pm** 3:32 pm
- ☽ ⚹ ♆ 9:49 pm

27 SUNDAY
- ☽ ⚹ ♆ **12:49 am**
- ☽ ☌ ♀ **4:06 am** 1:06 am
- ☽ ☌ ♂ **5:06 am** 2:06 am
- ☽ ☌ ♇ **9:49 am** 6:49 am

28 MONDAY
- ☽ ⚺ ☉ **5:59 am** 2:59 am
- ☽ □ ♅ **8:50 am** 5:50 am
- ☽ ⚺ ♃ **12:37 pm** 9:37 am
- ☽ ☌ ☿ **5:11 pm** 2:11 pm
- ☽ ☌ ♄ **9:01 pm** 6:01 pm

Eastern time in bold type
Pacific time in medium type

FEBRUARY 2022

DATE	SID.TIME	SUN	MOON	NODE	MERCURY	VENUS	MARS	JUPITER	SATURN	URANUS	NEPTUNE	PLUTO	CERES	PALLAS	JUNO	VESTA	CHIRON
1 T	8 44 44	12♒05 17	8♒48	28♉47℞	25♑03℞	11♑13	5♑26	7♓13	15♒29	10♉54	21♓26	26♑57	28♉55	25♓29	29♑37	10♑58	9♈16
2 W	8 48 40	13 06 12	23 25	28 35	24 41	11 20	6 10	7 27	15 36	10 55	21 28	26 59	29 02	25 49	0♒01	11 29	9 18
3 Th	8 52 37	14 07 07	7♓42	28 23	24 28	11 30	6 54	7 40	15 43	10 55	21 30	27 01	29 09	26 09	0 25	12 01	9 21
4 F	8 56 33	15 08 00	21 35	28 12	24 23D	11 42	7 37	7 54	15 51	10 56	21 32	27 03	29 17	26 29	0 49	12 32	9 23
5 Sa	9 0 30	16 08 52	5♈01	28 04	24 25	11 56	8 21	8 08	15 58	10 57	21 33	27 05	29 25	26 49	1 13	13 03	9 25
6 Su	9 4 26	17 09 42	18 00	27 58	24 35	12 12	9 05	8 22	16 05	10 58	21 35	27 07	29 33	27 09	1 37	13 34	9 28
7 M	9 8 23	18 10 31	0♉35	27 55	24 51	12 30	9 49	8 36	16 12	10 59	21 37	27 08	29 41	27 30	2 01	14 05	9 30
8 T	9 12 19	19 11 19	12 50	27 54D	25 13	12 50	10 33	8 50	16 19	11 00	21 39	27 10	29 50	27 50	2 24	14 36	9 33
9 W	9 16 16	20 12 05	24 50	27 54℞	25 41	13 12	11 17	9 05	16 27	11 01	21 41	27 12	29 59	28 11	2 48	15 07	9 35
10 Th	9 20 13	21 12 50	6♊41	27 54	26 15	13 35	12 01	9 19	16 34	11 02	21 43	27 14	0♊09	28 31	3 12	15 38	9 38
11 F	9 24 9	22 13 33	18 28	27 52	26 53	14 01	12 45	9 33	16 41	11 03	21 45	27 16	0 18	28 52	3 36	16 09	9 40
12 Sa	9 28 6	23 14 14	0♋16	27 49	27 35	14 28	13 30	9 47	16 48	11 05	21 47	27 18	0 28	29 13	4 00	16 39	9 43
13 Su	9 32 2	24 14 54	12 11	27 42	28 21	14 57	14 14	10 01	16 55	11 06	21 49	27 19	0 39	29 34	4 24	17 10	9 45
14 M	9 35 59	25 15 33	24 15	27 33	29 11	15 27	14 58	10 16	17 02	11 07	21 52	27 21	0 49	29 55	4 48	17 41	9 48
15 T	9 39 55	26 16 10	6♌32	27 21	0♒05	15 59	15 42	10 30	17 10	11 09	21 54	27 23	1 00	0♈16	5 12	18 11	9 51
16 W	9 43 52	27 16 45	19 02	27 08	1 01	16 32	16 26	10 44	17 17	11 10	21 56	27 25	1 12	0 37	5 36	18 42	9 54
17 Th	9 47 48	28 17 19	1♍46	26 54	2 01	17 07	17 11	10 59	17 24	11 11	21 58	27 27	1 23	0 59	6 00	19 13	9 56
18 F	9 51 45	29 17 51	14 43	26 40	3 03	17 43	17 55	11 13	17 31	11 13	22 00	27 28	1 35	1 20	6 24	19 43	9 59
19 Sa	9 55 42	0♓18 22	27 52	26 29	4 07	18 20	18 39	11 27	17 38	11 15	22 02	27 30	1 47	1 42	6 47	20 13	10 02
20 Su	9 59 38	1 18 51	11♎13	26 20	5 14	18 59	19 24	11 42	17 45	11 16	22 04	27 32	2 00	2 03	7 11	20 44	10 05
21 M	10 3 35	2 19 19	24 43	26 14	6 23	19 39	20 08	11 56	17 52	11 18	22 06	27 33	2 12	2 25	7 35	21 14	10 08
22 T	10 7 31	3 19 46	8♏22	26 11	7 34	20 20	20 52	12 10	17 59	11 20	22 09	27 35	2 25	2 47	7 59	21 44	10 11
23 W	10 11 28	4 20 11	22 11	26 10	8 47	21 02	21 37	12 25	18 06	11 21	22 11	27 37	2 38	3 09	8 23	22 14	10 14
24 Th	10 15 24	5 20 35	6♐08	26 10	10 01	21 45	22 21	12 39	18 13	11 23	22 13	27 38	2 52	3 31	8 47	22 44	10 17
25 F	10 19 21	6 20 58	20 15	26 10	11 18	22 29	23 06	12 54	18 20	11 25	22 15	27 40	3 05	3 53	9 10	23 14	10 20
26 Sa	10 23 17	7 21 20	4♑30	26 08	12 35	23 14	23 51	13 08	18 27	11 27	22 17	27 42	3 19	4 15	9 34	23 44	10 23
27 Su	10 27 14	8 21 40	18 51	26 03	13 55	24 00	24 35	13 23	18 34	11 29	22 20	27 43	3 33	4 37	9 58	24 14	10 26
28 M	10 31 11	9 21 58	3♒15	25 55	15 15	24 47	25 20	13 37	18 41	11 31	22 22	27 45	3 48	5 00	10 22	24 44	10 29

EPHEMERIS CALCULATED FOR 12 MIDNIGHT GREENWICH MEAN TIME. ALL OTHER DATA AND FACING ASPECTARIAN PAGE IN **EASTERN TIME (BOLD)** AND PACIFIC TIME (REGULAR).

MARCH 2022

☽ Last Aspect day	ET / hr:mn / PT	asp	☽ Ingress sign day	ET / hr:mn / PT
2/28	**9:01 pm** 6:01 pm	☌ ♄	♓ 1	**3:53 pm** 12:53 pm
3	**4:45 pm** 1:45 pm	⚹ ♂	♈ 3	**7:52 pm** 4:52 pm
5	**11:02 pm** 8:02 pm	□ ♇	♉ 6	**3:00 am** 12:00 am
8	**9:35 am** 6:35 am	△ ♇	♊ 8	**1:40 pm** 10:40 am
10	**11:43 am** 8:43 am	□ ♆	♋ 10	11:24 pm
10	**11:43 am** 8:43 am	□ ♆	♋ 11	**2:24 am**
13	**11:44 am** 8:44 am	☍ ♇	♌ 13	**3:32 pm** 12:32 pm
15	**6:56 am** 3:56 am	☍ ♄	♍ 15	9:59 pm
15	**6:56 am** 3:56 am	☍ ♄	♍ 16	**12:59 am**
18	**4:11 am** 1:11 am	△ ♇	♎ 18	**7:26 am** 4:26 am
20	**8:40 am** 5:40 am	□ ♇	♏ 20	**11:45 am** 8:45 am
22	**12:01 pm** 9:01 am	⚹ ♇	♐ 22	**2:59 pm** 11:59 am
24	**8:59 am** 5:59 am	□ ☿	♑ 24	**5:54 pm** 2:54 pm
26	**7:51 pm** 4:51 pm	⚹ ☿	♒ 26	**8:55 pm** 5:55 pm
28	**10:11 am** 7:11 am	☌ ♄	♓ 28	9:32 pm
28	**10:11 am** 7:11 am	☌ ♄	♓ 29	**12:32 am**
30	11:37 pm	⚹ ♇	♈ 31	**5:30 am** 2:30 am
31	**2:37 am**	⚹ ♇	♈ 31	**5:30 am** 2:30 am

☽ Phases & Eclipses phase	day	ET / hr:mn / PT
New Moon	2	**12:35 pm** 9:35 am
2nd Quarter	10	**5:45 am** 2:45 am
Full Moon	18	**3:18 am** 12:18 am
4th Quarter	24	10:37 pm
4th Quarter	25	**1:37 am**
New Moon	31	11:24 pm
New Moon	4/1	**2:24 am**

Planet Ingress	day	ET / hr:mn / PT
♂ ♒	5	10:23 pm
♂ ♒	6	**1:23 am**
♀ ♒	5	10:30 pm
♀ ♒	6	**1:30 am**
☿ ♓	9	**8:32 pm** 5:32 pm
⚶ ♒	10	**1:22 pm** 10:22 am
☉ ♈	20	**11:33 am** 8:33 am
☿ ♈	27	**3:44 am** 12:44 am

Planetary Motion	day	ET / hr:mn / PT

1 TUESDAY
☽ ⚺ ♆ **3:05 am** 12:05 am
☽ ⚺ ♀ **9:14 am** 6:14 am
☽ ⚺ ♂ **10:02 am** 7:02 am
☽ ⚺ ♇ **12:09 pm** 9:09 am
☉ ⚹ ♅ 9:05 pm

2 WEDNESDAY
☉ ⚹ ♅ **12:05 am**
☿ ☌ ♄ **11:33 am** 8:33 am
☽ ⚹ ♅ **11:43 am** 8:43 am
☽ ☌ ☉ **12:35 pm** 9:35 am
☽ ☌ ♃ **4:24 pm** 1:24 pm
☽ ⚺ ♄ 9:37 pm
☽ ⚺ ☿ 11:00 pm

3 THURSDAY
☽ ⚺ ♄ **12:37 am**
☽ ⚺ ☿ **2:00 am**
♂ ☌ ♇ **3:43 am** 12:43 am
☽ ☌ ♆ **6:37 am** 3:37 am
♀ ☌ ♇ **12:56 pm** 9:56 am
☽ ⚹ ♇ **4:03 pm** 1:03 pm
☽ ⚹ ♀ **4:15 pm** 1:15 pm
☽ ⚹ ♂ **4:45 pm** 1:45 pm

4 FRIDAY
☽ ⚺ ♅ **4:55 pm** 1:55 pm
☽ ⚺ ☉ **10:05 pm** 7:05 pm
☽ ⚺ ♃ **10:45 pm** 7:45 pm
☿ ⚺ ♆ **10:50 pm** 7:50 pm

5 SATURDAY
☽ ⚹ ♄ **6:56 am** 3:56 am
☉ ☌ ♃ **9:06 am** 6:06 am
☽ ⚺ ♆ **1:01 pm** 10:01 am
☽ ⚹ ☿ **2:49 pm** 11:49 am
☽ □ ♇ **11:02 pm** 8:02 pm
♀ ☌ ♂ 11:12 pm

6 SUNDAY
♀ ☌ ♂ **2:12 am**
☽ □ ♂ **3:06 am** 12:06 am
☽ □ ♀ **3:07 am** 12:07 am
☽ ☌ ♅ 10:38 pm

7 MONDAY
☽ ☌ ♅ **1:38 am**
☽ ⚹ ♃ **8:49 am** 5:49 am
☽ ⚹ ☉ **12:03 pm** 9:03 am
☽ □ ♄ **4:56 pm** 1:56 pm
☽ ⚹ ♆ **11:03 pm** 8:03 pm

8 TUESDAY
☽ □ ☿ **9:04 am** 6:04 am
☽ △ ♇ **9:35 am** 6:35 am
☿ ⚺ ♇ **1:05 pm** 10:05 am
☽ △ ♂ **5:40 pm** 2:40 pm
☽ △ ♀ **6:27 pm** 3:27 pm

9 WEDNESDAY
☽ ⚺ ♅ **1:35 pm** 10:35 am
☽ □ ♃ **10:07 pm** 7:07 pm

10 THURSDAY
☽ □ ☉ **5:45 am** 2:45 am
☽ △ ♄ **5:48 am** 2:48 am
☉ ⚺ ♄ **6:17 am** 3:17 am
☽ □ ♆ **11:43 am** 8:43 am
☽ ⚻ ♇ **10:23 pm** 7:23 pm

11 FRIDAY
☽ △ ☿ **7:00 am** 4:00 am
☽ ⚻ ♂ **10:34 am** 7:34 am
☽ ⚻ ♀ **12:19 pm** 9:19 am
☽ ⚹ ♅ 11:37 pm

12 SATURDAY
☽ ⚹ ♅ **2:37 am**
☽ △ ♃ **12:07 pm** 9:07 am
☽ ⚻ ♄ **6:59 pm** 3:59 pm
☽ △ ☉ **11:52 pm** 8:52 pm
☽ △ ♆ 9:25 pm

13 SUNDAY
☽ △ ♆ **12:25 am**
☿ ⚺ ♂ **5:44 am** 1:44 am
☉ ☌ ♆ **7:43 am** 4:43 am
☽ ☍ ♇ **11:44 am** 8:44 am

14 MONDAY
☽ ☍ ♂ **3:17 am** 12:17 am
☽ ⚻ ☿ **5:05 am** 2:05 am
☽ ☍ ♀ **6:00 am** 3:00 am
☽ □ ♅ **3:02 pm** 12:02 pm
☿ ⚺ ♀ **7:51 pm** 4:51 pm
☽ ⚻ ♃ 10:02 pm

15 TUESDAY
☽ ⚻ ♃ **1:02 am**
☽ ☍ ♄ **6:56 am** 3:56 am
☽ ⚻ ♆ **11:46 am** 8:46 am
☽ ⚻ ☉ **4:01 pm** 1:01 pm
☽ ⚻ ♇ **9:29 pm** 6:29 pm

16 WEDNESDAY
☽ ⚻ ♂ **3:35 pm** 12:35 pm
☽ ⚻ ♀ **7:09 pm** 4:09 pm
☽ ☍ ☿ **10:08 pm** 7:08 pm
☽ △ ♅ **11:25 pm** 8:25 pm

17 THURSDAY
☿ ⚹ ♅ **8:13 am** 5:13 am
☽ ☍ ♃ **9:44 am** 6:44 am
☽ ⚻ ♄ **2:44 pm** 11:44 am
☽ ☍ ♆ **7:02 pm** 4:02 pm

18 FRIDAY
☽ ☍ ☉ **3:18 am** 12:18 am
☽ △ ♇ **4:11 am** 1:11 am
☉ ⚹ ♇ **3:37 pm** 12:37 pm
☽ △ ♂ 9:29 pm

19 SATURDAY
☽ △ ♂ **12:29 am**
☽ △ ♀ **4:52 am** 1:52 am
☽ ⚻ ♅ **5:02 am** 2:02 am
♀ □ ♅ **7:16 am** 4:16 am
☽ ⚻ ☿ **11:20 am** 8:20 am
☽ ⚻ ♃ **3:43 pm** 12:43 pm

☽ △ ♄ **7:59 pm** 4:59 pm
☽ ⚻ ♆ **11:53 pm** 8:53 pm

20 SUNDAY
☽ □ ♇ **8:40 am** 5:40 am
☽ ⚻ ☉ **11:45 am** 8:45 am
☿ ☌ ♃ 11:06 pm

21 MONDAY
☿ ☌ ♃ **2:06 am**
☽ □ ♂ **7:17 am** 4:17 am
☽ ☍ ♅ **8:58 am** 5:58 am
☽ □ ♀ **12:34 pm** 9:34 am
☽ △ ♃ **8:09 pm** 5:09 pm
☽ △ ☿ **10:26 pm** 7:26 pm
☽ □ ♄ **11:49 pm** 8:49 pm

22 TUESDAY
☽ △ ♆ **3:26 am** 12:26 am
☿ ⚺ ♄ **9:48 am** 6:48 am
☽ ⚹ ♇ **12:01 pm** 9:01 am
♂ □ ♅ **4:44 pm** 1:44 pm
☽ △ ☉ **6:52 pm** 3:52 pm

23 WEDNESDAY
☽ ⚻ ♅ **12:10 pm** 9:10 am
☽ ⚹ ♂ **1:12 pm** 10:12 am
☿ ☌ ♆ **1:44 pm** 10:44 am
☽ ⚹ ♀ **7:29 pm** 4:29 pm
☽ □ ♃ **11:59 pm** 8:59 pm

24 THURSDAY
☽ ⚹ ♄ **3:09 am** 12:09 am
☽ □ ♆ **6:30 am** 3:30 am
☽ □ ☿ **8:59 am** 5:59 am

☽ ⚺ ♇ **3:00 pm** 12:00 pm
☽ □ ☉ 10:37 pm

25 FRIDAY
☽ □ ☉ **1:37 am**
☽ △ ♅ **3:16 pm** 12:16 pm
☽ ⚺ ♂ **6:59 pm** 3:59 pm
☽ ⚺ ♀ 11:22 pm

26 SATURDAY
☽ ⚺ ♀ **2:22 am**
☽ ⚹ ♃ **3:48 am** 12:48 am
☽ ⚺ ♄ **6:27 am** 3:27 am
☿ ⚹ ♇ **6:35 am** 3:35 am
☽ ⚹ ♆ **9:37 am** 6:37 am
☽ ☌ ♇ **6:04 pm** 3:04 pm
☽ ⚹ ☿ **7:51 pm** 4:51 pm

27 SUNDAY
♀ ⚺ ♃ **3:34 am** 12:34 am
☽ ⚹ ☉ **8:35 am** 5:35 am
☽ □ ♅ **6:38 pm** 3:38 pm
☽ ☌ ♂ 10:08 pm

28 MONDAY
☽ ☌ ♂ **1:08 am**
☽ ⚺ ♃ **8:02 am** 5:02 am
☽ ☌ ♀ **9:48 am** 6:48 am
☽ ☌ ♄ **10:11 am** 7:11 am
☽ ⚺ ♆ **1:10 pm** 10:10 am
♀ ☌ ♄ **3:27 pm** 12:27 pm
☽ ⚺ ♇ **9:40 pm** 6:40 pm

29 TUESDAY
☽ ⚺ ☿ **7:52 am** 4:52 am
☽ ⚺ ☉ **4:27 pm** 1:27 pm
☽ ⚹ ♅ **10:54 pm** 7:54 pm

30 WEDNESDAY
♀ ⚺ ♆ **8:15 am** 5:15 am
☽ ⚺ ♂ **8:27 am** 5:27 am
☽ ☌ ♃ **1:24 pm** 10:24 am
☽ ⚺ ♄ **3:04 pm** 12:04 pm
☽ ☌ ♆ **5:55 pm** 2:55 pm
☽ ⚺ ♀ **6:42 pm** 3:42 pm
☽ ⚹ ♇ 11:37 pm

31 THURSDAY
☽ ⚹ ♇ **2:37 am**
☽ ☌ ☿ **10:35 pm** 7:35 pm
☽ ☌ ☉ 11:24 pm

Eastern time in bold type
Pacific time in medium type

MARCH 2022

DATE	SID.TIME	SUN	MOON	NODE	MERCURY	VENUS	MARS	JUPITER	SATURN	URANUS	NEPTUNE	PLUTO	CERES	PALLAS	JUNO	VESTA	CHIRON
1 T	10 35 7	10♓22 15	17♒36	25♉45℞	16♒38	25♑35	26♑04	13♓52	18♒48	11♉33	22♓24	27♑46	4♊02	5♈22	10♒46	25♑14	10♈32
2 W	10 39 4	11 22 31	1♓50	25 33	18 01	26 24	26 49	14 06	18 55	11 35	22 26	27 48	4 17	5 45	11 09	25 43	10 35
3 Th	10 43 0	12 22 44	15 50	25 21	19 26	27 13	27 34	14 21	19 02	11 37	22 29	27 50	4 32	6 07	11 33	26 13	10 38
4 F	10 46 57	13 22 56	29 30	25 10	20 52	28 03	28 19	14 35	19 08	11 39	22 31	27 51	4 48	6 30	11 57	26 42	10 42
5 Sa	10 50 53	14 23 06	12♈50	25 01	22 19	28 54	29 03	14 50	19 15	11 41	22 33	27 53	5 03	6 53	12 20	27 12	10 45
6 Su	10 54 50	15 23 13	25 46	24 55	23 48	29 46	29 48	15 04	19 22	11 43	22 35	27 54	5 19	7 15	12 44	27 41	10 48
7 M	10 58 46	16 23 19	8♉21	24 51	25 18	0♒38	0♒33	15 19	19 29	11 46	22 38	27 55	5 35	7 38	13 07	28 11	10 51
8 T	11 2 43	17 23 23	20 38	24 50D	26 49	1 31	1 18	15 33	19 35	11 48	22 40	27 57	5 51	8 01	13 31	28 40	10 55
9 W	11 6 39	18 23 25	2♊40	24 50	28 21	2 25	2 03	15 48	19 42	11 50	22 42	27 58	6 08	8 24	13 55	29 09	10 58
10 Th	11 10 36	19 23 24	14 32	24 51℞	29 54	3 19	2 47	16 02	19 49	11 53	22 44	28 00	6 24	8 48	14 18	29 38	11 01
11 F	11 14 33	20 23 22	26 21	24 51	1♓28	4 13	3 32	16 17	19 55	11 55	22 47	28 01	6 41	9 11	14 42	0♒07	11 05
12 Sa	11 18 29	21 23 17	8♋12	24 49	3 04	5 09	4 17	16 31	20 02	11 58	22 49	28 02	6 58	9 34	15 05	0 36	11 08
13 Su	11 22 26	22 23 10	20 09	24 45	4 41	6 04	5 02	16 46	20 08	12 00	22 51	28 04	7 15	9 57	15 29	1 04	11 11
14 M	11 26 22	23 23 01	2♌17	24 39	6 19	7 01	5 47	17 00	20 14	12 03	22 54	28 05	7 33	10 21	15 52	1 33	11 15
15 T	11 30 19	24 22 50	14 40	24 30	7 58	7 58	6 32	17 15	20 21	12 05	22 56	28 06	7 50	10 44	16 15	2 02	11 18
16 W	11 34 15	25 22 36	27 20	24 21	9 38	8 55	7 17	17 29	20 27	12 08	22 58	28 07	8 08	11 08	16 39	2 30	11 22
17 Th	11 38 12	26 22 21	10♍19	24 10	11 20	9 53	8 02	17 44	20 34	12 10	23 00	28 09	8 26	11 32	17 02	2 59	11 25
18 F	11 42 8	27 22 03	23 35	24 00	13 02	10 51	8 47	17 58	20 40	12 13	23 03	28 10	8 44	11 55	17 25	3 27	11 28
19 Sa	11 46 5	28 21 43	7♎07	23 51	14 46	11 49	9 32	18 13	20 46	12 16	23 05	28 11	9 02	12 19	17 48	3 55	11 32
20 Su	11 50 2	29 21 22	20 53	23 45	16 31	12 48	10 17	18 27	20 52	12 18	23 07	28 12	9 21	12 43	18 12	4 23	11 35
21 M	11 53 58	0♈20 58	4♏48	23 41	18 18	13 48	11 02	18 41	20 58	12 21	23 09	28 13	9 39	13 07	18 35	4 51	11 39
22 T	11 57 55	1 20 33	18 51	23 39D	20 05	14 48	11 47	18 56	21 04	12 24	23 12	28 14	9 58	13 31	18 58	5 19	11 42
23 W	12 1 51	2 20 06	2♐57	23 39	21 54	15 48	12 33	19 10	21 10	12 27	23 14	28 15	10 17	13 55	19 21	5 47	11 46
24 Th	12 5 48	3 19 37	17 06	23 40	23 45	16 48	13 18	19 24	21 16	12 30	23 16	28 17	10 36	14 19	19 44	6 15	11 49
25 F	12 9 44	4 19 07	1♑14	23 41℞	25 36	17 49	14 03	19 39	21 22	12 33	23 18	28 18	10 56	14 43	20 07	6 43	11 53
26 Sa	12 13 41	5 18 34	15 22	23 41	27 29	18 51	14 48	19 53	21 28	12 35	23 21	28 19	11 15	15 07	20 30	7 10	11 56
27 Su	12 17 37	6 18 01	29 28	23 38	29 23	19 52	15 33	20 07	21 34	12 38	23 23	28 20	11 35	15 32	20 53	7 38	12 00
28 M	12 21 34	7 17 25	13♒29	23 34	1♈18	20 54	16 19	20 21	21 40	12 41	23 25	28 20	11 54	15 56	21 16	8 05	12 03
29 T	12 25 31	8 16 47	27 24	23 28	3 15	21 56	17 04	20 36	21 46	12 44	23 27	28 21	12 14	16 20	21 39	8 32	12 07
30 W	12 29 27	9 16 08	11♓09	23 21	5 13	22 59	17 49	20 50	21 51	12 47	23 30	28 22	12 34	16 45	22 01	8 59	12 10
31 Th	12 33 24	10 15 27	24 42	23 13	7 12	24 02	18 34	21 04	21 57	12 50	23 32	28 23	12 54	17 09	22 24	9 26	12 14

EPHEMERIS CALCULATED FOR 12 MIDNIGHT GREENWICH MEAN TIME. ALL OTHER DATA AND FACING ASPECTARIAN PAGE IN **EASTERN TIME (BOLD)** AND PACIFIC TIME (REGULAR).

APRIL 2022

☽ Last Aspect day	ET / hr:mn	PT	asp	☽ Ingress sign	day	ET / hr:mn	PT
2	**9:51 am**	6:51 am	□♇	♉	2	**12:50 pm**	9:50 am
4	**9:53 pm**	6:53 pm	□♀	♊	4	**11:04 pm**	8:04 pm
6	**11:15 pm**	8:15 pm	△♂	♋	7	**11:30 am**	8:30 am
9	**9:01 pm**	6:01 pm	☍♇	♌	9		9:00 pm
9	**9:01 pm**	6:01 pm	☍♇	♌	10	**12:00 am**	
12	**6:16 am**	3:16 am	☍♂	♍	12	**10:07 am**	7:07 am
14	**2:11 pm**	11:11 am	△♇	♎	14	**4:46 pm**	1:46 pm
16	**5:57 pm**	2:57 pm	□♇	♏	16	**8:23 pm**	5:23 pm
18	**7:55 pm**	4:55 pm	⚹♇	♐	18	**10:16 pm**	7:16 pm
20	**4:56 pm**	1:56 pm	□♃	♑	20	**11:52 pm**	8:52 pm

☽ Last Aspect day	ET / hr:mn	PT	asp	☽ Ingress sign	day	ET / hr:mn	PT
22	**11:53 pm**	8:53 pm	☌♇	♒	22		11:17 pm
22	**11:53 pm**	8:53 pm	☌♇	♒	23	**2:17 am**	
24	**8:33 pm**	5:33 pm	□☿	♓	25	**6:15 am**	3:15 am
27	**9:36 am**	6:36 am	⚹♇	♈	27	**12:10 pm**	9:10 am
29	**5:38 pm**	2:38 pm	□♇	♉	29	**8:19 pm**	5:19 pm

☽ Phases & Eclipses phase	day	ET / hr:mn	PT
New Moon	3/31		11:24 pm
New Moon	1	**2:24 am**	
2nd Quarter	8		11:48 pm
2nd Quarter	9	**2:48 am**	
Full Moon	16	**2:55 pm**	11:55 am
4th Quarter	23	**7:56 am**	4:56 am
New Moon	30	**4:28 pm**	1:28 pm
●	30	10° ♉ 28'	

Planet Ingress		day	ET / hr:mn	PT
♀	♓	5	**11:18 am**	8:18 am
☿	♉	10	**10:09 pm**	7:09 pm
♂	♓	14	**11:06 pm**	8:06 pm
☉	♉	19	**10:24 pm**	7:24 pm
⚵	♓	20	**11:51 am**	8:51 am
☿	♊	29	**6:23 pm**	3:23 pm
⚳	♉	30	**4:50 am**	1:50 am

Planetary Motion		day	ET / hr:mn	PT
♇	℞	29	**2:38 pm**	11:38 am

1 FRIDAY

☽ ☌ ☉	**2:24 am**	
☽ ⚺ ♅	**4:59 am**	1:59 am
☽ ⚹ ♂	**6:07 pm**	3:07 pm
☽ ⚺ ♃	**8:57 pm**	5:57 pm
☽ ⚹ ♄	**10:04 pm**	7:04 pm
☽ ⚺ ♆		9:49 pm

2 SATURDAY

☽ ⚺ ♆	**12:49 am**	
☽ ⚹ ♀	**6:24 am**	3:24 am
☽ □ ♇	**9:51 am**	6:51 am
☉ ⚺ ♅	**2:10 pm**	11:10 am
☿ ⚺ ♅	**4:49 pm**	1:49 pm
☉ ☌ ☿	**7:11 pm**	4:11 pm

3 SUNDAY

☽ ☌ ♅	**1:47 pm**	10:47 am
☽ ⚺ ☉	**3:43 pm**	12:43 pm
☽ ⚺ ☿	**5:50 pm**	2:50 pm
♀ ⚺ ♇		9:16 pm

4 MONDAY

♀ ⚺ ♇	**12:16 am**	
☽ □ ♂	**7:09 am**	4:09 am
☽ ⚹ ♃	**7:29 am**	4:29 am
☽ □ ♄	**7:58 am**	4:58 am
☽ ⚹ ♆	**10:36 am**	7:36 am
♂ ⚺ ♃	**2:47 pm**	11:47 am
☽ △ ♇	**8:00 pm**	5:00 pm
♂ ☌ ♄	**9:51 pm**	6:51 pm
☽ □ ♀	**9:53 pm**	6:53 pm

5 TUESDAY

♃ ⚺ ♄	**11:24 pm**	8:24 pm
☽ ⚺ ♅		10:25 pm

6 WEDNESDAY

☽ ⚺ ♅	**1:25 am**	
☽ ⚹ ☉	**8:32 am**	5:32 am
♂ ⚺ ♆	**5:34 pm**	2:34 pm
☽ ⚹ ☿	**5:57 pm**	2:57 pm
☽ △ ♄	**8:26 pm**	5:26 pm
☽ □ ♃	**8:42 pm**	5:42 pm
☽ □ ♆	**10:54 pm**	7:54 pm
☽ △ ♂	**11:15 pm**	8:15 pm

7 THURSDAY

☽ ⚻ ♇	**8:25 am**	5:25 am
☿ ⚹ ♄	**8:37 am**	5:37 am
☿ ⚺ ♃	**11:14 am**	8:14 am
☽ △ ♀	**4:20 pm**	1:20 pm
☿ ⚺ ♆	**10:33 pm**	7:33 pm

8 FRIDAY

☿ ⚹ ♂	**2:19 pm**	11:19 am
☽ ⚹ ♅	**2:28 pm**	11:28 am
☽ □ ☉		11:48 pm

9 SATURDAY

☽ □ ☉	**2:48 am**	
☽ ⚻ ♄	**9:35 am**	6:35 am
☽ △ ♃	**10:36 am**	7:36 am
☽ △ ♆	**11:46 am**	8:46 am
☽ ⚻ ♂	**4:01 pm**	1:01 pm
☽ □ ☿	**7:25 pm**	4:25 pm
☽ ☍ ♇	**9:01 pm**	6:01 pm

10 SUNDAY

☿ □ ♇	**4:45 am**	1:45 am
☽ ⚻ ♀	**10:37 am**	7:37 am
☽ □ ♅		11:25 pm

11 MONDAY

☽ □ ♅	**2:25 am**	
☽ △ ☉	**7:01 pm**	4:01 pm
☽ ☍ ♄	**8:50 pm**	5:50 pm
☽ ⚻ ♃	**10:30 pm**	7:30 pm
☽ ⚻ ♆	**10:42 pm**	7:42 pm

12 TUESDAY

☽ ☍ ♂	**6:16 am**	3:16 am
☽ ⚻ ♇	**7:21 am**	4:21 am
♃ ☌ ♆	**10:42 am**	7:42 am
☽ △ ☿	**4:55 pm**	1:55 pm
☉ ⚹ ♄	**8:14 pm**	5:14 pm
♂ ⚺ ♇		9:30 pm
☽ ☍ ♀		10:27 pm

13 WEDNESDAY

♂ ⚺ ♇	**12:30 am**	
☽ ☍ ♀	**1:27 am**	
☽ △ ♅	**11:15 am**	8:15 am
☉ ⚺ ♆	**7:48 pm**	4:48 pm

14 THURSDAY

☉ ⚺ ♃	**4:14 am**	1:14 am
☽ ⚻ ♄	**4:37 am**	1:37 am
☽ ☍ ♆	**6:11 am**	3:11 am
☽ ☍ ♃	**6:49 am**	3:49 am
☽ ⚻ ☉	**6:58 am**	3:58 am
☽ △ ♇	**2:11 pm**	11:11 am
☽ ⚻ ♂	**4:23 pm**	1:23 pm

15 FRIDAY

☽ ⚻ ☿	**8:12 am**	5:12 am
☽ ⚻ ♀	**11:48 am**	8:48 am
☽ ⚻ ♅	**4:37 pm**	1:37 pm

16 SATURDAY

☽ △ ♄	**9:06 am**	6:06 am
☽ ⚻ ♆	**10:26 am**	7:26 am
☽ ⚻ ♃	**11:45 am**	8:45 am
☽ ☍ ☉	**2:55 pm**	11:55 am
☽ □ ♇	**5:57 pm**	2:57 pm
☽ △ ♂	**10:55 pm**	7:55 pm

17 SUNDAY

☽ ☍ ☿	**6:43 pm**	3:43 pm
☽ △ ♀	**6:51 pm**	3:51 pm
☽ ☍ ♅	**7:28 pm**	4:28 pm
☿ ⚹ ♀	**9:09 pm**	6:09 pm
☿ ☌ ♅		9:51 pm

18 MONDAY

☿ ☌ ♅	**12:51 am**	
♀ ⚹ ♅	**3:15 am**	12:15 am
☉ □ ♇	**11:14 am**	8:14 am
☽ □ ♄	**11:31 am**	8:31 am
☽ △ ♆	**12:40 pm**	9:40 am
☽ △ ♃	**2:37 pm**	11:37 am
☽ ⚹ ♇	**7:55 pm**	4:55 pm
☽ ⚻ ☉	**8:32 pm**	5:32 pm

19 TUESDAY

☽ □ ♂	**3:30 am**	12:30 am ☽
⚻ ♅	**9:15pm**	6:15pm
☽ □ ♀		9:33 pm

20 WEDNESDAY

☽ □ ♀	**12:33 am**	
☽ ⚻ ☿	**3:02 am**	12:02 am
☽ ⚹ ♄	**1:18 pm**	10:18 am
☽ □ ♆	**2:20 pm**	11:20 am
☽ □ ♃	**4:56 pm**	1:56 pm
☽ ⚺ ♇	**9:31 pm**	6:31 pm
☽ △ ☉		10:43 pm

21 THURSDAY

☽ △ ☉	**1:43 am**	
☽ ⚹ ♂	**7:53 am**	4:53 am
☽ △ ♅	**11:18 pm**	8:18 pm

22 FRIDAY

☽ ⚹ ♀	**6:43 am**	3:43 am
☽ △ ☿	**11:13 am**	8:13 am
☽ ⚺ ♄	**3:43 pm**	12:43 pm
☽ ⚹ ♆	**4:38 pm**	1:38 pm
☽ ⚹ ♃	**7:58 pm**	4:58 pm
☽ ☌ ♇	**11:53 pm**	8:53 pm

23 SATURDAY

☽ □ ☉	**7:56 am**	4:56 am
☽ ⚺ ♂	**1:24 pm**	10:24 am
☽ □ ♅		11:35 pm

24 SUNDAY

☽ □ ♅	**2:35 am**	
☿ □ ♄	**9:50 am**	6:50 am
☽ ⚺ ♀	**2:33 pm**	11:33 am
☿ ⚹ ♆	**6:37 pm**	3:37 pm
☽ ☌ ♄	**7:33 pm**	4:33 pm
☽ ⚺ ♆	**8:22 pm**	5:22 pm
☽ □ ☿	**8:33 pm**	5:33 pm
☽ ⚺ ♃		9:32 pm

25 MONDAY

☽ ⚺ ♃	**12:32 am**	
☽ ⚺ ♇	**3:46 am**	12:46 am
☽ ⚹ ☉	**4:09 pm**	1:09 pm
☽ ☌ ♂	**8:51 pm**	5:51 pm

26 TUESDAY

☽ ⚹ ♅	**7:39 am**	4:39 am
☽ ☌ ♀		9:50 pm
☿ ⚹ ♃		10:11 pm
☽ ⚺ ♄		10:18 pm
☽ ☌ ♆		11:02 pm

27 WEDNESDAY

☽ ☌ ♀	**12:50 am**	
☿ ⚹ ♃	**1:11 am**	
☽ ⚺ ♄	**1:18 am**	
☽ ☌ ♆	**2:02 am**	
♀ ⚺ ♄	**6:43 am**	3:43 am
☽ ☌ ♃	**7:07 am**	4:07 am
☽ ⚹ ☿	**7:35 am**	4:35 am
☽ ⚹ ♇	**9:36 am**	6:36 am
♀ ☌ ♆	**3:12 pm**	12:12 pm
☽ ⚺ ☉		11:52 pm

28 THURSDAY

☽ ⚺ ☉	**2:52 am**	
☽ ⚺ ♂	**6:45 am**	3:45 am
☿ △ ♇	**8:05 am**	5:05 am
☽ ⚺ ♅	**2:52 pm**	11:52 am

29 FRIDAY

☽ ⚹ ♄	**9:16 am**	6:16 am
☽ ⚺ ♆	**9:53 am**	6:53 am
☽ ⚺ ♀	**1:59 pm**	10:59 am
☽ ⚺ ♃	**4:01 pm**	1:01 pm
☽ □ ♇	**5:38 pm**	2:38 pm
☽ ⚺ ☿	**8:28 pm**	5:28 pm

30 SATURDAY

☽ ☌ ☉	**4:28 pm**	1:28 pm
♀ ☌ ♃	**5:14 pm**	2:14 pm
☽ ⚹ ♂	**7:23 pm**	4:23 pm
☽ ☌ ♅		9:24 pm

Eastern time in bold type
Pacific time in medium type

APRIL 2022

DATE	SID.TIME	SUN	MOON	NODE	MERCURY	VENUS	MARS	JUPITER	SATURN	URANUS	NEPTUNE	PLUTO	CERES	PALLAS	JUNO	VESTA	CHIRON
1 F	12 37 20	11♈14 43	8♈00	23♉06℞	9♈12	25♒05	19♒20	21♓18	22♒02	12♉53	23♓34	28♑24	13♊15	17♈34	22♒47	9♒53	12♈17
2 Sa	12 41 17	12 13 58	21 02	23 01	11 13	26 08	20 05	21 32	22 08	12 56	23 36	28 25	13 35	17 59	23 09	10 20	12 21
3 Su	12 45 13	13 13 10	3♉46	22 57	13 15	27 11	20 50	21 46	22 13	13 00	23 38	28 26	13 56	18 23	23 32	10 46	12 24
4 M	12 49 10	14 12 21	16 14	22 55D	15 18	28 15	21 35	22 00	22 19	13 03	23 41	28 26	14 16	18 48	23 54	11 13	12 28
5 T	12 53 6	15 11 29	28 27	22 55	17 22	29 19	22 21	22 14	22 24	13 06	23 43	28 27	14 37	19 13	24 17	11 39	12 31
6 W	12 57 3	16 10 35	10♊28	22 56	19 27	0♓23	23 06	22 28	22 29	13 09	23 45	28 28	14 58	19 38	24 39	12 06	12 35
7 Th	13 1 0	17 09 39	22 21	22 58	21 31	1 28	23 51	22 42	22 34	13 12	23 47	28 28	15 19	20 03	25 02	12 32	12 38
8 F	13 4 56	18 08 41	4♋11	23 00	23 36	2 32	24 37	22 56	22 39	13 15	23 49	28 29	15 40	20 28	25 24	12 58	12 42
9 Sa	13 8 53	19 07 40	16 02	23 01℞	25 41	3 37	25 22	23 09	22 44	13 19	23 51	28 30	16 02	20 53	25 46	13 24	12 45
10 Su	13 12 49	20 06 37	28 00	23 00	27 45	4 42	26 07	23 23	22 49	13 22	23 53	28 30	16 23	21 18	26 08	13 49	12 49
11 M	13 16 46	21 05 32	10♌08	22 59	29 49	5 48	26 53	23 37	22 54	13 25	23 55	28 31	16 44	21 43	26 30	14 15	12 52
12 T	13 20 42	22 04 25	22 33	22 56	1♉52	6 53	27 38	23 50	22 59	13 28	23 57	28 31	17 06	22 08	26 52	14 40	12 56
13 W	13 24 39	23 03 15	5♍17	22 52	3 53	7 59	28 23	24 04	23 04	13 32	24 00	28 32	17 28	22 34	27 14	15 06	12 59
14 Th	13 28 35	24 02 03	18 22	22 47	5 53	9 04	29 09	24 18	23 08	13 35	24 02	28 32	17 50	22 59	27 36	15 31	13 03
15 F	13 32 32	25 00 49	1♎50	22 43	7 50	10 10	29 54	24 31	23 13	13 38	24 04	28 33	18 12	23 24	27 58	15 56	13 06
16 Sa	13 36 29	25 59 32	15 39	22 39	9 45	11 16	0♓40	24 45	23 18	13 42	24 06	28 33	18 34	23 50	28 20	16 21	13 10
17 Su	13 40 25	26 58 14	29 47	22 36	11 38	12 23	1 25	24 58	23 22	13 45	24 08	28 34	18 56	24 15	28 41	16 46	13 13
18 M	13 44 22	27 56 54	14♏08	22 35D	13 27	13 29	2 10	25 11	23 26	13 48	24 10	28 34	19 18	24 41	29 03	17 10	13 17
19 T	13 48 18	28 55 32	28 37	22 35	15 13	14 36	2 56	25 25	23 31	13 52	24 12	28 34	19 41	25 06	29 24	17 35	13 20
20 W	13 52 15	29 54 08	13♐10	22 35	16 56	15 43	3 41	25 38	23 35	13 55	24 13	28 35	20 03	25 32	29 46	17 59	13 23
21 Th	13 56 11	0♉52 42	27 40	22 37	18 35	16 49	4 26	25 51	23 39	13 58	24 15	28 35	20 26	25 57	0♓07	18 23	13 27
22 F	14 0 8	1 51 15	12♑04	22 38	20 09	17 57	5 12	26 04	23 43	14 02	24 17	28 35	20 48	26 23	0 29	18 47	13 30
23 Sa	14 4 4	2 49 47	26 18	22 39℞	21 40	19 04	5 57	26 17	23 47	14 05	24 19	28 35	21 11	26 49	0 50	19 11	13 34
24 Su	14 8 1	3 48 16	10♒21	22 39	23 06	20 11	6 42	26 30	23 51	14 09	24 21	28 35	21 34	27 15	1 11	19 35	13 37
25 M	14 11 58	4 46 44	24 10	22 38	24 27	21 19	7 28	26 43	23 55	14 12	24 23	28 36	21 57	27 40	1 32	19 58	13 40
26 T	14 15 54	5 45 11	7♓46	22 36	25 44	22 26	8 13	26 56	23 59	14 16	24 25	28 36	22 20	28 06	1 53	20 22	13 44
27 W	14 19 51	6 43 36	21 08	22 34	26 57	23 34	8 59	27 09	24 02	14 19	24 27	28 36	22 43	28 32	2 14	20 45	13 47
28 Th	14 23 47	7 41 59	4♈16	22 32	28 04	24 42	9 44	27 21	24 06	14 22	24 28	28 36	23 06	28 58	2 34	21 08	13 50
29 F	14 27 44	8 40 20	17 10	22 30	29 06	25 50	10 29	27 34	24 10	14 26	24 30	28 36℞	23 30	29 24	2 55	21 31	13 54
30 Sa	14 31 40	9 38 40	29 50	22 29	0♊04	26 58	11 15	27 47	24 13	14 29	24 32	28 36	23 53	29 50	3 16	21 53	13 57

EPHEMERIS CALCULATED FOR 12 MIDNIGHT GREENWICH MEAN TIME. ALL OTHER DATA AND FACING ASPECTARIAN PAGE IN **EASTERN TIME (BOLD)** AND PACIFIC TIME (REGULAR).

MAY 2022

☽ Last Aspect day	ET / hr:mn / PT		asp	☽ Ingress sign	day	ET / hr:mn / PT	
2	**6:13 am**	3:13 am	⚹♀	♊	2	**6:47 am**	3:47 am
4	**4:37 pm**	1:37 pm	□♃	♋	4	**7:05 pm**	4:05 pm
7	**6:26 am**	3:26 am	△♃	♌	7	**7:50 am**	4:50 am
9	**8:39 am**	5:39 am	☍♄	♍	9	**6:53 pm**	3:53 pm
11		9:00 pm	△♇	♎	11		11:34 pm
12	**12:00 am**		△♇	♎	12	**2:34 am**	
14	**4:07 am**	1:07 am	□♇	♏	14	**6:34 am**	3:34 am
16	**5:28 am**	2:28 am	⚹♇	♐	16	**7:50 am**	4:50 am
17	**11:59 pm**	8:59 pm	⚹♄	♑	18	**8:02 am**	5:02 am
20	**8:00 am**	5:00 am	△☉	♒	20	**8:53 am**	5:53 am
22	**3:19 am**	12:19 am	☌♄	♓	22	**11:49 am**	8:49 am
24	**5:33 pm**	2:33 pm	☌♂	♈	24	**5:39 pm**	2:39 pm
26	**11:20 pm**	8:20 pm	□♇	♉	26		11:22 pm
26	**11:20 pm**	8:20 pm	□♇	♉	27	**2:22 am**	
29	**10:11 am**	7:11 am	△♇	♊	29	**1:23 pm**	10:23 am
31	**4:10 pm**	1:10 pm	△♄	♋	31		10:49 pm
31	**4:10 pm**	1:10 pm	△♄	♋	6/1	**1:49 am**	

☽ Phases & Eclipses phase	day	ET / hr:mn / PT	
2nd Quarter	8	**8:21 pm**	5:21 pm
Full Moon	15		9:14 pm
Full Moon	16	**12:14 am**	
⚫	15/16	25° ♏ 18'	
4th Quarter	22	**2:43 pm**	11:43 am
New Moon	30	**7:30 am**	4:30 am

Planet Ingress		day	ET / hr:mn / PT	
♀	♈	2	**12:10 pm**	9:10 am
♃	♈	10	**7:22 pm**	4:22 pm
⚳	♋	15	**3:11 am**	12:11 am
☉	♊	20	**9:23 pm**	6:23 pm
☿	♉	22	**9:15 pm**	6:15 pm
⚶	♓	24	**5:46 am**	2:46 am
♂	♈	24	**7:17 pm**	4:17 pm
♀	♉	28	**10:46 am**	7:46 am

Planetary Motion		day	ET / hr:mn / PT	
☿	℞	10	**7:47 am**	4:47 am

1 SUNDAY
☽☌♅ **12:24 am**
♀⚹♇ **6:37 am** 3:37 am
☽□♄ **7:33 pm** 4:33 pm
☽⚹♆ **8:04 pm** 5:04 pm

2 MONDAY
☽⚹♃ **3:19 am** 12:19 am
☽△♇ **4:00 am** 1:00 am
☽⚹♀ **6:13 am** 3:13 am
☽☌☿ **11:05 am** 8:05 am

3 TUESDAY
☽⚺☉ **8:54 am** 5:54 am
☽□♂ **10:41 am** 7:41 am
☽⚺♅ **12:10 pm** 9:10 am
♃⚹♇ **6:33 pm** 3:33 pm

4 WEDNESDAY
☽△♄ **7:51 am** 4:51 am
☽□♆ **8:16 am** 5:16 am
♂⚹♅ **11:47 am** 8:47 am
☽⚻♇ **4:14 pm** 1:14 pm
☽□♃ **4:37 pm** 1:37 pm
☽□♀ 9:57 pm
☽⚺☿ 11:33 pm

5 THURSDAY
☽□♀ **12:57 am**
☽⚺☿ **2:33 am**
☉☌♅ **3:22 am** 12:22 am

☽⚹♅ 10:13 pm
☿⚹♀ 11:01 pm

6 FRIDAY
☽⚹♅ **1:13 am**
☿⚹♀ **2:01 am**
☽⚹☉ **3:03 am** 12:03 am
☽△♂ **3:34 am** 12:34 am
☽⚻♄ **8:55 pm** 5:55 pm
☽△♆ **9:13 pm** 6:13 pm

7 SATURDAY
☽☍♇ **4:59 am** 1:59 am
☉⚹♂ **5:48 am** 2:48 am
☽△♃ **6:26 am** 3:26 am
☽⚹☿ **4:59 pm** 1:59 pm
☽△♀ **8:02 pm** 5:02 pm

8 SUNDAY
☽□♅ **1:41 pm** 10:41 am
☽⚻♂ **7:38 pm** 4:38 pm
☽□☉ **8:21 pm** 5:21 pm

9 MONDAY
☽☍♄ **8:39 am** 5:39 am
☽⚻♆ **8:50 am** 5:50 am
☽⚻♇ **4:09 pm** 1:09 pm
☽⚻♃ **6:30 pm** 3:30 pm

10 TUESDAY
☽□☿ **4:10 am** 1:10 am
☽⚻♀ **12:19 pm** 9:19 am
☽△♅ **11:27 pm** 8:27 pm

11 WEDNESDAY
☽☍♂ **8:17 am** 5:17 am
☽△☉ **10:02 am** 7:02 am
☽⚻♄ **5:10 pm** 2:10 pm
☽☍♆ **5:17 pm** 2:17 pm
☽△♇ 9:00 pm

12 THURSDAY
☽△♇ **12:00 am**
☽☍♃ **3:02 am** 12:02 am
☽△☿ **10:54 am** 7:54 am
☽☍♀ **11:49 pm** 8:49 pm

13 FRIDAY
☽⚻♅ **5:27 am** 2:27 am
☽⚻♂ **4:28 pm** 1:28 pm
☽⚻☉ **7:00 pm** 4:00 pm
☽△♄ **9:54 pm** 6:54 pm
☽⚻♆ **9:57 pm** 6:57 pm

14 SATURDAY
☽□♇ **4:07 am** 1:07 am
☽⚻♃ **7:42 am** 4:42 am
☽⚻☿ **1:31 pm** 10:31 am

15 SUNDAY
☽⚻♀ **6:55 am** 3:55 am
☽☍♅ **8:04 am** 5:04 am
☉□♄ **2:49 pm** 11:49 am
☉⚹♆ **3:15 pm** 12:15 pm
☽△♂ **9:02 pm** 6:02 pm
♀⚺♅ **10:14 pm** 7:14 pm

☽□♄ **11:38 pm** 8:38 pm
☽△♆ **11:40 pm** 8:40 pm
☽☍☉ 9:14 pm

16 MONDAY
☽☍☉ **12:14 am**
☽⚹♇ **5:28 am** 2:28 am
☽△♃ **9:34 am** 6:34 am
☽☍☿ **1:19 pm** 10:19 am

17 TUESDAY
☽⚻♅ **8:46 am** 5:46 am
☽△♀ **11:31 am** 8:31 am
♄⚺♆ **11:39 am** 8:39 am
☽□♂ **11:51 pm** 8:51 pm
☽□♆ **11:59 pm** 8:59 pm
☽⚹♄ **11:59 pm** 8:59 pm
♂☌♆ 11:33 pm
♂⚺♄ 11:43 pm

18 WEDNESDAY
♂☌♆ **2:33 am**
♂⚺♄ **2:43 am**
☽⚻☉ **3:48 am** 12:48 am
☽⚺♇ **5:39 am** 2:39 am
☽□♃ **10:21 am** 7:21 am
☽⚻☿ **12:00 pm** 9:00 am

19 THURSDAY
☉△♇ **8:11 am** 5:11 am
☽△♅ **9:16 am** 6:16 am
☽□♀ **4:02 pm** 1:02 pm
☿⚹♃ **9:33 pm** 6:33 pm
☽⚹♆ 9:41 pm
☽⚺♄ 9:43 pm

20 FRIDAY
☽⚹♆ **12:41 am**
☽⚺♄ **12:43 am**
☽⚹♂ **3:07 am** 12:07 am
☽☌♇ **6:24 am** 3:24 am
☽△☉ **8:00 am** 5:00 am
☽△☿ **11:11 am** 8:11 am
☽⚹♃ **11:54 am** 8:54 am

21 SATURDAY
☽□♅ **11:16 am** 8:16 am
☉☌☿ **3:18 pm** 12:18 pm
☽⚹♀ **10:40 pm** 7:40 pm

22 SUNDAY
☽⚺♆ **3:17 am** 12:17 am
☽☌♄ **3:19 am** 12:19 am
☽⚺♂ **8:39 am** 5:39 am
☽⚺♇ **9:11 am** 6:11 am
☽□☿ **12:12 pm** 9:12 am
☽□☉ **2:43 pm** 11:43 am
☽⚺♃ **3:40 pm** 12:40 pm
♂⚹♇ **6:15 pm** 3:15 pm

23 MONDAY
☉⚹♃ **7:05 am** 4:05 am
☽⚹♅ **3:54 pm** 12:54 pm
☿⚹♂ **11:27 pm** 8:27 pm

24 TUESDAY
♀⚺♆ **6:30 am** 3:30 am
♀⚹♄ **7:06 am** 4:06 am
☽☌♆ **8:41 am** 5:41 am
☽⚺♄ **8:45 am** 5:45 am

☽⚺♀ **8:54 am** 5:54 am
☽⚹♇ **2:49 pm** 11:49 am
☽⚹☿ **3:50 pm** 12:50 pm
☽☌♂ **5:33 pm** 2:33 pm
☽☌♃ **10:27 pm** 7:27 pm
☽⚹☉ 10:03 pm

25 WEDNESDAY
☽⚹☉ **1:03 am**
☿△♇ **5:49 pm** 2:49 pm
☽⚺♅ **11:33 pm** 8:33 pm

26 THURSDAY
☽⚺♆ **5:03 pm** 2:03 pm
☽⚹♄ **5:06 pm** 2:06 pm
☿⚺♀ **5:07 pm** 2:07 pm
☽⚺☿ **10:16 pm** 7:16 pm
☽☌♀ **11:00 pm** 8:00 pm
☽□♇ **11:20 pm** 8:20 pm
♀□♇ 11:29 pm

27 FRIDAY
♀□♇ **2:29 am**
☽⚺♂ **5:54 am** 2:54 am
☽⚺♃ **8:12 am** 5:12 am
☽⚺☉ **2:56 pm** 11:56 am

28 SATURDAY
☽☌♅ **9:50 am** 6:50 am

29 SUNDAY
☽⚹♆ **3:49 am** 12:49 am
☽□♄ **3:51 am** 12:51 am
♂☌♃ **6:31 am** 3:31 am
☽☌☿ **7:15 am** 4:15 am

☽△♇ **10:11 am** 7:11 am
☽⚺♀ **4:15 pm** 1:15 pm
☽⚹♃ **8:12 pm** 5:12 pm
☽⚹♂ **8:55 pm** 5:55 pm

30 MONDAY
☽☌☉ **7:30 am** 4:30 am
☽⚺♅ **10:00 pm** 7:00 pm

31 TUESDAY
♀⚺♃ **2:34 pm** 11:34 am
☽□♆ **4:10 pm** 1:10 pm
☽△♄ **4:10 pm** 1:10 pm
♄⚺♆ **6:03 pm** 3:03 pm
☽⚺☿ **6:19 pm** 3:19 pm
☽⚻♇ **10:30 pm** 7:30 pm

Eastern time in bold type
Pacific time in medium type

MAY 2022

DATE	SID.TIME	SUN	MOON	NODE	MERCURY	VENUS	MARS	JUPITER	SATURN	URANUS	NEPTUNE	PLUTO	CERES	PALLAS	JUNO	VESTA	CHIRON
1 Su	14 35 37	10♉36 58	12♉18	22♉28D	0♊56	28♓06	12♓00	27♓59	24♒16	14♉33	24♓34	28♑36℞	24♊16	0♉17	3♓36	22♒16	14♈00
2 M	14 39 33	11 35 14	24 33	22 28	1 43	29 14	12 45	28 12	24 20	14 36	24 35	28 36	24 40	0 43	3 57	22 38	14 03
3 T	14 43 30	12 33 29	6♊38	22 28	2 25	0♈22	13 30	28 24	24 23	14 40	24 37	28 36	25 04	1 09	4 17	23 00	14 06
4 W	14 47 27	13 31 42	18 36	22 29	3 02	1 31	14 16	28 36	24 26	14 43	24 39	28 36	25 27	1 35	4 37	23 22	14 10
5 Th	14 51 23	14 29 52	0♋27	22 30	3 33	2 39	15 01	28 49	24 29	14 47	24 40	28 36	25 51	2 01	4 57	23 43	14 13
6 F	14 55 20	15 28 01	12 16	22 30	3 59	3 48	15 46	29 01	24 32	14 50	24 42	28 35	26 15	2 28	5 17	24 05	14 16
7 Sa	14 59 16	16 26 09	24 08	22 31	4 20	4 57	16 31	29 13	24 35	14 54	24 43	28 35	26 39	2 54	5 37	24 26	14 19
8 Su	15 3 13	17 24 14	6♌05	22 31	4 36	6 05	17 17	29 25	24 37	14 57	24 45	28 35	27 03	3 21	5 57	24 47	14 22
9 M	15 7 9	18 22 17	18 12	22 32℞	4 46	7 14	18 02	29 37	24 40	15 01	24 47	28 35	27 27	3 47	6 16	25 08	14 25
10 T	15 11 6	19 20 18	0♍35	22 32	4 51℞	8 23	18 47	29 49	24 42	15 04	24 48	28 34	27 51	4 14	6 36	25 29	14 28
11 W	15 15 2	20 18 17	13 17	22 31	4 51	9 32	19 32	0♈00	24 45	15 07	24 50	28 34	28 15	4 40	6 55	25 49	14 31
12 Th	15 18 59	21 16 15	26 21	22 31	4 46	10 41	20 17	0 12	24 47	15 11	24 51	28 34	28 40	5 07	7 14	26 09	14 34
13 F	15 22 56	22 14 11	9♎50	22 31D	4 36	11 51	21 02	0 24	24 49	15 14	24 52	28 33	29 04	5 33	7 33	26 29	14 37
14 Sa	15 26 52	23 12 04	23 45	22 31	4 22	13 00	21 47	0 35	24 52	15 18	24 54	28 33	29 28	6 00	7 52	26 49	14 40
15 Su	15 30 49	24 09 57	8♏03	22 31℞	4 04	14 09	22 32	0 46	24 54	15 21	24 55	28 33	29 53	6 27	8 11	27 08	14 43
16 M	15 34 45	25 07 47	22 41	22 31	3 42	15 19	23 17	0 58	24 56	15 25	24 57	28 32	0♋17	6 53	8 30	27 28	14 46
17 T	15 38 42	26 05 37	7♐33	22 31	3 16	16 28	24 02	1 09	24 58	15 28	24 58	28 32	0 42	7 20	8 49	27 47	14 49
18 W	15 42 38	27 03 25	22 30	22 31	2 48	17 38	24 47	1 20	24 59	15 31	24 59	28 31	1 06	7 47	9 07	28 06	14 51
19 Th	15 46 35	28 01 12	7♑26	22 30	2 17	18 47	25 32	1 31	25 01	15 35	25 01	28 31	1 31	8 14	9 25	28 24	14 54
20 F	15 50 31	28 58 57	22 11	22 30	1 45	19 57	26 17	1 42	25 03	15 38	25 02	28 30	1 56	8 41	9 44	28 42	14 57
21 Sa	15 54 28	29 56 41	6♒41	22 29	1 11	21 07	27 02	1 53	25 04	15 42	25 03	28 30	2 21	9 08	10 02	29 00	15 00
22 Su	15 58 25	0♊54 25	20 51	22 29D	0 36	22 16	27 47	2 03	25 06	15 45	25 04	28 29	2 45	9 35	10 20	29 18	15 02
23 M	16 2 21	1 52 07	4♓40	22 29	0 02	23 26	28 32	2 14	25 07	15 48	25 05	28 28	3 10	10 02	10 37	29 36	15 05
24 T	16 6 18	2 49 48	18 08	22 29	29♉28	24 36	29 17	2 24	25 08	15 52	25 06	28 28	3 35	10 29	10 55	29 53	15 08
25 W	16 10 14	3 47 28	1♈16	22 30	28 55	25 46	0♈01	2 35	25 09	15 55	25 08	28 27	4 00	10 56	11 13	0♓10	15 10
26 Th	16 14 11	4 45 07	14 07	22 31	28 24	26 56	0 46	2 45	25 10	15 58	25 09	28 26	4 25	11 23	11 30	0 27	15 13
27 F	16 18 7	5 42 45	26 42	22 32	27 55	28 07	1 31	2 55	25 11	16 02	25 10	28 26	4 51	11 50	11 47	0 43	15 15
28 Sa	16 22 4	6 40 22	9♉04	22 33	27 28	29 17	2 15	3 05	25 12	16 05	25 11	28 25	5 16	12 18	12 04	0 59	15 18
29 Su	16 26 0	7 37 58	21 16	22 33℞	27 05	0♉27	3 00	3 15	25 13	16 08	25 12	28 24	5 41	12 45	12 21	1 15	15 20
30 M	16 29 57	8 35 33	3♊19	22 33	26 45	1 37	3 45	3 25	25 13	16 12	25 13	28 23	6 06	13 12	12 37	1 31	15 23
31 T	16 33 54	9 33 07	15 16	22 32	26 29	2 48	4 29	3 35	25 14	16 15	25 14	28 23	6 32	13 39	12 54	1 46	15 25

EPHEMERIS CALCULATED FOR 12 MIDNIGHT GREENWICH MEAN TIME. ALL OTHER DATA AND FACING ASPECTARIAN PAGE IN **EASTERN TIME (BOLD)** AND PACIFIC TIME (REGULAR).

JUNE 2022

☽ Last Aspect day	ET / hr:mn / PT		asp	☽ Ingress sign	day	ET / hr:mn / PT	
3	**11:15 am**	8:15 am	☍♇	♌	3	**2:38 pm**	11:38 am
5	**7:12 pm**	4:12 pm	□☿	♍	5		11:22 pm
5	**7:12 pm**	4:12 pm	□☿	♍	6	**2:22 am**	
8	**8:09 am**	5:09 am	△♇	♎	8	**11:23 am**	8:23 am
10	**1:36 pm**	10:36 am	□♇	♏	10	**4:41 pm**	1:41 pm
12	**5:40 pm**	2:40 pm	☍☿	♐	12	**6:31 pm**	3:31 pm
14	**10:58 am**	7:58 am	□♆	♑	14	**6:14 pm**	3:14 pm
16	**2:41 pm**	11:41 am	☌♇	♒	16	**5:44 pm**	2:44 pm
18	**2:50 pm**	11:50 am	△☉	♓	18	**7:01 pm**	4:01 pm
20	**11:11 pm**	8:11 pm	□☉	♈	20	**11:37 pm**	8:37 pm
23	**4:02 am**	1:02 am	□♇	♉	23	**7:58 am**	4:58 am
25	**3:02 pm**	12:02 pm	△♇	♊	25	**7:13 pm**	4:13 pm
27	**10:38 pm**	7:38 pm	□♆	♋	28	**7:53 am**	4:53 am
30	**4:14 pm**	1:14 pm	☍♇	♌	30	**8:40 pm**	5:40 pm

☽ Phases & Eclipses phase	day	ET / hr:mn / PT	
2nd Quarter	7	**10:48 am**	7:48 am
Full Moon	14	**7:52 am**	4:52 am
4th Quarter	20	**11:11 pm**	8:11 pm
New Moon	28	**10:52 pm**	7:52 pm

Planet Ingress		day	ET / hr:mn / PT	
☿	♊	13	**11:27 am**	8:27 am
☉	♋	21	**5:14 am**	2:14 am
♀	♊	22	**8:34 pm**	5:34 pm

Planetary Motion		day	ET / hr:mn / PT	
☿	D	3	**4:00 am**	1:00 am
♄	℞	4	**5:47 pm**	2:47 pm
♆	℞	28	**3:55 am**	12:55 am

1 WEDNESDAY
☽□♃ **9:35 am** 6:35 am
☽⚹♀ **11:24 am** 8:24 am
☽□♂ **1:31 pm** 10:31 am
☽⚺☉ 10:33 pm

2 THURSDAY
☽⚺☉ **1:33 am**
☽⚹♅ **11:05 am** 8:05 am

3 FRIDAY
☽⚻♄ **5:02 am** 2:02 am
☽△♆ **5:05 am** 2:05 am
☽⚹☿ **6:44 am** 3:44 am
☽☍♇ **11:15 am** 8:15 am
♀⚺♂ **5:18 pm** 2:18 pm
☽△♃ **11:09 pm** 8:09 pm

4 SATURDAY
☽△♂ **6:15 am** 3:15 am
☽□♀ **6:47 am** 3:47 am
☽⚹☉ **7:23 pm** 4:23 pm
☽□♅ **11:47 pm** 8:47 pm

5 SUNDAY
☽☍♄ **5:03 pm** 2:03 pm
☽⚻♆ **5:10 pm** 2:10 pm
☽□☿ **7:12 pm** 4:12 pm
☽⚻♇ **11:01 pm** 8:01 pm

6 MONDAY
☽⚻♃ **11:19 am** 8:19 am
☽⚻♂ **9:09 pm** 6:09 pm
☽△♀ 9:05 pm

7 TUESDAY
☽△♀ **12:05 am**
☉⚺♅ **5:36 am** 2:36 am
☽△♅ **10:26 am** 7:26 am
☽□☉ **10:48 am** 7:48 am
☽⚻♄ 11:34 pm
☽☍♆ 11:44 pm

8 WEDNESDAY
☽⚻♄ **2:34 am**
☽☍♆ **2:44 am**
☽△☿ **5:56 am** 2:56 am
☽△♇ **8:09 am** 5:09 am
☽☍♃ **8:26 pm** 5:26 pm

9 THURSDAY
☽☍♂ **8:16 am** 5:16 am
☽⚻♀ **1:08 pm** 10:08 am
☽⚻♅ **5:39 pm** 2:39 pm
☽△☉ **9:57 pm** 6:57 pm

10 FRIDAY
☽△♄ **8:27 am** 5:27 am
☽⚻♆ **8:41 am** 5:41 am
☽⚻☿ **1:27 pm** 10:27 am
☽□♇ **1:36 pm** 10:36 am
☿△♇ **5:21 pm** 2:21 pm
☽⚻♃ 10:38 pm

11 SATURDAY
☽⚻♃ **1:38 am**
☽⚻♂ **2:55 pm** 11:55 am
♀☌♅ **6:58 pm** 3:58 pm
☽☍♅ **9:05 pm** 6:05 pm
☽☍♀ **9:16 pm** 6:16 pm

12 SUNDAY
☽⚻☉ **4:29 am** 1:29 am
☽□♄ **10:45 am** 7:45 am
☽△♆ **11:01 am** 8:01 am
☽⚹♇ **3:34 pm** 12:34 pm
☽☍☿ **5:40 pm** 2:40 pm

13 MONDAY
☽△♃ **3:26 am** 12:26 am
☽△♂ **6:05 pm** 3:05 pm
☽⚻♅ **9:40 pm** 6:40 pm
☽⚻♀ 10:47 pm

14 TUESDAY
☽⚻♀ **1:47 am**
☽☍☉ **7:52 am** 4:52 am
☽⚹♄ **10:38 am** 7:38 am
☽□♆ **10:58 am** 7:58 am
☽⚺♇ **3:18 pm** 12:18 pm
☽⚻☿ **7:55 pm** 4:55 pm

15 WEDNESDAY
☽□♃ **3:21 am** 12:21 am
☽□♂ **7:50 pm** 4:50 pm
☽△♅ **9:10 pm** 6:10 pm

16 THURSDAY
☉△♄ **3:13 am** 12:13 am
☽△♀ **5:09 am** 2:09 am
☉□♆ **9:41 am** 6:41 am
☽⚺♄ **9:58 am** 6:58 am
☽⚹♆ **10:23 am** 7:23 am
☽⚻☉ **10:26 am** 7:26 am
☽☌♇ **2:41 pm** 11:41 am
☽△☿ **10:30 pm** 7:30 pm
♂⚺♅ 10:37 pm

17 FRIDAY
♂⚺♅ **1:37 am**
☽⚹♃ **3:28 am** 12:28 am
☽□♅ **9:37 pm** 6:37 pm
☽⚹♂ **10:35 pm** 7:35 pm

18 SATURDAY
☽□♀ **10:10 am** 7:10 am
☽☌♄ **10:47 am** 7:47 am
☽⚺♆ **11:19 am** 8:19 am
☽△☉ **2:50 pm** 11:50 am
☽⚺♇ **3:45 pm** 12:45 pm
♀□♄ **5:32 pm** 2:32 pm
♀⚹♆ 9:06 pm

19 SUNDAY
♀⚹♆ **12:06 am**
☽□☿ **4:01 am** 1:01 am
☉⚻♇ **4:10 am** 1:10 am
☽⚺♃ **5:45 am** 2:45 am
☽⚹♅ 9:50 pm

20 MONDAY
☽⚹♅ **12:50 am**
☿⚹♃ **3:44 am** 12:44 am
☽⚺♂ **4:35 am** 1:35 am
☽⚺♄ **2:41 pm** 11:41 am
☽☌♆ **3:21 pm** 12:21 pm
☽⚹♀ **7:11 pm** 4:11 pm
☽⚹♇ **8:01 pm** 5:01 pm
☽□☉ **11:11 pm** 8:11 pm

21 TUESDAY
♀△♇ **4:23 am** 1:23 am
☽☌♃ **11:37 am** 8:37 am
☽⚹☿ **2:34 pm** 11:34 am

22 WEDNESDAY
☽⚺♅ **7:50 am** 4:50 am
☽☌♂ **2:58 pm** 11:58 am
☽⚹♄ **10:19 pm** 7:19 pm
☽⚺♆ **11:10 pm** 8:10 pm

23 THURSDAY
☽□♇ **4:02 am** 1:02 am
☽⚺♀ **9:10 am** 6:10 am
☽⚹☉ **12:12 pm** 9:12 am
☽⚺♃ **9:13 pm** 6:13 pm

24 FRIDAY
☽⚺☿ **6:48 am** 3:48 am
☽☌♅ **6:15 pm** 3:15 pm

25 SATURDAY
☽⚺♂ **5:14 am** 2:14 am
☽□♄ **9:02 am** 6:02 am
☽⚹♆ **10:05 am** 7:05 am
☽△♇ **3:02 pm** 12:02 pm

26 SUNDAY
☽☌♀ **3:03 am** 12:03 am
☽⚺☉ **4:47 am** 1:47 am
☽⚹♃ **9:27 am** 6:27 am

27 MONDAY
☽☌☿ **3:22 am** 12:22 am
☽⚺♅ **6:44 am** 3:44 am
♂⚹♄ **6:29 pm** 3:29 pm
☽△♄ **9:23 pm** 6:23 pm
☽⚹♂ **9:35 pm** 6:35 pm
☽□♆ **10:38 pm** 7:38 pm

28 TUESDAY
☽⚻♇ **3:33 am** 12:33 am
☿⚺♅ **5:02 am** 2:02 am
♂⚺♆ **3:08 pm** 12:08 pm
☉□♃ **8:59 pm** 5:59 pm
☽⚺♀ **10:37 pm** 7:37 pm
☽□♃ **10:44 pm** 7:44 pm
☽☌☉ **10:52 pm** 7:52 pm
♀⚹♃ **11:52 pm** 8:52 pm

29 WEDNESDAY
☉⚺♀ **10:09 am** 7:09 am
☽⚹♅ **7:48 pm** 4:48 pm
☽⚺☿ 11:00 pm

30 THURSDAY
☽⚺☿ **2:00 am**
☽⚻♄ **10:01 am** 7:01 am
☽△♆ **11:28 am** 8:28 am
☽□♂ **2:17 pm** 11:17 am
☽☍♇ **4:14 pm** 1:14 pm

Eastern time in bold type
Pacific time in medium type

JUNE 2022

DATE	SID.TIME	SUN	MOON	NODE	MERCURY	VENUS	MARS	JUPITER	SATURN	URANUS	NEPTUNE	PLUTO	CERES	PALLAS	JUNO	VESTA	CHIRON
1 W	16 37 50	10♊30 40	27♊08	22♉30℞	26♉17℞	3♉58	5♈14	3♈44	25♒14	16♉18	25♓14	28♑22℞	6♋57	14♉07	13♓10	2♓01	15♈27
2 Th	16 41 47	11 28 12	8♋58	22 27	26 09	5 09	5 58	3 54	25 15	16 21	25 15	28 21	7 22	14 34	13 26	2 16	15 30
3 F	16 45 43	12 25 43	20 47	22 24	26 05D	6 19	6 42	4 03	25 15	16 25	25 16	28 20	7 48	15 02	13 42	2 30	15 32
4 Sa	16 49 40	13 23 12	2♌40	22 20	26 06	7 30	7 27	4 12	25 15℞	16 28	25 17	28 19	8 13	15 29	13 58	2 44	15 34
5 Su	16 53 36	14 20 40	14 38	22 18	26 11	8 40	8 11	4 21	25 15	16 31	25 18	28 18	8 39	15 57	14 13	2 58	15 36
6 M	16 57 33	15 18 07	26 45	22 15	26 21	9 51	8 55	4 30	25 15	16 34	25 18	28 17	9 04	16 24	14 29	3 11	15 38
7 T	17 1 29	16 15 33	9♍06	22 14D	26 35	11 01	9 39	4 39	25 15	16 37	25 19	28 16	9 30	16 52	14 44	3 24	15 40
8 W	17 5 26	17 12 58	21 44	22 14	26 54	12 12	10 23	4 48	25 15	16 40	25 20	28 15	9 56	17 19	14 59	3 37	15 42
9 Th	17 9 23	18 10 21	4♎43	22 15	27 17	13 23	11 07	4 57	25 14	16 43	25 20	28 14	10 21	17 47	15 14	3 49	15 44
10 F	17 13 19	19 07 43	18 06	22 16	27 44	14 34	11 51	5 05	25 14	16 47	25 21	28 13	10 47	18 15	15 28	4 01	15 46
11 Sa	17 17 16	20 05 04	1♏56	22 18	28 16	15 45	12 35	5 13	25 13	16 50	25 22	28 12	11 13	18 42	15 42	4 12	15 48
12 Su	17 21 12	21 02 25	16 13	22 19℞	28 52	16 56	13 19	5 21	25 13	16 53	25 22	28 11	11 39	19 10	15 56	4 24	15 50
13 M	17 25 9	21 59 44	0♐55	22 19	29 32	18 06	14 03	5 29	25 12	16 56	25 23	28 10	12 05	19 38	16 10	4 35	15 52
14 T	17 29 5	22 57 03	15 55	22 17	0♊16	19 17	14 47	5 37	25 11	16 59	25 23	28 09	12 30	20 06	16 24	4 45	15 54
15 W	17 33 2	23 54 21	1♑07	22 14	1 04	20 28	15 31	5 45	25 10	17 01	25 24	28 08	12 56	20 33	16 37	4 55	15 55
16 Th	17 36 59	24 51 38	16 20	22 10	1 56	21 40	16 14	5 53	25 09	17 04	25 24	28 07	13 22	21 01	16 51	5 05	15 57
17 F	17 40 55	25 48 55	1♒25	22 05	2 52	22 51	16 58	6 00	25 08	17 07	25 24	28 06	13 48	21 29	17 04	5 14	15 59
18 Sa	17 44 52	26 46 12	16 12	22 01	3 52	24 02	17 41	6 08	25 07	17 10	25 25	28 05	14 14	21 57	17 16	5 24	16 00
19 Su	17 48 48	27 43 28	0♓35	21 57	4 55	25 13	18 25	6 15	25 06	17 13	25 25	28 03	14 40	22 25	17 29	5 32	16 02
20 M	17 52 45	28 40 43	14 31	21 55	6 02	26 24	19 08	6 22	25 04	17 16	25 25	28 02	15 06	22 53	17 41	5 40	16 04
21 T	17 56 41	29 37 59	28 00	21 54D	7 12	27 36	19 51	6 29	25 03	17 19	25 26	28 01	15 33	23 21	17 53	5 48	16 05
22 W	18 0 38	0♋35 14	11♈04	21 54	8 26	28 47	20 35	6 35	25 01	17 21	25 26	28 00	15 59	23 49	18 05	5 56	16 06
23 Th	18 4 34	1 32 29	23 47	21 56	9 44	29 58	21 18	6 42	24 59	17 24	25 26	27 58	16 25	24 17	18 16	6 03	16 08
24 F	18 8 31	2 29 44	6♉11	21 57	11 05	1♊10	22 01	6 48	24 58	17 27	25 26	27 57	16 51	24 45	18 27	6 09	16 09
25 Sa	18 12 28	3 26 59	18 22	21 58℞	12 29	2 21	22 44	6 55	24 56	17 29	25 26	27 56	17 17	25 13	18 38	6 15	16 10
26 Su	18 16 24	4 24 14	0♊23	21 58	13 56	3 33	23 27	7 01	24 54	17 32	25 26	27 55	17 44	25 42	18 49	6 21	16 12
27 M	18 20 21	5 21 29	12 18	21 56	15 27	4 44	24 10	7 07	24 52	17 35	25 27	27 53	18 10	26 10	18 59	6 26	16 13
28 T	18 24 17	6 18 43	24 09	21 52	17 02	5 56	24 53	7 12	24 50	17 37	25 27℞	27 52	18 36	26 38	19 09	6 31	16 14
29 W	18 28 14	7 15 58	5♋58	21 45	18 39	7 07	25 35	7 18	24 47	17 40	25 27	27 51	19 03	27 06	19 19	6 35	16 15
30 Th	18 32 10	8 13 12	17 48	21 38	20 20	8 19	26 18	7 24	24 45	17 42	25 27	27 49	19 29	27 34	19 28	6 39	16 16

EPHEMERIS CALCULATED FOR 12 MIDNIGHT GREENWICH MEAN TIME. ALL OTHER DATA AND FACING ASPECTARIAN PAGE IN **EASTERN TIME (BOLD)** AND PACIFIC TIME (REGULAR).

JULY 2022

☽ Last Aspect day	ET / hr:mn / PT	asp	☽ Ingress sign	day	ET / hr:mn / PT
3	**5:59 am** 2:59 am	△♂	♍	3	**8:31 am** 5:31 am
5	**2:04 pm** 11:04 am	△♇	♎	5	**6:25 pm** 3:25 pm
7	**9:04 pm** 6:04 pm	□♇	♏	7	10:15 pm
7	**9:04 pm** 6:04 pm	□♇	♏	8	**1:15 am**
9	9:34 pm	⚹♇	♐	10	**4:34 am** 1:34 am
10	**12:34 am**	⚹♇	♐	10	**4:34 am** 1:34 am
11	**9:42 pm** 6:42 pm	□♆	♑	12	**5:01 am** 2:01 am
13	9:17 pm	☌♇	♒	14	**4:13 am** 1:13 am
14	**12:17 am**	☌♇	♒	14	**4:13 am** 1:13 am
15	9:36 pm	△♀	♓	16	**4:18 am** 1:18 am
16	**12:36 am**	△♀	♓	16	**4:18 am** 1:18 am
17	11:43 pm	⚹♇	♈	18	**7:17 am** 4:17 am
18	**2:43 am**	⚹♇	♈	18	**7:17 am** 4:17 am
20	**10:19 am** 7:19 am	□☉	♉	20	**2:23 pm** 11:23 am
22	**7:45 pm** 4:45 pm	△♇	♊	22	10:11 pm
22	**7:45 pm** 4:45 pm	△♇	♊	23	**1:11 am**
25	**4:14 am** 1:14 am	□♆	♋	25	**1:54 pm** 10:54 am
27	**8:54 pm** 5:54 pm	☍♇	♌	27	11:36 pm
27	**8:54 pm** 5:54 pm	☍♇	♌	28	**2:36 am**
29	9:29 pm	☍♄	♍	30	**2:11 pm** 11:11 am
30	**12:29 am**	☍♄	♍	30	**2:11 pm** 11:11 am

☽ Phases & Eclipses phase	day	ET / hr:mn / PT
2nd Quarter	6	**10:14 pm** 7:14 pm
Full Moon	13	**2:38 pm** 11:38 am
4th Quarter	20	**10:19 am** 7:19 am
New Moon	28	**1:55 pm** 10:55 am

Planet Ingress		day	ET / hr:mn / PT
♀	♊	4	**11:16 pm** 8:16 pm
♂	♉	4	11:04 pm
♂	♉	5	**2:04 am**
☿	♋	4	11:25 pm
☿	♋	5	**2:25 am**
♀	♋	17	**9:32 pm** 6:32 pm
☿	♌	19	**8:35 am** 5:35 am
☉	♌	22	**4:07 pm** 1:07 pm
⚳	♌	23	**1:29 pm** 10:29 am

Planetary Motion		day	ET / hr:mn / PT
♇	℞	7	**5:30 pm** 2:30 pm
⚷	℞	19	**11:21 am** 8:21 am
⚵	℞	24	11:48 pm
⚵	℞	25	**2:48 am**
♃	℞	28	**4:37 pm** 1:37 pm

1 FRIDAY
☽ △ ♃ **11:49 am** 8:49 am
☽ ⚺ ☉ **4:46 pm** 1:46 pm
☽ ⚹ ♀ **5:59 pm** 2:59 pm
♂ □ ♇ **10:14 pm** 7:14 pm

2 SATURDAY
☿ △ ♄ **6:39 am** 3:39 am
☽ □ ♅ **8:22 am** 5:22 am
☿ □ ♆ **4:53 pm** 1:53 pm
☽ ☍ ♄ **9:55 pm** 6:55 pm
☽ ⚻ ♆ **11:31 pm** 8:31 pm
☽ ⚹ ☿ 9:43 pm

3 SUNDAY
☽ ⚹ ☿ **12:43 am**
☽ ⚻ ♇ **4:05 am** 1:05 am
☽ △ ♂ **5:59 am** 2:59 am
☿ ⚻ ♇ **10:13 pm** 7:13 pm
☽ ⚻ ♃ **11:41 pm** 8:41 pm

4 MONDAY
☽ ⚹ ☉ **9:03 am** 6:03 am
☽ □ ♀ **11:38 am** 8:38 am
☽ △ ♅ **7:23 pm** 4:23 pm
☿ ⚹ ♂ 11:37 pm

5 TUESDAY
☿ ⚹ ♂ **2:37 am**
☽ ⚻ ♄ **8:02 am** 5:02 am
☽ ☍ ♆ **9:46 am** 6:46 am
☽ △ ♇ **2:04 pm** 11:04 am

☽ ⚻ ♂ **7:22 pm** 4:22 pm
☽ □ ☿ **9:20 pm** 6:20 pm

6 WEDNESDAY
☽ ☍ ♃ **9:13 am** 6:13 am
☽ □ ☉ **10:14 pm** 7:14 pm
☽ △ ♀ 10:54 pm

7 THURSDAY
☽ △ ♀ **1:54 am**
☽ ⚻ ♅ **3:43 am** 12:43 am
☽ △ ♄ **3:18 pm** 12:18 pm
☽ ⚻ ♆ **5:06 pm** 2:06 pm
☽ □ ♇ **9:04 pm** 6:04 pm
♀ ⚺ ♅ **10:27 pm** 7:27 pm

8 FRIDAY
☽ ☍ ♂ **5:06 am** 2:06 am
☽ △ ☿ **1:31 pm** 10:31 am
☽ ⚻ ♃ **3:23 pm** 12:23 pm
☿ □ ♃ 11:14 pm

9 SATURDAY
☿ □ ♃ **2:14 am**
☽ △ ☉ **7:10 am** 4:10 am
☽ ☍ ♅ **8:34 am** 5:34 am
☽ ⚻ ♀ **11:38 am** 8:38 am
☽ □ ♄ **7:04 pm** 4:04 pm
☽ △ ♆ **8:56 pm** 5:56 pm
☽ ⚹ ♇ 9:34 pm

10 SUNDAY
☽ ⚹ ♇ **12:34 am**
☉ ⚹ ♅ **4:39 am** 1:39 am
☽ ⚻ ♂ **10:44 am** 7:44 am
☽ △ ♃ **6:02 pm** 3:02 pm
☽ ⚻ ☿ 9:29 pm

11 MONDAY
☽ ⚻ ☿ **12:29 am**
☽ ⚻ ♅ **10:07 am** 7:07 am
☽ ⚻ ☉ **12:03 pm** 9:03 am
☽ ☍ ♀ **5:12 pm** 2:12 pm
☽ ⚹ ♄ **7:48 pm** 4:48 pm
☽ □ ♆ **9:42 pm** 6:42 pm
☽ ⚺ ♇ 10:07 pm

12 TUESDAY
☽ ⚺ ♇ **1:07 am**
☽ △ ♂ **1:12 pm** 10:12 am
☽ □ ♃ **6:07 pm** 3:07 pm
♀ △ ♄ 9:28 pm

13 WEDNESDAY
♀ △ ♄ **12:28 am**
☽ ☍ ☿ **7:59 am** 4:59 am
☽ △ ♅ **9:41 am** 6:41 am
☽ ☍ ☉ **2:38 pm** 11:38 am
☽ ⚺ ♄ **6:55 pm** 3:55 pm
☿ ⚹ ♅ **8:17 pm** 5:17 pm
☽ ⚻ ♀ **8:34 pm** 5:34 pm
☽ ⚹ ♆ **8:57 pm** 5:57 pm
☽ ☌ ♇ 9:17 pm
♀ □ ♆ 10:24 pm

14 THURSDAY
☽ ☌ ♇ **12:17 am**
♀ □ ♆ **1:24 am**
☽ □ ♂ **2:39 pm** 11:39 am
☽ ⚹ ♃ **5:30 pm** 2:30 pm

15 FRIDAY
☽ □ ♅ **9:16 am** 6:16 am
☽ ⚻ ☿ **3:25 pm** 12:25 pm
☽ ⚻ ☉ **5:30 pm** 2:30 pm
☽ ☌ ♄ **6:27 pm** 3:27 pm
♀ ⚻ ♇ **6:51 pm** 3:51 pm
☽ ⚺ ♆ **8:43 pm** 5:43 pm
☽ ⚺ ♇ 9:08 pm
☽ △ ♀ 9:36 pm

16 SATURDAY
☽ ⚺ ♇ **12:08 am**
☽ △ ♀ **12:36 am**
☉ ⚻ ♄ **7:34 am** 4:34 am
☿ ⚻ ♄ **11:55 am** 8:55 am
☉ ☌ ☿ **3:38 pm** 12:38 pm
☽ ⚹ ♂ **5:37 pm** 2:37 pm
☽ ⚺ ♃ **6:21 pm** 3:21 pm

17 SUNDAY
☿ △ ♆ **3:52 am** 12:52 am
♂ ⚺ ♃ **9:58 am** 6:58 am
☽ ⚹ ♅ **11:01 am** 8:01 am
☉ △ ♆ **6:55 pm** 3:55 pm
☽ ⚺ ♄ **8:31 pm** 5:31 pm
☽ ☌ ♆ **11:07 pm** 8:07 pm

☽ △ ☉ **11:26 pm** 8:26 pm
☽ △ ☿ 11:40 pm
☽ ⚹ ♇ 11:43 pm

18 MONDAY
☽ △ ☿ **2:40 am**
☽ ⚹ ♇ **2:43 am**
☿ ☍ ♇ **3:01 am** 12:01 am
☽ □ ♀ **8:15 am** 5:15 am
☽ ☌ ♃ **10:35 pm** 7:35 pm
☽ ⚺ ♂ 9:27 pm

19 TUESDAY
☽ ⚺ ♂ **12:27 am**
☽ ⚺ ♅ **4:35 pm** 1:35 pm
☉ ☍ ♇ **9:39 pm** 6:39 pm
☽ ⚹ ♄ 11:28 pm

20 WEDNESDAY
☽ ⚹ ♄ **2:28 am**
☽ ⚺ ♆ **5:30 am** 2:30 am
☽ □ ♇ **9:20 am** 6:20 am
☽ □ ☉ **10:19 am** 7:19 am
☽ □ ☿ **8:19 pm** 5:19 pm
☽ ⚹ ♀ **9:17 pm** 6:17 pm

21 THURSDAY
☽ ⚺ ♃ **6:58 am** 3:58 am
☿ ⚺ ♀ **9:02 am** 6:02 am
☽ ☌ ♂ **12:06 pm** 9:06 am
☽ ☌ ♅ 11:14 pm

22 FRIDAY
☽ ☌ ♅ **2:14 am**
☽ □ ♄ **12:18 pm** 9:18 am

☽ ⚹ ♆ **3:45 pm** 12:45 pm
☽ △ ♇ **7:45 pm** 4:45 pm
☽ ⚹ ☉ 10:58 pm

23 SATURDAY
☽ ⚹ ☉ **1:58 am**
☿ △ ♃ **1:52 pm** 10:52 am
☽ ⚺ ♀ **3:06 pm** 12:06 pm
☽ ⚹ ♃ **6:38 pm** 3:38 pm
☽ ⚹ ☿ **7:36 pm** 4:36 pm

24 SUNDAY
☽ ⚺ ♂ **3:26 am** 12:26 am
☽ ⚺ ♅ **2:36 pm** 11:36 am
☽ △ ♄ 9:27 pm
♀ □ ♃ 11:13 pm

25 MONDAY
☽ △ ♄ **12:27 am**
♀ □ ♃ **2:13 am**
☽ □ ♆ **4:14 am** 1:14 am
☽ ⚻ ♇ **8:15 am** 5:15 am
☽ ⚺ ☉ **8:02 pm** 5:02 pm

26 TUESDAY
☽ □ ♃ **7:35 am** 4:35 am
☽ ☌ ♀ **10:54 am** 7:54 am
☿ □ ♂ **3:13 pm** 12:13 pm
☽ ⚹ ♂ **7:57 pm** 4:57 pm
☽ ⚺ ☿ **8:33 pm** 5:33 pm

27 WEDNESDAY
☽ ⚹ ♅ **3:36 am** 12:36 am
☽ ⚻ ♄ **12:56 pm** 9:56 am

☽ △ ♆ **4:58 pm** 1:58 pm
☽ ☍ ♇ **8:54 pm** 5:54 pm

28 THURSDAY
☽ ☌ ☉ **1:55 pm** 10:55 am
☿ □ ♅ **5:16 pm** 2:16 pm
☽ △ ♃ **8:03 pm** 5:03 pm

29 FRIDAY
☽ ⚺ ♀ **6:04 am** 3:04 am
☽ □ ♂ **11:38 am** 8:38 am
☽ □ ♅ **3:48 pm** 12:48 pm
☽ ☌ ☿ **7:49 pm** 4:49 pm
☽ ☍ ♄ 9:29 pm

30 SATURDAY
☽ ☍ ♄ **12:29 am**
☽ ⚻ ♆ **4:42 am** 1:42 am
☽ ⚻ ♇ **8:30 am** 5:30 am
☿ ☍ ♄ 11:05 pm

31 SUNDAY
☿ ☍ ♄ **2:05 am**
☽ ⚺ ☉ **6:12 am** 3:12 am
☽ ⚻ ♃ **7:11 am** 4:11 am
☉ △ ♃ **6:36 pm** 3:36 pm
☽ ⚹ ♀ **11:19 pm** 8:19 pm
☽ △ ♂ 10:35 pm
☽ △ ♅ 11:30 pm

Eastern time in bold type
Pacific time in medium type

JULY 2022

DATE	SID.TIME	SUN	MOON	NODE	MERCURY	VENUS	MARS	JUPITER	SATURN	URANUS	NEPTUNE	PLUTO	CERES	PALLAS	JUNO	VESTA	CHIRON
1 F	18 36 7	9♋10 26	29♋40	21♉29℞	22♊04	9♊31	27♈00	7♈29	24♒43℞	17♉45	25♓26℞	27♑48℞	19♋55	28♉03	19♓37	6♓43	16♈17
2 Sa	18 40 3	10 07 39	11♌37	21 20	23 51	10 43	27 43	7 34	24 40	17 47	25 26	27 47	20 22	28 31	19 46	6 46	16 18
3 Su	18 44 0	11 04 53	23 40	21 12	25 41	11 54	28 25	7 39	24 38	17 49	25 26	27 45	20 48	28 59	19 54	6 48	16 19
4 M	18 47 57	12 02 06	5♍51	21 05	27 33	13 06	29 07	7 44	24 35	17 52	25 26	27 44	21 15	29 28	20 03	6 50	16 20
5 T	18 51 53	12 59 19	18 14	21 00	29 29	14 18	29 49	7 48	24 32	17 54	25 26	27 43	21 41	29 56	20 10	6 52	16 20
6 W	18 55 50	13 56 31	0♎51	20 57	1♋27	15 30	0♉31	7 53	24 30	17 56	25 26	27 41	22 08	0♊25	20 18	6 53	16 21
7 Th	18 59 46	14 53 44	13 46	20 56D	3 27	16 42	1 13	7 57	24 27	17 59	25 25	27 40	22 34	0 53	20 25	6 54℞	16 22
8 F	19 3 43	15 50 56	27 03	20 56	5 29	17 54	1 55	8 01	24 24	18 01	25 25	27 39	23 01	1 21	20 32	6 54	16 22
9 Sa	19 7 39	16 48 07	10♏44	20 57℞	7 33	19 06	2 37	8 05	24 21	18 03	25 25	27 37	23 27	1 50	20 38	6 54	16 23
10 Su	19 11 36	17 45 19	24 51	20 57	9 39	20 18	3 18	8 08	24 18	18 05	25 24	27 36	23 54	2 18	20 44	6 53	16 24
11 M	19 15 32	18 42 31	9♐24	20 56	11 46	21 30	4 00	8 12	24 15	18 07	25 24	27 34	24 20	2 47	20 50	6 52	16 24
12 T	19 19 29	19 39 43	24 19	20 53	13 54	22 42	4 41	8 15	24 11	18 09	25 24	27 33	24 47	3 15	20 56	6 50	16 24
13 W	19 23 26	20 36 54	9♑30	20 47	16 03	23 54	5 23	8 18	24 08	18 11	25 23	27 31	25 14	3 44	21 01	6 48	16 25
14 Th	19 27 22	21 34 06	24 47	20 39	18 12	25 06	6 04	8 21	24 05	18 13	25 23	27 30	25 40	4 12	21 05	6 45	16 25
15 F	19 31 19	22 31 19	9♒58	20 30	20 21	26 18	6 45	8 24	24 01	18 15	25 22	27 29	26 07	4 41	21 10	6 42	16 25
16 Sa	19 35 15	23 28 31	24 55	20 21	22 30	27 31	7 26	8 27	23 58	18 17	25 22	27 27	26 33	5 10	21 14	6 38	16 26
17 Su	19 39 12	24 25 44	9♓28	20 13	24 39	28 43	8 07	8 29	23 54	18 19	25 21	27 26	27 00	5 38	21 17	6 34	16 26
18 M	19 43 8	25 22 58	23 33	20 07	26 47	29 55	8 48	8 31	23 51	18 21	25 20	27 24	27 27	6 07	21 20	6 30	16 26
19 T	19 47 5	26 20 12	7♈08	20 04	28 54	1♋08	9 28	8 33	23 47	18 23	25 20	27 23	27 54	6 36	21 23	6 25	16 26℞
20 W	19 51 1	27 17 27	20 15	20 02D	1♌00	2 20	10 09	8 35	23 43	18 24	25 19	27 21	28 20	7 04	21 26	6 19	16 26
21 Th	19 54 58	28 14 43	2♉56	20 02	3 05	3 33	10 49	8 37	23 39	18 26	25 18	27 20	28 47	7 33	21 28	6 13	16 26
22 F	19 58 55	29 11 59	15 18	20 02℞	5 08	4 45	11 29	8 38	23 36	18 28	25 18	27 19	29 14	8 02	21 29	6 07	16 26
23 Sa	20 2 51	0♌09 16	27 25	20 02	7 10	5 58	12 09	8 40	23 32	18 29	25 17	27 17	29 40	8 30	21 30	6 00	16 26
24 Su	20 6 48	1 06 35	9♊21	20 01	9 11	7 10	12 49	8 41	23 28	18 31	25 16	27 16	0♌07	8 59	21 31	5 52	16 26
25 M	20 10 44	2 03 53	21 12	19 57	11 10	8 23	13 29	8 42	23 24	18 32	25 15	27 14	0 34	9 28	21 31℞	5 44	16 25
26 T	20 14 41	3 01 13	3♋00	19 50	13 08	9 36	14 09	8 42	23 20	18 34	25 14	27 13	1 01	9 56	21 31	5 36	16 25
27 W	20 18 37	3 58 34	14 50	19 41	15 04	10 48	14 49	8 43	23 16	18 35	25 14	27 11	1 28	10 25	21 31	5 28	16 25
28 Th	20 22 34	4 55 55	26 43	19 29	16 58	12 01	15 28	8 43℞	23 12	18 36	25 13	27 10	1 54	10 54	21 30	5 18	16 24
29 F	20 26 30	5 53 17	8♌41	19 16	18 50	13 14	16 07	8 43	23 07	18 38	25 12	27 09	2 21	11 23	21 29	5 09	16 24
30 Sa	20 30 27	6 50 40	20 46	19 03	20 41	14 27	16 46	8 43	23 03	18 39	25 11	27 07	2 48	11 51	21 27	4 59	16 23
31 Su	20 34 24	7 48 03	2♍58	18 50	22 30	15 40	17 25	8 43	22 59	18 40	25 10	27 06	3 15	12 20	21 24	4 49	16 23

EPHEMERIS CALCULATED FOR 12 MIDNIGHT GREENWICH MEAN TIME. ALL OTHER DATA AND FACING ASPECTARIAN PAGE IN **EASTERN TIME (BOLD)** AND PACIFIC TIME (REGULAR).

AUGUST 2022

☽ Last Aspect day	ET / hr:mn / PT	asp	☽ Ingress sign day	ET / hr:mn / PT
1	**6:29 pm** 3:29 pm	△♇	♎ 1	9:06 pm
1	**6:29 pm** 3:29 pm	△♇	♎ 2	**12:06 am**
3	11:20 pm	□♇	♏ 4	**7:47 am** 4:47 am
4	**2:20 am**	□♇	♏ 4	**7:47 am** 4:47 am
6	**7:24 am** 4:24 am	⚹♇	♐ 6	**12:39 pm** 9:39 am
8	**6:30 am** 3:30 am	□♆	♑ 8	**2:39 pm** 11:39 am
10	**12:39 pm** 9:39 am	☍♀	♒ 10	**2:45 pm** 11:45 am
12	**7:07 am** 4:07 am	□♂	♓ 12	**2:44 pm** 11:44 am
14	**11:11 am** 8:11 am	⚹♇	♈ 14	**4:43 pm** 1:43 pm
16	**4:18 pm** 1:18 pm	□♇	♉ 16	**10:22 pm** 7:22 pm
19	**7:06 am** 4:06 am	☌♂	♊ 19	**8:06 am** 5:06 am
21	**6:06 pm** 3:06 pm	⚹☉	♋ 21	**8:29 pm** 5:29 pm
24	**5:40 am** 2:40 am	⚹☿	♌ 24	**9:09 am** 6:09 am
25	11:55 pm	☍♄	♍ 26	**8:25 pm** 5:25 pm
26	**2:55 am**	☍♄	♍ 26	**8:25 pm** 5:25 pm
28	**11:08 pm** 8:08 pm	△♇	♎ 29	**5:45 am** 2:45 am
31	**6:43 am** 3:43 am	□♇	♏ 31	**1:11 pm** 10:11 am

☽ Phases & Eclipses phase	day	ET / hr:mn / PT
2nd Quarter	5	**7:07 am** 4:07 am
Full Moon	11	**9:36 pm** 6:36 pm
4th Quarter	18	9:36 pm
4th Quarter	19	**12:36 am**
New Moon	27	**4:17 am** 1:17 am

Planet Ingress	day	ET / hr:mn / PT
☿ ♍	3	11:58 pm
☿ ♍	4	**2:58 am**
♀ ♌	11	**2:30 pm** 11:30 am
♂ ♊	20	**3:56 am** 12:56 am
⚶ ♒	21	**6:33 am** 3:33 am
☉ ♍	22	**11:16 pm** 8:16 pm
☿ ♎	25	**9:03 pm** 6:03 pm

Planetary Motion	day	ET / hr:mn / PT
♅ ℞	24	**9:54 am** 6:54 am

1 MONDAY
☽ △ ♂ **1:35 am**
☽ △ ♅ **2:30 am**
☿ ⚻ ♆ **7:23 am** 4:23 am
☽ ⚻ ♄ **10:30 am** 7:30 am
☽ ☍ ♆ **2:50 pm** 11:50 am
☽ ⚺ ☿ **4:03 pm** 1:03 pm
☽ △ ♇ **6:29 pm** 3:29 pm
♂ ☌ ♅ **7:53 pm** 4:53 pm

2 TUESDAY
♀ ⚹ ♅ **8:25 am** 5:25 am
☿ ⚻ ♇ **9:24 am** 6:24 am
☽ ☍ ♃ **4:27 pm** 1:27 pm
☽ ⚹ ☉ **8:12 pm** 5:12 pm
♀ ⚹ ♂ **10:00 pm** 7:00 pm

3 WEDNESDAY
☽ ⚻ ♅ **11:11 am** 8:11 am
☽ ⚻ ♂ **1:10 pm** 10:10 am
☽ □ ♀ **1:54 pm** 10:54 am
☽ △ ♄ **6:28 pm** 3:28 pm
☽ ⚻ ♆ **10:51 pm** 7:51 pm
☽ □ ♇ 11:20 pm

4 THURSDAY
☽ □ ♇ **2:20 am**
☽ ⚹ ☿ **8:29 am** 5:29 am
☽ ⚻ ♃ **11:18 pm** 8:18 pm

5 FRIDAY
☽ □ ☉ **7:07 am** 4:07 am
♀ ⚻ ♄ **12:23 pm** 9:23 am
☽ ☍ ♅ **5:13 pm** 2:13 pm
☽ ☍ ♂ **9:38 pm** 6:38 pm
☽ □ ♄ **11:46 pm** 8:46 pm
☽ △ ♀ 9:56 pm

6 SATURDAY
☽ △ ♀ **12:56 am**
☽ △ ♆ **4:08 am** 1:08 am
☽ ⚹ ♇ **7:24 am** 4:24 am
☽ □ ☿ **8:18 pm** 5:18 pm

7 SUNDAY
☽ △ ♃ **3:12 am** 12:12 am
♀ △ ♆ **12:43 pm** 9:43 am
☽ △ ☉ **2:21 pm** 11:21 am
♂ □ ♄ **3:57 pm** 12:57 pm
☽ ⚻ ♅ **8:17 pm** 5:17 pm
☽ ⚹ ♄ 11:11 pm
☽ ⚻ ♂ 11:42 pm

8 MONDAY
☽ ⚹ ♄ **2:11 am**
☽ ⚻ ♂ **2:42 am**
☽ □ ♆ **6:30 am** 3:30 am
☽ ⚻ ♀ **8:08 am** 5:08 am
☽ ⚺ ♇ **9:35 am** 6:35 am
♀ ☍ ♇ 10:18 pm

9 TUESDAY
♀ ☍ ♇ **1:18 am**
☽ △ ☿ **3:51 am** 12:51 am
☽ □ ♃ **4:24 am** 1:24 am
☿ ⚻ ♃ **9:06 am** 6:06 am
☽ ⚻ ☉ **6:33 pm** 3:33 pm
☽ △ ♅ **8:58 pm** 5:58 pm
☽ ⚺ ♄ 11:23 pm

10 WEDNESDAY
☽ ⚺ ♄ **2:23 am**
☽ △ ♂ **5:12 am** 2:12 am
☽ ⚹ ♆ **6:45 am** 3:45 am
☽ ☌ ♇ **9:45 am** 6:45 am
☽ ☍ ♀ **12:39 pm** 9:39 am

11 THURSDAY
☽ ⚹ ♃ **4:08 am** 1:08 am
☉ □ ♅ **8:53 am** 5:53 am
☽ ⚻ ☿ **9:05 am** 6:05 am
♂ ⚹ ♆ **5:44 pm** 2:44 pm
☽ □ ♅ **8:47 pm** 5:47 pm
☽ ☍ ☉ **9:36 pm** 6:36 pm
☽ ☌ ♄ 10:58 pm

12 FRIDAY
☽ ☌ ♄ **1:58 am**
☽ ⚺ ♆ **6:33 am** 3:33 am
☽ □ ♂ **7:07 am** 4:07 am
☽ ⚺ ♇ **9:35 am** 6:35 am
☽ ⚻ ♀ **4:55 pm** 1:55 pm

13 SATURDAY
☽ ⚺ ♃ **4:19 am** 1:19 am
☽ ☍ ☿ **3:02 pm** 12:02 pm
☽ ⚹ ♅ **9:49 pm** 6:49 pm
☽ ⚻ ☉ 11:10 pm
☽ ⚺ ♄ 11:58 pm

14 SUNDAY
☽ ⚻ ☉ **2:10 am**
☽ ⚺ ♄ **2:58 am**
☽ ☌ ♆ **7:58 am** 4:58 am
☽ ⚹ ♂ **10:53 am** 7:53 am
☽ ⚹ ♇ **11:11 am** 8:11 am
☉ ☍ ♄ **1:11 pm** 10:11 am
♂ △ ♇ **5:28 pm** 2:28 pm
☽ △ ♀ **11:53 pm** 8:53 pm

15 MONDAY
☽ ☌ ♃ **6:59 am** 3:59 am
☽ ⚻ ☿ 9:41 pm
☽ ⚺ ♅ 11:01 pm

16 TUESDAY
☽ ⚻ ☿ **12:41 am**
☽ ⚺ ♅ **2:01 am**
☽ ⚹ ♄ **7:14 am** 4:14 am
☽ △ ☉ **10:48 am** 7:48 am
☽ ⚺ ♆ **12:50 pm** 9:50 am
☿ △ ♅ **1:46 pm** 10:46 am
☽ □ ♇ **4:18 pm** 1:18 pm
☽ ⚺ ♂ **6:39 pm** 3:39 pm

17 WEDNESDAY
☽ □ ♀ **11:54 am** 8:54 am
☽ ⚺ ♃ **1:32 pm** 10:32 am
☉ ⚻ ♆ **1:57 pm** 10:57 am

18 THURSDAY
♀ △ ♃ **4:03 am** 1:03 am
☽ ☌ ♅ **10:20 am** 7:20 am
☿ ⚻ ♄ **3:06 pm** 12:06 pm
☽ □ ♄ **3:34 pm** 12:34 pm
☽ △ ☿ **3:37 pm** 12:37 pm
☽ ⚹ ♆ **9:49 pm** 6:49 pm
☽ □ ☉ 9:36 pm
☽ △ ♇ 10:32 pm

19 FRIDAY
☽ □ ☉ **12:36 am**
☽ △ ♇ **1:32 am**
☽ ☌ ♂ **7:06 am** 4:06 am
☉ ⚻ ♇ **12:10 pm** 9:10 am
☽ ⚹ ♃ **11:52 pm** 8:52 pm

20 SATURDAY
☽ ⚹ ♀ **5:09 am** 2:09 am
☽ ⚺ ♅ **10:01 pm** 7:01 pm

21 SUNDAY
☽ △ ♄ **3:04 am** 12:04 am
☿ ☍ ♆ **3:40 am** 12:40 am
☽ □ ♆ **9:47 am** 6:47 am
☽ □ ☿ **10:29 am** 7:29 am
☽ ⚻ ♇ **1:38 pm** 10:38 am
☽ ⚹ ☉ **6:06 pm** 3:06 pm
☽ ⚺ ♂ **10:35 pm** 7:35 pm

22 MONDAY
☽ □ ♃ **12:10 pm** 9:10 am
☿ △ ♇ **5:59 pm** 2:59 pm
☽ ⚺ ♀ 9:55 pm

23 TUESDAY
☽ ⚺ ♀ **12:55 am**
☽ ⚹ ♅ **10:51 am** 7:51 am
☽ ⚻ ♄ **3:30 pm** 12:30 pm
☽ △ ♆ **10:26 pm** 7:26 pm
☽ ☍ ♇ 11:17 pm

24 WEDNESDAY
☽ ☍ ♇ **2:17 am**
☽ ⚹ ☿ **5:40 am** 2:40 am
☽ ⚺ ☉ **12:07 pm** 9:07 am
☽ ⚹ ♂ **2:16 pm** 11:16 am
☽ △ ♃ 9:10 pm

25 THURSDAY
☽ △ ♃ **12:10 am**
☽ ☌ ♀ **7:50 pm** 4:50 pm
☽ □ ♅ **10:45 pm** 7:45 pm
☽ ☍ ♄ 11:55 pm

26 FRIDAY
☽ ☍ ♄ **2:55 am**
☽ ⚻ ♆ **9:53 am** 6:53 am
☽ ⚻ ♇ **1:39 pm** 10:39 am
☽ ⚺ ☿ **10:28 pm** 7:28 pm
♀ □ ♅ 9:34 pm
☉ □ ♂ 10:27 pm

27 SATURDAY
♀ □ ♅ **12:34 am**
☉ □ ♂ **1:27 am**
☽ □ ♂ **4:11 am** 1:11 am
☽ ☌ ☉ **4:17 am** 1:17 am
☽ ⚻ ♃ **10:33 am** 7:33 am

28 SUNDAY
☽ △ ♅ **8:47 am** 5:47 am
☽ ⚺ ♀ **12:17 pm** 9:17 am
☽ ⚻ ♄ **12:30 pm** 9:30 am
♀ ☍ ♄ **2:27 pm** 11:27 am
☽ ☍ ♆ **7:27 pm** 4:27 pm
☽ △ ♇ **11:08 pm** 8:08 pm

29 MONDAY
☽ ☌ ☿ **12:10 pm** 9:10 am
☽ △ ♂ **3:50 pm** 12:50 pm
☽ ⚺ ☉ **6:00 pm** 3:00 pm
☽ ☍ ♃ **7:00 pm** 4:00 pm

30 TUESDAY
☉ ⚻ ♃ **6:09 am** 3:09 am
☽ ⚻ ♅ **4:54 pm** 1:54 pm
☽ △ ♄ **8:13 pm** 5:13 pm
☽ ⚹ ♀ 11:07 pm

31 WEDNESDAY
☽ ⚹ ♀ **2:07 am**
☽ ⚻ ♆ **3:08 am** 12:08 am
☽ □ ♇ **6:43 am** 3:43 am
♀ ⚻ ♆ **12:37 pm** 9:37 am
☽ ⚺ ☿ **10:54 pm** 7:54 pm
☽ ⚻ ♂ 10:16 pm
☽ ⚻ ♃ 10:35 pm

Eastern time in bold type
Pacific time in medium type

AUGUST 2022

DATE	SID.TIME	SUN	MOON	NODE	MERCURY	VENUS	MARS	JUPITER	SATURN	URANUS	NEPTUNE	PLUTO	CERES	PALLAS	JUNO	VESTA	CHIRON
1 M	20 38 20	8♌45 27	15♍20	18♉40℞	24♌18	16♋52	18♉04	8♈42℞	22♒55℞	18♉41	25♓09℞	27♑04℞	3♌42	12♊49	21♓22℞	4♓38℞	16♈22℞
2 T	20 42 17	9 42 52	27 51	18 31	26 04	18 05	18 43	8 41	22 50	18 43	25 08	27 03	4 09	13 18	21 19	4 27	16 21
3 W	20 46 13	10 40 18	10♎34	18 26	27 48	19 18	19 21	8 40	22 46	18 44	25 07	27 02	4 35	13 46	21 15	4 15	16 21
4 Th	20 50 10	11 37 44	23 32	18 23	29 31	20 31	20 00	8 39	22 42	18 45	25 06	27 00	5 02	14 15	21 11	4 04	16 20
5 F	20 54 6	12 35 10	6♏47	18 22	1♍11	21 44	20 38	8 38	22 37	18 46	25 05	26 59	5 29	14 44	21 07	3 51	16 19
6 Sa	20 58 3	13 32 38	20 22	18 22	2 51	22 58	21 16	8 36	22 33	18 47	25 04	26 57	5 56	15 13	21 02	3 39	16 18
7 Su	21 1 59	14 30 06	4♐19	18 22	4 28	24 11	21 54	8 35	22 29	18 48	25 02	26 56	6 23	15 41	20 57	3 26	16 17
8 M	21 5 56	15 27 35	18 38	18 20	6 04	25 24	22 31	8 33	22 24	18 48	25 01	26 55	6 50	16 10	20 51	3 13	16 16
9 T	21 9 53	16 25 05	3♑18	18 15	7 39	26 37	23 09	8 31	22 20	18 49	25 00	26 53	7 17	16 39	20 45	3 00	16 15
10 W	21 13 49	17 22 35	18 14	18 08	9 12	27 50	23 46	8 29	22 15	18 50	24 59	26 52	7 43	17 08	20 38	2 46	16 14
11 Th	21 17 46	18 20 07	3♒18	17 59	10 43	29 03	24 23	8 26	22 11	18 51	24 58	26 51	8 10	17 36	20 31	2 33	16 13
12 F	21 21 42	19 17 39	18 22	17 48	12 12	0♌17	25 00	8 23	22 06	18 51	24 56	26 50	8 37	18 05	20 24	2 19	16 12
13 Sa	21 25 39	20 15 13	3♓14	17 37	13 40	1 30	25 37	8 21	22 02	18 52	24 55	26 48	9 04	18 34	20 16	2 05	16 11
14 Su	21 29 35	21 12 47	17 47	17 27	15 06	2 44	26 13	8 17	21 57	18 52	24 54	26 47	9 31	19 02	20 08	1 50	16 10
15 M	21 33 32	22 10 23	1♈54	17 19	16 31	3 57	26 50	8 14	21 53	18 53	24 52	26 46	9 58	19 31	19 59	1 36	16 08
16 T	21 37 28	23 08 01	15 33	17 14	17 54	5 10	27 26	8 11	21 48	18 53	24 51	26 44	10 24	20 00	19 50	1 21	16 07
17 W	21 41 25	24 05 40	28 43	17 11	19 15	6 24	28 02	8 07	21 44	18 54	24 50	26 43	10 51	20 28	19 41	1 06	16 06
18 Th	21 45 22	25 03 20	11♉28	17 10D	20 34	7 37	28 37	8 03	21 39	18 54	24 48	26 42	11 18	20 57	19 31	0 52	16 04
19 F	21 49 18	26 01 02	23 52	17 10℞	21 51	8 51	29 13	7 59	21 35	18 54	24 47	26 41	11 45	21 26	19 21	0 37	16 03
20 Sa	21 53 15	26 58 46	5♊59	17 10	23 07	10 05	29 48	7 55	21 30	18 55	24 46	26 40	12 12	21 54	19 11	0 22	16 01
21 Su	21 57 11	27 56 32	17 55	17 08	24 21	11 18	0♊23	7 51	21 26	18 55	24 44	26 38	12 38	22 23	19 00	0 07	16 00
22 M	22 1 8	28 54 19	29 46	17 05	25 32	12 32	0 58	7 46	21 21	18 55	24 43	26 37	13 05	22 51	18 49	29♒52	15 58
23 T	22 5 4	29 52 07	11♋35	16 58	26 42	13 46	1 33	7 42	21 17	18 55	24 41	26 36	13 32	23 20	18 37	29 37	15 56
24 W	22 9 1	0♍49 58	23 27	16 50	27 49	15 00	2 07	7 37	21 13	18 55℞	24 40	26 35	13 59	23 48	18 25	29 22	15 55
25 Th	22 12 57	1 47 50	5♌25	16 38	28 55	16 13	2 42	7 32	21 08	18 55	24 38	26 34	14 26	24 17	18 13	29 07	15 53
26 F	22 16 54	2 45 43	17 32	16 26	29 57	17 27	3 16	7 27	21 04	18 55	24 37	26 33	14 52	24 45	18 00	28 52	15 51
27 Sa	22 20 51	3 43 38	29 47	16 13	0♎58	18 41	3 49	7 21	20 59	18 55	24 35	26 32	15 19	25 13	17 48	28 37	15 49
28 Su	22 24 47	4 41 35	12♍13	16 01	1 55	19 55	4 23	7 16	20 55	18 55	24 34	26 31	15 46	25 42	17 35	28 22	15 47
29 M	22 28 44	5 39 33	24 50	15 50	2 50	21 09	4 56	7 10	20 51	18 55	24 32	26 29	16 13	26 10	17 21	28 08	15 46
30 T	22 32 40	6 37 32	7♎37	15 42	3 42	22 23	5 29	7 05	20 47	18 55	24 31	26 28	16 39	26 38	17 08	27 53	15 44
31 W	22 36 37	7 35 33	20 35	15 37	4 31	23 37	6 01	6 59	20 42	18 54	24 29	26 27	17 06	27 06	16 54	27 39	15 42

EPHEMERIS CALCULATED FOR 12 MIDNIGHT GREENWICH MEAN TIME. ALL OTHER DATA AND FACING ASPECTARIAN PAGE IN **EASTERN TIME (BOLD)** AND PACIFIC TIME (REGULAR).

SEPTEMBER 2022

☽ Last Aspect day	ET / hr:mn / PT	asp	☽ Ingress sign	day	ET / hr:mn / PT
2	**1:22 pm** 10:22 am	□♀	♐	2	**6:39 pm** 3:39 pm
4	**9:51 pm** 6:51 pm	△♀	♑	4	**10:03 pm** 7:03 pm
6	**5:43 pm** 2:43 pm	☌♇	♒	6	**11:41 pm** 8:41 pm
8	**8:34 am** 5:34 am	☌♄	♓	8	9:42 pm
8	**8:34 am** 5:34 am	☌♄	♓	9	**12:42 am**
10	**8:29 pm** 5:29 pm	⚹♇	♈	10	11:47 pm
10	**8:29 pm** 5:29 pm	⚹♇	♈	11	**2:47 am**
12	9:53 pm	□♇	♉	13	**7:39 am** 4:39 am
13	**12:53 am**	□♇	♉	13	**7:39 am** 4:39 am
15	**8:59 am** 5:59 am	△♇	♊	15	**4:16 pm** 1:16 pm
17	**5:52 pm** 2:52 pm	□☉	♋	18	**3:59 am** 12:59 am
20	**11:57 am** 8:57 am	⚹☉	♌	20	**4:38 pm** 1:38 pm
22	**7:07 am** 4:07 am	☍♄	♍	23	**3:53 am** 12:53 am
25	**8:49 am** 5:49 am	☌☿	♎	25	**12:43 pm** 9:43 am
27	**12:21 pm** 9:21 am	□♇	♏	27	**7:15 pm** 4:15 pm
29	**5:20 pm** 2:20 pm	⚹♇	♐	29	9:03 pm
29	**5:20 pm** 2:20 pm	⚹♇	♐	30	**12:03 am**

☽ Phases & Eclipses phase	day	ET / hr:mn / PT
2nd Quarter	3	**2:08 pm** 11:08 am
Full Moon	10	**5:59 am** 2:59 am
4th Quarter	17	**5:52 pm** 2:52 pm
New Moon	25	**5:55 pm** 2:55 pm

Planet Ingress		day	ET / hr:mn / PT
♀	♍	4	9:05 pm
♀	♍	5	**12:05 am**
⚴	♋	5	10:04 pm
⚴	♋	6	**1:04 am**
☉	♎	22	**9:04 pm** 6:04 pm
☿	♍	23	**8:04 am** 5:04 am
♀	♎	29	**3:49 am** 12:49 am
⚳	♍	29	**4:59 am** 1:59 am

Planetary Motion		day	ET / hr:mn / PT
☿	℞	9	**11:38 pm** 8:38 pm

1 THURSDAY

☽⚻♂	**1:16 am**	
☽⚻♃	**1:35 am**	
☽⚹☉	**5:20 am**	2:20 am
♂⚹♃	**7:52 am**	4:52 am
☽☍♅	**11:06 pm**	8:06 pm
☽□♄		11:02 pm
♀⚻♇		11:33 pm

2 FRIDAY

☽□♄	**2:02 am**	
♀⚻♇	**2:33 am**	
☽△♆	**8:52 am**	5:52 am
☽⚹♇	**12:23 pm**	9:23 am
☽□♀	**1:22 pm**	10:22 am
☿☍♃	**9:49 pm**	6:49 pm

3 SATURDAY

☽△♃	**6:10 am**	3:10 am
☽⚹☿	**6:37 am**	3:37 am
☽☍♂	**8:23 am**	5:23 am
☽□☉	**2:08 pm**	11:08 am

4 SUNDAY

☽⚻♅	**3:13 am**	12:13 am
☽⚹♄	**5:50 am**	2:50 am
☽□♆	**12:32 pm**	9:32 am
☽⚺♇	**3:57 pm**	12:57 pm
☽△♀	**9:51 pm**	6:51 pm

5 MONDAY

☽□♃	**8:44 am**	5:44 am
☽□☿	**11:21 am**	8:21 am
☽⚻♂	**1:09 pm**	10:09 am
☽△☉	**8:25 pm**	5:25 pm

6 TUESDAY

☽△♅	**5:23 am**	2:23 am
☽⚺♄	**7:43 am**	4:43 am
☽⚹♆	**2:21 pm**	11:21 am
☽☌♇	**5:43 pm**	2:43 pm

7 WEDNESDAY

☽⚻♀	**4:04 am**	1:04 am
☽⚹♃	**9:45 am**	6:45 am
☽△☿	**1:48 pm**	10:48 am
☽△♂	**4:13 pm**	1:13 pm
☽⚻☉		10:04 pm

8 THURSDAY

☽⚻☉	**1:04 am**	
☽□♅	**6:26 am**	3:26 am
☽☌♄	**8:34 am**	5:34 am
☽⚺♆	**3:17 pm**	12:17 pm
☽⚺♇	**6:41 pm**	3:41 pm

9 FRIDAY

☽☍♀	**9:39 am**	6:39 am
☽⚺♃	**10:26 am**	7:26 am
☽⚻☿	**3:24 pm**	12:24 pm
♀⚻♃	**6:06 pm**	3:06 pm
☽□♂	**7:08 pm**	4:08 pm

10 SATURDAY

☽☍☉	**5:59 am**	2:59 am
☽⚹♅	**7:51 am**	4:51 am
☽⚺♄	**9:52 am**	6:52 am
☽☌♆	**4:56 pm**	1:56 pm
☽⚹♇	**8:29 pm**	5:29 pm

11 SUNDAY

☉△♅	**9:09 am**	6:09 am
☽☌♃	**12:31 pm**	9:31 am
☽⚻♀	**5:05 pm**	2:05 pm
☽☍☿	**5:52 pm**	2:52 pm
☽⚹♂	**11:56 pm**	8:56 pm
☿⚺♀		9:49 pm

12 MONDAY

☿⚺♀	**12:49 am**	
☽⚺♅	**11:27 am**	8:27 am
☉⚻♄	**12:09 pm**	9:09 am
☽⚹♄	**1:25 pm**	10:25 am
☽⚻☉	**1:31 pm**	10:31 am
☽⚺♆	**9:02 pm**	6:02 pm
☽□♇		9:53 pm

13 TUESDAY

☽□♇	**12:53 am**	
☽⚺♃	**5:33 pm**	2:33 pm
☽⚻☿	**10:32 pm**	7:32 pm

14 WEDNESDAY

☽△♀	**4:41 am**	1:41 am
☽⚺♂	**8:23 am**	5:23 am
☽☌♅	**6:34 pm**	3:34 pm
☽□♄	**8:30 pm**	5:30 pm
☽△☉		10:31 pm

15 THURSDAY

☽△☉	**1:31 am**	
☽⚹♆	**4:47 am**	1:47 am
☽△♇	**8:59 am**	5:59 am
☽⚹♃		11:14 pm

16 FRIDAY

☽⚹♃	**2:14 am**	
☽△☿	**5:36 am**	2:36 am
♀□♂	**2:49 pm**	11:49 am
☉☍♆	**6:21 pm**	3:21 pm
☽☌♂	**8:52 pm**	5:52 pm
☽□♀	**9:18 pm**	6:18 pm

17 SATURDAY

☽⚺♅	**5:13 am**	2:13 am
☽△♄	**7:04 am**	4:04 am
☽□♆	**3:54 pm**	12:54 pm
☽□☉	**5:52 pm**	2:52 pm
☽⚻♇	**8:21 pm**	5:21 pm

18 SUNDAY

☽□♃	**1:38 pm**	10:38 am
☽□☿	**1:56 pm**	10:56 am
☿☍♃	**6:34 pm**	3:34 pm
☉△♇	**11:58 pm**	8:58 pm

19 MONDAY

☽⚺♂	**11:41 am**	8:41 am
☽⚹♀	**4:53 pm**	1:53 pm
☽⚹♅	**5:43 pm**	2:43 pm
☽⚻♄	**7:25 pm**	4:25 pm
♀△♅		9:44 pm

20 TUESDAY

♀△♅	**12:44 am**	
☽△♆	**4:25 am**	1:25 am
☽☍♇	**8:58 am**	5:58 am
☽⚹☉	**11:57 am**	8:57 am
♀⚻♄	**4:12 pm**	1:12 pm
☽⚹☿	**9:52 pm**	6:52 pm
☽△♃		10:32 pm

21 WEDNESDAY

☽△♃	**1:32 am**	
☽⚹♂		11:00 pm

22 THURSDAY

☽⚹♂	**2:00 am**	
☽□♅	**5:36 am**	2:36 am
☽☍♄	**7:07 am**	4:07 am
☽⚺♀	**11:42 am**	8:42 am
☽⚻♆	**3:57 pm**	12:57 pm
☽⚻♇	**8:28 pm**	5:28 pm
☉☌☿		11:50 pm

23 FRIDAY

☉☌☿	**2:50 am**	
☽⚺☿	**4:13 am**	1:13 am
☽⚺☉	**4:28 am**	1:28 am
☽⚻♃	**11:50 am**	8:50 am

24 SATURDAY

♀☍♆	**4:51 am**	1:51 am
☽□♂	**1:51 pm**	10:51 am
☽△♅	**3:17 pm**	12:17 pm
☽⚻♄	**4:38 pm**	1:38 pm
☽☍♆		10:10 pm

25 SUNDAY

☽☍♆	**1:10 am**	
☽☌♀	**3:24 am**	12:24 am
☽△♇	**5:35 am**	2:35 am
☽☌☿	**8:49 am**	5:49 am
☽☌☉	**5:55 pm**	2:55 pm
☽☍♃	**7:45 pm**	4:45 pm
♀△♇		10:46 pm

26 MONDAY

♀△♇	**1:46 am**	
♂⚺♅	**10:14 am**	7:14 am
☿☌♀	**1:59 pm**	10:59 am
☉☍♃	**3:33 pm**	12:33 pm
☽⚻♅	**10:31 pm**	7:31 pm
☽△♂	**10:54 pm**	7:54 pm
☽△♄	**11:44 pm**	8:44 pm

27 TUESDAY

☽⚻♆	**8:01 am**	5:01 am
☿△♇	**8:56 am**	5:56 am
☽⚺☿	**12:10 pm**	9:10 am
☽□♇	**12:21 pm**	9:21 am
☽⚺♀	**3:54 pm**	12:54 pm
☽⚻♃		10:29 pm
♂△♄		10:49 pm

28 WEDNESDAY

☽⚻♃	**1:29 am**	
♂△♄	**1:49 am**	
☽⚺☉	**4:31 am**	1:31 am

29 THURSDAY

☽☍♅	**3:49 am**	12:49 am
☽□♄	**4:57 am**	1:57 am
☽⚻♂	**5:46 am**	2:46 am
☽△♆	**1:03 pm**	10:03 am
☽⚹☿	**2:58 pm**	11:58 am
☽⚹♇	**5:20 pm**	2:20 pm
☽⚹♀		11:04 pm

30 FRIDAY

☽⚹♀	**2:04 am**	
☽△♃	**5:38 am**	2:38 am
☽⚹☉	**1:05 pm**	10:05 am

Eastern time in bold type
Pacific time in medium type

SEPTEMBER 2022

DATE	SID.TIME	SUN	MOON	NODE	MERCURY	VENUS	MARS	JUPITER	SATURN	URANUS	NEPTUNE	PLUTO	CERES	PALLAS	JUNO	VESTA	CHIRON
1 Th	22 40 33	8♍33 35	3♏46	15♉35D	5♎17	24♌51	6♊34	6♈53℞	20♒38℞	18♉54℞	24♓28℞	26♑26℞	17♌33	27♊34	16♓40℞	27♒25℞	15♈40℞
2 F	22 44 30	9 31 39	17 09	15 34	5 59	26 05	7 06	6 46	20 34	18 53	24 26	26 25	17 59	28 02	16 26	27 11	15 38
3 Sa	22 48 26	10 29 44	0♐46	15 35℞	6 37	27 19	7 37	6 40	20 30	18 53	24 24	26 25	18 26	28 30	16 12	26 58	15 36
4 Su	22 52 23	11 27 51	14 39	15 35	7 11	28 33	8 09	6 33	20 26	18 53	24 23	26 24	18 53	28 58	15 57	26 44	15 33
5 M	22 56 20	12 25 59	28 47	15 34	7 41	29 47	8 40	6 27	20 22	18 52	24 21	26 23	19 19	29 26	15 43	26 31	15 31
6 T	23 0 16	13 24 08	13♑10	15 31	8 06	1♍02	9 11	6 20	20 18	18 51	24 20	26 22	19 46	29 54	15 28	26 18	15 29
7 W	23 4 13	14 22 19	27 45	15 25	8 27	2 16	9 42	6 13	20 14	18 51	24 18	26 21	20 12	0♋22	15 13	26 06	15 27
8 Th	23 8 9	15 20 32	12♒26	15 17	8 42	3 30	10 12	6 06	20 10	18 50	24 16	26 20	20 39	0 50	14 59	25 54	15 25
9 F	23 12 6	16 18 45	27 08	15 09	8 51	4 44	10 42	5 59	20 06	18 49	24 15	26 19	21 06	1 17	14 44	25 42	15 22
10 Sa	23 16 2	17 17 01	11♓42	14 59	8 55℞	5 59	11 11	5 52	20 03	18 49	24 13	26 19	21 32	1 45	14 29	25 30	15 20
11 Su	23 19 59	18 15 18	26 01	14 51	8 53	7 13	11 41	5 45	19 59	18 48	24 11	26 18	21 59	2 12	14 14	25 19	15 18
12 M	23 23 55	19 13 37	9♈59	14 45	8 45	8 27	12 10	5 38	19 55	18 47	24 10	26 17	22 25	2 40	13 59	25 08	15 15
13 T	23 27 52	20 11 58	23 34	14 40	8 30	9 42	12 38	5 30	19 52	18 46	24 08	26 16	22 51	3 07	13 44	24 58	15 13
14 W	23 31 49	21 10 21	6♉43	14 38D	8 08	10 56	13 07	5 23	19 48	18 45	24 07	26 16	23 18	3 34	13 30	24 48	15 11
15 Th	23 35 45	22 08 46	19 29	14 38	7 39	12 11	13 35	5 15	19 45	18 44	24 05	26 15	23 44	4 01	13 15	24 38	15 08
16 F	23 39 42	23 07 13	1♊55	14 39	7 04	13 25	14 02	5 07	19 41	18 43	24 03	26 14	24 11	4 28	13 00	24 29	15 06
17 Sa	23 43 38	24 05 42	14 04	14 40℞	6 22	14 40	14 29	5 00	19 38	18 42	24 02	26 14	24 37	4 55	12 46	24 20	15 03
18 Su	23 47 35	25 04 14	26 03	14 41	5 34	15 54	14 56	4 52	19 35	18 41	24 00	26 13	25 03	5 22	12 32	24 12	15 01
19 M	23 51 31	26 02 48	7♋55	14 40	4 41	17 09	15 22	4 44	19 32	18 39	23 58	26 13	25 29	5 49	12 17	24 04	14 58
20 T	23 55 28	27 01 24	19 46	14 37	3 43	18 23	15 48	4 36	19 29	18 38	23 57	26 12	25 56	6 16	12 03	23 56	14 56
21 W	23 59 24	28 00 02	1♌41	14 32	2 42	19 38	16 14	4 28	19 26	18 37	23 55	26 12	26 22	6 42	11 50	23 49	14 53
22 Th	0 3 21	28 58 42	13 43	14 26	1 38	20 52	16 39	4 20	19 23	18 36	23 53	26 11	26 48	7 09	11 36	23 43	14 51
23 F	0 7 18	29 57 24	25 56	14 18	0 33	22 07	17 04	4 12	19 20	18 34	23 52	26 11	27 14	7 35	11 23	23 36	14 48
24 Sa	0 11 14	0♎56 09	8♍22	14 10	29♍28	23 22	17 28	4 04	19 17	18 33	23 50	26 10	27 40	8 01	11 10	23 31	14 45
25 Su	0 15 11	1 54 55	21 02	14 02	28 26	24 37	17 52	3 56	19 14	18 31	23 48	26 10	28 06	8 27	10 57	23 25	14 43
26 M	0 19 7	2 53 43	3♎57	13 56	27 28	25 51	18 15	3 48	19 12	18 30	23 47	26 09	28 32	8 53	10 44	23 21	14 40
27 T	0 23 4	3 52 34	17 05	13 51	26 35	27 06	18 38	3 40	19 09	18 28	23 45	26 09	28 58	9 19	10 32	23 16	14 37
28 W	0 27 0	4 51 26	0♏25	13 49D	25 48	28 21	19 01	3 32	19 07	18 27	23 43	26 09	29 24	9 44	10 20	23 12	14 35
29 Th	0 30 57	5 50 20	13 58	13 48	25 10	29 36	19 23	3 24	19 04	18 25	23 42	26 08	29 50	10 10	10 08	23 09	14 32
30 F	0 34 53	6 49 17	27 40	13 48	24 41	0♎50	19 44	3 16	19 02	18 24	23 40	26 08	0♍16	10 35	9 57	23 06	14 29

EPHEMERIS CALCULATED FOR 12 MIDNIGHT GREENWICH MEAN TIME. ALL OTHER DATA AND FACING ASPECTARIAN PAGE IN **EASTERN TIME (BOLD)** AND PACIFIC TIME (REGULAR).

OCTOBER 2022

☽ Last Aspect day	ET / hr:mn / PT		asp	☽ Ingress sign	day	ET / hr:mn / PT	
1	**5:46 pm**	2:46 pm	□☿	♑	2	**3:38 am**	12:38 am
3	**11:49 pm**	8:49 pm	☌♇	♒	4	**6:20 am**	3:20 am
5	**6:46 pm**	3:46 pm	△♂	♓	6	**8:47 am**	5:47 am
8	**7:10 am**	4:10 am	☍☿	♈	8	**11:57 am**	8:57 am
10	**10:02 am**	7:02 am	□♇	♉	10	**5:04 pm**	2:04 pm
12	**5:42 pm**	2:42 pm	△♇	♊	12		10:08 pm
12	**5:42 pm**	2:42 pm	△♇	♊	13	**1:08 am**	
14		9:11 pm	☌♂	♋	15	**12:11 pm**	9:11 am
15	**12:11 am**		☌♂	♋	15	**12:11 pm**	9:11 am
17	**4:56 pm**	1:56 pm	☍♇	♌	17		9:45 pm
17	**4:56 pm**	1:56 pm	☍♇	♌	18	**12:45 am**	
20	**6:35 am**	3:35 am	⚹☉	♍	20	**12:25 pm**	9:25 am
22	**2:17 pm**	11:17 am	△♇	♎	22	**9:24 pm**	6:24 pm
24	**8:36 pm**	5:36 pm	□♇	♏	25	**3:18 am**	12:18 am
26		9:27 pm	⚹♇	♐	27	**6:55 am**	3:55 am
27	**12:27 am**		⚹♇	♐	27	**6:55 am**	3:55 am
29	**9:10 am**	6:10 am	□♃	♑	29	**9:21 am**	6:21 am
31	**11:14 am**	8:14 am	⚹♃	♒	31	**11:43 am**	8:43 am

☽ Phases & Eclipses phase	day	ET / hr:mn / PT	
2nd Quarter	2	**8:14 pm**	5:14 pm
Full Moon	9	**4:55 pm**	1:55 pm
4th Quarter	17	**1:15 pm**	10:15 am
New Moon	25	**6:49 am**	3:49 am
●	25	2° ♏ 00'	
2nd Quarter	31		11:37 pm
2nd Quarter	11/1	**2:37 am**	

Planet Ingress		day	ET / hr:mn / PT	
☿	♎	10	**7:51 pm**	4:51 pm
♀	♏	23	**3:52 am**	12:52 am
☉	♏	23	**6:36 am**	3:36 am
♃	♓	27		10:10 pm
♃	♓	28	**1:10 am**	
☿	♏	29	**3:22 pm**	12:22 pm

Planetary Motion		day	ET / hr:mn / PT	
☿	D	2	**5:07 am**	2:07 am
⚴	D	5	**2:10 pm**	11:10 am
♇	D	8	**5:56 pm**	2:56 pm
♄	D	22		9:07 pm
♄	D	23	**12:07 am**	
⚵	D	23	**9:05 am**	6:05 pm
♂	℞	30	**9:26 am**	6:26 am

1 SATURDAY

☽ ⚻ ♅ **7:43 am** 4:43 am
☽ ⚹ ♄ **8:48 am** 5:48 am
☽ ☍ ♂ **11:03 am** 8:03 am
♀ ☍ ♃ **2:12 pm** 11:12 am
☽ □ ♆ **4:45 pm** 1:45 pm
☽ □ ☿ **5:46 pm** 2:46 pm
☽ ⚺ ♇ **9:02 pm** 6:02 pm

2 SUNDAY

☽ □ ♃ **8:37 am** 5:37 am
☽ □ ♀ **10:35 am** 7:35 am
☽ □ ☉ **8:14 pm** 5:14 pm

3 MONDAY

☽ △ ♅ **10:37 am** 7:37 am
☽ ⚺ ♄ **11:39 am** 8:39 am
☽ ⚻ ♂ **3:12 pm** 12:12 pm
☽ ⚹ ♆ **7:31 pm** 4:31 pm
☽ △ ☿ **8:59 pm** 5:59 pm
☽ ☌ ♇ **11:49 pm** 8:49 pm

4 TUESDAY

☽ ⚹ ♃ **10:48 am** 7:48 am
☽ △ ♀ **6:04 pm** 3:04 pm
☽ △ ☉ 11:31 pm

5 WEDNESDAY

☽ △ ☉ **2:31 am**
☽ □ ♅ **12:58 pm** 9:58 am
☽ ☌ ♄ **2:00 pm** 11:00 am
☽ △ ♂ **6:46 pm** 3:46 pm
☽ ⚺ ♆ **9:51 pm** 6:51 pm
☽ ⚻ ☿ 10:06 pm
☽ ⚺ ♇ 11:14 pm

6 THURSDAY

☽ ⚻ ☿ **1:06 am**
☽ ⚺ ♇ **2:14 am**
☽ ⚺ ♃ **12:49 pm** 9:49 am
☿ △ ♇ **11:56 pm** 8:56 pm
☽ ⚻ ♀ 10:28 pm

7 FRIDAY

☽ ⚻ ♀ **1:28 am**
☽ ⚻ ☉ **8:54 am** 5:54 am
☽ ⚹ ♅ **3:35 pm** 12:35 pm
☽ ⚺ ♄ **4:39 pm** 1:39 pm
☽ □ ♂ **10:40 pm** 7:40 pm
☽ ☌ ♆ 9:40 pm

8 SATURDAY

☽ ☌ ♆ **12:40 am**
☽ ⚹ ♇ **5:14 am** 2:14 am
☽ ☍ ☿ **7:10 am** 4:10 am
☽ ☌ ♃ **3:37 pm** 12:37 pm

9 SUNDAY

☽ ☍ ♀ **10:20 am** 7:20 am
☽ ☍ ☉ **4:55 pm** 1:55 pm
☽ ⚺ ♅ **7:39 pm** 4:39 pm
☽ ⚹ ♄ **8:48 pm** 5:48 pm

10 MONDAY

☽ ⚹ ♂ **4:14 am** 1:14 am
☽ ⚺ ♆ **5:09 am** 2:09 am
☽ □ ♇ **10:02 am** 7:02 am
☽ ⚻ ☿ **4:47 pm** 1:47 pm
☽ ⚺ ♃ **8:25 pm** 5:25 pm

11 TUESDAY

☉ ⚻ ♅ **5:13 am** 2:13 am
☉ △ ♄ **9:07 pm** 6:07 pm
☽ ⚻ ♀ **10:29 pm** 7:29 pm
♂ □ ♆ 10:46 pm
☽ ☌ ♅ 11:20 pm

12 WEDNESDAY

♂ □ ♆ **1:46 am**
☽ ☌ ♅ **2:20 am**
☿ ☍ ♃ **3:24 am** 12:24 am
☽ □ ♄ **3:37 am** 12:37 am
☽ ⚻ ☉ **4:10 am** 1:10 am
☽ ⚹ ♆ **12:25 pm** 9:25 am
☽ ⚺ ♂ **12:38 pm** 9:38 am
☽ △ ♇ **5:42 pm** 2:42 pm

13 THURSDAY

☽ ⚹ ♃ **4:08 am** 1:08 am
☽ △ ☿ **7:29 am** 4:29 am
♀ ⚻ ♅ **12:57 pm** 9:57 am
♀ △ ♄ 11:21 pm

14 FRIDAY

♀ △ ♄ **2:21 am**
☽ ⚺ ♅ **12:07 pm** 9:07 am
☽ △ ♄ **1:33 pm** 10:33 am
☽ △ ♀ **2:51 pm** 11:51 am
☽ △ ☉ **7:23 pm** 4:23 pm
☽ □ ♆ **10:46 pm** 7:46 pm
☽ ☌ ♂ 9:11 pm

15 SATURDAY

☽ ☌ ♂ **12:11 am**
☽ ⚻ ♇ **4:26 am** 1:26 am
☽ □ ♃ **2:44 pm** 11:44 am

16 SUNDAY

☽ □ ☿ **3:19 am** 12:19 am
☉ ⚻ ♆ **11:39 am** 8:39 am
☽ ⚹ ♅ 9:09 pm
☽ ⚻ ♄ 10:44 pm

17 MONDAY

☽ ⚹ ♅ **12:09 am**
☽ ⚻ ♄ **1:44 am**
☽ □ ♀ **10:14 am** 7:14 am
☽ △ ♆ **11:04 am** 8:04 am
☽ □ ☉ **1:15 pm** 10:15 am
☽ ⚺ ♂ **1:35 pm** 10:35 am
☽ ☍ ♇ **4:56 pm** 1:56 pm
♀ ⚻ ♆ **6:00 pm** 3:00 pm
☉ △ ♂ **6:05 pm** 3:05 pm
☽ △ ♃ 11:44 pm

18 TUESDAY

☽ △ ♃ **2:44 am**
♀ △ ♂ **10:20 pm** 7:20 pm
☽ ⚹ ☿ 10:16 pm

19 WEDNESDAY

☽ ⚹ ☿ **1:16 am**
☉ □ ♇ **9:33 am** 6:33 am
☽ □ ♅ **12:17 pm** 9:17 am
☽ ☍ ♄ **1:59 pm** 10:59 am
☽ ⚻ ♆ **11:02 pm** 8:02 pm
♀ □ ♇ 11:03 pm
☽ ⚹ ♂ 11:23 pm

20 THURSDAY

♀ □ ♇ **2:03 am**
☽ ⚹ ♂ **2:23 am**
☽ ⚻ ♇ **4:53 am** 1:53 am
☽ ⚹ ♀ **5:13 am** 2:13 am
☽ ⚹ ☉ **6:35 am** 3:35 am
☽ ⚻ ♃ **1:50 pm** 10:50 am

21 FRIDAY

☽ ⚺ ☿ **8:54 pm** 5:54 pm
☽ △ ♅ **10:19 pm** 7:19 pm
☽ ⚻ ♄ 9:06 pm

22 SATURDAY

☽ ⚻ ♄ **12:06 am**
☿ ⚻ ♅ **7:24 am** 4:24 am
☽ ☍ ♆ **8:37 am** 5:37 am
☽ □ ♂ **12:27 pm** 9:27 am
☽ △ ♇ **2:17 pm** 11:17 am
☉ ☌ ♀ **5:17 pm** 2:17 pm
☽ ⚺ ☉ **8:38 pm** 5:38 pm
☽ ⚺ ♀ **8:43 pm** 5:43 pm
☿ △ ♄ **9:00 pm** 6:00 pm
☽ ☍ ♃ **10:17 pm** 7:17 pm

23 SUNDAY

♀ ⚻ ♃ **11:58 am** 8:58 am
☉ ⚻ ♃ **4:21 pm** 1:21 pm

24 MONDAY

☽ ⚻ ♅ **5:18 am** 2:18 am
☽ △ ♄ **7:08 am** 4:08 am
☽ ☌ ☿ **12:01 pm** 9:01 am
☽ ⚻ ♆ **3:07 pm** 12:07 pm
☽ △ ♂ **7:12 pm** 4:12 pm
☽ □ ♇ **8:36 pm** 5:36 pm

25 TUESDAY

☽ ⚻ ♃ **3:46 am** 12:46 am
☽ ☌ ☉ **6:49 am** 3:49 am
☽ ☌ ♀ **8:04 am** 5:04 am
☿ ⚻ ♆ **12:30 pm** 9:30 am

26 WEDNESDAY

☽ ☍ ♅ **9:34 am** 6:34 am
☽ □ ♄ **11:30 am** 8:30 am
☽ △ ♆ **7:04 pm** 4:04 pm
☽ ⚺ ☿ **11:17 pm** 8:17 pm
☽ ⚻ ♂ **11:19 pm** 8:19 pm
☿ △ ♂ **11:37 pm** 8:37 pm
☽ ⚹ ♇ 9:27 pm

27 THURSDAY

☽ ⚹ ♇ **12:27 am**
☽ △ ♃ **7:01 am** 4:01 am
☿ □ ♇ **9:09 am** 6:09 am
☽ ⚺ ☉ **2:11 pm** 11:11 am
☽ ⚺ ♀ **4:30 pm** 1:30 pm

28 FRIDAY

☽ ⚻ ♅ **12:13 pm** 9:13 am
☽ ⚹ ♄ **2:17 pm** 11:17 am
☽ □ ♆ **9:37 pm** 6:37 pm
☽ ☍ ♂ 10:59 pm

29 SATURDAY

☽ ☍ ♂ **1:59 am**
☽ ⚺ ♇ **3:01 am** 12:01 am
☽ ⚹ ☿ **8:34 am** 5:34 am
☽ □ ♃ **9:10 am** 6:10 am
☿ ⚻ ♃ **1:32 pm** 10:32 am
☽ ⚹ ☉ **8:20 pm** 5:20 pm
☽ ⚹ ♀ **11:41 pm** 8:41 pm

30 SUNDAY

☽ △ ♅ **2:21 pm** 11:21 am
☽ ⚺ ♄ **4:36 pm** 1:36 pm
☽ ⚹ ♆ **11:51 pm** 8:51 pm

31 MONDAY

☽ ⚻ ♂ **4:19 am** 1:19 am
☽ ☌ ♇ **5:23 am** 2:23 am
☽ ⚹ ♃ **11:14 am** 8:14 am
☽ □ ☿ **5:37 pm** 2:37 pm
☽ □ ☉ 11:37 pm

Eastern time in bold type
Pacific time in medium type

OCTOBER 2022

DATE	SID.TIME	SUN	MOON	NODE	MERCURY	VENUS	MARS	JUPITER	SATURN	URANUS	NEPTUNE	PLUTO	CERES	PALLAS	JUNO	VESTA	CHIRON
1 Sa	0 38 50	7♎48 15	11♐32	13♉50	24♍22℞	2♎05	20♊05	3♈08℞	19♒00℞	18♉22℞	23♓39℞	26♑08℞	0♍42	11♋00	9♓46℞	23♒03℞	14♈27℞
2 Su	0 42 47	8 47 14	25 32	13 51	24 13D	3 20	20 25	3 00	18 58	18 20	23 37	26 08	1 08	11 25	9 36	23 02	14 24
3 M	0 46 43	9 46 16	9♑39	13 52℞	24 14	4 35	20 45	2 52	18 56	18 18	23 35	26 07	1 34	11 50	9 26	23 00	14 21
4 T	0 50 40	10 45 19	23 51	13 51	24 26	5 50	21 04	2 44	18 54	18 17	23 34	26 07	1 59	12 15	9 16	22 59	14 19
5 W	0 54 36	11 44 24	8♒08	13 49	24 47	7 05	21 23	2 36	18 52	18 15	23 32	26 07	2 25	12 39	9 07	22 58D	14 16
6 Th	0 58 33	12 43 31	22 25	13 45	25 19	8 20	21 41	2 29	18 50	18 13	23 31	26 07	2 50	13 03	8 58	22 58	14 13
7 F	1 2 29	13 42 39	6♓38	13 41	26 00	9 35	21 59	2 21	18 48	18 11	23 29	26 07	3 16	13 27	8 50	22 59	14 11
8 Sa	1 6 26	14 41 49	20 44	13 37	26 49	10 50	22 16	2 13	18 47	18 09	23 28	26 07D	3 41	13 51	8 42	22 59	14 08
9 Su	1 10 22	15 41 01	4♈38	13 33	27 46	12 04	22 32	2 06	18 45	18 07	23 26	26 07	4 07	14 15	8 35	23 01	14 05
10 M	1 14 19	16 40 15	18 17	13 29	28 50	13 19	22 48	1 58	18 44	18 05	23 25	26 07	4 32	14 38	8 28	23 02	14 02
11 T	1 18 15	17 39 31	1♉37	13 28D	0♎00	14 34	23 03	1 51	18 43	18 03	23 23	26 07	4 57	15 02	8 21	23 04	14 00
12 W	1 22 12	18 38 49	14 38	13 27	1 17	15 49	23 18	1 43	18 42	18 01	23 22	26 07	5 23	15 25	8 15	23 07	13 57
13 Th	1 26 9	19 38 10	27 19	13 28	2 37	17 04	23 32	1 36	18 41	17 59	23 20	26 07	5 48	15 47	8 10	23 10	13 54
14 F	1 30 5	20 37 32	9♊44	13 29	4 03	18 19	23 45	1 29	18 40	17 57	23 19	26 07	6 13	16 10	8 05	23 14	13 52
15 Sa	1 34 2	21 36 57	21 54	13 31	5 31	19 35	23 58	1 22	18 39	17 55	23 18	26 08	6 38	16 32	8 00	23 17	13 49
16 Su	1 37 58	22 36 24	3♋54	13 32	7 03	20 50	24 10	1 15	18 38	17 53	23 16	26 08	7 03	16 54	7 56	23 22	13 46
17 M	1 41 55	23 35 54	15 47	13 33℞	8 37	22 05	24 21	1 08	18 37	17 50	23 15	26 08	7 28	17 16	7 52	23 27	13 44
18 T	1 45 51	24 35 26	27 39	13 33	10 13	23 20	24 31	1 01	18 37	17 48	23 13	26 08	7 53	17 38	7 49	23 32	13 41
19 W	1 49 48	25 35 00	9♌35	13 33	11 51	24 35	24 41	0 55	18 36	17 46	23 12	26 08	8 18	17 59	7 47	23 37	13 38
20 Th	1 53 45	26 34 36	21 38	13 31	13 30	25 50	24 50	0 48	18 36	17 44	23 11	26 09	8 43	18 20	7 45	23 43	13 36
21 F	1 57 41	27 34 14	3♍54	13 29	15 09	27 05	24 59	0 42	18 36	17 41	23 09	26 09	9 07	18 41	7 43	23 50	13 33
22 Sa	2 1 38	28 33 55	16 25	13 27	16 50	28 20	25 06	0 35	18 35	17 39	23 08	26 09	9 32	19 01	7 42	23 57	13 30
23 Su	2 5 34	29 33 38	29 15	13 25	18 31	29 35	25 13	0 29	18 35D	17 37	23 07	26 10	9 56	19 21	7 42D	24 04	13 28
24 M	2 9 31	0♏33 23	12♎23	13 23	20 12	0♏51	25 19	0 23	18 35	17 34	23 06	26 10	10 21	19 41	7 42	24 11	13 25
25 T	2 13 27	1 33 10	25 51	13 22	21 54	2 06	25 24	0 18	18 35	17 32	23 04	26 11	10 45	20 00	7 42	24 19	13 23
26 W	2 17 24	2 32 59	9♏35	13 22D	23 35	3 21	25 28	0 12	18 36	17 30	23 03	26 11	11 10	20 19	7 43	24 28	13 20
27 Th	2 21 20	3 32 50	23 35	13 22	25 17	4 36	25 31	0 06	18 36	17 27	23 02	26 12	11 34	20 38	7 45	24 36	13 18
28 F	2 25 17	4 32 43	7♐45	13 22	26 58	5 51	25 34	0 01	18 37	17 25	23 01	26 12	11 58	20 56	7 47	24 46	13 15
29 Sa	2 29 13	5 32 37	22 02	13 23	28 39	7 06	25 36	29♓56	18 37	17 23	23 00	26 13	12 22	21 14	7 49	24 55	13 13
30 Su	2 33 10	6 32 34	6♑21	13 24	0♏19	8 22	25 37℞	29 51	18 38	17 20	22 59	26 14	12 46	21 32	7 52	25 05	13 10
31 M	2 37 7	7 32 32	20 40	13 24	2 00	9 37	25 37	29 46	18 38	17 18	22 58	26 14	13 10	21 49	7 56	25 15	13 08

EPHEMERIS CALCULATED FOR 12 MIDNIGHT GREENWICH MEAN TIME. ALL OTHER DATA AND FACING ASPECTARIAN PAGE IN **EASTERN TIME (BOLD)** AND PACIFIC TIME (REGULAR).

NOVEMBER 2022

☽ Last Aspect day	ET / hr:mn / PT	asp	☽ Ingress sign day	ET / hr:mn / PT
2	**7:08 am** 4:08 am	△♂	♓ 2	**2:46 pm** 11:46 am
4	**6:05 pm** 3:05 pm	☌♃	♈ 4	**7:07 pm** 4:07 pm
6	**5:30 pm** 2:30 pm	□♇	♉ 6	9:15 pm
6	**5:30 pm** 2:30 pm	□♇	♉ 7	**12:15 am**
9	**7:00 am** 4:00 am	⚹♃	♊ 9	**8:37 am** 5:37 am
11	**5:28 pm** 2:28 pm	□♃	♋ 11	**7:22 pm** 4:22 pm
14	**5:41 am** 2:41 am	△♃	♌ 14	**7:48 am** 4:48 am
16	**6:55 pm** 3:55 pm	□☿	♍ 16	**8:04 pm** 5:04 pm
19	**3:47 am** 12:47 am	☍♃	♎ 19	**5:58 am** 2:58 am
21	**6:14 am** 3:14 am	□♇	♏ 21	**12:16 pm** 9:16 am

☽ Last Aspect day	ET / hr:mn / PT	asp	☽ Ingress sign day	ET / hr:mn / PT
23	**1:16 pm** 10:16 am	△♃	♐ 23	**3:16 pm** 12:16 pm
25	**2:22 pm** 11:22 am	□♃	♑ 25	**4:18 pm** 1:18 pm
27	**3:11 pm** 12:11 pm	⚹♃	♒ 27	**5:07 pm** 2:07 pm
28	10:53 pm	☌♄	♓ 29	**7:15 pm** 4:15 pm
29	**1:53 am**	☌♄	♓ 29	**7:15 pm** 4:15 pm

☽ Phases & Eclipses phase	day	ET / hr:mn / PT
2nd Quarter	10/31	11:37 pm
2nd Quarter	1	**2:37 am**
Full Moon	8	**6:02 am** 3:02 am
●	8	16° ♉ 01'
4th Quarter	16	**8:27 am** 5:27 am
New Moon	23	**5:57 pm** 2:57 pm
2nd Quarter	30	**9:37 am** 6:37 am

Planet Ingress	day	ET / hr:mn / PT
♀ ♐	15	10:09 pm
♀ ♐	16	**1:09 am**
☿ ♐	17	**3:42 am** 12:42 am
⚶ ♓	20	**4:25 pm** 1:25 pm
☉ ♐	22	**3:20 am** 12:20 am

Planetary Motion		day	ET / hr:mn / PT
♃	D	23	**6:02 pm** 3:02 pm
♀	℞	30	**3:33 am** 12:33 am

1 TUESDAY
☽□☉ **2:37 am**
☽□♀ **7:05 am** 4:05 am
☽□♅ **4:54 pm** 1:54 pm
☽☌♄ **7:22 pm** 4:22 pm
☽⚺♆ 11:38 pm

2 WEDNESDAY
☽⚺♆ **2:38 am**
☽△♂ **7:08 am** 4:08 am
☽⚺♇ **8:21 am** 5:21 am
☽⚺♃ **2:01 pm** 11:01 am

3 THURSDAY
☽△☿ **3:43 am** 12:43 am
☽△☉ **10:01 am** 7:01 am
☽△♀ **3:43 pm** 12:43 pm
☽⚹♅ **8:28 pm** 5:28 pm
☽⚺♄ **11:14 pm** 8:14 pm

4 FRIDAY
☽☌♆ **6:34 am** 3:34 am
☽□♂ **11:02 am** 8:02 am
☽⚹♇ **12:34 pm** 9:34 am
☽☌♃ **6:05 pm** 3:05 pm

5 SATURDAY
☽⚻☿ **3:49 pm** 12:49 pm
♀☍♅ **6:22 pm** 3:22 pm
☽⚻☉ **7:15 pm** 4:15 pm
☽⚺♅ 10:37 pm
☽⚻♀ 11:23 pm

6 SUNDAY
☽⚺♅ **1:37 am**
☽⚻♀ **1:23 am**
☽⚹♄ **3:44 am** 1:44 am
☽⚺♆ **11:10 am** 8:10 am
☽⚹♂ **3:30 pm** 12:30 pm
☽□♇ **5:30 pm** 2:30 pm
☽⚺♃ **10:56 pm** 7:56 pm
♀□♄ 11:34 pm

7 MONDAY
♀□♄ **2:34 am**

8 TUESDAY
☽☍☿ **5:44 am** 2:44 am
☽☍☉ **6:02 am** 3:02 am
☽☌♅ **7:47 am** 4:47 am
☽□♄ **11:20 am** 8:20 am
☉☌☿ **11:42 am** 8:42 am
☽☍♀ **2:51 pm** 11:51 am
☽⚹♆ **6:54 pm** 3:54 pm
☿☍♅ **9:40 pm** 6:40 pm
☽⚺♂ **10:57 pm** 7:57 pm
☽△♇ 10:38 pm

9 WEDNESDAY
☽△♇ **1:38 am**
☉☍♅ **3:26 am** 12:26 am
☽⚹♃ **7:00 am** 4:00 am
☿□♄ 11:52 pm

10 THURSDAY
☿□♄ **2:52 am**
♀△♆ **7:22 am** 4:22 am
☽⚺♅ **5:20 pm** 2:20 pm
☽⚻☉ **8:52 pm** 5:52 pm
☽△♄ **9:22 pm** 6:22 pm
☽⚻☿ 9:06 pm

11 FRIDAY
☽⚻☿ **12:06 am**
☉□♄ **3:04 am** 12:04 am
☽□♆ **5:03 am** 2:03 am
☽⚻♀ **7:34 am** 4:34 am
☽☌♂ **8:34 am** 5:34 am
☽⚻♇ **12:12 pm** 9:12 am
♀⚻♂ **4:07 pm** 1:07 pm
☽□♃ **5:28 pm** 2:28 pm

12 SATURDAY
☿△♆ **1:36 pm** 10:36 am

13 SUNDAY
♀⚹♇ **4:41 am** 1:41 am
☽⚹♅ **4:59 am** 1:59 am
☽⚻♄ **9:30 am** 6:30 am
☿⚻♂ **10:47 am** 7:47 am
☽△☉ **2:22 pm** 11:22 am
☽△♆ **5:08 pm** 2:08 pm
☽⚺♂ **7:50 pm** 4:50 pm
☽△☿ **9:25 pm** 6:25 pm
☽☍♇ 9:35 pm
☽△♀ 11:54 pm

14 MONDAY
☽☍♇ **12:35 am**
☽△♀ **2:54 am**
☽△♃ **5:41 am** 2:41 am
☿⚹♇ **9:27 pm** 6:27 pm
☉△♆ **10:43 pm** 7:43 pm

15 TUESDAY
♀△♃ **4:36 am** 1:36 am
☽□♅ **5:23 pm** 2:23 pm
☉⚻♂ **8:07 pm** 5:07 pm
☽☍♄ **10:17 pm** 7:17 pm

16 WEDNESDAY
☽⚻♆ **5:36 am** 2:36 am
☽⚹♂ **7:12 am** 4:12 am
☽□☉ **8:27 am** 5:27 am
☿△♃ **10:43 am** 7:43 am
☽⚻♇ **1:04 pm** 10:04 am
☽⚻♃ **5:51 pm** 2:51 pm
☽□☿ **6:55 pm** 3:55 pm
☽□♀ **10:14 pm** 7:14 pm

18 FRIDAY
☽△♅ **4:23 am** 1:23 am
☽⚻♄ **9:28 am** 6:28 am
☽☍♆ **4:12 pm** 1:12 pm
☽□♂ **4:35 pm** 1:35 pm
☉⚹♇ **4:38 pm** 1:38 pm
☽△♇ **11:26 pm** 8:26 pm
☽⚹☉ 9:00 pm

19 SATURDAY
☽⚹☉ **12:00 am**
☽☍♃ **3:47 am** 12:47 am
♂□♆ **10:43 am** 7:43 am
☽⚹☿ **12:54 pm** 9:54 am
☽⚹♀ **2:15 pm** 11:15 am

20 SUNDAY
☽⚻♅ **12:11 pm** 9:11 am
☽△♄ **5:18 pm** 2:18 pm
☽△♂ **10:37 pm** 7:37 pm
☉△♃ **11:07 pm** 8:07 pm
☽⚻♆ **11:22 pm** 8:22 pm

21 MONDAY
☽□♇ **6:14 am** 3:14 am
☽⚻♃ **10:10 am** 7:10 am
☽⚺☉ **11:04 am** 8:04 am
☿☌♀ **5:55 pm** 2:55 pm
☽⚺♀ 10:21 pm
☽⚺☿ 10:32 pm

22 TUESDAY
☽⚺♀ **1:21 am**
☽⚺☿ **1:32 am**
☽☍♅ **4:24 pm** 1:24 pm
☽□♄ **9:33 pm** 6:33 pm
☽⚻♂ 10:16 pm

23 WEDNESDAY
☽⚻♂ **1:16 am**
☽△♆ **3:03 am** 12:03 am
☽⚹♇ **9:38 am** 6:38 am
☽△♃ **1:16 pm** 10:16 am
☽☌☉ **5:57 pm** 2:57 pm

24 THURSDAY
☽☌♀ **8:26 am** 5:26 am
☽☌☿ **9:49 am** 6:49 am
☽⚻♅ **6:00 pm** 3:00 pm
☽⚹♄ **11:16 pm** 8:16 pm
☽☍♂ 10:36 pm

25 FRIDAY
☽☍♂ **1:36 am**
☽□♆ **4:24 am** 1:24 am
☽⚺♇ **10:53 am** 7:53 am
☽□♃ **2:22 pm** 11:22 am
☽⚺☉ **10:32 pm** 7:32 pm

26 SATURDAY
☽⚺♀ **1:43 pm** 10:43 am
☽⚺☿ **4:14 pm** 1:14 pm
☽△♅ **6:35 pm** 3:35 pm
☽⚺♄ 9:09 pm
☽⚻♂ 10:11 pm

27 SUNDAY
☽⚺♄ **12:09 am**
☽⚻♂ **1:11 am**
☽⚹♆ **5:06 am** 2:06 am
☽☌♇ **11:43 am** 8:43 am
☿⚻♅ **2:16 pm** 11:16 am
☽⚹♃ **3:11 pm** 12:11 pm

28 MONDAY
☽⚹☉ **3:06 am** 12:06 am
♂△♄ **12:56 pm** 9:56 am
☽⚹♀ **7:40 pm** 4:40 pm
☽□♅ **7:48 pm** 4:48 pm
♀⚻♅ **9:19 pm** 6:19 pm
☽⚹☿ **11:26 pm** 8:26 pm
☽△♂ 10:31 pm
☽☌♄ 10:53 pm

29 TUESDAY
☽△♂ **1:31 am**
☽☌♄ **1:53 am**
☽⚺♆ **6:47 am** 3:47 am
☽⚺♇ **1:44 pm** 10:44 am
☿☍♂ **3:30 pm** 12:30 pm
☽⚺♃ **5:19 pm** 2:19 pm
☿⚹♄ **11:18 pm** 8:18 pm

30 WEDNESDAY
☽□☉ **9:37 am** 6:37 am
☽⚹♅ **10:58 pm** 7:58 pm
♀☍♂ 9:28 pm

Eastern time in bold type
Pacific time in medium type

NOVEMBER 2022

DATE	SID.TIME	SUN	MOON	NODE	MERCURY	VENUS	MARS	JUPITER	SATURN	URANUS	NEPTUNE	PLUTO	CERES	PALLAS	JUNO	VESTA	CHIRON
1 T	2 41 3	8♏32 32	4♒54	13♉24℞	3♏40	10♏52	25♊36℞	29♓42℞	18♒39	17♉15℞	22♓57℞	26♑15	13♍34	22♋06	8♓00	25♒26	13♈05℞
2 W	2 45 0	9 32 33	19 02	13 24	5 19	12 07	25 34	29 37	18 40	17 13	22 56	26 15	13 57	22 22	8 04	25 37	13 03
3 Th	2 48 56	10 32 36	3♓02	13 24	6 58	13 23	25 32	29 33	18 41	17 10	22 55	26 16	14 21	22 38	8 09	25 48	13 01
4 F	2 52 53	11 32 40	16 52	13 24	8 37	14 38	25 28	29 29	18 43	17 08	22 54	26 17	14 44	22 54	8 15	25 59	12 58
5 Sa	2 56 49	12 32 45	0♈30	13 24D	10 15	15 53	25 24	29 25	18 44	17 05	22 53	26 18	15 08	23 09	8 21	26 11	12 56
6 Su	3 0 46	13 32 53	13 56	13 24	11 53	17 08	25 19	29 21	18 45	17 03	22 52	26 19	15 31	23 24	8 27	26 24	12 54
7 M	3 4 42	14 33 02	27 09	13 24	13 31	18 23	25 13	29 18	18 47	17 00	22 51	26 19	15 54	23 38	8 34	26 36	12 52
8 T	3 8 39	15 33 13	10♉07	13 24℞	15 08	19 39	25 06	29 14	18 48	16 58	22 50	26 20	16 17	23 52	8 41	26 49	12 49
9 W	3 12 36	16 33 25	22 52	13 24	16 44	20 54	24 58	29 11	18 50	16 55	22 49	26 21	16 40	24 05	8 49	27 02	12 47
10 Th	3 16 32	17 33 39	5♊23	13 24	18 21	22 09	24 49	29 08	18 52	16 53	22 48	26 22	17 03	24 18	8 58	27 16	12 45
11 F	3 20 29	18 33 56	17 42	13 23	19 57	23 24	24 40	29 05	18 54	16 51	22 48	26 23	17 26	24 30	9 06	27 29	12 43
12 Sa	3 24 25	19 34 14	29 49	13 22	21 32	24 40	24 29	29 03	18 56	16 48	22 47	26 24	17 48	24 42	9 16	27 43	12 41
13 Su	3 28 22	20 34 34	11♋47	13 21	23 08	25 55	24 18	29 00	18 58	16 46	22 46	26 25	18 11	24 53	9 25	27 58	12 39
14 M	3 32 18	21 34 56	23 41	13 20	24 43	27 10	24 06	28 58	19 00	16 43	22 45	26 26	18 33	25 04	9 35	28 12	12 37
15 T	3 36 15	22 35 19	5♌32	13 19	26 17	28 25	23 53	28 56	19 02	16 41	22 45	26 27	18 56	25 14	9 46	28 27	12 35
16 W	3 40 12	23 35 45	17 26	13 19D	27 52	29 41	23 39	28 55	19 04	16 38	22 44	26 28	19 18	25 24	9 57	28 42	12 33
17 Th	3 44 8	24 36 12	29 28	13 19	29 26	0♐56	23 25	28 53	19 07	16 36	22 44	26 29	19 40	25 33	10 08	28 58	12 31
18 F	3 48 5	25 36 41	11♍41	13 19	1♐00	2 11	23 09	28 52	19 09	16 33	22 43	26 30	20 02	25 41	10 20	29 13	12 29
19 Sa	3 52 1	26 37 12	24 11	13 20	2 34	3 27	22 53	28 50	19 12	16 31	22 43	26 31	20 24	25 49	10 32	29 29	12 28
20 Su	3 55 58	27 37 45	7♎01	13 22	4 07	4 42	22 36	28 50	19 15	16 28	22 42	26 33	20 45	25 56	10 45	29 45	12 26
21 M	3 59 54	28 38 20	20 14	13 23	5 40	5 57	22 19	28 49	19 18	16 26	22 42	26 34	21 07	26 03	10 58	0♓02	12 24
22 T	4 3 51	29 38 56	3♏52	13 24℞	7 13	7 12	22 01	28 48	19 21	16 24	22 41	26 35	21 28	26 09	11 11	0 18	12 23
23 W	4 7 47	0♐39 34	17 53	13 24	8 46	8 28	21 42	28 48D	19 24	16 21	22 41	26 36	21 49	26 14	11 25	0 35	12 21
24 Th	4 11 44	1 40 13	2♐16	13 23	10 19	9 43	21 22	28 48	19 27	16 19	22 40	26 37	22 10	26 19	11 39	0 52	12 19
25 F	4 15 40	2 40 54	16 53	13 21	11 51	10 58	21 02	28 48	19 30	16 16	22 40	26 39	22 31	26 23	11 54	1 10	12 18
26 Sa	4 19 37	3 41 36	1♑40	13 19	13 24	12 14	20 42	28 48	19 33	16 14	22 40	26 40	22 52	26 26	12 09	1 27	12 16
27 Su	4 23 34	4 42 20	16 27	13 16	14 56	13 29	20 21	28 49	19 37	16 12	22 40	26 41	23 13	26 29	12 24	1 45	12 15
28 M	4 27 30	5 43 04	1♒09	13 13	16 28	14 44	19 59	28 50	19 40	16 09	22 39	26 43	23 33	26 31	12 40	2 03	12 14
29 T	4 31 27	6 43 50	15 38	13 11	18 00	16 00	19 37	28 51	19 44	16 07	22 39	26 44	23 53	26 32	12 56	2 22	12 12
30 W	4 35 23	7 44 36	29 51	13 09D	19 32	17 15	19 15	28 52	19 47	16 05	22 39	26 46	24 14	26 33℞	13 12	2 40	12 11

EPHEMERIS CALCULATED FOR 12 MIDNIGHT GREENWICH MEAN TIME. ALL OTHER DATA AND FACING ASPECTARIAN PAGE IN **EASTERN TIME (BOLD)** AND PACIFIC TIME (REGULAR).

DECEMBER 2022

☽ Last Aspect day	ET	PT	asp	☽ Ingress sign	day	ET	PT
1	**9:44 pm**	6:44 pm	☌ ♃	♈	1	**11:41 pm**	8:41 pm
3		9:46 pm	□ ♇	♉	4	**6:38 am**	3:38 am
4	**12:46 am**		□ ♇	♉	4	**6:38 am**	3:38 am
6	**2:02 pm**	11:02 am	⚹ ♃	♊	6	**3:49 pm**	12:49 pm
8		10:13 pm	□ ♃	♋	8		11:49 pm
9	**1:13 am**		□ ♃	♋	9	**2:49 am**	
11	**1:49 pm**	10:49 am	△ ♃	♌	11	**3:09 pm**	12:09 pm
13	**10:52 am**	7:52 am	△ ☉	♍	14	**3:45 am**	12:45 am
16	**2:13 pm**	11:13 am	☍ ♃	♎	16	**2:49 pm**	11:49 am
18	**5:35 pm**	2:35 pm	□ ♇	♏	18	**10:31 pm**	7:31 pm
20	**9:45 pm**	6:45 pm	⚹ ♇	♐	20		11:12 pm

☽ Last Aspect day	ET	PT	asp	☽ Ingress sign	day	ET	PT
20	**9:45 pm**	6:45 pm	⚹ ♇	♐	21	**2:12 am**	
22	**3:16 pm**	12:16 pm	□ ♆	♑	22		11:49 pm
22	**3:16 pm**	12:16 pm	□ ♆	♑	23	**2:49 am**	
24	**10:11 pm**	7:11 pm	☌ ♇	♒	24		11:14 pm
24	**10:11 pm**	7:11 pm	☌ ♇	♒	25	**2:14 am**	
26	**1:19 pm**	10:19 am	☌ ♄	♓	26		11:34 pm
26	**1:19 pm**	10:19 am	☌ ♄	♓	27	**2:34 am**	
28		10:21 pm	⚹ ♇	♈	29	**5:36 am**	2:36 am
29	**1:21 am**		⚹ ♇	♈	29	**5:36 am**	2:36 am
31	**7:44 am**	4:44 am	□ ♇	♉	31	**12:08 pm**	9:08 am

☽ Phases & Eclipses phase	day	ET	PT
Full Moon	7	**11:08 pm**	8:08 pm
4th Quarter	16	**3:56 am**	12:56 am
New Moon	23	**5:17 am**	2:17 am
2nd Quarter	29	**8:21 pm**	5:21 pm

Planet Ingress		day	ET	PT
☿	♑	6	**5:08 pm**	2:08 pm
♀	♑	9	**10:54 pm**	7:54 pm
⚳	♎	18	**6:34 pm**	3:34 pm
♃	♈	20	**9:32 am**	6:32 am
☉	♑	21	**4:48 pm**	1:48 pm

Planetary Motion		day	ET	PT
♆	D	3	**7:15 pm**	4:15 pm
⚷	D	23	**4:31 am**	1:31 am
☿	℞	29	**4:32 am**	1:32 am

1 THURSDAY
♀ ☍ ♂ **12:28 am**
☽ □ ♂ **3:42 am** 12:42 am
☽ □ ♀ **4:08 am** 1:08 am
☽ ⚺ ♄ **5:43 am** 2:43 am
☽ □ ☿ **9:23 am** 6:23 am
☽ ☌ ♆ **10:36 am** 7:36 am
☽ ⚹ ♇ **5:59 pm** 2:59 pm
☿ □ ♆ **8:08 pm** 5:08 pm
☽ ☌ ♃ **9:44 pm** 6:44 pm
♀ ⚹ ♄ **10:09 pm** 7:09 pm

2 FRIDAY
☽ △ ☉ **7:10 pm** 4:10 pm

3 SATURDAY
☽ ⚺ ♅ **4:36 am** 1:36 am
☽ ⚹ ♂ **8:11 am** 5:11 am
☽ ⚹ ♄ **12:06 pm** 9:06 am
☽ △ ♀ **3:57 pm** 12:57 pm
☽ ⚺ ♆ **4:56 pm** 1:56 pm
☽ △ ☿ **10:53 pm** 7:53 pm
☽ □ ♇ 9:46 pm
♀ □ ♆ 11:12 pm

4 SUNDAY
☽ □ ♇ **12:46 am**
♀ □ ♆ **2:12 am**
☽ ⚺ ♃ **4:44 am** 1:44 am
☿ ⚺ ♇ **3:11 pm** 12:11 pm

5 MONDAY
☽ ⚻ ☉ **7:50 am** 4:50 am
☽ ☌ ♅ **12:38 pm** 9:38 am
☽ ⚺ ♂ **2:50 pm** 11:50 am
☽ □ ♄ **8:54 pm** 5:54 pm
☽ ⚹ ♆ 10:37 pm
☿ □ ♃ 11:05 pm

6 TUESDAY
☽ ⚹ ♆ **1:37 am**
☿ □ ♃ **2:05 am**
☽ ⚻ ♀ **6:55 am** 3:55 am
☽ △ ♇ **9:51 am** 6:51 am
☽ ⚹ ♃ **2:02 pm** 11:02 am
☽ ⚻ ☿ **3:38 pm** 12:38 pm

7 WEDNESDAY
♀ ⚺ ♇ **12:33 pm** 9:33 am
☉ ⚻ ♅ **5:35 pm** 2:35 pm
☽ ⚺ ♅ **10:40 pm** 7:40 pm
☽ ☍ ☉ **11:08 pm** 8:08 pm
☽ ☌ ♂ **11:19 pm** 8:19 pm
☉ ☍ ♂ 9:42 pm

8 THURSDAY
☉ ☍ ♂ **12:42 am**
☽ △ ♄ **7:41 am** 4:41 am
☽ □ ♆ **12:13 pm** 9:13 am
☽ ⚻ ♇ **8:49 pm** 5:49 pm
♂ ⚺ ♅ **10:05 pm** 7:05 pm
☽ ☍ ♀ 9:29 pm
☽ □ ♃ 10:13 pm

9 FRIDAY
☽ ☍ ♀ **12:29 am**
☽ □ ♃ **1:13 am**
♀ □ ♃ **7:55 am** 4:55 am
☽ ☍ ☿ **10:55 am** 7:55 am

10 SATURDAY
☽ ⚺ ♂ **9:16 am** 6:16 am
☽ ⚹ ♅ **10:17 am** 7:17 am
☽ ⚻ ☉ **4:30 pm** 1:30 pm
☽ ⚻ ♄ **8:03 pm** 5:03 pm
☽ △ ♆ 9:18 pm

11 SUNDAY
☽ △ ♆ **12:18 am**
☽ ☍ ♇ **9:11 am** 6:11 am
☽ △ ♃ **1:49 pm** 10:49 am
☽ ⚻ ♀ **7:54 pm** 4:54 pm

12 MONDAY
☽ ⚻ ☿ **7:47 am** 4:47 am
☉ ⚹ ♄ **1:12 pm** 10:12 am
☽ ⚹ ♂ **8:04 pm** 5:04 pm
☽ □ ♅ **10:47 pm** 7:47 pm

13 TUESDAY
☽ ☍ ♄ **9:09 am** 6:09 am
☽ △ ☉ **10:52 am** 7:52 am
☽ ⚻ ♆ **1:01 pm** 10:01 am
☽ ⚻ ♇ **9:59 pm** 6:59 pm
☽ ⚻ ♃ 11:46 pm

14 WEDNESDAY
☽ ⚻ ♃ **2:46 am**
☉ □ ♆ **12:10 pm** 9:10 am
☽ △ ♀ **3:32 pm** 12:32 pm

15 THURSDAY
☽ △ ☿ **4:02 am** 1:02 am
☽ □ ♂ **6:29 am** 3:29 am
☽ △ ♅ **10:41 am** 7:41 am
☽ ⚻ ♄ **9:18 pm** 6:18 pm
☿ ⚻ ♂ **10:12 pm** 7:12 pm
☽ ☍ ♆ 9:41 pm

16 FRIDAY
☽ ☍ ♆ **12:41 am**
☽ □ ☉ **3:56 am** 12:56 am
☽ △ ♇ **9:25 am** 6:25 am
☽ ☍ ♃ **2:13 pm** 11:13 am

17 SATURDAY
☽ □ ♀ **8:28 am** 5:28 am
☽ △ ♂ **2:44 pm** 11:44 am
☿ △ ♅ **4:37 pm** 1:37 pm
☽ ⚻ ♅ **8:03 pm** 5:03 pm
☽ □ ☿ **8:26 pm** 5:26 pm

18 SUNDAY
☽ △ ♄ **6:31 am** 3:31 am
☽ ⚻ ♆ **9:20 am** 6:20 am
☽ ⚹ ☉ **5:03 pm** 2:03 pm
☽ □ ♇ **5:35 pm** 2:35 pm
☽ ⚻ ♃ **10:17 pm** 7:17 pm
☉ ⚺ ♇ 9:26 pm

19 MONDAY
☉ ⚺ ♇ **12:26 am**
♀ ⚻ ♂ **12:37 pm** 9:37 am
☽ ⚻ ♂ **7:30 pm** 4:30 pm
☽ ⚹ ♀ **8:22 pm** 5:22 pm
☽ ☍ ♅ 10:33 pm

20 TUESDAY
☽ ☍ ♅ **1:33 am**
☽ ⚹ ☿ **6:58 am** 3:58 am
☽ □ ♄ **11:41 am** 8:41 am
☽ △ ♆ **2:01 pm** 11:01 am
☽ ⚹ ♇ **9:45 pm** 6:45 pm
☽ ⚺ ☉ 10:06 pm
☽ △ ♃ 11:19 pm

21 WEDNESDAY
☽ ⚺ ☉ **1:06 am**
☽ △ ♃ **2:19 am**
☉ □ ♃ **7:50 pm** 4:50 pm
☽ ☍ ♂ **8:48 pm** 5:48 pm

22 THURSDAY
☽ ⚺ ♀ **3:15 am** 12:15 am
☽ ⚻ ♅ **3:23 am** 12:23 am
♀ △ ♅ **4:48 am** 1:48 am
☽ ⚺ ☿ **12:15 pm** 9:15 am
☽ ⚹ ♄ **1:19 pm** 10:19 am
☽ □ ♆ **3:16 pm** 12:16 pm
☽ ⚺ ♇ **10:40 pm** 7:40 pm

23 FRIDAY
☽ □ ♃ **3:13 am** 12:13 am
☽ ☌ ☉ **5:17 am** 2:17 am
☿ ⚺ ♄ **8:08 am** 5:08 am
☽ ⚻ ♂ **7:51 pm** 4:51 pm

24 SATURDAY
☽ △ ♅ **3:02 am** 12:02 am
☽ ☌ ♀ **7:16 am** 4:16 am
☽ ⚺ ♄ **1:09 pm** 10:09 am
☽ ☌ ☿ **2:32 pm** 11:32 am
☽ ⚹ ♆ **2:48 pm** 11:48 am
☿ ⚹ ♆ **8:17 pm** 5:17 pm
☽ ☌ ♇ **10:11 pm** 7:11 pm
☽ ⚹ ♃ 11:56 pm

25 SUNDAY
☽ ⚹ ♃ **2:56 am**
☽ ⚺ ☉ **8:07 am** 5:07 am
☽ △ ♂ **6:34 pm** 3:34 pm
☽ □ ♅ 11:35 pm

26 MONDAY
☽ □ ♅ **2:35 am**
☽ ⚺ ♀ **11:24 am** 8:24 am
☽ ☌ ♄ **1:19 pm** 10:19 am
☽ ⚺ ♆ **2:46 pm** 11:46 am
☽ ⚺ ☿ **4:24 pm** 1:24 pm
☽ ⚺ ♇ **10:28 pm** 7:28 pm

27 TUESDAY
☽ ⚺ ♃ **3:39 am** 12:39 am
♀ ⚺ ♄ **11:53 am** 8:53 am
☽ ⚹ ☉ **12:23 pm** 9:23 am
☽ □ ♂ **6:54 pm** 3:54 pm

28 WEDNESDAY
♀ ⚹ ♆ **3:32 am** 12:32 am
☽ ⚹ ♅ **4:02 am** 1:02 am
☽ ⚺ ♄ **3:51 pm** 12:51 pm
☽ ☌ ♆ **5:05 pm** 2:05 pm
☽ ⚹ ♀ **6:25 pm** 3:25 pm
☽ ⚹ ☿ **7:43 pm** 4:43 pm
☽ ⚹ ♇ 10:21 pm

29 THURSDAY
☽ ⚹ ♇ **1:21 am**
☽ ☌ ♃ **7:11 am** 4:11 am
☿ ☌ ♀ **8:58 am** 5:58 am
☽ □ ☉ **8:21 pm** 5:21 pm
☽ ⚹ ♂ **10:17 pm** 7:17 pm

30 FRIDAY
☽ ⚺ ♅ **8:45 am** 5:45 am
☉ ⚻ ♂ **6:21 pm** 3:21 pm
☽ ⚹ ♄ **9:52 pm** 6:52 pm
☽ ⚺ ♆ **10:51 pm** 7:51 pm
☽ □ ☿ 10:00 pm

31 SATURDAY
☽ □ ☿ **1:00 am**
☽ □ ♀ **5:59 am** 2:59 am
☽ □ ♇ **7:44 am** 4:44 am
☽ ⚺ ♃ **2:20 pm** 11:20 am
♀ ☌ ♇ 9:25 pm

Eastern time in bold type
Pacific time in medium type

DECEMBER 2022

DATE	SID.TIME	SUN	MOON	NODE	MERCURY	VENUS	MARS	JUPITER	SATURN	URANUS	NEPTUNE	PLUTO	CERES	PALLAS	JUNO	VESTA	CHIRON
1 Th	4 39 20	8♐45 24	13♓46	13♉09	21♐03	18♐30	18♊53℞	28♓53	19♒51	16♉03℞	22♓39℞	26♑47	24♍34	26♋33℞	13♓29	2♓59	12♈10℞
2 F	4 43 16	9 46 12	27 23	13 10	22 34	19 46	18 30	28 55	19 55	16 00	22 39	26 48	24 53	26 32	13 46	3 18	12 09
3 Sa	4 47 13	10 47 01	10♈42	13 12	24 06	21 01	18 07	28 56	19 59	15 58	22 39	26 50	25 13	26 30	14 03	3 37	12 08
4 Su	4 51 10	11 47 51	23 45	13 13	25 36	22 16	17 44	28 58	20 03	15 56	22 39D	26 51	25 32	26 28	14 21	3 56	12 06
5 M	4 55 6	12 48 41	6♉35	13 15℞	27 07	23 31	17 21	29 01	20 07	15 54	22 39	26 53	25 52	26 25	14 39	4 16	12 05
6 T	4 59 3	13 49 33	19 12	13 15	28 37	24 47	16 58	29 03	20 11	15 52	22 39	26 54	26 11	26 22	14 57	4 35	12 04
7 W	5 2 59	14 50 26	1♊39	13 13	0♑07	26 02	16 34	29 06	20 15	15 50	22 39	26 56	26 30	26 17	15 16	4 55	12 04
8 Th	5 6 56	15 51 20	13 56	13 10	1 36	27 17	16 11	29 08	20 20	15 48	22 39	26 57	26 48	26 12	15 35	5 15	12 03
9 F	5 10 52	16 52 15	26 04	13 05	3 05	28 32	15 48	29 11	20 24	15 46	22 39	26 59	27 07	26 06	15 55	5 35	12 02
10 Sa	5 14 49	17 53 10	8♋06	12 59	4 33	29 48	15 25	29 14	20 29	15 44	22 39	27 01	27 25	25 59	16 14	5 56	12 01
11 Su	5 18 45	18 54 07	20 02	12 52	6 01	1♑03	15 03	29 18	20 33	15 42	22 40	27 02	27 43	25 52	16 34	6 16	12 00
12 M	5 22 42	19 55 05	1♌54	12 45	7 27	2 18	14 40	29 21	20 38	15 40	22 40	27 04	28 01	25 44	16 54	6 37	12 00
13 T	5 26 39	20 56 04	13 45	12 38	8 53	3 34	14 18	29 25	20 42	15 38	22 40	27 05	28 19	25 35	17 15	6 58	11 59
14 W	5 30 35	21 57 03	25 39	12 33	10 17	4 49	13 57	29 29	20 47	15 36	22 40	27 07	28 36	25 26	17 36	7 19	11 59
15 Th	5 34 32	22 58 04	7♍38	12 30	11 40	6 04	13 35	29 33	20 52	15 34	22 41	27 09	28 54	25 15	17 57	7 40	11 58
16 F	5 38 28	23 59 06	19 47	12 29D	13 01	7 19	13 14	29 38	20 57	15 32	22 41	27 11	29 11	25 04	18 18	8 01	11 58
17 Sa	5 42 25	25 00 09	2♎11	12 29	14 20	8 35	12 54	29 42	21 02	15 30	22 42	27 12	29 27	24 53	18 40	8 23	11 57
18 Su	5 46 21	26 01 12	14 55	12 30	15 36	9 50	12 34	29 47	21 07	15 29	22 42	27 14	29 44	24 41	19 02	8 44	11 57
19 M	5 50 18	27 02 17	28 03	12 31	16 50	11 05	12 14	29 52	21 12	15 27	22 43	27 16	0♎00	24 28	19 24	9 06	11 57
20 T	5 54 14	28 03 22	11♏38	12 32℞	18 01	12 20	11 55	29 57	21 18	15 25	22 43	27 17	0 16	24 14	19 46	9 28	11 56
21 W	5 58 11	29 04 29	25 41	12 31	19 08	13 36	11 37	0♈02	21 23	15 24	22 44	27 19	0 32	24 00	20 09	9 50	11 56
22 Th	6 2 8	0♑05 36	10♐12	12 28	20 10	14 51	11 20	0 08	21 28	15 22	22 44	27 21	0 48	23 45	20 32	10 12	11 56
23 F	6 6 4	1 06 44	25 05	12 23	21 08	16 06	11 03	0 13	21 34	15 21	22 45	27 23	1 03	23 30	20 55	10 35	11 56D
24 Sa	6 10 1	2 07 52	10♑13	12 16	21 59	17 21	10 46	0 19	21 39	15 19	22 46	27 25	1 18	23 14	21 18	10 57	11 56
25 Su	6 13 57	3 09 01	25 26	12 08	22 44	18 37	10 31	0 25	21 45	15 18	22 46	27 26	1 33	22 57	21 42	11 20	11 56
26 M	6 17 54	4 10 09	10♒32	12 00	23 22	19 52	10 16	0 31	21 50	15 16	22 47	27 28	1 48	22 40	22 06	11 42	11 56
27 T	6 21 50	5 11 18	25 24	11 53	23 51	21 07	10 02	0 37	21 56	15 15	22 48	27 30	2 02	22 23	22 30	12 05	11 56
28 W	6 25 47	6 12 27	9♓52	11 48	24 11	22 22	9 49	0 44	22 02	15 14	22 49	27 32	2 16	22 05	22 54	12 28	11 57
29 Th	6 29 44	7 13 36	23 56	11 45	24 21℞	23 37	9 36	0 51	22 07	15 12	22 50	27 34	2 30	21 46	23 19	12 51	11 57
30 F	6 33 40	8 14 45	7♈33	11 44D	24 19	24 53	9 25	0 57	22 13	15 11	22 50	27 36	2 43	21 28	23 44	13 14	11 57
31 Sa	6 37 37	9 15 54	20 46	11 44	24 07	26 08	9 14	1 04	22 19	15 10	22 51	27 38	2 56	21 09	24 09	13 38	11 58

EPHEMERIS CALCULATED FOR 12 MIDNIGHT GREENWICH MEAN TIME. ALL OTHER DATA AND FACING ASPECTARIAN PAGE IN **EASTERN TIME (BOLD)** AND PACIFIC TIME (REGULAR).

JANUARY 2023

☽ Last Aspect day	ET / hr:mn / PT	asp	☽ Ingress sign	day	ET / hr:mn / PT
2	**5:16 pm** 2:16 pm	△♇	♊	2	**9:44 pm** 6:44 pm
4	**7:08 pm** 4:08 pm	□♆	♋	5	**9:15 am** 6:15 am
7	**5:23 pm** 2:23 pm	☍♇	♌	7	**9:40 pm** 6:40 pm
9	**8:52 pm** 5:52 pm	☍♄	♍	10	**10:15 am** 7:15 am
12	**6:06 pm** 3:06 pm	△♇	♎	12	**9:56 pm** 6:56 pm
15	**3:40 am** 12:40 am	□♇	♏	15	**7:08 am** 4:08 am
17	**9:27 am** 6:27 am	⚹♇	♐	17	**12:33 pm** 9:33 am
19	**5:09 am** 2:09 am	⚹♄	♑	19	**2:11 pm** 11:11 am
21	**10:52 am** 7:52 am	☌♇	♒	21	**1:29 pm** 10:29 am
23	**5:19 am** 2:19 am	☌♀	♓	23	**12:36 pm** 9:36 am

☽ Last Aspect day	ET / hr:mn / PT	asp	☽ Ingress sign	day	ET / hr:mn / PT
25	**11:12 am** 8:12 am	⚹♇	♈	25	**1:48 pm** 10:48 am
27	**4:01 pm** 1:01 pm	□♇	♉	27	**6:42 pm** 3:42 pm
29	9:52 pm	△♇	♊	30	**3:35 am** 12:35 am
30	**12:52 am**	△♇	♊	30	**3:35 am** 12:35 am

☽ Phases & Eclipses phase	day	ET / hr:mn / PT
Full Moon	6	**6:08 pm** 3:08 pm
4th Quarter	14	**9:10 pm** 6:10 pm
New Moon	21	**3:53 pm** 12:53 pm
2nd Quarter	28	**10:19 am** 7:19 am

Planet Ingress		day	ET / hr:mn / PT
♀	♒	2	**9:09 pm** 6:09 pm
⚵	♈	12	10:30 pm
⚵	♈	13	**1:30 am**
☉	♒	20	**3:30 am** 12:30 am
♀	♓	26	**9:33 pm** 6:33 pm

Planetary Motion		day	ET / hr:mn / PT
♂	D	12	**3:56 pm** 12:56 pm
☿	D	18	**8:12 am** 5:12 am
♅	D	22	**5:59 pm** 2:59 pm

1 SUNDAY
♀ ☌ ♇ **12:25 am**
☽ ⚺ ♂ **5:09 am** 2:09 am
☽ △ ☉ **8:42 am** 5:42 am
☽ ☌ ♅ **4:52 pm** 1:52 pm
☿ ⚹ ♆ 10:44 pm

2 MONDAY
☿ ⚹ ♆ **1:44 am**
☽ □ ♄ **7:15 am** 4:15 am
☽ △ ☿ **7:30 am** 4:30 am
☽ ⚹ ♆ **7:53 am** 4:53 am
☿ ⚺ ♄ **10:59 am** 7:59 am
☽ △ ♇ **5:16 pm** 2:16 pm
☽ △ ♀ **9:48 pm** 6:48 pm
☽ ⚹ ♃ 9:37 pm

3 TUESDAY
☽ ⚹ ♃ **12:37 am**
☽ ☌ ♂ **2:47 pm** 11:47 am
☽ ⚻ ☉ 9:30 pm

4 WEDNESDAY
☽ ⚻ ☉ **12:30 am**
☽ ⚺ ♅ **3:30 am** 12:30 am
♀ ⚹ ♃ **4:08 am** 1:08 am
☽ ⚻ ☿ **2:10 pm** 11:10 am
☽ △ ♄ **6:54 pm** 3:54 pm
☽ □ ♆ **7:08 pm** 4:08 pm

5 THURSDAY
☽ ⚻ ♇ **4:50 am** 1:50 am
☉ △ ♅ **11:43 am** 8:43 am

☽ □ ♃ **12:50 pm** 9:50 am
☽ ⚻ ♀ **4:16 pm** 1:16 pm
☽ ⚺ ♂ 11:08 pm
♄ ⚺ ♆ 11:56 pm

6 FRIDAY
☽ ⚺ ♂ **2:08 am**
♄ ⚺ ♆ **2:56 am**
☽ ⚹ ♅ **3:30 pm** 12:30 pm
☽ ☍ ☉ **6:08 pm** 3:08 pm
☽ ☍ ☿ **8:36 pm** 5:36 pm

7 SATURDAY
☽ △ ♆ **7:30 am** 4:30 am
☽ ⚻ ♄ **7:42 am** 4:42 am
☉ ☌ ☿ **7:57 am** 4:57 am
☽ ☍ ♇ **5:23 pm** 2:23 pm
☽ △ ♃ 11:00 pm

8 SUNDAY
☽ △ ♃ **2:00 am**
☽ ☍ ♀ **11:52 am** 8:52 am
☽ ⚹ ♂ **2:19 pm** 11:19 am
☿ △ ♅ **6:23 pm** 3:23 pm

9 MONDAY
☽ ⚻ ☿ **3:05 am** 12:05 am
☽ □ ♅ **4:02 am** 1:02 am
♀ △ ♂ **10:22 am** 7:22 am
☽ ⚻ ☉ **12:26 pm** 9:26 am
☽ ⚻ ♆ **8:13 pm** 5:13 pm
☽ ☍ ♄ **8:52 pm** 5:52 pm

10 TUESDAY
☽ ⚻ ♇ **6:09 am** 3:09 am
☽ ⚻ ♃ **3:17 pm** 12:17 pm
☽ □ ♂ 11:36 pm

11 WEDNESDAY
☽ □ ♂ **2:36 am**
☽ ⚻ ♀ **7:25 am** 4:25 am
☽ △ ☿ **9:58 am** 6:58 am
☽ △ ♅ **4:17 pm** 1:17 pm
☿ ⚺ ♀ **10:02 pm** 7:02 pm

12 THURSDAY
☽ △ ☉ **6:08 am** 3:08 am
☽ ☍ ♆ **8:21 am** 5:21 am
☽ ⚻ ♄ **9:25 am** 6:25 am
☽ △ ♇ **6:06 pm** 3:06 pm

13 FRIDAY
☽ ☍ ♃ **3:34 am** 12:34 am
☉ ⚹ ♆ **9:11 am** 6:11 am
☽ △ ♂ **1:46 pm** 10:46 am
☽ □ ☿ **4:55 pm** 1:55 pm
☽ △ ♀ 9:58 pm
☉ ⚺ ♄ 10:47 pm
☽ ⚻ ♅ 11:54 pm

14 SATURDAY
☽ △ ♀ **12:58 am**
☉ ⚺ ♄ **1:47 am**
☽ ⚻ ♅ **2:54 am**
☽ ⚻ ♆ **6:22 pm** 3:22 pm
☽ △ ♄ **7:47 pm** 4:47 pm

♀ □ ♅ **8:22 pm** 5:22 pm
☽ □ ☉ **9:10 pm** 6:10 pm

15 SUNDAY
☽ □ ♇ **3:40 am** 12:40 am
☽ ⚻ ♃ **1:07 pm** 10:07 am
☽ ⚻ ♂ **10:08 pm** 7:08 pm
☽ ⚹ ☿ **10:47 pm** 7:47 pm

16 MONDAY
☽ ☍ ♅ **10:17 am** 7:17 am
☽ □ ♀ **2:09 pm** 11:09 am
☽ △ ♆ 9:48 pm
☿ ⚻ ♂ 10:42 pm
☽ □ ♄ 11:27 pm

17 TUESDAY
☽ △ ♆ **12:48 am**
☿ ⚻ ♂ **1:42 am**
☽ □ ♄ **2:27 am**
☽ ⚹ ☉ **7:36 am** 4:36 am
☽ ⚹ ♇ **9:27 am** 6:27 am
☽ △ ♃ **6:41 pm** 3:41 pm
☽ ⚺ ☿ 11:21 pm
☽ ☍ ♂ 11:39 pm

18 WEDNESDAY
☽ ⚺ ☿ **2:21 am**
☽ ☍ ♂ **2:39 am**
☉ ☌ ♇ **9:44 am** 6:44 am
☽ ⚻ ♅ **1:42 pm** 10:42 am
☽ ⚹ ♀ **10:05 pm** 7:05 pm

19 THURSDAY
☽ □ ♆ **3:17 am** 12:17 am
☽ ⚹ ♄ **5:09 am** 2:09 am
☽ ⚺ ♇ **11:24 am** 8:24 am
☽ ⚺ ☉ **1:13 pm** 10:13 am
☽ □ ♃ **8:29 pm** 5:29 pm

20 FRIDAY
☽ ☌ ☿ **3:30 am** 12:30 am
☽ ⚻ ♂ **3:42 am** 12:42 am
☽ △ ♅ **1:55 pm** 10:55 am
☿ ⚻ ♂ **8:06 pm** 5:06 pm
☽ ⚺ ♀ 11:10 pm

21 SATURDAY
☽ ⚺ ♀ **2:10 am**
☽ ⚹ ♆ **3:01 am** 12:01 am
☽ ⚺ ♄ **5:04 am** 2:04 am
☽ ☌ ♇ **10:52 am** 7:52 am
♀ ⚺ ♆ **12:43 pm** 9:43 am
☽ ☌ ☉ **3:53 pm** 12:53 pm
☽ ⚹ ♃ **8:09 pm** 5:09 pm

22 SUNDAY
☽ △ ♂ **3:02 am** 12:02 am
☽ ⚺ ☿ **3:36 am** 12:36 am
☽ □ ♅ **12:49 pm** 9:49 am
♀ ☌ ♄ **5:13 pm** 2:13 pm
☽ ⚺ ♆ 11:03 pm

23 MONDAY
☽ ⚺ ♆ **2:03 am**
☽ ☌ ♄ **4:25 am** 1:25 am
☽ ☌ ♀ **5:19 am** 2:19 am

☽ ⚺ ♇ **10:02 am** 7:02 am
☽ ⚺ ☉ **6:30 pm** 3:30 pm
☽ ⚺ ♃ **7:59 pm** 4:59 pm
☽ □ ♂ 11:56 pm

24 TUESDAY
☽ □ ♂ **2:56 am**
☽ ⚹ ☿ **4:59 am** 1:59 am
☽ ⚹ ♅ **12:43 pm** 9:43 am
☉ ⚹ ♃ **8:30 pm** 5:30 pm
☽ ☌ ♆ 11:42 pm

25 WEDNESDAY
☽ ☌ ♆ **2:42 am**
☽ ⚺ ♄ **5:30 am** 2:30 am
☽ ⚺ ♀ **10:45 am** 7:45 am
☽ ⚹ ♇ **11:12 am** 8:12 am
♀ ⚺ ♇ **3:59 pm** 12:59 pm
☽ ☌ ♃ **10:18 pm** 7:18 pm
☽ ⚹ ☉ **11:59 pm** 8:59 pm

26 THURSDAY
☽ ⚹ ♂ **5:40 am** 2:40 am
☽ □ ☿ **10:08 am** 7:08 am
☽ ⚺ ♅ **3:38 pm** 12:38 pm

27 FRIDAY
☽ ⚺ ♆ **6:50 am** 3:50 am
☽ ⚹ ♄ **10:13 am** 7:13 am
☽ □ ♇ **4:01 pm** 1:01 pm
☽ ⚹ ♀ **8:56 pm** 5:56 pm

28 SATURDAY
☽ ⚺ ♃ **4:39 am** 1:39 am
☽ □ ☉ **10:19 am** 7:19 am

☽ ⚺ ♂ **12:34 pm** 9:34 am
☽ △ ☿ **8:44 pm** 5:44 pm
☽ ☌ ♅ **10:37 pm** 7:37 pm

29 SUNDAY
☽ ⚹ ♆ **3:02 pm** 12:02 pm
☽ □ ♄ **7:03 pm** 4:03 pm
☉ △ ♂ **8:45 pm** 5:45 pm
☿ △ ♅ **9:16 pm** 6:16 pm
☽ △ ♇ 9:52 pm

30 MONDAY
☽ △ ♇ **12:52 am**
☽ □ ♀ **12:24 pm** 9:24 am
☽ ⚹ ♃ **3:01 pm** 12:01 pm
☽ ☌ ♂ **11:27 pm** 8:27 pm
☽ △ ☉ 10:24 pm

31 TUESDAY
☽ △ ☉ **1:24 am**
☽ ⚺ ♅ **9:06 am** 6:06 am
☽ ⚻ ☿ **12:27 pm** 9:27 am
♀ ⚺ ♃ **6:14 pm** 3:14 pm
☽ □ ♆ 11:21 pm

Eastern time in bold type
Pacific time in medium type

JANUARY 2023

DATE	SID.TIME	SUN	MOON	NODE	MERCURY	VENUS	MARS	JUPITER	SATURN	URANUS	NEPTUNE	PLUTO	CERES	PALLAS	JUNO	VESTA	CHIRON
1 Su	6 41 33	10♑17 02	3♉39	11♉45℞	23♑42℞	27♑23	9♊04℞	1♈12	22♒25	15♉09℞	22♓52	27♑39	3♎09	20♋49℞	24♓34	14♓01	11♈58
2 M	6 45 30	11 18 11	16 14	11 45	23 06	28 38	8 55	1 19	22 31	15 08	22 53	27 41	3 22	20 30	25 00	14 25	11 59
3 T	6 49 26	12 19 19	28 36	11 44	22 18	29 53	8 46	1 26	22 37	15 07	22 54	27 43	3 34	20 10	25 25	14 48	11 59
4 W	6 53 23	13 20 27	10♊48	11 39	21 20	1♒08	8 39	1 34	22 43	15 06	22 55	27 45	3 46	19 50	25 51	15 12	12 00
5 Th	6 57 19	14 21 35	22 53	11 33	20 13	2 23	8 32	1 42	22 49	15 05	22 56	27 47	3 58	19 30	26 17	15 36	12 00
6 F	7 1 16	15 22 43	4♋52	11 23	18 59	3 39	8 26	1 50	22 56	15 04	22 57	27 49	4 09	19 10	26 43	16 00	12 01
7 Sa	7 5 13	16 23 51	16 47	11 11	17 40	4 54	8 21	1 58	23 02	15 03	22 59	27 51	4 20	18 50	27 10	16 24	12 02
8 Su	7 9 9	17 24 59	28 41	10 58	16 20	6 09	8 17	2 06	23 08	15 02	23 00	27 53	4 31	18 29	27 37	16 48	12 03
9 M	7 13 6	18 26 06	10♌33	10 44	15 00	7 24	8 14	2 14	23 15	15 02	23 01	27 55	4 41	18 09	28 03	17 12	12 04
10 T	7 17 2	19 27 14	22 26	10 32	13 42	8 39	8 11	2 23	23 21	15 01	23 02	27 57	4 51	17 49	28 30	17 37	12 05
11 W	7 20 59	20 28 21	4♍21	10 21	12 31	9 54	8 09	2 32	23 28	15 00	23 03	27 59	5 01	17 29	28 58	18 01	12 06
12 Th	7 24 55	21 29 29	16 21	10 13	11 26	11 09	8 08D	2 40	23 34	15 00	23 05	28 01	5 10	17 09	29 25	18 26	12 07
13 F	7 28 52	22 30 36	28 30	10 08	10 30	12 24	8 08	2 49	23 41	14 59	23 06	28 03	5 19	16 49	29 53	18 50	12 08
14 Sa	7 32 48	23 31 43	10♎51	10 05	9 42	13 39	8 08	2 58	23 47	14 59	23 07	28 05	5 28	16 29	0♈20	19 15	12 09
15 Su	7 36 45	24 32 50	23 29	10 04D	9 05	14 54	8 09	3 08	23 54	14 58	23 09	28 07	5 36	16 10	0 48	19 40	12 10
16 M	7 40 42	25 33 57	6♏28	10 05℞	8 37	16 09	8 11	3 17	24 00	14 58	23 10	28 09	5 44	15 51	1 16	20 05	12 11
17 T	7 44 38	26 35 04	19 53	10 04	8 19	17 24	8 14	3 26	24 07	14 57	23 11	28 11	5 52	15 32	1 44	20 29	12 13
18 W	7 48 35	27 36 10	3♐47	10 02	8 09D	18 39	8 18	3 36	24 14	14 57	23 13	28 12	5 59	15 13	2 13	20 54	12 14
19 Th	7 52 31	28 37 17	18 10	9 58	8 09	19 54	8 22	3 46	24 21	14 57	23 14	28 14	6 06	14 55	2 41	21 20	12 15
20 F	7 56 28	29 38 23	3♑00	9 51	8 17	21 08	8 27	3 56	24 27	14 57	23 16	28 16	6 12	14 38	3 10	21 45	12 17
21 Sa	8 0 24	0♒39 29	18 11	9 41	8 32	22 23	8 32	4 06	24 34	14 57	23 17	28 18	6 18	14 20	3 39	22 10	12 18
22 Su	8 4 21	1 40 34	3♒32	9 30	8 54	23 38	8 39	4 16	24 41	14 56D	23 19	28 20	6 23	14 04	4 08	22 35	12 20
23 M	8 8 17	2 41 38	18 53	9 18	9 22	24 53	8 46	4 26	24 48	14 56	23 21	28 22	6 29	13 47	4 37	23 01	12 22
24 T	8 12 14	3 42 42	4♓00	9 07	9 56	26 08	8 53	4 36	24 55	14 56	23 22	28 24	6 33	13 32	5 06	23 26	12 23
25 W	8 16 11	4 43 44	18 46	8 59	10 35	27 23	9 02	4 47	25 02	14 57	23 24	28 26	6 38	13 16	5 36	23 52	12 25
26 Th	8 20 7	5 44 46	3♈03	8 53	11 19	28 37	9 10	4 57	25 09	14 57	23 25	28 28	6 42	13 02	6 05	24 17	12 27
27 F	8 24 4	6 45 46	16 51	8 51	12 07	29 52	9 20	5 08	25 16	14 57	23 27	28 30	6 45	12 48	6 35	24 43	12 28
28 Sa	8 28 0	7 46 46	0♉10	8 50	12 58	1♓07	9 30	5 19	25 23	14 57	23 29	28 32	6 48	12 34	7 05	25 08	12 30
29 Su	8 31 57	8 47 44	13 03	8 50	13 54	2 21	9 41	5 30	25 30	14 57	23 31	28 34	6 51	12 22	7 35	25 34	12 32
30 M	8 35 53	9 48 41	25 35	8 49	14 52	3 36	9 52	5 41	25 37	14 58	23 32	28 36	6 53	12 09	8 05	26 00	12 34
31 T	8 39 50	10 49 37	7♊51	8 47	15 53	4 51	10 04	5 52	25 44	14 58	23 34	28 38	6 55	11 58	8 36	26 26	12 36

EPHEMERIS CALCULATED FOR 12 MIDNIGHT GREENWICH MEAN TIME. ALL OTHER DATA AND FACING ASPECTARIAN PAGE IN **EASTERN TIME (BOLD)** AND PACIFIC TIME (REGULAR).

FEBRUARY 2023

☽ Last Aspect day	ET / hr:mn / PT	asp	☽ Ingress sign	day	ET / hr:mn / PT
1	**6:58 am** 3:58 am	△♄	♋	1	**3:11 pm** 12:11 pm
3	10:19 pm	☍♇	♌	4	**3:48 am** 12:48 am
4	**1:19 am**	☍♇	♌	4	**3:48 am** 12:48 am
6	**9:15 am** 6:15 am	☍♄	♍	6	**4:14 pm** 1:14 pm
8	10:40 pm	△♇	♎	9	**3:47 am** 12:47 am
9	**1:40 am**	△♇	♎	9	**3:47 am** 12:47 am
11	**11:41 am** 8:41 am	□♇	♏	11	**1:34 pm** 10:34 am
13	**6:52 pm** 3:52 pm	⚹♇	♐	13	**8:31 pm** 5:31 pm
15	**8:06 pm** 5:06 pm	⚹♄	♑	15	9:00 pm
15	**8:06 pm** 5:06 pm	⚹♄	♑	16	**12:00 am**

☽ Last Aspect day	ET / hr:mn / PT	asp	☽ Ingress sign	day	ET / hr:mn / PT
17	**11:18 pm** 8:18 pm	☌♇	♒	17	9:35 pm
17	**11:18 pm** 8:18 pm	☌♇	♒	18	**12:35 am**
19	**9:00 pm** 6:00 pm	☌♄	♓	19	**11:56 pm** 8:56 pm
21	**11:06 pm** 8:06 pm	⚹♇	♈	21	9:14 pm
21	**11:06 pm** 8:06 pm	⚹♇	♈	22	**12:14 am**
23	11:22 pm	□♇	♉	24	**3:29 am** 12:29 am
24	**2:22 am**	□♇	♉	24	**3:29 am** 12:29 am
26	**9:42 am** 6:42 am	△♇	♊	26	**10:48 am** 7:48 am
28	**8:07 pm** 5:07 pm	△♄	♋	28	**9:40 pm** 6:40 pm

☽ Phases & Eclipses phase	day	ET / hr:mn / PT
Full Moon	5	**1:29 pm** 10:29 am
4th Quarter	13	**11:01 am** 8:01 am
New Moon	19	11:06 pm
New Moon	20	**2:06 am**
2nd Quarter	27	**3:06 am** 12:06 am

Planet Ingress		day	ET / hr:mn / PT
⚵	♈	7	**11:47 pm** 8:47 pm
☿	♒	11	**6:22 am** 3:22 am
☉	♓	18	**5:34 pm** 2:34 pm
♀	♈	19	11:56 pm
♀	♈	20	**2:56 am**

Planetary Motion		day	ET / hr:mn / PT
⚳	℞	3	**2:13 pm** 11:13 am
⚴	D	16	**9:26 am** 6:26 am

1 WEDNESDAY
☽ □ ♆ **2:21 am**
☽ △ ♄ **6:58 am** 3:58 am
☽ ⊼ ♇ **12:33 pm** 9:33 am

2 THURSDAY
☽ □ ♃ **3:55 am** 12:55 am
☽ △ ♀ **7:15 am** 4:15 am
☽ ⊻ ♂ **12:42 pm** 9:42 am
☽ ⊼ ☉ **7:12 pm** 4:12 pm
☽ ⚹ ♅ **9:27 pm** 6:27 pm

3 FRIDAY
☽ ☍ ☿ **7:09 am** 3:09 am
☽ △ ♆ **3:02 pm** 12:02 pm
☽ ⊼ ♄ **8:09 pm** 5:09 pm
☉ □ ♅ **9:50 pm** 6:50 pm
☽ ☍ ♇ 10:19 pm

4 SATURDAY
☽ ☍ ♇ **1:19 am**
☽ △ ♃ **5:34 pm** 2:34 pm
♀ □ ♂ **10:29 pm** 7:29 pm
☽ ⚹ ♂ 11:35 pm
☽ ⊼ ♀ 11:58 pm

5 SUNDAY
☽ ⚹ ♂ **2:35 am**
☽ ⊼ ♀ **2:58 am**
☽ □ ♅ **10:08 am** 7:08 am
☽ ☍ ☉ **1:29 pm** 10:29 am
☽ ⊼ ☿ 11:37 pm

6 MONDAY
☽ ⊼ ☿ **2:37 am**
☽ ⊼ ♆ **3:44 am** 12:44 am
☽ ☍ ♄ **9:15 am** 6:15 am
☿ ⚹ ♆ **1:26 pm** 10:26 am
☽ ⊼ ♇ **1:56 pm** 10:56 am

7 TUESDAY
☽ ⊼ ♃ **6:51 am** 3:51 am
☽ □ ♂ **4:05 pm** 1:05 pm
☽ ☍ ♀ **10:01 pm** 7:01 pm
☽ △ ♅ **10:16 pm** 7:16 pm
♀ ⚹ ♅ 9:29 pm

8 WEDNESDAY
♀ ⚹ ♅ **12:29 am**
☽ ⊼ ☉ **6:58 am** 3:58 am
☽ ☍ ♆ **3:40 pm** 12:40 pm
☽ △ ☿ **9:30 pm** 6:30 pm
☽ ⊼ ♄ **9:32 pm** 6:32 pm
☿ ⊻ ♄ **9:49 pm** 6:49 pm
☽ △ ♇ 10:40 pm

9 THURSDAY
☽ △ ♇ **1:40 am**
☽ ☍ ♃ **7:02 pm** 4:02 pm

10 FRIDAY
☽ △ ♂ **4:25 am** 1:25 am
☽ ⊼ ♅ **9:08 am** 6:08 am
☿ ☌ ♇ **12:16 pm** 9:16 am
☽ ⊼ ♀ **3:18 pm** 12:18 pm
☽ △ ☉ **10:39 pm** 7:39 pm
☽ ⊼ ♆ 11:04 pm

11 SATURDAY
☽ ⊼ ♆ **2:04 am**
☽ △ ♄ **8:07 am** 5:07 am
☽ □ ♇ **11:41 am** 8:41 am
☽ □ ☿ **2:27 pm** 11:27 am

12 SUNDAY
☽ ⊼ ♃ **5:07 am** 2:07 am
☽ ⊼ ♂ **2:28 pm** 11:28 am
☽ ☍ ♅ **5:43 pm** 2:43 pm
☉ ⊻ ♆ **6:37 pm** 3:37 pm

13 MONDAY
☽ △ ♀ **5:16 am** 2:16 am
☽ △ ♆ **9:49 am** 6:49 am
☽ □ ☉ **11:01 am** 8:01 am
☽ □ ♄ **3:53 pm** 12:53 pm
☽ ⚹ ♇ **6:52 pm** 3:52 pm

14 TUESDAY
☽ ⚹ ☿ **3:39 am** 12:39 am
☽ △ ♃ **11:56 am** 8:56 am
☽ ☍ ♂ **9:06 pm** 6:06 pm
☽ ⊼ ♅ **10:59 pm** 7:59 pm

15 WEDNESDAY
♀ ☌ ♆ **7:25 am** 4:25 am
☽ □ ♆ **2:06 pm** 11:06 am
☽ □ ♀ **2:43 pm** 11:43 am
☽ ⚹ ☉ **7:03 pm** 4:03 pm
☽ ⚹ ♄ **8:06 pm** 5:06 pm
☽ ⊻ ♇ **10:33 pm** 7:33 pm

16 THURSDAY
☉ ☌ ♄ **11:48 am** 8:48 am
☽ ⊻ ☿ **12:17 pm** 9:17 am
☽ □ ♃ **3:11 pm** 12:11 pm
☽ ⊼ ♂ 9:12 pm
☽ △ ♅ 9:55 pm

17 FRIDAY
☽ ⊼ ♂ **12:12 am**
☽ △ ♅ **12:55 am**
☽ ⚹ ♆ **3:16 pm** 12:16 pm
☽ ⚹ ♀ **8:06 pm** 5:06 pm
☿ ⚹ ♃ **9:13 pm** 6:13 pm
☽ ⊻ ♄ **9:15 pm** 6:15 pm
☉ ⊻ ♇ **10:23 pm** 7:23 pm
☽ ☌ ♇ **11:18 pm** 8:18 pm
☽ ⊻ ☉ **11:22 pm** 8:22 pm

18 SATURDAY
♂ ⊻ ♅ **9:51 am** 6:51 am
♀ ⊻ ♄ **11:32 am** 8:32 am
☽ ⚹ ♃ **3:51 pm** 12:51 pm
☽ ☌ ☿ **5:35 pm** 2:35 pm
☽ □ ♅ 9:42 pm
☽ △ ♂ 10:01 pm

19 SUNDAY
☽ □ ♅ **12:42 am**
☽ △ ♂ **1:01 am**
♀ ⚹ ♇ **12:05 pm** 9:05 am
☽ ⊻ ♆ **2:48 pm** 11:48 am
☽ ☌ ♄ **9:00 pm** 6:00 pm
☽ ⊻ ♇ **10:45 pm** 7:45 pm
☽ ⊻ ♀ **11:40 pm** 8:40 pm
☽ ☌ ☉ 11:06 pm

20 MONDAY
☽ ☌ ☉ **2:06 am**
☽ ⊻ ♃ **3:57 pm** 12:57 pm
☽ ⊻ ☿ **10:24 pm** 7:24 pm
☽ ⚹ ♅ 9:20 pm
☽ □ ♂ 10:44 pm

21 TUESDAY
☽ ⚹ ♅ **12:20 am**
☽ □ ♂ **1:44 am**
☽ ☌ ♆ **2:52 pm** 11:52 am
☿ □ ♅ **5:22 pm** 2:22 pm
☽ ⊻ ♄ **9:35 pm** 6:35 pm
☽ ⚹ ♇ **11:06 pm** 8:06 pm

22 WEDNESDAY
☽ ☌ ♀ **4:26 am** 1:26 am
☽ ⊻ ☉ **6:07 am** 3:07 am
☿ △ ♂ **3:14 pm** 12:14 pm
☽ ☌ ♃ **5:48 pm** 2:48 pm
☽ ⊻ ♅ 11:01 pm

23 THURSDAY
☽ ⊻ ♅ **2:01 am**
☽ ⚹ ♂ **4:44 am** 1:44 am
☽ ⚹ ☿ **6:03 am** 3:03 am
☽ ⊻ ♆ **5:34 pm** 2:34 pm
☽ ⚹ ♄ 10:06 pm
☽ □ ♇ 11:22 pm

24 FRIDAY
☽ ⚹ ♄ **1:06 am**
☽ □ ♇ **2:22 am**
☽ ⊻ ♀ **1:12 pm** 10:12 am
☽ ⚹ ☉ **2:02 pm** 11:02 am
☽ ⊻ ♃ **11:19 pm** 8:19 pm

25 SATURDAY
☽ ☌ ♅ **7:25 am** 4:25 am
☽ ⊻ ♂ **11:51 am** 8:51 am
☽ □ ☿ **7:16 pm** 4:16 pm
☽ ⚹ ♆ 9:15 pm

26 SUNDAY
☽ ⚹ ♆ **12:15 am**
☽ □ ♄ **8:45 am** 5:45 am
☽ △ ♇ **9:42 am** 6:42 am
☉ ⊻ ♀ **11:11 am** 8:11 am

27 MONDAY
☽ □ ☉ **3:06 am** 12:06 am
☽ ⚹ ♀ **3:24 am** 12:24 am
☽ ⚹ ♃ **9:08 am** 6:08 am
☿ ⊻ ♆ **11:03 am** 8:03 am
☽ ⊻ ♅ **4:51 pm** 1:51 pm
☽ ☌ ♂ **11:21 pm** 8:21 pm

28 TUESDAY
☽ □ ♆ **10:46 am** 7:46 am
☽ △ ☿ **2:27 pm** 11:27 am
☽ △ ♄ **8:07 pm** 5:07 pm
☽ ⊼ ♇ **8:40 pm** 5:40 pm

Eastern time in bold type
Pacific time in medium type

FEBRUARY 2023

DATE	SID.TIME	SUN	MOON	NODE	MERCURY	VENUS	MARS	JUPITER	SATURN	URANUS	NEPTUNE	PLUTO	CERES	PALLAS	JUNO	VESTA	CHIRON
1 W	8 43 46	11♒50 31	19♊56	8♉42℞	16♑57	6♓05	10♊17	6♈03	25♒51	14♉59	23♓36	28♑40	6♎57	11♋47℞	9♈06	26♓52	12♈38
2 Th	8 47 43	12 51 25	1♋54	8 35	18 03	7 20	10 30	6 15	25 58	14 59	23 38	28 42	6 58	11 37	9 37	27 18	12 40
3 F	8 51 40	13 52 17	13 47	8 24	19 12	8 34	10 43	6 26	26 05	15 00	23 40	28 44	6 58℞	11 28	10 07	27 44	12 42
4 Sa	8 55 36	14 53 08	25 39	8 11	20 22	9 49	10 57	6 38	26 13	15 00	23 41	28 46	6 58	11 19	10 38	28 10	12 45
5 Su	8 59 33	15 53 58	7♌31	7 56	21 35	11 03	11 12	6 49	26 20	15 01	23 43	28 48	6 58	11 11	11 09	28 36	12 47
6 M	9 3 29	16 54 46	19 25	7 41	22 49	12 18	11 27	7 01	26 27	15 02	23 45	28 49	6 57	11 03	11 40	29 02	12 49
7 T	9 7 26	17 55 34	1♍23	7 27	24 04	13 32	11 43	7 13	26 34	15 02	23 47	28 51	6 56	10 56	12 11	29 28	12 51
8 W	9 11 22	18 56 20	13 25	7 15	25 21	14 46	11 59	7 25	26 41	15 03	23 49	28 53	6 54	10 50	12 42	29 55	12 54
9 Th	9 15 19	19 57 05	25 32	7 06	26 40	16 01	12 15	7 37	26 48	15 04	23 51	28 55	6 52	10 45	13 14	0♈21	12 56
10 F	9 19 15	20 57 49	7♎48	7 00	28 00	17 15	12 32	7 49	26 56	15 05	23 53	28 57	6 50	10 40	13 45	0 47	12 58
11 Sa	9 23 12	21 58 32	20 13	6 56	29 21	18 29	12 49	8 01	27 03	15 06	23 55	28 59	6 47	10 36	14 17	1 14	13 01
12 Su	9 27 9	22 59 14	2♏53	6 55D	0♒43	19 43	13 07	8 13	27 10	15 07	23 57	29 01	6 44	10 33	14 48	1 40	13 03
13 M	9 31 5	23 59 54	15 50	6 55℞	2 07	20 58	13 25	8 25	27 17	15 08	23 59	29 02	6 40	10 30	15 20	2 07	13 06
14 T	9 35 2	25 00 34	29 09	6 55	3 32	22 12	13 44	8 38	27 25	15 09	24 01	29 04	6 36	10 28	15 52	2 33	13 08
15 W	9 38 58	26 01 13	12♐51	6 54	4 57	23 26	14 03	8 50	27 32	15 10	24 03	29 06	6 31	10 27	16 24	3 00	13 11
16 Th	9 42 55	27 01 51	27 00	6 51	6 24	24 40	14 22	9 03	27 39	15 12	24 05	29 08	6 26	10 26D	16 56	3 26	13 14
17 F	9 46 51	28 02 27	11♑34	6 45	7 52	25 54	14 42	9 15	27 46	15 13	24 07	29 10	6 20	10 26	17 28	3 53	13 16
18 Sa	9 50 48	29 03 02	26 30	6 37	9 21	27 08	15 02	9 28	27 54	15 14	24 09	29 11	6 14	10 26	18 00	4 20	13 19
19 Su	9 54 45	0♓03 36	11♒39	6 27	10 51	28 22	15 23	9 41	28 01	15 16	24 11	29 13	6 08	10 28	18 33	4 46	13 22
20 M	9 58 41	1 04 09	26 53	6 16	12 22	29 36	15 44	9 54	28 08	15 17	24 14	29 15	6 01	10 29	19 05	5 13	13 24
21 T	10 2 38	2 04 39	11♓59	6 07	13 53	0♈49	16 05	10 07	28 16	15 18	24 16	29 17	5 54	10 32	19 38	5 40	13 27
22 W	10 6 34	3 05 09	26 49	5 59	15 26	2 03	16 27	10 20	28 23	15 20	24 18	29 18	5 46	10 35	20 10	6 07	13 30
23 Th	10 10 31	4 05 36	11♈14	5 54	17 00	3 17	16 49	10 33	28 30	15 21	24 20	29 20	5 38	10 39	20 43	6 34	13 33
24 F	10 14 27	5 06 01	25 11	5 52D	18 35	4 31	17 11	10 46	28 37	15 23	24 22	29 22	5 30	10 43	21 16	7 01	13 36
25 Sa	10 18 24	6 06 25	8♉39	5 51	20 10	5 44	17 33	10 59	28 44	15 25	24 24	29 23	5 21	10 48	21 49	7 27	13 39
26 Su	10 22 20	7 06 47	21 39	5 52	21 47	6 58	17 56	11 12	28 52	15 26	24 27	29 25	5 12	10 53	22 22	7 54	13 42
27 M	10 26 17	8 07 07	4♊17	5 53℞	23 24	8 11	18 19	11 25	28 59	15 28	24 29	29 26	5 02	10 59	22 55	8 21	13 45
28 T	10 30 13	9 07 25	16 35	5 52	25 03	9 25	18 43	11 39	29 06	15 30	24 31	29 28	4 53	11 06	23 28	8 48	13 48

EPHEMERIS CALCULATED FOR 12 MIDNIGHT GREENWICH MEAN TIME. ALL OTHER DATA AND FACING ASPECTARIAN PAGE IN **EASTERN TIME (BOLD)** AND PACIFIC TIME (REGULAR).

MARCH 2023

☽ Last Aspect day	ET / hr:mn / PT	asp	☽ Ingress sign	day	ET / hr:mn / PT
3	**9:22 am** 6:22 am	☍♇	♌	3	**10:16 am** 7:16 am
5	**10:18 pm** 7:18 pm	☍♄	♍	5	**10:38 pm** 7:38 pm
8	**9:07 am** 6:07 am	△♇	♎	8	**9:44 am** 6:44 am
10	**6:37 pm** 3:37 pm	□♇	♏	10	**7:06 pm** 4:06 pm
12	11:58 pm	⚹♇	♐	13	**3:21 am** 12:21 am
13	**2:58 am**	⚹♇	♐	13	**3:21 am** 12:21 am
15	**4:50 am** 1:50 am	△♀	♑	15	**8:06 am** 5:06 am
17	**10:14 am** 7:14 am	☌♇	♒	17	**10:25 am** 7:25 am
19	**6:33 am** 3:33 am	△♂	♓	19	**11:12 am** 8:12 am
21	**11:58 am** 8:58 am	⚹♇	♈	21	**12:01 pm** 9:01 am
23	**1:13 pm** 10:13 am	⚹♂	♉	23	**2:42 pm** 11:42 am
25	**12:19 pm** 9:19 am	⚹♆	♊	25	**8:42 pm** 5:42 pm
27	**9:39 pm** 6:39 pm	□♆	♋	28	**6:22 am** 3:22 am
30	**9:45 am** 6:45 am	△♆	♌	30	**6:31 pm** 3:31 pm

☽ Phases & Eclipses phase	day	ET / hr:mn / PT
Full Moon	7	**7:40 am** 4:40 am
4th Quarter	14	**10:08 pm** 7:08 pm
New Moon	21	**1:23 pm** 10:23 am
2nd Quarter	28	**10:32 pm** 7:32 pm

Planet Ingress		day	ET / hr:mn / PT
☿	♓	2	**5:52 pm** 2:52 pm
♄	♓	7	**8:35 am** 5:35 am
⚵	♉	11	**11:15 am** 8:15 am
♀	♉	16	**6:34 pm** 3:34 pm
☿	♈	18	9:24 pm
☿	♈	19	**12:24 am**
☉	♈	20	**5:24 pm** 2:24 pm
⚳	♍	22	**11:38 pm** 8:38 pm
♇	♒	23	**8:13 am** 5:13 am
♂	♋	25	**7:45 am** 4:45 am

Planetary Motion day	ET / hr:mn / PT

1 WEDNESDAY
☽△☉ **8:10 pm** 5:10 pm
☽□♀ **9:50 pm** 6:50 pm
☽□♃ **10:04 pm** 7:04 pm
♀☌♃ 9:36 pm

2 THURSDAY
♀☌♃ **12:36 am**
☽⚹♅ **5:03 am** 2:03 am
☿☌♄ **9:34 am** 6:34 am
☿⚺♇ **11:21 am** 8:21 am
☽⚺♂ **1:39 pm** 10:39 am
☽△♆ **11:23 pm** 8:23 pm
☉⚺♃ 9:40 pm

3 FRIDAY
☉⚺♃ **12:40 am**
☽⚻♄ **9:19 am** 6:19 am
☽☍♇ **9:22 am** 6:22 am
☽⚻☿ **1:01 pm** 10:01 am
♄⚺♇ **5:26 pm** 2:26 pm

4 SATURDAY
☽△♃ **11:56 am** 8:56 am
☽⚻☉ **2:27 pm** 11:27 am
☽△♀ **5:28 pm** 2:28 pm
☽□♅ **5:54 pm** 2:54 pm
♀⚺♅ **9:46 pm** 6:46 pm

5 SUNDAY
☽⚹♂ **4:26 am** 1:26 am
☽⚻♆ **12:06 pm** 9:06 am
☽⚻♇ **9:54 pm** 6:54 pm
☽☍♄ **10:18 pm** 7:18 pm

6 MONDAY
☉⚹♅ **8:42 am** 5:42 am
☽☍☿ **11:32 am** 8:32 am
☽⚻♃ 10:00 pm

7 TUESDAY
☽⚻♃ **1:00 am**
☽△♅ **5:51 am** 2:51 am
☽☍☉ **7:40 am** 4:40 am
☽⚻♀ **11:53 am** 8:53 am
☽□♂ **6:06 pm** 3:06 pm
☽☍♆ **11:39 pm** 8:39 pm

8 WEDNESDAY
☽△♇ **9:07 am** 6:07 am
☽⚻♄ **9:58 am** 6:58 am

9 THURSDAY
☽⚻☿ **8:10 am** 5:10 am
☽☍♃ **12:27 pm** 9:27 am
☽⚻♅ **4:15 pm** 1:15 pm
☽⚻☉ **10:52 pm** 7:52 pm

10 FRIDAY
☽☍♀ **4:07 am** 1:07 am
☽△♂ **6:00 am** 3:00 am
☽⚻♆ **9:30 am** 6:30 am
☿⚺♃ **5:04 pm** 2:04 pm
☽□♇ **6:37 pm** 3:37 pm
☽△♄ **7:51 pm** 4:51 pm

11 SATURDAY
♀⚹♂ **10:05 am** 7:05 am
☿⚹♅ **4:04 pm** 1:04 pm
☽⚻♃ **9:55 pm** 6:55 pm
☽☍♅ 9:43 pm
☽△☿ 11:07 pm

12 SUNDAY
☽☍♅ **12:43 am**
☽△☿ **3:07 am**
☽△☉ **12:32 pm** 9:32 am
♀⚺♆ **3:09 pm** 12:09 pm
☽⚻♂ **4:43 pm** 1:43 pm
☽△♆ **6:18 pm** 3:18 pm
☽⚻♀ **6:37 pm** 3:37 pm
☽⚹♇ 11:58 pm

13 MONDAY
☽⚹♇ **2:58 am**
☽□♄ **4:34 am** 1:34 am

14 TUESDAY
☽△♃ **5:57 am** 2:57 am
☽⚻♅ **7:49 am** 4:49 am
☽□☿ **5:38 pm** 2:38 pm
♂□♆ **7:39 pm** 4:39 pm
☽□☉ **10:08 pm** 7:08 pm
☽□♆ **11:38 pm** 8:38 pm
☽☍♂ **11:45 pm** 8:45 pm

15 WEDNESDAY
☽△♀ **4:50 am** 1:50 am
☽⚺♇ **7:49 am** 4:49 am
☽⚹♄ **9:41 am** 6:41 am
☉☌♆ **7:39 pm** 4:39 pm

16 THURSDAY
☽□♃ **10:17 am** 7:17 am
☽△♅ **11:22 am** 8:22 am
☿☌♆ **1:13 pm** 10:13 am
☉□♂ **2:10 pm** 11:10 am
♀□♇ **3:59 pm** 12:59 pm
☿□♂ 9:49 pm
☽⚹♆ 11:26 pm

17 FRIDAY
☿□♂ **12:49 am**
☽⚹♆ **2:26 am**
☽⚻♂ **4:04 am** 1:04 am
☽⚹☿ **4:28 am** 1:28 am
☽⚹☉ **4:37 am** 1:37 am
☉☌☿ **6:45 am** 3:45 am
☽☌♇ **10:14 am** 7:14 am
☽□♀ **11:50 am** 8:50 am
☽⚺♄ **12:20 pm** 9:20 am
♀⚹♄ **6:25 pm** 3:25 pm

18 SATURDAY
☽⚹♃ **12:27 pm** 9:27 am
☽□♅ **12:50 pm** 9:50 am
☿⚹♇ **11:24 pm** 8:24 pm

19 SUNDAY
☽⚺♆ **3:30 am** 12:30 am
☽△♂ **6:33 am** 3:33 am
☽⚺☉ **9:02 am** 6:02 am
☽⚺♇ **11:05 am** 8:05 am
☽⚺☿ **12:52 pm** 9:52 am
☽☌♄ **1:28 pm** 10:28 am
☽⚹♀ **4:54 pm** 1:54 pm
☿⚺♄ **5:30 pm** 2:30 pm
♃⚺♅ **6:06 pm** 3:06 pm

20 MONDAY
☽⚹♅ **1:34 pm** 10:34 am
☽⚺♃ **1:49 pm** 10:49 am
☉⚹♇ **4:12 pm** 1:12 pm

21 TUESDAY
☽☌♆ **4:20 am** 1:20 am
☽□♂ **8:55 am** 5:55 am
☽⚹♇ **11:58 am** 8:58 am
☽☌☉ **1:23 pm** 10:23 am
☽⚺♄ **2:43 pm** 11:43 am
☽☌☿ **9:34 pm** 6:34 pm
☽⚺♀ **10:17 pm** 7:17 pm

22 WEDNESDAY
☿⚺♀ **9:14 am** 6:14 am
☉⚺♄ **11:00 am** 8:00 am
☽⚺♅ **3:19 pm** 12:19 pm
☽☌♃ **4:17 pm** 1:17 pm

23 THURSDAY
☽⚺♆ **6:44 am** 3:44 am
☽⚹♂ **1:13 pm** 10:13 am
☽□♇ **2:42 pm** 11:42 am
☽⚹♄ **5:57 pm** 2:57 pm
☽⚺☉ **8:05 pm** 5:05 pm

24 FRIDAY
☽☌♀ **6:31 am** 3:31 am
☽⚺☿ **9:45 am** 6:45 am
☽☌♅ **7:52 pm** 4:52 pm
☽⚺♃ **9:40 pm** 6:40 pm

25 SATURDAY
♂⚻♇ **9:34 am** 6:34 am
☽⚹♆ **12:19 pm** 9:19 am
☽△♇ **8:46 pm** 5:46 pm
☽⚺♂ **9:12 pm** 6:12 pm
☽□♄ 9:38 pm

26 SUNDAY
☽□♄ **12:38 am**
☽⚹☉ **7:03 am** 4:03 am
☽⚺♀ **7:25 pm** 4:25 pm

27 MONDAY
☽⚹☿ **3:39 am** 12:39 am
☽⚺♅ **4:08 am** 1:08 am
☿⚺♅ **6:45 am** 3:45 am
☽⚹♃ **6:57 am** 3:57 am
☽□♆ **9:39 pm** 6:39 pm
☿☌♃ 11:50 pm

28 TUESDAY
☿☌♃ **2:50 am**
☽⚻♇ **6:32 am** 3:32 am
☽☌♂ **9:19 am** 6:19 am
☽△♄ **11:04 am** 8:04 am
☽□☉ **10:32 pm** 7:32 pm

29 WEDNESDAY
☽⚹♀ **12:50 pm** 9:50 am
☽⚹♅ **3:40 pm** 12:40 pm
☽□♃ **7:35 pm** 4:35 pm
☽□☿ 11:30 pm

30 THURSDAY
☽□☿ **2:30 am**
☽△♆ **9:45 am** 6:45 am
♂△♄ **3:03 pm** 12:03 pm
♀☌♅ **6:26 pm** 3:26 pm
☽☍♇ **6:46 pm** 3:46 pm
☽⚻♄ **11:51 pm** 8:51 pm
☽⚺♂ 9:10 pm

31 FRIDAY
☽⚺♂ **12:10 am**
☽△☉ **4:29 pm** 1:29 pm
☿⚺♆ 10:39 pm

Eastern time in bold type
Pacific time in medium type

MARCH 2023

DATE	SID.TIME	SUN	MOON	NODE	MERCURY	VENUS	MARS	JUPITER	SATURN	URANUS	NEPTUNE	PLUTO	CERES	PALLAS	JUNO	VESTA	CHIRON
1 W	10 34 10	10♓07 41	28♊40	5♉50R	26♒43	10♈38	19♊07	11♈52	29♒13	15♉32	24♓33	29♑30	4♎42R	11♋13	24♈01	9♈15	13♈51
2 Th	10 38 7	11 07 55	10♋36	5 46	28 23	11 52	19 31	12 06	29 20	15 34	24 35	29 31	4 32	11 20	24 34	9 42	13 54
3 F	10 42 3	12 08 06	22 28	5 39	0♓05	13 05	19 55	12 19	29 28	15 36	24 38	29 33	4 21	11 29	25 08	10 09	13 57
4 Sa	10 46 0	13 08 16	4♌19	5 31	1 48	14 18	20 19	12 33	29 35	15 38	24 40	29 34	4 10	11 37	25 41	10 36	14 00
5 Su	10 49 56	14 08 24	16 12	5 21	3 31	15 31	20 44	12 46	29 42	15 40	24 42	29 36	3 59	11 46	26 15	11 03	14 03
6 M	10 53 53	15 08 30	28 11	5 11	5 16	16 44	21 09	13 00	29 49	15 42	24 44	29 37	3 47	11 56	26 48	11 31	14 06
7 T	10 57 49	16 08 34	10♍15	5 01	7 02	17 58	21 35	13 14	29 56	15 44	24 47	29 39	3 35	12 06	27 22	11 58	14 10
8 W	11 1 46	17 08 36	22 27	4 53	8 49	19 10	22 00	13 27	0♓03	15 46	24 49	29 40	3 23	12 17	27 56	12 25	14 13
9 Th	11 5 42	18 08 36	4♎47	4 47	10 37	20 23	22 26	13 41	0 10	15 48	24 51	29 42	3 11	12 28	28 29	12 52	14 16
10 F	11 9 39	19 08 35	17 17	4 43	12 26	21 36	22 52	13 55	0 17	15 50	24 53	29 43	2 58	12 39	29 03	13 19	14 19
11 Sa	11 13 36	20 08 32	29 57	4 42D	14 17	22 49	23 18	14 09	0 24	15 52	24 56	29 45	2 45	12 51	29 37	13 46	14 23
12 Su	11 17 32	21 08 27	12♏50	4 42	16 08	24 02	23 45	14 23	0 31	15 55	24 58	29 46	2 32	13 03	0♉11	14 13	14 26
13 M	11 21 29	22 08 20	25 56	4 43	18 01	25 14	24 11	14 37	0 38	15 57	25 00	29 47	2 19	13 16	0 45	14 41	14 29
14 T	11 25 25	23 08 12	9♐19	4 44	19 54	26 27	24 38	14 51	0 45	15 59	25 02	29 49	2 06	13 29	1 19	15 08	14 32
15 W	11 29 22	24 08 02	22 59	4 45R	21 49	27 39	25 05	15 05	0 52	16 02	25 05	29 50	1 52	13 42	1 53	15 35	14 36
16 Th	11 33 18	25 07 50	6♑59	4 44	23 45	28 52	25 32	15 19	0 59	16 04	25 07	29 51	1 39	13 56	2 27	16 02	14 39
17 F	11 37 15	26 07 37	21 17	4 42	25 42	0♉04	26 00	15 33	1 06	16 07	25 09	29 52	1 25	14 10	3 02	16 29	14 43
18 Sa	11 41 11	27 07 22	5♒51	4 38	27 40	1 17	26 27	15 47	1 12	16 09	25 12	29 54	1 11	14 25	3 36	16 57	14 46
19 Su	11 45 8	28 07 06	20 36	4 33	29 38	2 29	26 55	16 01	1 19	16 12	25 14	29 55	0 58	14 40	4 10	17 24	14 49
20 M	11 49 5	29 06 47	5♓27	4 28	1♈38	3 41	27 23	16 15	1 26	16 14	25 16	29 56	0 44	14 55	4 45	17 51	14 53
21 T	11 53 1	0♈06 27	20 14	4 23	3 38	4 53	27 51	16 30	1 33	16 17	25 18	29 57	0 30	15 11	5 19	18 19	14 56
22 W	11 56 58	1 06 04	4♈49	4 18	5 38	6 05	28 20	16 44	1 39	16 20	25 21	29 58	0 16	15 27	5 53	18 46	15 00
23 Th	12 0 54	2 05 40	19 07	4 16	7 39	7 17	28 48	16 58	1 46	16 22	25 23	29 59	0 02	15 43	6 28	19 13	15 03
24 F	12 4 51	3 05 13	3♉02	4 15D	9 40	8 29	29 17	17 12	1 52	16 25	25 25	0♒01	29♍48	16 00	7 03	19 40	15 07
25 Sa	12 8 47	4 04 45	16 32	4 16	11 41	9 41	29 46	17 27	1 59	16 28	25 27	0 02	29 34	16 17	7 37	20 08	15 10
26 Su	12 12 44	5 04 14	29 38	4 17	13 41	10 52	0♋15	17 41	2 05	16 31	25 30	0 03	29 21	16 34	8 12	20 35	15 13
27 M	12 16 40	6 03 41	12♊20	4 19	15 41	12 04	0 44	17 55	2 12	16 33	25 32	0 04	29 07	16 52	8 46	21 02	15 17
28 T	12 20 37	7 03 06	24 44	4 20	17 40	13 15	1 13	18 10	2 18	16 36	25 34	0 05	28 54	17 09	9 21	21 30	15 20
29 W	12 24 34	8 02 28	6♋52	4 21R	19 38	14 27	1 43	18 24	2 25	16 39	25 36	0 06	28 40	17 27	9 56	21 57	15 24
30 Th	12 28 30	9 01 48	18 51	4 20	21 33	15 38	2 12	18 38	2 31	16 42	25 39	0 07	28 27	17 46	10 31	22 24	15 27
31 F	12 32 27	10 01 06	0♌44	4 19	23 27	16 49	2 42	18 53	2 37	16 45	25 41	0 07	28 14	18 04	11 06	22 52	15 31

EPHEMERIS CALCULATED FOR 12 MIDNIGHT GREENWICH MEAN TIME. ALL OTHER DATA AND FACING ASPECTARIAN PAGE IN **EASTERN TIME (BOLD)** AND PACIFIC TIME (REGULAR).

APRIL 2023

☽ Last Aspect day	ET / hr:mn	PT	asp	☽ Ingress sign	day	ET / hr:mn	PT
1		11:03 pm	△☿	♍	2	**6:57 am**	3:57 am
2	**2:03 am**		△☿	♍	2	**6:57 am**	3:57 am
4	**9:50 am**	6:50 am	☍♆	♎	4	**5:51 pm**	2:51 pm
6	**8:43 am**	5:43 am	☍♃	♏	6		11:29 pm
6	**8:43 am**	5:43 am	☍♃	♏	7	**2:29 am**	
9	**5:09 am**	2:09 am	☍♀	♐	9	**8:57 am**	5:57 am
11	**6:48 am**	3:48 am	□♆	♑	11	**1:33 pm**	10:33 am
13	**10:14 am**	7:14 am	✶♆	♒	13	**4:42 pm**	1:42 pm
15	**11:16 am**	8:16 am	✶⊙	♓	15	**6:57 pm**	3:57 pm
17	**2:57 pm**	11:57 am	☌♆	♈	17	**9:09 pm**	6:09 pm

☽ Last Aspect day	ET / hr:mn	PT	asp	☽ Ingress sign	day	ET / hr:mn	PT
19		9:13 pm	☌⊙	♉	19		9:30 pm
20	**12:13 am**		☌⊙	♉	20	**12:30 am**	
21	**11:41 pm**	8:41 pm	✶♆	♊	22	**6:11 am**	3:11 am
24	**8:15 am**	5:15 am	□♆	♋	24	**2:58 pm**	11:58 am
26	**7:41 pm**	4:41 pm	△♆	♌	26		11:30 pm
26	**7:41 pm**	4:41 pm	△♆	♌	27	**2:30 am**	
29	**6:53 am**	3:53 am	△♃	♍	29	**2:59 pm**	11:59 am

☽ Phases & Eclipses phase	day	ET / hr:mn	PT
Full Moon	5		9:34 pm
Full Moon	6	**12:34 am**	
4th Quarter	13	**5:11 am**	2:11 am
New Moon	19		9:13 pm
New Moon	20	**12:13 am**	
●	20	29° ♈ 50'	
2nd Quarter	27	**5:20 pm**	2:20 pm

Planet Ingress		day	ET / hr:mn	PT
☿	♉	3	**12:22 pm**	9:22 am
♀	♊	10		9:47 pm
♀	♊	11	**12:47 am**	
⚳	♉	15	**1:01 pm**	10:01 am
⊙	♉	20	**4:14 am**	1:14 am

Planetary Motion		day	ET / hr:mn	PT
☿	R	21	**4:35 am**	1:35 am

1 SATURDAY
☿ ⚺ ♆ **1:39 am**
☽ □ ♅ **4:30 am** 1:30 am
☽ □ ♀ **8:06 am** 5:06 am
☽ △ ♃ **9:25 am** 6:25 am
☽ ⚻ ♆ **10:28 pm** 7:28 pm
♀ ⚺ ♃ 9:18 pm
☽ △ ☿ 11:03 pm

2 SUNDAY
♀ ⚺ ♃ **12:18 am**
☽ △ ☿ **2:03 am**
☽ ⚻ ♇ **7:16 am** 4:16 am
☽ ☍ ♄ **12:44 pm** 9:44 am
☽ ✶ ♂ **3:08 pm** 12:08 pm

3 MONDAY
☽ ⚻ ⊙ **9:49 am** 6:49 am
☿ □ ♇ **2:55 pm** 11:55 am
☽ △ ♅ **4:28 pm** 1:28 pm
☽ ⚻ ♃ **10:12 pm** 7:12 pm
☽ △ ♀ 11:04 pm

4 TUESDAY
☽ △ ♀ **2:04 am**
☽ ☍ ♆ **9:50 am** 6:50 am
☽ △ ♇ **6:13 pm** 3:13 pm
☽ ⚻ ☿ **10:16 pm** 7:16 pm
☽ ⚻ ♄ **11:54 pm** 8:54 pm

5 WEDNESDAY
☽ □ ♂ **4:12 am** 1:12 am
☿ ✶ ♄ **12:21 pm** 9:21 am
☽ ☍ ⊙ 9:34 pm
☽ ⚻ ♅ 11:21 pm

6 THURSDAY
☽ ☍ ⊙ **12:34 am**
☽ ⚻ ♅ **2:21 am**
☽ ☍ ♃ **8:43 am** 5:43 am
☽ ⚻ ♀ **5:06 pm** 2:06 pm
☽ ⚻ ♆ **6:57 pm** 3:57 pm
⊙ ⚺ ♅ 9:42 pm
☽ □ ♇ 11:54 pm

7 FRIDAY
⊙ ⚺ ♅ **12:42 am**
☽ □ ♇ **2:54 am**
☽ △ ♄ **8:44 am** 5:44 am
☽ ☍ ☿ **1:53 pm** 10:53 am
♀ ✶ ♆ **1:58 pm** 10:58 am
☽ △ ♂ **2:42 pm** 11:42 am
☿ ✶ ♂ 11:29 pm

8 SATURDAY
☿ ✶ ♂ **2:29 am**
☽ ☍ ♅ **9:56 am** 6:56 am
☽ ⚻ ⊙ **12:27 pm** 9:27 am
☽ ⚻ ♃ **4:51 pm** 1:51 pm
☽ △ ♆ 10:50 pm

9 SUNDAY
☽ △ ♆ **1:50 am**
☽ ☍ ♀ **5:09 am** 2:09 am
☽ ✶ ♇ **9:23 am** 6:23 am
☽ □ ♄ **3:21 pm** 12:21 pm
☽ ⚻ ♂ **10:51 pm** 7:51 pm
☽ ⚻ ☿ 10:23 pm

10 MONDAY
☽ ⚻ ☿ **1:23 am**
☽ ⚻ ♅ **3:29 pm** 12:29 pm
☽ △ ⊙ **9:48 pm** 6:48 pm
☽ △ ♃ **10:55 pm** 7:55 pm

11 TUESDAY
♀ △ ♇ **6:14 am** 3:14 am
☽ □ ♆ **6:48 am** 3:48 am
☽ ⚺ ♇ **2:01 pm** 11:01 am
☽ ⚻ ♀ **2:43 pm** 11:43 am
⊙ ☌ ♃ **6:07 pm** 3:07 pm
☽ ✶ ♄ **8:08 pm** 5:08 pm

12 WEDNESDAY
☽ ☍ ♂ **5:03 am** 2:03 am
☽ △ ☿ **9:35 am** 6:35 am
☽ △ ♅ **7:24 pm** 4:24 pm

13 THURSDAY
☽ □ ♃ **3:20 am** 12:20 am
☽ □ ⊙ **5:11 am** 2:11 am
☽ ✶ ♆ **10:14 am** 7:14 am
☽ ☌ ♇ **5:11 pm** 2:11 pm
☽ △ ♀ **10:23 pm** 7:23 pm
☽ ⚺ ♄ **11:28 pm** 8:28 pm

14 FRIDAY
☽ ⚻ ♂ **9:47 am** 6:47 am
♀ □ ♄ **12:38 pm** 9:38 am
☽ □ ☿ **3:16 pm** 12:16 pm
☽ □ ♅ **10:08 pm** 7:08 pm

15 SATURDAY
☽ ✶ ♃ **6:36 am** 3:36 am
☽ ✶ ⊙ **11:16 am** 8:16 am
☽ ⚺ ♆ **12:41 pm** 9:41 am
☽ ⚺ ♇ **7:27 pm** 4:27 pm
☽ ☌ ♄ 10:58 pm

16 SUNDAY
☽ ☌ ♄ **1:58 am**
☽ □ ♀ **4:58 am** 1:58 am
⊙ ⚺ ♆ **8:43 am** 5:43 am
☽ △ ♂ **1:49 pm** 10:49 am
☽ ✶ ☿ **7:24 pm** 4:24 pm
☽ ✶ ♅ 9:25 pm

17 MONDAY
☽ ✶ ♅ **12:25 am**
☽ ⚺ ♃ **9:35 am** 6:35 am
☽ ☌ ♆ **2:57 pm** 11:57 am
☽ ⚺ ⊙ **5:06 pm** 2:06 pm
☽ ✶ ♇ **9:42 pm** 6:42 pm

18 TUESDAY
☽ ⚺ ♄ **4:34 am** 1:34 am
☽ ✶ ♀ **11:47 am** 8:47 am
☽ □ ♂ **6:16 pm** 3:16 pm
☽ ⚺ ☿ **11:15 pm** 8:15 pm

19 WEDNESDAY
☽ ⚺ ♅ **3:20 am** 12:20 am
☽ ☌ ♃ **1:27 pm** 10:27 am
☽ ⚺ ♆ **6:12 pm** 3:12 pm
☽ ☌ ⊙ 9:13 pmc
☽ □ ♇ 10:04 pm

20 THURSDAY
☽ ☌ ⊙ **12:13 am**
☽ □ ♇ **1:04 am**
☽ ✶ ♄ **8:30 am** 5:30 am
⊙ □ ♇ **12:27 pm** 9:27 am
☽ ⚺ ♀ **8:29 pm** 5:29 pm
☽ ✶ ♂ 9:37 pm

21 FRIDAY
☽ ✶ ♂ **12:37 am**
☽ ☌ ☿ **4:05 am** 1:05 am
☽ ☌ ♅ **8:09 am** 5:09 am
☽ ⚺ ♃ **7:32 pm** 4:32 pm
☽ ✶ ♆ **11:41 pm** 8:41 pm

22 SATURDAY
☽ △ ♇ **6:49 am** 3:49 am
☽ ⚺ ⊙ **10:14 am** 7:14 am
☽ □ ♄ **3:00 pm** 12:00 pm

23 SUNDAY
☽ ☌ ♀ **8:43 am** 5:43 am
☽ ⚺ ♂ **10:06 am** 7:06 am
☽ ⚺ ☿ **10:54 am** 7:54 am
☽ ⚺ ♅ **3:55 pm** 12:55 pm
☿ ✶ ♂ **11:19 pm** 8:19 pm

24 MONDAY
☽ ✶ ♃ **4:49 am** 1:49 am
☿ ⚺ ♀ **5:04 am** 2:04 am
☽ □ ♆ **8:15 am** 5:15 am
♀ ⚺ ♂ **12:50 pm** 9:50 am
☽ ⚻ ♇ **3:40 pm** 12:40 pm
☽ ✶ ⊙ 9:11 pm
☽ △ ♄ 9:40 pm

25 TUESDAY
☽ ✶ ⊙ **12:11 am**
☽ △ ♄ **12:40 am**
⊙ ✶ ♄ **6:48 am** 3:48 am
☽ ✶ ☿ **7:47 pm** 4:47 pm
☽ ☌ ♂ **11:08 pm** 8:08 pm
☽ ⚺ ♀ 10:00 pm
☽ ✶ ♅ 11:45 pm

26 WEDNESDAY
☽ ⚺ ♀ **1:00 am**
☽ ✶ ♅ **2:45 am**
☽ □ ♃ **5:09 pm** 2:09 pm
☽ △ ♆ **7:41 pm** 4:41 pm
♀ ⚺ ♅ **8:35 pm** 5:35 pm

27 THURSDAY
☽ ☍ ♇ **3:13 am** 12:13 am
☽ ⚻ ♄ **12:54 pm** 9:54 am
☽ □ ⊙ **5:20 pm** 2:20 pm

28 FRIDAY
☽ □ ☿ **5:44 am** 2:44 am
☽ ⚺ ♂ **2:22 pm** 11:22 am
☽ □ ♅ **3:26 pm** 12:26 pm
☽ ✶ ♀ **7:42 pm** 4:42 pm

29 SATURDAY
☽ △ ♃ **6:53 am** 3:53 am
☽ ⚻ ♆ **8:20 am** 5:20 am
☽ ⚻ ♇ **3:43 pm** 12:43 pm
♂ ✶ ♅ **4:05 pm** 1:05 pm
☽ ☍ ♄ 10:41 pm

30 SUNDAY
☽ ☍ ♄ **1:41 am**
☽ △ ⊙ **10:59 am** 7:59 am
☽ △ ☿ **3:05 pm** 12:05 pm

Eastern time in bold type
Pacific time in medium type

LOWE'S

LOWE'S HOME CENTERS, LLC
1482 CENTRAL AVENUE
COLONIE, NY 12205 (518) 956-9407

-GIFT CARD ACTIVATION-

SALES #: S1973PXN 4007104 11-29-21

257604 AMAZON.COM MULTI 30 6157 30.00
CARD#: XXXXXXXXXXXXXXX6157
APPROVAL CODE: 000000
ACTIVATION AMOUNT: 30.00
STORE: 1973 TERMINAL: 23

****

THANK YOU FOR SHOPPING LOWE'S.

PLEASE KEEP FOR YOUR RECORDS

THANK YOU FOR SHOPPING LOWE'S.
REFUNDS OR EXCHANGES WILL NOT BE GIVEN ON ACTIVATED
GIFT CARDS, EXCEPT WHERE REQUIRED BY LAW
STORE MANAGER: KEN LANZO

April 2023

DATE	SID.TIME	SUN	MOON	NODE	MERCURY	VENUS	MARS	JUPITER	SATURN	URANUS	NEPTUNE	PLUTO	CERES	PALLAS	JUNO	VESTA	CHIRON
1 Sa	12 36 23	11♈00 21	12♌36	4♉16℞	25♈18	18♉01	3♋12	19♈07	2♓44	16♉48	25♓43	0♒08	28♍01℞	18♋23	11♉41	23♈19	15♈35
2 Su	12 40 20	11 59 34	24 31	4 13	27 06	19 12	3 42	19 22	2 50	16 51	25 45	0 09	27 48	18 42	12 15	23 46	15 38
3 M	12 44 16	12 58 45	6♍33	4 09	28 51	20 22	4 12	19 36	2 56	16 54	25 48	0 10	27 36	19 02	12 50	24 13	15 42
4 T	12 48 13	13 57 54	18 45	4 06	0♉32	21 33	4 42	19 51	3 02	16 57	25 50	0 11	27 24	19 21	13 25	24 41	15 45
5 W	12 52 9	14 57 00	1♎07	4 03	2 09	22 44	5 13	20 05	3 08	17 00	25 52	0 12	27 12	19 41	14 00	25 08	15 49
6 Th	12 56 6	15 56 05	13 42	4 01	3 41	23 55	5 43	20 20	3 14	17 03	25 54	0 12	27 00	20 01	14 35	25 35	15 52
7 F	13 0 2	16 55 07	26 30	4 00D	5 09	25 05	6 14	20 34	3 20	17 06	25 56	0 13	26 48	20 21	15 10	26 03	15 56
8 Sa	13 3 59	17 54 07	9♏32	4 00	6 32	26 16	6 45	20 48	3 26	17 09	25 58	0 14	26 37	20 42	15 45	26 30	15 59
9 Su	13 7 56	18 53 06	22 46	4 01	7 49	27 26	7 16	21 03	3 32	17 12	26 01	0 14	26 26	21 02	16 21	26 57	16 03
10 M	13 11 52	19 52 02	6♐14	4 02	9 01	28 36	7 47	21 17	3 37	17 15	26 03	0 15	26 16	21 23	16 56	27 24	16 06
11 T	13 15 49	20 50 57	19 53	4 03	10 08	29 46	8 18	21 32	3 43	17 19	26 05	0 16	26 05	21 44	17 31	27 52	16 10
12 W	13 19 45	21 49 51	3♑44	4 04	11 08	0♊56	8 49	21 46	3 49	17 22	26 07	0 16	25 55	22 06	18 06	28 19	16 13
13 Th	13 23 42	22 48 42	17 46	4 04℞	12 03	2 06	9 20	22 01	3 54	17 25	26 09	0 17	25 45	22 27	18 41	28 46	16 17
14 F	13 27 38	23 47 32	1♒57	4 04	12 51	3 16	9 52	22 15	4 00	17 28	26 11	0 17	25 36	22 49	19 16	29 13	16 20
15 Sa	13 31 35	24 46 20	16 16	4 04	13 34	4 25	10 23	22 30	4 05	17 32	26 13	0 18	25 27	23 10	19 52	29 41	16 24
16 Su	13 35 32	25 45 07	0♓38	4 03	14 10	5 35	10 55	22 44	4 11	17 35	26 15	0 18	25 18	23 32	20 27	0♉08	16 27
17 M	13 39 28	26 43 51	15 00	4 02	14 40	6 44	11 26	22 59	4 16	17 38	26 17	0 19	25 10	23 54	21 02	0 35	16 31
18 T	13 43 25	27 42 34	29 19	4 01	15 03	7 53	11 58	23 13	4 22	17 41	26 19	0 19	25 02	24 17	21 38	1 02	16 34
19 W	13 47 21	28 41 15	13♈29	4 01	15 21	9 02	12 30	23 28	4 27	17 45	26 21	0 20	24 55	24 39	22 13	1 30	16 38
20 Th	13 51 18	29 39 54	27 25	4 00D	15 32	10 11	13 02	23 42	4 32	17 48	26 23	0 20	24 48	25 02	22 48	1 57	16 41
21 F	13 55 14	0♉38 31	11♉05	4 00	15 37℞	11 20	13 34	23 57	4 37	17 51	26 25	0 20	24 41	25 24	23 24	2 24	16 45
22 Sa	13 59 11	1 37 07	24 26	4 01	15 36	12 29	14 06	24 11	4 42	17 55	26 27	0 20	24 34	25 47	23 59	2 51	16 48
23 Su	14 3 7	2 35 40	7♊27	4 01	15 30	13 37	14 39	24 25	4 47	17 58	26 29	0 21	24 29	26 10	24 34	3 18	16 52
24 M	14 7 4	3 34 12	20 10	4 01℞	15 18	14 46	15 11	24 40	4 52	18 02	26 31	0 21	24 23	26 33	25 10	3 45	16 55
25 T	14 11 0	4 32 41	2♋35	4 01	15 00	15 54	15 43	24 54	4 57	18 05	26 33	0 21	24 18	26 57	25 45	4 12	16 58
26 W	14 14 57	5 31 08	14 46	4 01	14 39	17 02	16 16	25 08	5 02	18 08	26 35	0 21	24 13	27 20	26 20	4 40	17 02
27 Th	14 18 54	6 29 33	26 46	4 01D	14 13	18 10	16 49	25 23	5 06	18 12	26 37	0 22	24 09	27 43	26 56	5 07	17 05
28 F	14 22 50	7 27 56	8♌41	4 01	13 43	19 18	17 21	25 37	5 11	18 15	26 38	0 22	24 05	28 07	27 31	5 34	17 09
29 Sa	14 26 47	8 26 17	20 34	4 01	13 10	20 26	17 54	25 51	5 15	18 19	26 40	0 22	24 02	28 31	28 07	6 01	17 12
30 Su	14 30 43	9 24 36	2♍30	4 01	12 35	21 33	18 27	26 06	5 20	18 22	26 42	0 22	23 58	28 55	28 42	6 28	17 15

EPHEMERIS CALCULATED FOR 12 MIDNIGHT GREENWICH MEAN TIME. ALL OTHER DATA AND FACING ASPECTARIAN PAGE IN **EASTERN TIME (BOLD)** AND PACIFIC TIME (REGULAR).

MAY 2023

☽ Last Aspect day	ET / hr:mn / PT		asp	☽ Ingress sign	day	ET / hr:mn / PT	
1	**7:53 pm**	4:53 pm	☍♆	♎	1		11:09 pm
1	**7:53 pm**	4:53 pm	☍♆	♎	2	**2:09 am**	
4	**5:17 am**	2:17 am	☍♃	♏	4	**10:32 am**	7:32 am
6	**10:38 am**	7:38 am	△♆	♐	6	**4:04 pm**	1:04 pm
8	**4:28 pm**	1:28 pm	△♃	♑	8	**7:33 pm**	4:33 pm
10	**7:52 pm**	4:52 pm	□♃	♒	10	**10:05 pm**	7:05 pm
12	**11:15 pm**	8:15 pm	⚹♃	♓	12		9:39 pm
12	**11:15 pm**	8:15 pm	⚹♃	♓	13	**12:39 am**	
14	**10:56 pm**	7:56 pm	☌♆	♈	15	**3:56 am**	12:56 am
17	**5:10 am**	2:10 am	□♂	♉	17	**8:28 am**	5:28 am

☽ Last Aspect day	ET / hr:mn / PT		asp	☽ Ingress sign	day	ET / hr:mn / PT	
19	**1:51 pm**	10:51 am	⚹♂	♊	19	**2:48 pm**	11:48 am
21	**6:12 pm**	3:12 pm	□♆	♋	21	**11:28 pm**	8:28 pm
24	**5:12 am**	2:12 am	△♆	♌	24	**10:35 am**	7:35 am
25		11:38 pm	□♅	♍	26	**11:05 pm**	8:05 pm
26	**2:38 am**		□♅	♍	26	**11:05 pm**	8:05 pm
29	**5:46 am**	2:46 am	☍♆	♎	29	**10:51 am**	7:51 am
31	**10:53 am**	7:53 am	□♀	♏	31	**7:45 pm**	4:45 pm

☽ Phases & Eclipses phase	day	ET / hr:mn / PT	
Full Moon	5	**1:34 pm**	10:34 am
(eclipse)	5	14° ♏ 58'	
4th Quarter	12	**10:28 am**	7:28 am
New Moon	19	**11:53 am**	8:53 am
2nd Quarter	27	**11:22 am**	8:22 am

Planet Ingress		day	ET / hr:mn / PT	
⚵	♊	1		9:50 pm
⚵	♊	2	**12:50 am**	
♀	♌	2	**1:03 pm**	10:03 am
♀	♋	7	**10:25 am**	7:25 am
♃	♉	16	**1:20 pm**	10:20 am
♂	♌	20	**11:31 am**	8:31 am
☉	♊	21	**3:09 am**	12:09 am

Planetary Motion		day	ET / hr:mn / PT	
♇	℞	1	**1:09 pm**	10:09 am
⚳	D	6	**3:24 pm**	12:24 pm
☿	D	14	**11:17 pm**	8:17 pm

1 MONDAY
☽△♅ **3:38 am** 12:38 am
☽⚹♂ **5:08 am** 2:08 am
☽□♀ **1:31 pm** 10:31 am
☉☌☿ **7:28 pm** 4:28 pm
☽⚻♃ **7:30 pm** 4:30 pm
☽☍♆ **7:53 pm** 4:53 pm
☽△♇ 11:51 pm

2 TUESDAY
☽△♇ **2:51 am**
☽⚻♄ **12:46 pm** 9:46 am
♃⚺♆ **6:03 pm** 3:03 pm
☽⚻☿ **10:26 pm** 7:26 pm
☽⚻☉ 11:09 pm

3 WEDNESDAY
☽⚻☉ **2:09 am**
☽⚻♅ **1:26 pm** 10:26 am
☽□♂ **5:10 pm** 2:10 pm

4 THURSDAY
☽△♀ **3:54 am** 12:54 am
☽⚻♆ **4:43 am** 1:43 am
☽☍♃ **5:17 am** 2:17 am
☽□♇ **11:12 am** 8:12 am
♀□♆ **1:40 pm** 10:40 am
☽△♄ **8:53 pm** 5:53 pm
♀⚹♃ 9:03 pm

5 FRIDAY
♀⚹♃ **12:03 am**
☽☍☿ **3:15 am** 12:15 am
☽☍☉ **1:34 pm** 10:34 am
☽☍♅ **8:13 pm** 5:13 pm
☽△♂ 10:51 pm

6 SATURDAY
☽△♂ **1:51 am**
☽△♆ **10:38 am** 7:38 am
☽⚻♃ **11:59 am** 8:59 am
☽⚻♀ **2:28 pm** 11:28 am
☽⚹♇ **4:41 pm** 1:41 pm
☽□♄ 11:12 pm

7 SUNDAY
☽□♄ **2:12 am**
☽⚻☿ **5:58 am** 2:58 am
♀⚻♇ **6:10 pm** 3:10 pm
☽⚻☉ **9:50 pm** 6:50 pm
☽⚻♅ 9:34 pm

8 MONDAY
☽⚻♅ **12:34 am**
☽⚻♂ **7:55 am** 4:55 am
☽□♆ **2:22 pm** 11:22 am
☽△♃ **4:28 pm** 1:28 pm
☽⚺♇ **8:09 pm** 5:09 pm
☽☍♀ **10:20 pm** 7:20 pm

9 TUESDAY
☽⚹♄ **5:39 am** 2:39 am
☽△☿ **7:28 am** 4:28 am
☉☌♅ **3:56 pm** 12:56 pm

10 WEDNESDAY
☽△♅ **3:32 am** 12:32 am
☽△☉ **4:20 am** 1:20 am
☽☍♂ **12:38 pm** 9:38 am
☽⚹♆ **5:03 pm** 2:03 pm
☽□♃ **7:52 pm** 4:52 pm
☽☌♇ **10:40 pm** 7:40 pm

11 THURSDAY
☽⚻♀ **5:01 am** 2:01 am
☽⚺♄ **8:20 am** 5:20 am
☽□☿ **8:45 am** 5:45 am

12 FRIDAY
☿⚹♄ **4:42 am** 1:42 am
☽□♅ **6:12 am** 3:12 am
☽□☉ **10:28 am** 7:28 am
☽⚻♂ **5:13 pm** 2:13 pm
☽⚺♆ **7:40 pm** 4:40 pm
☿⚹♀ **10:44 pm** 7:44 pm
☽⚹♃ **11:15 pm** 8:15 pm
☽⚺♇ 10:13 pm
♀△♄ 11:57 pm

13 SATURDAY
☽⚺♇ **1:13 am**
♀△♄ **2:57 am**
☽⚹☿ **10:44 am** 7:44 am
☽☌♄ **11:12 am** 8:12 am
☽△♀ **11:51 am** 8:51 am

14 SUNDAY
☽⚹♅ **9:22 am** 6:22 am
☽⚹☉ **5:17 pm** 2:17 pm
☽△♂ **10:30 pm** 7:30 pm
☽☌♆ **10:56 pm** 7:56 pm

15 MONDAY
☽⚺♃ **3:22 am** 12:22 am
☽⚹♇ **4:29 am** 1:29 am
♂△♆ **9:44 am** 6:44 am
☽⚺☿ **2:05 pm** 11:05 am
☽⚺♄ **2:54 pm** 11:54 am
☽□♀ **7:42 pm** 4:42 pm

16 TUESDAY
☽⚺♅ **1:37 pm** 10:37 am
☽⚺☉ 10:30 pm

17 WEDNESDAY
☽⚺☉ **1:30 am**
☽⚺♆ **3:25 am** 12:25 am
☽□♂ **5:10 am** 2:10 am
☽☌♃ **8:47 am** 5:47 am
☽□♇ **9:00 am** 6:00 am
☽☌☿ **7:27 pm** 4:27 pm
☽⚹♄ **7:57 pm** 4:57 pm
♃□♇ **9:11 pm** 6:11 pm

18 THURSDAY
☉⚹♆ **5:00 am** 2:00 am
☽⚹♀ **5:18 am** 2:18 am
☽☌♅ **7:28 pm** 4:28 pm
☿⚹♄ 11:40 pm

19 FRIDAY
☿⚹♄ **2:40 am**
☽⚹♆ **9:39 am** 6:39 am
☽☌☉ **11:53 am** 8:53 am
☽⚹♂ **1:51 pm** 10:51 am
☽△♇ **3:20 pm** 12:20 pm
☽⚺♃ **4:06 pm** 1:06 pm
☽□♄ 11:58 pm

20 SATURDAY
☽□♄ **2:58 am**
☽⚺☿ **3:33 am** 12:33 am
☽⚺♀ **5:28 pm** 2:28 pm
♂☍♇ **11:12 pm** 8:12 pm

21 SUNDAY
☽⚺♅ **3:32 am** 12:32 am
☉△♇ **9:58 am** 6:58 am
☽□♆ **6:12 pm** 3:12 pm
☽⚻♇ 9:00 pm
☽⚺☉ 10:11 pm
☽⚺♂ 10:12 pm
☽⚹♃ 10:54 pm
☉⚹♂ 10:57 pm

22 MONDAY
☽⚻♇ **12:00 am**
☽⚺☉ **1:11 am**
☽⚺♂ **1:12 am**
☽⚹♃ **1:54 am**
☉⚹♂ **1:57 am**
☽△♄ **12:24 pm** 9:24 am
☉⚺♃ **12:55 pm** 9:55 am
☽⚹☿ **3:07 pm** 12:07 pm
♂□♃ 10:13 pm

23 TUESDAY
♂□♃ **1:13 am**
☽☌♀ **8:45 am** 5:45 am
☽⚹♅ **2:07 pm** 11:07 am

24 WEDNESDAY
☽△♆ **5:12 am** 2:12 am
☽☍♇ **11:04 am** 8:04 am
☽□♃ **2:13 pm** 11:13 am
☽☌♂ **3:21 pm** 12:21 pm
☽⚹☉ **5:31 pm** 2:31 pm
☽⚻♄ 9:09 pm

25 THURSDAY
☽⚻♄ **12:09 am**
☽□☿ **6:11 am** 3:11 am
☽⚺♀ 11:33 pm
☽□♅ 11:38 pm

26 FRIDAY
☽⚺♀ **2:33 am**
☽□♅ **2:38 am**
♀⚹♅ **3:37 am** 12:37 am
☽⚻♆ **5:45 pm** 2:45 pm
☽⚻♇ **11:31 pm** 8:31 pm

27 SATURDAY
☽△♃ **3:53 am** 12:53 am
☽⚺♂ **6:57 am** 3:57 am
☽□☉ **11:22 am** 8:22 am
☽☍♄ **12:53 pm** 9:53 am
☽△☿ **11:07 pm** 8:07 pm

28 SUNDAY
☉□♄ **6:46 am** 3:46 am
☽△♅ **3:12 pm** 12:12 pm
☽⚹♀ **8:19 pm** 5:19 pm

29 MONDAY
☽☍♆ **5:46 am** 2:46 am
☽△♇ **11:13 am** 8:13 am
☽⚻♃ **4:33 pm** 1:33 pm
☽⚹♂ **9:21 pm** 6:21 pm
☽⚻♄ 9:18 pm

30 TUESDAY
☽⚻♄ **12:18 am**
☽△☉ **3:39 am** 12:39 am
☽⚻☿ **2:50 pm** 11:50 am
☽⚻♅ 10:29 pm

31 WEDNESDAY
☽⚻♅ **1:29 am**
☽□♀ **10:53 am** 7:53 am
☽⚻♆ **3:02 pm** 12:02 pm
☽□♇ **8:02 pm** 5:02 pm
☽☍♃ 11:04 pm

Eastern time in bold type
Pacific time in medium type

MAY 2023

DATE	SID.TIME	SUN	MOON	NODE	MERCURY	VENUS	MARS	JUPITER	SATURN	URANUS	NEPTUNE	PLUTO	CERES	PALLAS	JUNO	VESTA	CHIRON
1 M	14 34 40	10♉22 52	14♍34	4♉02	11♉57℞	22♊40	19♋00	26♈20	5♓24	18♉26	26♓44	0♒22℞	23♍56℞	29♋19	29♉17	6♉55	17♈19
2 T	14 38 36	11 21 07	26 49	4 02	11 19	23 48	19 33	26 34	5 29	18 29	26 46	0 22	23 54	29 43	29 53	7 22	17 22
3 W	14 42 33	12 19 19	9♎19	4 03	10 40	24 55	20 06	26 48	5 33	18 32	26 47	0 22	23 52	0♌07	0♊28	7 49	17 25
4 Th	14 46 29	13 17 30	22 06	4 04℞	10 02	26 01	20 39	27 02	5 37	18 36	26 49	0 22	23 51	0 31	1 04	8 16	17 28
5 F	14 50 26	14 15 39	5♏12	4 04	9 24	27 08	21 12	27 17	5 41	18 39	26 51	0 22	23 50	0 56	1 39	8 43	17 32
6 Sa	14 54 23	15 13 46	18 35	4 03	8 48	28 14	21 45	27 31	5 45	18 43	26 52	0 22	23 49D	1 20	2 15	9 09	17 35
7 Su	14 58 19	16 11 52	2♐16	4 03	8 14	29 20	22 19	27 45	5 49	18 46	26 54	0 21	23 49	1 45	2 50	9 36	17 38
8 M	15 2 16	17 09 56	16 10	4 01	7 43	0♋26	22 52	27 59	5 53	18 50	26 56	0 21	23 49	2 09	3 25	10 03	17 41
9 T	15 6 12	18 07 59	0♑16	3 59	7 15	1 32	23 26	28 13	5 57	18 53	26 57	0 21	23 50	2 34	4 01	10 30	17 44
10 W	15 10 9	19 06 00	14 29	3 58	6 50	2 38	23 59	28 27	6 00	18 57	26 59	0 21	23 51	2 59	4 36	10 57	17 48
11 Th	15 14 5	20 04 00	28 45	3 56	6 30	3 43	24 33	28 41	6 04	19 00	27 00	0 21	23 52	3 24	5 12	11 24	17 51
12 F	15 18 2	21 01 58	13♒02	3 55D	6 13	4 48	25 06	28 55	6 07	19 04	27 02	0 20	23 54	3 49	5 47	11 50	17 54
13 Sa	15 21 59	21 59 55	27 15	3 55	6 01	5 53	25 40	29 09	6 11	19 07	27 03	0 20	23 57	4 14	6 22	12 17	17 57
14 Su	15 25 55	22 57 51	11♓23	3 56	5 54	6 58	26 14	29 23	6 14	19 11	27 05	0 20	23 59	4 39	6 58	12 44	18 00
15 M	15 29 52	23 55 46	25 24	3 57	5 51D	8 02	26 48	29 36	6 17	19 14	27 06	0 19	24 02	5 04	7 33	13 10	18 03
16 T	15 33 48	24 53 39	9♈16	3 59	5 53	9 06	27 22	29 50	6 21	19 18	27 08	0 19	24 06	5 30	8 08	13 37	18 06
17 W	15 37 45	25 51 31	22 58	4 00℞	5 59	10 10	27 56	0♉04	6 24	19 21	27 09	0 19	24 10	5 55	8 44	14 04	18 09
18 Th	15 41 41	26 49 22	6♉28	4 00	6 10	11 14	28 30	0 17	6 27	19 25	27 11	0 18	24 14	6 21	9 19	14 30	18 12
19 F	15 45 38	27 47 12	19 45	3 59	6 25	12 17	29 04	0 31	6 30	19 28	27 12	0 18	24 19	6 46	9 54	14 57	18 15
20 Sa	15 49 34	28 45 00	2♊49	3 57	6 45	13 21	29 38	0 45	6 32	19 31	27 13	0 17	24 24	7 12	10 30	15 24	18 17
21 Su	15 53 31	29 42 47	15 38	3 54	7 09	14 24	0♌12	0 58	6 35	19 35	27 14	0 17	24 29	7 37	11 05	15 50	18 20
22 M	15 57 28	0♊40 33	28 12	3 50	7 38	15 26	0 46	1 12	6 38	19 38	27 16	0 16	24 35	8 03	11 40	16 17	18 23
23 T	16 1 24	1 38 17	10♋33	3 45	8 10	16 28	1 21	1 25	6 40	19 42	27 17	0 16	24 41	8 29	12 16	16 43	18 26
24 W	16 5 21	2 35 59	22 42	3 41	8 47	17 31	1 55	1 39	6 43	19 45	27 18	0 15	24 47	8 55	12 51	17 10	18 29
25 Th	16 9 17	3 33 40	4♌42	3 37	9 27	18 32	2 29	1 52	6 45	19 49	27 19	0 14	24 54	9 21	13 26	17 36	18 31
26 F	16 13 14	4 31 20	16 36	3 34	10 11	19 34	3 04	2 05	6 47	19 52	27 21	0 14	25 01	9 47	14 01	18 02	18 34
27 Sa	16 17 10	5 28 57	28 28	3 33D	10 59	20 35	3 38	2 18	6 49	19 55	27 22	0 13	25 09	10 13	14 37	18 29	18 37
28 Su	16 21 7	6 26 34	10♍24	3 32	11 50	21 35	4 13	2 32	6 52	19 59	27 23	0 12	25 16	10 39	15 12	18 55	18 39
29 M	16 25 3	7 24 09	22 27	3 33	12 45	22 36	4 48	2 45	6 53	20 02	27 24	0 12	25 25	11 05	15 47	19 21	18 42
30 T	16 29 0	8 21 42	4♎42	3 35	13 43	23 36	5 22	2 58	6 55	20 05	27 25	0 11	25 33	11 31	16 22	19 47	18 44
31 W	16 32 57	9 19 15	17 15	3 36	14 45	24 35	5 57	3 11	6 57	20 09	27 26	0 10	25 42	11 57	16 57	20 14	18 47

EPHEMERIS CALCULATED FOR 12 MIDNIGHT GREENWICH MEAN TIME. ALL OTHER DATA AND FACING ASPECTARIAN PAGE IN **EASTERN TIME (BOLD)** AND PACIFIC TIME (REGULAR).

JUNE 2023

☽ Last Aspect day	ET / hr:mn / PT	asp	☽ Ingress sign	day	ET / hr:mn / PT
2	**8:51 pm** 5:51 pm	△♀	♐	2	10:03 pm
2	**8:51 pm** 5:51 pm	△♀	♐	3	**1:03 am**
4	**11:24 pm** 8:24 pm	□♆	♑	5	**3:31 am** 12:31 am
6	9:40 pm	⚹♆	♒	7	**4:42 am** 1:42 am
7	**12:40 am**	⚹♆	♒	7	**4:42 am** 1:42 am
8	9:24 pm	□☿	♓	9	**6:14 am** 3:14 am
9	**12:24 am**	□☿	♓	9	**6:14 am** 3:14 am
11	**9:20 am** 6:20 am	⚹♇	♈	11	**9:20 am** 6:20 am
13	**2:27 pm** 11:27 am	□♇	♉	13	**2:31 pm** 11:31 am
15	**9:36 pm** 6:36 pm	△♇	♊	15	**9:46 pm** 6:46 pm

☽ Last Aspect day	ET / hr:mn / PT	asp	☽ Ingress sign	day	ET / hr:mn / PT
17	11:24 pm	□♆	♋	18	**6:58 am** 3:58 am
18	**2:24 am**	□♆	♋	18	**6:58 am** 3:58 am
20	**5:43 pm** 2:43 pm	☍♇	♌	20	**6:04 pm** 3:04 pm
22	**1:01 pm** 10:01 am	□♅	♍	23	**6:35 am** 3:35 am
25	**6:24 pm** 3:24 pm	△♇	♎	25	**6:57 pm** 3:57 pm
28	**4:19 am** 1:19 am	□♇	♏	28	**4:55 am** 1:55 am
30	**10:20 am** 7:20 am	⚹♇	♐	30	**10:59 am** 7:59 am

☽ Phases & Eclipses phase	day	ET / hr:mn / PT
Full Moon	3	**11:42 pm** 8:42 pm
4th Quarter	10	**3:31 pm** 12:31 pm
New Moon	17	9:37 pm
New Moon	18	**12:37 am**
2nd Quarter	26	**3:50 am** 12:50 am

Planet Ingress		day	ET / hr:mn / PT
♀	♌	5	**9:46 am** 6:46 am
♇	♑	11	**5:47 am** 2:47 am
☿	♊	11	**6:27 am** 3:27 am
⚳	♎	21	**7:30 am** 4:30 am
☉	♋	21	**10:58 am** 7:58 am
⚵	♋	22	**7:40 am** 4:40 am
⚶	♊	22	**3:17 pm** 12:17 pm
☿	♋	26	**8:24 pm** 5:24 pm

Planetary Motion		day	ET / hr:mn / PT
♄	℞	17	**1:27 pm** 10:27 am
♆	℞	30	**5:07 pm** 2:07 pm

1 THURSDAY
☽☍♃ **2:04 am**
☽□♂ **8:11 am** 5:11 am
☽△♄ **8:30 am** 5:30 am
♂⚻♄ **3:31 pm** 12:31 pm
☽⚻☉ **3:50 pm** 12:50 pm
☽☍☿ 11:53 pm

2 FRIDAY
☽☍☿ **2:53 am**
☽☍♅ **8:10 am** 5:10 am
♀△♆ **6:42 pm** 3:42 pm
☽△♆ **8:42 pm** 5:42 pm
☽△♀ **8:51 pm** 5:51 pm
☽⚹♇ 10:16 pm

3 SATURDAY
☽⚹♇ **1:16 am**
☽⚻♃ **7:48 am** 4:48 am
☽□♄ **1:07 pm** 10:07 am
☽△♂ **2:59 pm** 11:59 am
☽☍☉ **11:42 pm** 8:42 pm

4 SUNDAY
☽⚻☿ **11:12 am** 8:12 am
☽⚻♅ **11:35 am** 8:35 am
☿☌♅ **3:49 pm** 12:49 pm
☽□♆ **11:24 pm** 8:24 pm

5 MONDAY
☽⚻♀ **3:05 am** 12:05 am
☽⚺♇ **3:40 am** 12:40 am
☽△♃ **10:44 am** 7:44 am

♀☍♇ **12:05 pm** 9:05 am
☽⚹♄ **3:12 pm** 12:12 pm
☽⚻♂ **7:00 pm** 4:00 pm

6 TUESDAY
☽⚻☉ **4:51 am** 1:51 am
☽△♅ **1:10 pm** 10:10 am
☽△☿ **5:34 pm** 2:34 pm
☽⚹♆ 9:40 pm

7 WEDNESDAY
☽⚹♆ **12:40 am**
☽☌♇ **4:48 am** 1:48 am
☽☍♀ **7:39 am** 4:39 am
☽□♃ **12:35 pm** 9:35 am
☽⚺♄ **4:23 pm** 1:23 pm
☽☍♂ **10:11 pm** 7:11 pm

8 THURSDAY
☽△☉ **9:29 am** 6:29 am
☽□♅ **2:37 pm** 11:37 am
☽□☿ 9:24 pm
☽⚺♆ 11:10 pm

9 FRIDAY
☽□☿ **12:24 am**
☽⚺♆ **2:10 am**
☽⚺♇ **6:17 am** 3:17 am
☽⚻♀ **12:41 pm** 9:41 am
☽⚹♃ **3:02 pm** 12:02 pm
☿⚹♆ **5:14 pm** 2:14 pm
☽☌♄ **6:16 pm** 3:16 pm
☽⚻♂ 11:20 pm

10 SATURDAY
☽⚻♂ **2:20 am**
☽□☉ **3:31 pm** 12:31 pm
☽⚹♅ **5:21 pm** 2:21 pm

11 SUNDAY
☽☌♆ **5:09 am** 2:09 am
☿△♇ **6:26 am** 3:26 am
☽⚹♇ **9:20 am** 6:20 am
☽⚹☿ **9:43 am** 6:43 am
♀□♃ **11:40 am** 8:40 am
☽⚺♃ **7:16 pm** 4:16 pm
☉⚺♅ **7:37 pm** 4:37 pm
☽△♀ **7:40 pm** 4:40 pm
☽⚺♄ **9:53 pm** 6:53 pm

12 MONDAY
☽△♂ **8:35 am** 5:35 am
☽⚺♅ **10:04 pm** 7:04 pm
☽⚹☉ **11:59 pm** 8:59 pm

13 TUESDAY
♀⚻♄ **5:59 am** 2:59 am
☽⚺♆ **10:12 am** 7:12 am
☽□♇ **2:27 pm** 11:27 am
☽⚺☿ **10:35 pm** 7:35 pm
☽☌♃ 10:40 pm

14 WEDNESDAY
☽☌♃ **1:40 am**
☽⚹♄ **3:36 am** 12:36 am
☽□♀ **5:08 am** 2:08 am
☽□♂ **5:15 pm** 2:15 pm
☿⚺♃ 9:24 pm

15 THURSDAY
☿⚺♃ **12:24 am**
☽☌♅ **4:55 am** 1:55 am
☽⚺☉ **11:04 am** 8:04 am
☿□♄ **12:09 pm** 9:09 am
☽⚹♆ **5:19 pm** 2:19 pm
☽△♇ **9:36 pm** 6:36 pm

16 FRIDAY
☽⚺♃ **10:12 am** 7:12 am
☽□♄ **11:20 am** 8:20 am
☽☌☿ **3:12 pm** 12:12 pm
☽⚹♀ **4:57 pm** 1:57 pm

17 SATURDAY
☽⚹♂ **4:14 am** 1:14 am
☿⚹♀ **11:29 am** 8:29 am
☽⚺♅ **1:45 pm** 10:45 am
☽☌☉ 9:37 pm
☽□♆ 11:24 pm

18 SUNDAY
☽☌☉ **12:37 am**
☽□♆ **2:24 am**
☽⚻♇ **6:43 am** 3:43 am
☽⚹♃ **8:45 pm** 5:45 pm
☽△♄ **9:00 pm** 6:00 pm
☉□♆ **11:54 pm** 8:54 pm

19 MONDAY
☽⚺♀ **7:02 am** 4:02 am
☽⚺☿ **11:41 am** 8:41 am
♃⚹♄ **11:53 am** 8:53 am

☽⚺♂ **5:28 pm** 2:28 pm
☽⚹♅ 9:33 pm

20 TUESDAY
☽⚹♅ **12:33 am**
☽△♆ **1:24 pm** 10:24 am
☽⚺☉ **4:37 pm** 1:37 pm
☽☍♇ **5:43 pm** 2:43 pm

21 WEDNESDAY
☉⚻♇ **6:20 am** 3:20 am
☽⚻♄ **8:30 am** 5:30 am
☽□♃ **9:15 am** 6:15 am
☿⚹♂ **11:23 am** 8:23 am
☽☌♀ **11:08 pm** 8:08 pm

22 THURSDAY
☽☌♂ **8:41 am** 5:41 am
☽⚹☿ **11:51 am** 8:51 am
☽□♅ **1:01 pm** 10:01 am
☿⚺♅ **6:37 pm** 3:37 pm
☽⚻♆ 10:52 pm

23 FRIDAY
☽⚻♆ **1:52 am**
☽⚻♇ **6:08 am** 3:08 am
☽⚹☉ **10:24 am** 7:24 am
☽☍♄ **9:07 pm** 6:07 pm
☽△♃ **10:53 pm** 7:53 pm

24 SATURDAY
☽⚺♀ **3:59 pm** 12:59 pm
☽⚺♂ 9:33 pm
☽△♅ 10:53 pm

25 SUNDAY
☽⚺♂ **12:33 am**
☽△♅ **1:53 am**
☽□☿ **1:25 pm** 10:25 am
☽☍♆ **2:20 pm** 11:20 am
☽△♇ **6:24 pm** 3:24 pm
☿□♆ **6:36 pm** 3:36 pm

26 MONDAY
☽□☉ **3:50 am** 12:50 am
♂□♅ **5:23 am** 2:23 am
☽⚻♄ **9:04 am** 6:04 am
☽⚻♃ **11:44 am** 8:44 am
☿⚻♇ **5:07 pm** 2:07 pm

27 TUESDAY
☽⚹♀ **6:56 am** 3:56 am
☽⚻♅ **12:58 pm** 9:58 am
☽⚹♂ **2:26 pm** 11:26 am
☽⚻♆ 9:35 pm

28 WEDNESDAY
☽⚻♆ **12:35 am**
☽□♇ **4:19 am** 1:19 am
☽△☿ **11:32 am** 8:32 am
☽△☉ **5:49 pm** 2:49 pm
☽△♄ **6:07 pm** 3:07 pm
☽☍♃ **9:29 pm** 6:29 pm
☉△♄ **9:43 pm** 6:43 pm

29 THURSDAY
☽□♀ **5:32 pm** 2:32 pm
☽☍♅ **8:22 pm** 5:22 pm

☽□♂ 9:05 pm
☿△♄ 11:24 pm

30 FRIDAY
☽□♂ **12:05 am**
☿△♄ **2:24 am**
☽△♆ **6:58 am** 3:58 am
☽⚹♇ **10:20 am** 7:20 am
☽□♄ **11:08 pm** 8:08 pm
☉☌☿ 10:06 pm
☽⚻☉ 11:48 pm
☽⚻☿ 11:58 pm

Eastern time in bold type
Pacific time in medium type

JUNE 2023

DATE	SID.TIME	SUN	MOON	NODE	MERCURY	VENUS	MARS	JUPITER	SATURN	URANUS	NEPTUNE	PLUTO	CERES	PALLAS	JUNO	VESTA	CHIRON
1 Th	16 36 53	10♊16 45	0♏08	3♉37℞	15♉49	25♋35	6♌32	3♉24	6♓59	20♉12	27♓27	0♒09℞	25♍51	12♌23	17♊32	20♉40	18♈49
2 F	16 40 50	11 14 15	13 24	3 37	16 57	26 33	7 07	3 37	7 00	20 15	27 28	0 09	26 00	12 50	18 07	21 06	18 52
3 Sa	16 44 46	12 11 44	27 04	3 35	18 08	27 32	7 41	3 49	7 02	20 19	27 29	0 08	26 10	13 16	18 42	21 32	18 54
4 Su	16 48 43	13 09 11	11♐07	3 31	19 21	28 30	8 16	4 02	7 03	20 22	27 30	0 07	26 20	13 42	19 18	21 58	18 57
5 M	16 52 39	14 06 38	25 27	3 26	20 38	29 27	8 51	4 15	7 05	20 25	27 30	0 06	26 30	14 09	19 53	22 24	18 59
6 T	16 56 36	15 04 03	10♑01	3 20	21 58	0♌24	9 26	4 28	7 06	20 28	27 31	0 05	26 41	14 35	20 27	22 50	19 01
7 W	17 0 32	16 01 28	24 41	3 14	23 20	1 21	10 01	4 40	7 07	20 32	27 32	0 04	26 52	15 02	21 02	23 16	19 04
8 Th	17 4 29	16 58 52	9♒20	3 08	24 46	2 17	10 36	4 53	7 08	20 35	27 33	0 03	27 03	15 28	21 37	23 42	19 06
9 F	17 8 26	17 56 16	23 52	3 04	26 14	3 13	11 12	5 05	7 09	20 38	27 33	0 02	27 15	15 55	22 12	24 08	19 08
10 Sa	17 12 22	18 53 38	8♓12	3 02D	27 45	4 08	11 47	5 17	7 10	20 41	27 34	0 01	27 26	16 22	22 47	24 33	19 10
11 Su	17 16 19	19 51 01	22 17	3 01	29 18	5 02	12 22	5 30	7 10	20 44	27 35	0 00	27 39	16 48	23 22	24 59	19 12
12 M	17 20 15	20 48 22	6♈07	3 02	0♊55	5 56	12 57	5 42	7 11	20 47	27 35	29♑59	27 51	17 15	23 57	25 25	19 14
13 T	17 24 12	21 45 44	19 41	3 03	2 34	6 50	13 33	5 54	7 12	20 51	27 36	29 58	28 03	17 42	24 32	25 51	19 16
14 W	17 28 8	22 43 05	3♉02	3 04℞	4 16	7 43	14 08	6 06	7 12	20 54	27 37	29 57	28 16	18 08	25 06	26 16	19 18
15 Th	17 32 5	23 40 25	16 09	3 03	6 01	8 35	14 43	6 18	7 12	20 57	27 37	29 56	28 29	18 35	25 41	26 42	19 20
16 F	17 36 1	24 37 45	29 04	3 00	7 48	9 26	15 19	6 30	7 12	21 00	27 38	29 55	28 43	19 02	26 16	27 07	19 22
17 Sa	17 39 58	25 35 05	11♊47	2 55	9 38	10 17	15 54	6 41	7 13℞	21 03	27 38	29 54	28 56	19 29	26 50	27 33	19 24
18 Su	17 43 55	26 32 24	24 20	2 47	11 30	11 08	16 30	6 53	7 13	21 06	27 39	29 53	29 10	19 56	27 25	27 58	19 26
19 M	17 47 51	27 29 42	6♋42	2 38	13 25	11 57	17 05	7 05	7 13	21 09	27 39	29 52	29 24	20 22	28 00	28 24	19 27
20 T	17 51 48	28 27 00	18 54	2 28	15 22	12 46	17 41	7 16	7 12	21 12	27 39	29 51	29 38	20 49	28 34	28 49	19 29
21 W	17 55 44	29 24 17	0♌58	2 18	17 22	13 34	18 17	7 28	7 12	21 15	27 40	29 49	29 53	21 16	29 09	29 14	19 31
22 Th	17 59 41	0♋21 34	12 55	2 08	19 24	14 22	18 53	7 39	7 12	21 18	27 40	29 48	0♎08	21 43	29 43	29 40	19 32
23 F	18 3 37	1 18 50	24 47	2 01	21 27	15 08	19 28	7 50	7 11	21 20	27 40	29 47	0 23	22 10	0♋18	0♊05	19 34
24 Sa	18 7 34	2 16 05	6♍37	1 55	23 33	15 54	20 04	8 02	7 11	21 23	27 40	29 46	0 38	22 37	0 52	0 30	19 35
25 Su	18 11 30	3 13 20	18 31	1 52	25 40	16 39	20 40	8 13	7 10	21 26	27 41	29 45	0 53	23 04	1 26	0 55	19 37
26 M	18 15 27	4 10 34	0♎32	1 51D	27 48	17 22	21 16	8 24	7 09	21 29	27 41	29 43	1 09	23 31	2 01	1 20	19 38
27 T	18 19 24	5 07 47	12 45	1 51	29 58	18 05	21 52	8 34	7 08	21 32	27 41	29 42	1 25	23 58	2 35	1 45	19 40
28 W	18 23 20	6 05 00	25 15	1 51℞	2♋08	18 47	22 28	8 45	7 07	21 34	27 41	29 41	1 41	24 26	3 09	2 10	19 41
29 Th	18 27 17	7 02 13	8♏08	1 51	4 19	19 28	23 04	8 56	7 06	21 37	27 41	29 40	1 57	24 53	3 44	2 35	19 42
30 F	18 31 13	7 59 25	21 27	1 50	6 30	20 08	23 40	9 06	7 05	21 40	27 41℞	29 38	2 14	25 20	4 18	3 00	19 43

EPHEMERIS CALCULATED FOR 12 MIDNIGHT GREENWICH MEAN TIME. ALL OTHER DATA AND FACING ASPECTARIAN PAGE IN **EASTERN TIME (BOLD)** AND PACIFIC TIME (REGULAR).

JULY 2023

☽ Last Aspect day	ET / hr:mn / PT	asp	☽ Ingress sign day	ET / hr:mn / PT
2	**9:33 am** 6:33 am	□♆	♑ 2	**1:20 pm** 10:20 am
4	**12:45 pm** 9:45 am	☌♇	♒ 4	**1:30 pm** 10:30 am
6	**9:42 am** 6:42 am	☍♂	♓ 6	**1:33 pm** 10:33 am
8	**2:22 pm** 11:22 am	✶♇	♈ 8	**3:19 pm** 12:19 pm
10	**7:11 pm** 4:11 pm	□☿	♉ 10	**7:55 pm** 4:55 pm
12	11:11 pm	△♇	♊ 13	**3:26 am** 12:26 am
13	**2:11 am**	△♇	♊ 13	**3:26 am** 12:26 am
15	**8:35 am** 5:35 am	□♆	♋ 15	**1:13 pm** 10:13 am
17	**11:06 pm** 8:06 pm	☍♇	♌ 18	9:39 pm
17	**11:06 pm** 8:06 pm	☍♇	♌ 18	**12:39 am**

☽ Last Aspect day	ET / hr:mn / PT	asp	☽ Ingress sign day	ET / hr:mn / PT
20	**10:08 am** 7:08 am	☌♀	♍ 20	**1:13 pm** 10:13 am
22	9:06 pm	△♇	♎ 22	10:54 pm
23	**12:06 am**	△♇	♎ 23	**1:54 am**
25	**11:05 am** 8:05 am	□♇	♏ 25	**12:55 pm** 9:55 am
27	**6:36 pm** 3:36 pm	✶♇	♐ 27	**8:24 pm** 5:24 pm
29	**7:51 pm** 4:51 pm	△♀	♑ 29	**11:44 pm** 8:44 pm
31	**10:13 pm** 7:13 pm	☌♇	♒ 31	**11:58 pm** 8:58 pm

☽ Phases & Eclipses

phase	day	ET / hr:mn / PT
Full Moon	3	**7:39 am** 4:39 am
4th Quarter	9	**9:48 pm** 6:48 pm
New Moon	17	**2:32 pm** 11:32 am
2nd Quarter	25	**6:07 pm** 3:07 pm

Planet Ingress

	day	ET / hr:mn / PT
♀ ♍	9	11:55 pm
♀ ♍	10	**2:55 am**
♂ ♍	10	**7:40 am** 4:40 am
☿ ♌	10	9:11 pm
☿ ♌	11	**12:11 am**
☉ ♌	22	**9:50 pm** 6:50 pm
☿ ♍	28	**5:31 pm** 2:31 pm

Planetary Motion

		day	ET / hr:mn / PT
♀	℞	22	**9:33 pm** 6:33 pm
⚷	℞	23	**8:42 am** 5:42 am

1 SATURDAY
☉☌☿ **1:06 am**
☽⚻☉ **2:48 am**
☽⚻☿ **2:58 am**
☽⚻♃ **3:00 am** 12:00 am
☿✶♃ **3:10 am** 12:10 am
☉✶♃ **6:26 am** 3:26 am
☽△♀ **11:21 pm** 8:21 pm
☽⚻♅ **11:48 pm** 8:48 pm

2 SUNDAY
☽△♂ **5:19 am** 2:19 am
☽□♆ **9:33 am** 6:33 am
♀□♅ **10:34 am** 7:34 am
☽⚺♇ **12:39 pm** 9:39 am
☽✶♄ 9:43 pm

3 MONDAY
☽✶♄ **12:43 am**
☽△♃ **5:02 am** 2:02 am
☽☍☉ **7:39 am** 4:39 am
☽☍☿ **12:50 pm** 9:50 am
☽△♅ 9:30 pm
☽⚻♀ 10:55 pm

4 TUESDAY
☽△♅ **12:30 am**
☽⚻♀ **1:55 am**
☽⚻♂ **7:43 am** 4:43 am
☽✶♆ **9:49 am** 6:49 am
☽☌♇ **12:45 pm** 9:45 am
☽⚺♄ 9:35 pm

Eastern time in bold type
Pacific time in medium type

5 WEDNESDAY
☽⚺♄ **12:35 am**
☽□♃ **5:28 am** 2:28 am
☽⚻☉ **10:46 am** 7:46 am
☽⚻☿ **8:36 pm** 5:36 pm
☽□♅ 9:30 pm

6 THURSDAY
☽□♅ **12:30 am**
☽☍♀ **3:38 am** 12:38 am
☽☍♂ **9:42 am** 6:42 am
☽⚺♆ **9:47 am** 6:47 am
♂⚻♆ **11:48 am** 8:48 am
☽⚺♇ **12:43 pm** 9:43 am
☽☌♄ 9:47 pm
☿✶♅ 9:55 pm

7 FRIDAY
☽☌♄ **12:47 am**
☿✶♅ **12:55 am**
☽✶♃ **6:28 am** 3:28 am
☽△☉ **2:48 pm** 11:48 am
☽✶♅ 10:48 pm

8 SATURDAY
☽✶♅ **1:48 am**
☽△☿ **5:56 am** 2:56 am
☽⚻♀ **6:42 am** 3:42 am
☽☌♆ **11:22 am** 8:22 am
☿⚺♀ **12:45 pm** 9:45 am
☽⚻♂ **1:30 pm** 10:30 am
☽✶♇ **2:22 pm** 11:22 am

9 SUNDAY
☽⚺♄ **3:02 am** 12:02 am
♂⚻♇ **8:54 am** 5:54 am
☽⚺♃ **9:44 am** 6:44 am
☿△♆ **7:57 pm** 4:57 pm
☽□☉ **9:48 pm** 6:48 pm

10 MONDAY
☽⚺♅ **5:45 am** 2:45 am
☽△♀ **12:34 pm** 9:34 am
☽⚺♆ **3:43 pm** 12:43 pm
☿☍♇ **4:48 pm** 1:48 pm
☽□♀ **6:50 pm** 3:50 pm
☽□☿ **7:11 pm** 4:11 pm
☽△♂ **8:31 pm** 5:31 pm

11 TUESDAY
☿⚺♂ **7:36 am** 4:36 am
☽✶♄ **8:11 am** 5:11 am
☽☌♃ **4:04 pm** 1:04 pm

12 WEDNESDAY
☽✶☉ **8:30 am** 5:30 am
☽☌♅ **12:42 pm** 9:42 am
☽□♀ **9:24 pm** 6:24 pm
☽✶♆ **10:59 pm** 7:59 pm
☽△♇ 11:11 pm

13 THURSDAY
☽△♇ **2:11 am**
☽□♂ **6:51 am** 3:51 am
☽✶☿ **12:40 pm** 9:40 am
☽□♄ **4:06 pm** 1:06 pm
☽⚺♃ 10:11 pm

14 FRIDAY
☽⚺♃ **1:11 am**
☿⚻♄ **11:17 am** 8:17 am
☉✶♅ **7:02 pm** 4:02 pm
☽⚺♅ **10:08 pm** 7:08 pm
☽⚺☉ **10:23 pm** 7:23 pm

15 SATURDAY
☽✶♀ **8:27 am** 5:27 am
☽□♆ **8:35 am** 5:35 am
☽⚻♇ **11:49 am** 8:49 am
♀⚻♆ **2:42 pm** 11:42 am
☽✶♂ **7:48 pm** 4:48 pm
☽△♄ 11:06 pm

16 SUNDAY
☽△♄ **2:06 am**
☽⚺☿ **9:08 am** 6:08 am
☽✶♃ **12:23 pm** 9:23 am

17 MONDAY
☿□♃ **8:49 am** 5:49 am
☽✶♅ **9:21 am** 6:21 am
☽☌☉ **2:32 pm** 11:32 am
☽△♆ **7:52 pm** 4:52 pm
☽⚺♀ **8:55 pm** 5:55 pm
☽☍♇ **11:06 pm** 8:06 pm

18 TUESDAY
☽⚺♂ **10:37 am** 7:37 am
☽⚻♄ **1:36 pm** 10:36 am
☽□♃ 10:02 pm

19 WEDNESDAY
☽□♃ **1:02 am**
☽☌☿ **7:23 am** 4:23 am
☽□♅ **9:51 pm** 6:51 pm

20 THURSDAY
☽⚺☉ **8:14 am** 5:14 am
☽⚻♆ **8:19 am** 5:19 am
☉△♆ **9:07 am** 6:07 am
☽☌♀ **10:08 am** 7:08 am
☽⚻♇ **11:31 am** 8:31 am
♂☍♄ **4:39 pm** 1:39 pm
☽☍♄ 11:03 pm
☽☌♂ 11:36 pm

21 FRIDAY
☽☍♄ **2:03 am**
☽☌♂ **2:36 am**
☉⚺♀ **9:39 am** 6:39 am
☽△♃ **2:30 pm** 11:30 am
☉☍♇ **11:53 pm** 8:53 pm

22 SATURDAY
☽⚺☿ **6:07 am** 3:07 am
☽△♅ **10:48 am** 7:48 am
☽☍♆ **9:00 pm** 6:00 pm
☽⚺♀ **11:06 pm** 8:06 pm
☽△♇ 9:06 pm
☽✶☉ 11:15 pm

23 SUNDAY
☽△♇ **12:06 am**
☽✶☉ **2:15 am**
☽⚻♄ **2:18 pm** 11:18 am

☿□♅ **5:39 pm** 2:39 pm
☽⚺♂ **6:22 pm** 3:22 pm

24 MONDAY
☽⚻♃ 3:24 am 12:24 am
☽⚻♅ **10:35 pm** 7:35 pm
☽✶☿ 11:39 pm

25 TUESDAY
☽✶☿ **2:39 am**
☽⚻♆ **8:10 am** 5:10 am
☽✶♀ **10:00 am** 7:00 am
☽□♇ **11:05 am** 8:05 am
☽□☉ **6:07 pm** 3:07 pm
☽△♄ 9:27 pm

26 WEDNESDAY
☽△♄ **12:27 am**
☽✶♂ **7:31 am** 4:31 am
☽☍♃ **1:38 pm** 10:38 am
☿⚻♆ 9:00 pm

27 THURSDAY
☿⚻♆ **12:00 am**
☽☍♅ **7:10 am** 4:10 am
☿☌♀ **11:16 am** 8:16 am
☽△♆ **3:56 pm** 12:56 pm
☽□♀ **5:06 pm** 2:06 pm
☽□☿ **5:53 pm** 2:53 pm
☽✶♇ **6:36 pm** 3:36 pm
☿⚻♇ 9:24 pm

28 FRIDAY
☿⚻♇ **12:24 am**
☽△☉ **5:22 am** 2:22 am

☽□♄ **6:52 am** 3:52 am
☽□♂ **4:09 pm** 1:09 pm
☽⚻♃ **7:44 pm** 4:44 pm
☉⚻♄ 10:38 pm

29 SATURDAY
☉⚻♄ **1:38 am**
☽⚻♅ **11:35 am** 8:35 am
☽□♆ **7:32 pm** 4:32 pm
☽△♀ **7:51 pm** 4:51 pm
☽⚺♇ **9:59 pm** 6:59 pm
☽△☿ 11:55 pm

30 SUNDAY
☽△☿ **2:55 am**
☽✶♄ **9:15 am** 6:15 am
☽⚻☉ **11:35 am** 8:35 am
♀⚻♆ **12:25 pm** 9:25 am
☽△♂ **8:18 pm** 5:18 pm
☽△♃ **9:51 pm** 6:51 pm

31 MONDAY
☽△♅ **12:29 pm** 9:29 am
☽⚻♀ **7:17 pm** 4:17 pm
☽✶♆ **7:55 pm** 4:55 pm
☽☌♇ **10:13 pm** 7:13 pm

JULY 2023

DATE	SID.TIME	SUN	MOON	NODE	MERCURY	VENUS	MARS	JUPITER	SATURN	URANUS	NEPTUNE	PLUTO	CERES	PALLAS	JUNO	VESTA	CHIRON
1 Sa	18 35 10	8♋56 36	5♐14	1♉46℞	8♋41	20♌47	24♌16	9♉17	7♓04℞	21♉42	27♓41℞	29♑37℞	2♎30	25♌47	4♋52	3♊25	19♈45
2 Su	18 39 6	9 53 48	19 28	1 40	10 52	21 24	24 52	9 27	7 03	21 45	27 41	29 36	2 47	26 14	5 26	3 49	19 46
3 M	18 43 3	10 50 59	4♑06	1 31	13 02	22 00	25 28	9 38	7 01	21 47	27 41	29 34	3 04	26 41	6 00	4 14	19 47
4 T	18 47 0	11 48 10	19 01	1 22	15 11	22 36	26 04	9 48	7 00	21 50	27 41	29 33	3 21	27 09	6 34	4 39	19 48
5 W	18 50 56	12 45 21	4♒05	1 12	17 19	23 09	26 41	9 58	6 58	21 52	27 41	29 32	3 39	27 36	7 08	5 03	19 49
6 Th	18 54 53	13 42 32	19 07	1 03	19 26	23 42	27 17	10 08	6 56	21 55	27 41	29 30	3 56	28 03	7 42	5 28	19 50
7 F	18 58 49	14 39 43	3♓58	0 56	21 32	24 13	27 53	10 17	6 55	21 57	27 41	29 29	4 14	28 30	8 16	5 52	19 51
8 Sa	19 2 46	15 36 55	18 32	0 51	23 36	24 42	28 29	10 27	6 53	22 00	27 40	29 28	4 32	28 58	8 49	6 16	19 51
9 Su	19 6 42	16 34 06	2♈45	0 49	25 39	25 11	29 06	10 37	6 51	22 02	27 40	29 26	4 50	29 25	9 23	6 41	19 52
10 M	19 10 39	17 31 18	16 34	0 48D	27 40	25 37	29 42	10 46	6 49	22 04	27 40	29 25	5 08	29 52	9 57	7 05	19 53
11 T	19 14 35	18 28 31	0♉03	0 48℞	29 39	26 02	0♍19	10 56	6 46	22 07	27 40	29 23	5 26	0♍19	10 31	7 29	19 54
12 W	19 18 32	19 25 44	13 11	0 48	1♌37	26 25	0 55	11 05	6 44	22 09	27 39	29 22	5 45	0 47	11 04	7 53	19 54
13 Th	19 22 29	20 22 58	26 04	0 46	3 33	26 47	1 32	11 14	6 42	22 11	27 39	29 21	6 04	1 14	11 38	8 17	19 55
14 F	19 26 25	21 20 12	8♊42	0 41	5 26	27 07	2 08	11 23	6 39	22 13	27 38	29 19	6 22	1 41	12 11	8 41	19 55
15 Sa	19 30 22	22 17 26	21 10	0 34	7 18	27 25	2 45	11 32	6 37	22 15	27 38	29 18	6 41	2 09	12 45	9 05	19 56
16 Su	19 34 18	23 14 41	3♋27	0 24	9 08	27 41	3 22	11 40	6 34	22 17	27 38	29 16	7 01	2 36	13 18	9 28	19 56
17 M	19 38 15	24 11 57	15 37	0 11	10 57	27 55	3 58	11 49	6 32	22 19	27 37	29 15	7 20	3 04	13 52	9 52	19 57
18 T	19 42 11	25 09 13	27 40	29♈58	12 43	28 07	4 35	11 58	6 29	22 21	27 37	29 14	7 39	3 31	14 25	10 16	19 57
19 W	19 46 8	26 06 29	9♌38	29 44	14 27	28 18	5 12	12 06	6 26	22 23	27 36	29 12	7 59	3 58	14 58	10 39	19 57
20 Th	19 50 4	27 03 45	21 31	29 31	16 10	28 26	5 49	12 14	6 23	22 25	27 35	29 11	8 19	4 26	15 32	11 03	19 57
21 F	19 54 1	28 01 02	3♍21	29 20	17 51	28 31	6 26	12 22	6 20	22 27	27 35	29 09	8 39	4 53	16 05	11 26	19 58
22 Sa	19 57 58	28 58 19	15 11	29 12	19 29	28 35	7 03	12 30	6 17	22 29	27 34	29 08	8 59	5 21	16 38	11 50	19 58
23 Su	20 1 54	29 55 36	27 04	29 07	21 06	28 36℞	7 40	12 38	6 14	22 31	27 33	29 06	9 19	5 48	17 11	12 13	19 58℞
24 M	20 5 51	0♌52 54	9♎04	29 04	22 42	28 35	8 17	12 45	6 11	22 33	27 33	29 05	9 39	6 16	17 44	12 36	19 58
25 T	20 9 47	1 50 12	21 15	29 03	24 15	28 32	8 54	12 53	6 08	22 34	27 32	29 04	9 59	6 43	18 17	12 59	19 58
26 W	20 13 44	2 47 31	3♏42	29 03	25 46	28 26	9 31	13 00	6 04	22 36	27 31	29 02	10 20	7 11	18 50	13 22	19 58
27 Th	20 17 40	3 44 49	16 32	29 02	27 16	28 18	10 08	13 07	6 01	22 37	27 30	29 01	10 40	7 38	19 23	13 45	19 57
28 F	20 21 37	4 42 09	29 47	29 01	28 43	28 07	10 45	13 14	5 57	22 39	27 30	28 59	11 01	8 06	19 55	14 08	19 57
29 Sa	20 25 33	5 39 28	13♐31	28 57	0♍09	27 54	11 22	13 21	5 54	22 41	27 29	28 58	11 22	8 33	20 28	14 30	19 57
30 Su	20 29 30	6 36 49	27 44	28 51	1 32	27 39	12 00	13 28	5 50	22 42	27 28	28 56	11 43	9 01	21 01	14 53	19 57
31 M	20 33 27	7 34 10	12♑26	28 42	2 54	27 21	12 37	13 35	5 46	22 44	27 27	28 55	12 04	9 28	21 33	15 15	19 56

EPHEMERIS CALCULATED FOR 12 MIDNIGHT GREENWICH MEAN TIME. ALL OTHER DATA AND FACING ASPECTARIAN PAGE IN **EASTERN TIME (BOLD)** AND PACIFIC TIME (REGULAR).

AUGUST 2023

☽ Last Aspect day	ET / hr:mn / PT	asp	☽ Ingress sign	day	ET / hr:mn / PT
2	**5:15 pm** 2:15 pm	☍♀	♓	2	**11:05 pm** 8:05 pm
4	**9:21 pm** 6:21 pm	⚹♇	♈	4	**11:19 pm** 8:19 pm
6	9:13 pm	□♇	♉	6	11:25 pm
7	**12:13 am**	□♇	♉	7	**2:25 am**
9	**6:39 am** 3:39 am	△♇	♊	9	**9:05 am** 6:05 am
11	**1:27 pm** 10:27 am	□♆	♋	11	**6:52 pm** 3:52 pm
14	**3:46 am** 12:46 am	☍♇	♌	14	**6:36 am** 3:36 am
16	**5:38 am** 2:38 am	☌☉	♍	16	**7:14 pm** 4:14 pm
19	**4:51 am** 1:51 am	△♇	♎	19	**7:53 am** 4:53 am
21	**4:31 pm** 1:31 pm	⚹☉	♏	21	**7:22 pm** 4:22 pm
23	10:10 pm	⚹♇	♐	24	**4:07 am** 1:07 am
24	**1:10 am**	⚹♇	♐	24	**4:07 am** 1:07 am
26	**7:56 am** 4:56 am	□♂	♑	27	**9:05 am** 6:05 am
28	**7:49 am** 4:49 am	☌♇	♒	28	**10:32 am** 7:32 am
29	**11:04 pm** 8:04 pm	□♅	♓	30	**9:56 am** 6:56 am

☽ Phases & Eclipses phase	day	ET / hr:mn / PT
Full Moon	1	**2:32 pm** 11:32 am
4th Quarter	8	**6:28 am** 3:28 am
New Moon	16	**5:38 am** 2:38 am
2nd Quarter	24	**5:57 am** 2:57 am
Full Moon	30	**9:36 pm** 6:36 pm

Planet Ingress	day	ET / hr:mn / PT
✷ ♌	15	**3:29 pm** 12:29 pm
☉ ♍	23	**5:01 am** 2:01 am
♂ ♎	27	**9:20 am** 6:20 am

Planetary Motion	day	ET / hr:mn / PT
☿ ℞	23	**3:59 pm** 12:59 pm
♅ ℞	28	**10:39 pm** 7:39 pm

1 TUESDAY
☽⚻☿ **7:37 am** 4:37 am
☽⚺♄ **8:54 am** 5:54 am
☽☍☉ **2:32 pm** 11:32 am
♂△♃ **4:45 pm** 1:45 pm
☽□♃ **9:38 pm** 6:38 pm
☽⚻♂ **9:48 pm** 6:48 pm
☿☍♄ **10:18 pm** 7:18 pm

2 WEDNESDAY
☽□♅ **11:44 am** 8:44 am
☽☍♀ **5:15 pm** 2:15 pm
☽⚺♆ **7:00 pm** 4:00 pm
☽⚺♇ **9:16 pm** 6:16 pm

3 THURSDAY
☽☌♄ **7:53 am** 4:53 am
☽☍☿ **11:03 am** 8:03 am
☽⚻☉ **4:59 pm** 1:59 pm
☽⚹♃ **9:20 pm** 6:20 pm
☽☍♂ **11:15 pm** 8:15 pm

4 FRIDAY
☽⚹♅ **11:35 am** 8:35 am
☽⚻♀ **3:49 pm** 12:49 pm
☽☌♆ **7:00 pm** 4:00 pm
☽⚹♇ **9:21 pm** 6:21 pm

5 SATURDAY
☽⚺♄ **8:18 am** 5:18 am
☽⚻☿ **4:14 pm** 1:14 pm
☽△☉ **9:40 pm** 6:40 pm
☽⚺♃ **11:03 pm** 8:03 pm

6 SUNDAY
☽⚻♂ **3:03 am** 12:03 am
☽⚺♅ **1:57 pm** 10:57 am
☽△♀ **4:35 pm** 1:35 pm
☉□♃ **8:03 pm** 5:03 pm
☽⚺♆ **9:43 pm** 6:43 pm
☽□♇ 9:13 pm

7 MONDAY
☽□♇ **12:13 am**
☽⚹♄ **11:46 am** 8:46 am
☽△☿ 10:10 pm

8 TUESDAY
☽△☿ **1:10 am**
☽☌♃ **4:11 am** 1:11 am
☽□☉ **6:28 am** 3:28 am
☽△♂ **10:46 am** 7:46 am
☽☌♅ **7:50 pm** 4:50 pm
☽□♀ **8:21 pm** 5:21 pm

9 WEDNESDAY
☽⚹♆ **4:00 am** 1:00 am
☽△♇ **6:39 am** 3:39 am
♀□♅ **7:08 am** 4:08 am
☽□♄ **6:45 pm** 3:45 pm
☿△♃ **8:47 pm** 5:47 pm

10 THURSDAY
☽⚺♃ **12:51 pm** 9:51 am
☽□☿ **2:02 pm** 11:02 am
☽⚹☉ **7:37 pm** 4:37 pm

☽□♂ **10:28 pm** 7:28 pm
☽⚹♀ 11:52 pm

11 FRIDAY
☽⚹♀ **2:52 am**
☽⚺♅ **5:03 am** 2:03 am
☽□♆ **1:27 pm** 10:27 am
☽⚻♇ **4:13 pm** 1:13 pm

12 SATURDAY
☽△♄ **4:37 am** 1:37 am
♀⚺♂ **8:15 pm** 5:15 pm
☽⚹♃ 9:06 pm

13 SUNDAY
☽⚹♃ **12:06 am**
☽⚹☿ **5:26 am** 2:26 am
☉☌♀ **7:16 am** 4:16 am
☽⚺♀ **11:17 am** 8:17 am
☽⚺☉ **11:51 am** 8:51 am
☽⚹♂ **12:56 pm** 9:56 am
☽⚹♅ **4:30 pm** 1:30 pm
☽△♆ 9:57 pm

14 MONDAY
☽△♆ **12:57 am**
☽☍♇ **3:46 am** 12:46 am
☽⚻♄ **4:12 pm** 1:12 pm
☉⚺♂ 10:10 pm

15 TUESDAY
☉⚺♂ **1:10 am**
☽□♃ **12:44 pm** 9:44 am
☿⚺♀ **1:04 pm** 10:04 am
☽☌♀ **8:44 pm** 5:44 pm

☽⚺☿ **9:34 pm** 6:34 pm
☉□♅ **10:35 pm** 7:35 pm

16 WEDNESDAY
☽⚺♂ **4:48 am** 1:48 am
☽□♅ **5:04 am** 2:04 am
☽☌☉ **5:38 am** 2:38 am
♂△♅ **9:53 am** 6:53 am
☽⚻♆ **1:26 pm** 10:26 am
☽⚻♇ **4:17 pm** 1:17 pm

17 THURSDAY
☽☍♄ **4:32 am** 1:32 am
☽△♃ 10:48 pm

18 FRIDAY
☽△♃ **1:48 am**
☽⚺♀ **6:35 am** 3:35 am
☽☌☿ **1:09 pm** 10:09 am
☽△♅ **5:51 pm** 2:51 pm
☽☌♂ **8:57 pm** 5:57 pm
☽⚺☉ **11:42 pm** 8:42 pm
☽☍♆ 11:01 pm

19 SATURDAY
☽☍♆ **2:01 am**
☽△♇ **4:51 am** 1:51 am
☽⚻♄ **4:43 pm** 1:43 pm

20 SUNDAY
☉⚻♆ **3:40 am** 12:40 am
☽⚻♃ **2:19 pm** 11:19 am
☽⚹♀ **4:07 pm** 1:07 pm
☽⚺☿ 11:50 pm

21 MONDAY
☽⚺☿ **2:50 am**
☽⚻♅ **5:47 am** 2:47 am
☽⚺♂ **12:02 pm** 9:02 am
☽⚻♆ **1:34 pm** 10:34 am
☉⚻♇ **2:07 pm** 11:07 am
☽□♇ **4:19 pm** 1:19 pm
☽⚹☉ **4:31 pm** 1:31 pm

22 TUESDAY
☽△♄ **3:33 am** 12:33 am
♀□♃ **8:16 am** 5:16 am
♂☍♆ **4:34 pm** 1:34 pm
☽□♀ 9:10 pm
☽☍♃ 9:48 pm

23 WEDNESDAY
☽□♀ **12:10 am**
☽☍♃ **12:48 am**
☽⚹☿ **1:03 pm** 10:03 am
☽☍♅ **3:19 pm** 12:19 pm
☽△♆ **10:33 pm** 7:33 pm
☽⚹♂ 9:09 pm
☽⚹♇ 10:10 pm

24 THURSDAY
☽⚹♂ **12:09 am**
☽⚹♇ **1:10 am**
☽□☉ **5:57 am** 2:57 am
☽□♄ **11:29 am** 8:29 am
♂△♇ **8:23 pm** 5:23 pm

25 FRIDAY
☽△♀ **5:27 am** 2:27 am
☽⚻♃ **7:49 am** 4:49 am

☽□☿ **6:43 pm** 3:43 pm
☽⚻♅ **9:12 pm** 6:12 pm

26 SATURDAY
☽□♆ **3:49 am** 12:49 am
☽⚺♇ **6:16 am** 3:16 am
☽□♂ **7:56 am** 4:56 am
☽△☉ **2:39 pm** 11:39 am
☽⚹♄ **3:39 pm** 12:39 pm

27 SUNDAY
☉☍♄ **4:28 am** 1:28 am
☽⚻♀ **7:28 am** 4:28 am
☽△♃ **10:58 am** 7:58 am
☽△☿ **8:00 pm** 5:00 pm
☽△♅ **11:22 pm** 8:22 pm

28 MONDAY
☽⚹♆ **5:29 am** 2:29 am
☽☌♇ **7:49 am** 4:49 am
☽△♂ **11:39 am** 8:39 am
☽⚺♄ **4:29 pm** 1:29 pm
☽⚻☉ **7:08 pm** 4:08 pm

29 TUESDAY
☽☍♀ **6:56 am** 3:56 am
☽□♃ **11:11 am** 8:11 am
☽⚻☿ **6:18 pm** 3:18 pm
☽□♅ **11:04 pm** 8:04 pm

30 WEDNESDAY
☽⚺♆ **4:56 am** 1:56 am
☽⚺♇ **7:14 am** 4:14 am
☽⚻♂ **1:07 pm** 10:07 am

☽☌♄ **3:33 pm** 12:33 pm
☽☍☉ **9:36 pm** 6:36 pm

31 THURSDAY
☽⚻♀ **5:33 am** 2:33 am
☽⚹♃ **10:25 am** 7:25 am
☽☍☿ **3:29 pm** 12:29 pm
☽⚹♅ **10:20 pm** 7:20 pm

Eastern time in bold type
Pacific time in medium type

AUGUST 2023

DATE	SID.TIME	SUN	MOON	NODE	MERCURY	VENUS	MARS	JUPITER	SATURN	URANUS	NEPTUNE	PLUTO	CERES	PALLAS	JUNO	VESTA	CHIRON
1 T	20 37 23	8♌ 31 31	27♑29	28♈32℞	4♍14	27♌01℞	13♍14	13♉41	5♓43℞	22♉45	27♓26℞	28♑54℞	12♎25	9♍56	22♋06	15♊38	19♈56℞
2 W	20 41 20	9 28 53	12♒45	28 21	5 31	26 39	13 51	13 47	5 39	22 46	27 25	28 52	12 47	10 23	22 38	16 00	19 55
3 Th	20 45 16	10 26 16	28 02	28 11	6 47	26 15	14 29	13 53	5 35	22 48	27 24	28 51	13 08	10 51	23 11	16 22	19 55
4 F	20 49 13	11 23 40	13♓10	28 04	8 00	25 49	15 06	13 59	5 31	22 49	27 23	28 49	13 30	11 18	23 43	16 45	19 54
5 Sa	20 53 9	12 21 05	27 59	27 59	9 11	25 20	15 44	14 05	5 27	22 50	27 22	28 48	13 51	11 46	24 15	17 07	19 54
6 Su	20 57 6	13 18 31	12♈23	27 56	10 20	24 50	16 21	14 11	5 23	22 51	27 21	28 47	14 13	12 13	24 47	17 29	19 53
7 M	21 1 2	14 15 59	26 21	27 55D	11 26	24 19	16 59	14 16	5 19	22 52	27 20	28 45	14 35	12 41	25 20	17 50	19 52
8 T	21 4 59	15 13 28	9♉52	27 55℞	12 30	23 46	17 36	14 21	5 15	22 53	27 19	28 44	14 57	13 08	25 52	18 12	19 52
9 W	21 8 56	16 10 58	23 00	27 55	13 31	23 11	18 14	14 26	5 11	22 54	27 18	28 43	15 19	13 36	26 24	18 34	19 51
10 Th	21 12 52	17 08 29	5♊47	27 54	14 30	22 36	18 52	14 31	5 07	22 55	27 17	28 41	15 41	14 04	26 56	18 55	19 50
11 F	21 16 49	18 06 02	18 17	27 50	15 25	22 00	19 29	14 36	5 03	22 56	27 15	28 40	16 03	14 31	27 28	19 17	19 49
12 Sa	21 20 45	19 03 36	0♋35	27 44	16 18	21 23	20 07	14 41	4 58	22 57	27 14	28 39	16 25	14 59	27 59	19 38	19 48
13 Su	21 24 42	20 01 12	12 42	27 35	17 08	20 46	20 45	14 45	4 54	22 58	27 13	28 37	16 48	15 26	28 31	19 59	19 47
14 M	21 28 38	20 58 49	24 43	27 24	17 54	20 08	21 23	14 49	4 50	22 59	27 12	28 36	17 10	15 54	29 03	20 20	19 46
15 T	21 32 35	21 56 27	6♌39	27 12	18 37	19 31	22 01	14 53	4 45	23 00	27 10	28 35	17 33	16 21	29 34	20 41	19 45
16 W	21 36 31	22 54 06	18 32	27 00	19 16	18 54	22 39	14 57	4 41	23 00	27 09	28 33	17 55	16 49	0♌06	21 02	19 44
17 Th	21 40 28	23 51 47	0♍23	26 49	19 51	18 18	23 17	15 01	4 37	23 01	27 08	28 32	18 18	17 17	0 37	21 22	19 42
18 F	21 44 25	24 49 29	12 13	26 39	20 22	17 43	23 55	15 05	4 32	23 01	27 07	28 31	18 41	17 44	1 09	21 43	19 41
19 Sa	21 48 21	25 47 12	24 06	26 32	20 49	17 08	24 33	15 08	4 28	23 02	27 05	28 30	19 04	18 12	1 40	22 03	19 40
20 Su	21 52 18	26 44 56	6♎02	26 27	21 12	16 35	25 11	15 11	4 23	23 02	27 04	28 28	19 27	18 39	2 11	22 24	19 39
21 M	21 56 14	27 42 42	18 06	26 25D	21 29	16 03	25 49	15 14	4 19	23 03	27 02	28 27	19 50	19 07	2 43	22 44	19 37
22 T	22 0 11	28 40 28	0♏19	26 25	21 42	15 33	26 27	15 17	4 14	23 03	27 01	28 26	20 13	19 35	3 14	23 04	19 36
23 W	22 4 7	29 38 16	12 48	26 26	21 49℞	15 04	27 05	15 19	4 10	23 04	27 00	28 25	20 36	20 02	3 45	23 24	19 34
24 Th	22 8 4	0♍36 05	25 35	26 27℞	21 51	14 38	27 44	15 22	4 05	23 04	26 58	28 24	20 59	20 30	4 16	23 43	19 33
25 F	22 12 0	1 33 55	8♐46	26 26	21 47	14 13	28 22	15 24	4 01	23 04	26 57	28 23	21 23	20 57	4 46	24 03	19 31
26 Sa	22 15 57	2 31 47	22 23	26 25	21 38	13 50	29 00	15 26	3 56	23 04	26 55	28 21	21 46	21 25	5 17	24 22	19 30
27 Su	22 19 54	3 29 40	6♑28	26 21	21 22	13 30	29 39	15 28	3 52	23 04	26 54	28 20	22 09	21 52	5 48	24 42	19 28
28 M	22 23 50	4 27 34	21 00	26 15	21 00	13 12	0♎17	15 29	3 47	23 04	26 52	28 19	22 33	22 20	6 19	25 01	19 26
29 T	22 27 47	5 25 29	5♒56	26 08	20 33	12 56	0 56	15 31	3 43	23 05℞	26 51	28 18	22 57	22 48	6 49	25 20	19 24
30 W	22 31 43	6 23 25	21 07	26 01	20 00	12 43	1 34	15 32	3 38	23 05	26 49	28 17	23 20	23 15	7 20	25 39	19 23
31 Th	22 35 40	7 21 23	6♓24	25 54	19 21	12 32	2 13	15 33	3 34	23 04	26 48	28 16	23 44	23 43	7 50	25 57	19 21

EPHEMERIS CALCULATED FOR 12 MIDNIGHT GREENWICH MEAN TIME. ALL OTHER DATA AND FACING ASPECTARIAN PAGE IN **EASTERN TIME (BOLD)** AND PACIFIC TIME (REGULAR).

SEPTEMBER 2023

☽ Last Aspect / ☽ Ingress

day	ET / hr:mn / PT		asp	sign	day	ET / hr:mn / PT	
1	**6:36 am**	3:36 am	⚹♇	♈	1	**9:25 am**	6:25 am
3	**7:57 am**	4:57 am	□♇	♉	3	**11:00 am**	8:00 am
5	**12:46 pm**	9:46 am	△♇	♊	5	**4:07 pm**	1:07 pm
7	**6:22 pm**	3:22 pm	□♆	♋	7		10:00 pm
7	**6:22 pm**	3:22 pm	□♆	♋	8	**1:00 am**	
10	**8:47 am**	5:47 am	☍♇	♌	10	**12:36 pm**	9:36 am
12	**11:06 am**	8:06 am	□♅	♍	12		10:18 pm
12	**11:06 am**	8:06 am	□♅	♍	13	**1:18 am**	
15	**9:49 am**	6:49 am	△♇	♎	15	**1:44 pm**	10:44 am
17	**9:06 pm**	6:06 pm	□♇	♏	17		9:58 pm
17	**9:06 pm**	6:06 pm	□♇	♏	18	**12:58 am**	
20	**6:21 am**	3:21 am	⚹♇	♐	20	**10:06 am**	7:06 am
22	**3:32 pm**	12:32 pm	□☉	♑	22	**4:20 pm**	1:20 pm
24	**4:05 pm**	1:05 pm	☌♇	♒	24	**7:29 pm**	4:29 pm
26	**8:38 am**	5:38 am	□♅	♓	26	**8:18 pm**	5:18 pm
28	**4:58 pm**	1:58 pm	⚹♇	♈	28	**8:17 pm**	5:17 pm
30	**5:50 pm**	2:50 pm	□♇	♉	30	**9:18 pm**	6:18 pm

☽ Phases & Eclipses

phase	day	ET / hr:mn / PT	
4th Quarter	6	**6:21 pm**	3:21 pm
New Moon	14	**9:40 pm**	6:40 pm
2nd Quarter	22	**3:32 pm**	12:32 pm
Full Moon	29	**5:58 am**	2:58 am

Planet Ingress

	day	ET / hr:mn / PT	
♀ ♎	13	**12:38 pm**	9:38 am
⚶ ♋	13	**7:28 pm**	4:28 pm
⚵ ♏	15	**8:50 am**	5:50 am
☉ ♎	22		11:50 pm
☉ ♎	23	**2:50 am**	

Planetary Motion

		day	ET / hr:mn / PT	
♀	D	3	**9:20 pm**	6:20 pm
♃	℞	4	**10:10 am**	7:10 am
☿	D	15	**4:21 pm**	1:21 pm

1 FRIDAY
☽☌♆ **4:13 am** 1:13 am
☽⚹♇ **6:36 am** 3:36 am
☽☍♂ **2:50 pm** 11:50 am
☽⚺♄ **2:56 pm** 11:56 am
♂⚻♄ **5:01 pm** 2:01 pm
☽⚻☉ 9:46 pm

2 SATURDAY
☽⚻☉ **12:46 am**
☽△♀ **5:19 am** 2:19 am
☽⚺♃ **10:47 am** 7:47 am
☽⚻☿ **1:25 pm** 10:25 am
☽⚺♅ **11:15 pm** 8:15 pm

3 SUNDAY
☽⚺♆ **5:24 am** 2:24 am
☽□♇ **7:57 am** 4:57 am
☽⚹♄ **4:36 pm** 1:36 pm
☽⚻♂ **7:10 pm** 4:10 pm

4 MONDAY
☿△♃ **6:29 am** 3:29 am
☽△☉ **7:12 am** 4:12 am
☽□♀ **8:08 am** 5:08 am
☽△☿ **1:35 pm** 10:35 am
☽☌♃ **2:06 pm** 11:06 am
☉⚺♀ **8:42 pm** 5:42 pm

5 TUESDAY
☽☌♅ **3:28 am** 12:28 am
☽⚹♆ **9:59 am** 6:59 am
☽△♇ **12:46 pm** 9:46 am
☽□♄ **9:50 pm** 6:50 pm

6 WEDNESDAY
☽△♂ **3:45 am** 12:45 am
☉☌☿ **7:09 am** 4:09 am
☽⚹♀ **3:06 pm** 12:06 pm
☽□☿ **4:46 pm** 1:46 pm
☽□☉ **6:21 pm** 3:21 pm
☽⚺♃ **9:12 pm** 6:12 pm

7 THURSDAY
☽⚺♅ **11:30 am** 8:30 am
☿⚺♀ **12:18 pm** 9:18 am
☽□♆ **6:22 pm** 3:22 pm
☽⚻♇ **9:22 pm** 6:22 pm

8 FRIDAY
☽△♄ **6:43 am** 3:43 am
☉△♃ **7:13 am** 4:13 am
☽□♂ **4:34 pm** 1:34 pm
☽⚹☿ **10:57 pm** 7:57 pm
☽⚺♀ 11:02 pm

9 SATURDAY
☽⚺♀ **2:02 am**
☽⚹♃ **7:38 am** 4:38 am
☽⚹☉ **9:49 am** 6:49 am
☽⚹♅ **10:34 pm** 7:34 pm

10 SUNDAY
☽△♆ **5:36 am** 2:36 am
☽☍♇ **8:47 am** 5:47 am
☽⚻♄ **6:09 pm** 3:09 pm

11 MONDAY
☿⚺♂ **3:22 am** 12:22 am
☽⚺☿ **7:37 am** 4:37 am
☽⚹♂ **8:06 am** 5:06 am
☽☌♀ **3:32 pm** 12:32 pm
☽□♃ **7:54 pm** 4:54 pm

12 TUESDAY
☽⚺☉ **3:37 am** 12:37 am
☽□♅ **11:06 am** 8:06 am
☽⚻♆ **6:07 pm** 3:07 pm
☽⚻♇ **9:24 pm** 6:24 pm

13 WEDNESDAY
☽☍♄ **6:31 am** 3:31 am
☽☌☿ **6:04 pm** 3:04 pm
☽⚺♂ 9:22 pm

14 THURSDAY
☽⚺♂ **12:22 am**
☽⚺♀ **5:56 am** 2:56 am
☽△♃ **8:27 am** 5:27 am
☽☌☉ **9:40 pm** 6:40 pm
☽△♅ **11:38 pm** 8:38 pm

15 FRIDAY
☽☍♆ **6:30 am** 3:30 am
☽△♇ **9:49 am** 6:49 am
☽⚻♄ **6:32 pm** 3:32 pm
☉△♅ **9:24 pm** 6:24 pm

16 SATURDAY
☽⚺☿ **5:45 am** 2:45 am
☽☌♂ **3:53 pm** 12:53 pm
☽⚹♀ **7:57 pm** 4:57 pm
☽⚻♃ **8:12 pm** 5:12 pm
♀□♃ 11:10 pm

17 SUNDAY
♀□♃ **2:10 am**
☽⚻♅ **11:09 am** 8:09 am
☽⚺☉ **2:27 pm** 11:27 am
☽⚻♆ **5:47 pm** 2:47 pm
☽□♇ **9:06 pm** 6:06 pm

18 MONDAY
☽△♄ **5:19 am** 2:19 am
☽⚹☿ **5:52 pm** 2:52 pm

19 TUESDAY
☽⚺♂ **5:31 am** 2:31 am
☽☍♃ **6:16 am** 3:16 am
☉☍♆ **7:17 am** 4:17 am
☽□♀ **8:29 am** 5:29 am
♂⚻♃ **6:48 pm** 3:48 pm
☽☍♅ **8:46 pm** 5:46 pm

20 WEDNESDAY
☽△♆ **3:06 am** 12:06 am
☽⚹☉ **4:47 am** 1:47 am
☽⚹♇ **6:21 am** 3:21 am
☽□♄ **1:58 pm** 10:58 am
☉△♇ 10:21 pm

21 THURSDAY
☉△♇ **1:21 am**
☽□☿ **5:13 am** 2:13 am
☽⚻♃ **1:47 pm** 10:47 am
☽⚹♂ **4:12 pm** 1:12 pm
☽△♀ **6:25 pm** 3:25 pm

22 FRIDAY
☽⚻♅ **3:40 am** 12:40 am
☽□♆ **9:37 am** 6:37 am
☽⚺♇ **12:46 pm** 9:46 am
☽□☉ **3:32 pm** 12:32 pm
☽⚹♄ **7:44 pm** 4:44 pm

23 SATURDAY
☽△☿ **2:24 pm** 11:24 am
☽△♃ **6:12 pm** 3:12 pm
☽□♂ **11:17 pm** 8:17 pm
☽□⚷ 9:07 pm
☽⚻♀ 10:04 pm

24 SUNDAY
☽⚻♀ **1:04 am**
☽△♅ **7:27 am** 4:27 am
☽⚹♆ **1:03 pm** 10:03 am
☽☌♇ **4:05 pm** 1:05 pm
☽△☉ **10:26 pm** 7:26 pm
☽⚺♄ **10:29 pm** 7:29 pm
☉⚻♄ **11:10 pm** 8:10 pm

25 MONDAY
☿△♃ **8:10 am** 5:10 am
☽□♃ **7:49 pm** 4:49 pm
☽⚻☿ **9:02 pm** 6:02 pm

26 TUESDAY
☽△♂ **3:13 am** 12:13 am
☽☍♀ **4:47 am** 1:47 am
☽□♅ **8:38 am** 5:38 am
☽⚺♆ **2:00 pm** 11:00 am
☽⚺♇ **5:00 pm** 2:00 pm
☽☌♄ **11:01 pm** 8:01 pm
☽⚻☉ 11:33 pm

27 WEDNESDAY
☽⚻☉ **2:33 am**
☽⚹♃ **7:46 pm** 4:46 pm
☽☍☿ 11:18 pm

28 THURSDAY
☽☍☿ **2:18 am**
☽⚻♂ **5:30 am** 2:30 am
☽⚻♀ **7:06 am** 4:06 am
☽⚹♅ **8:35 am** 5:35 am
☽☌♆ **1:54 pm** 10:54 am
☽⚹♇ **4:58 pm** 1:58 pm
☽⚺♄ **10:49 pm** 7:49 pm

29 FRIDAY
☽☍☉ **5:58 am** 2:58 am
♀□♅ **1:53 pm** 10:53 am
☽⚺♃ **7:46 pm** 4:46 pm

30 SATURDAY
☿⚺♂ **4:35 am** 1:35 am
☽☍♂ **8:20 am** 5:20 am
☽⚻☿ **8:36 am** 5:36 am
☽⚺♅ **9:06 am** 6:06 am
☽△♀ **10:08 am** 7:08 am
☿△♅ **12:55 pm** 9:55 am
☽⚺♆ **2:35 pm** 11:35 am
☽□♇ **5:50 pm** 2:50 pm
☽⚹♄ **11:45 pm** 8:45 pm
♂⚻♅ 9:38 pm

Eastern time in bold type
Pacific time in medium type

SEPTEMBER 2023

DATE	SID.TIME	SUN	MOON	NODE	MERCURY	VENUS	MARS	JUPITER	SATURN	URANUS	NEPTUNE	PLUTO	CERES	PALLAS	JUNO	VESTA	CHIRON
1 F	22 39 36	8♍19 23	21♓36	25♈48℞	18♍37℞	12♌23℞	2♎51	15♉34	3♓29℞	23♉04℞	26♓46℞	28♑15℞	24♎08	24♍10	8♌20	26♊16	19♈19℞
2 Sa	22 43 33	9 17 24	6♈33	25 45	17 48	12 17	3 30	15 34	3 25	23 04	26 45	28 14	24 32	24 38	8 50	26 34	19 17
3 Su	22 47 29	10 15 27	21 07	25 43D	16 55	12 14	4 09	15 35	3 20	23 04	26 43	28 13	24 56	25 05	9 21	26 52	19 15
4 M	22 51 26	11 13 32	5♉15	25 43	16 00	12 12D	4 47	15 35℞	3 16	23 04	26 42	28 12	25 20	25 33	9 51	27 10	19 13
5 T	22 55 23	12 11 39	18 54	25 45	15 02	12 13	5 26	15 35	3 11	23 03	26 40	28 11	25 44	26 01	10 21	27 28	19 11
6 W	22 59 19	13 09 48	2♊07	25 46℞	14 04	12 17	6 05	15 35	3 07	23 03	26 38	28 10	26 08	26 28	10 50	27 46	19 09
7 Th	23 3 16	14 07 59	14 56	25 46	13 06	12 22	6 44	15 34	3 02	23 03	26 37	28 09	26 32	26 56	11 20	28 03	19 07
8 F	23 7 12	15 06 12	27 26	25 46	12 10	12 30	7 23	15 34	2 58	23 02	26 35	28 08	26 56	27 23	11 50	28 21	19 05
9 Sa	23 11 9	16 04 27	9♋41	25 43	11 16	12 40	8 02	15 33	2 53	23 02	26 34	28 08	27 20	27 51	12 20	28 38	19 03
10 Su	23 15 5	17 02 44	21 44	25 39	10 27	12 52	8 41	15 32	2 49	23 01	26 32	28 07	27 45	28 18	12 49	28 55	19 01
11 M	23 19 2	18 01 03	3♌40	25 33	9 44	13 07	9 20	15 31	2 45	23 00	26 30	28 06	28 09	28 46	13 18	29 11	18 58
12 T	23 22 58	18 59 24	15 32	25 26	9 07	13 23	9 59	15 29	2 40	23 00	26 29	28 05	28 33	29 13	13 48	29 28	18 56
13 W	23 26 55	19 57 47	27 23	25 20	8 37	13 41	10 38	15 28	2 36	22 59	26 27	28 04	28 58	29 41	14 17	29 44	18 54
14 Th	23 30 52	20 56 12	9♍15	25 13	8 16	14 01	11 17	15 26	2 32	22 58	26 25	28 04	29 22	0♎08	14 46	0♋00	18 51
15 F	23 34 48	21 54 39	21 09	25 08	8 04D	14 23	11 56	15 24	2 28	22 57	26 24	28 03	29 47	0 36	15 15	0 16	18 49
16 Sa	23 38 45	22 53 07	3♎08	25 05	8 00	14 47	12 36	15 22	2 24	22 57	26 22	28 02	0♏11	1 03	15 44	0 32	18 47
17 Su	23 42 41	23 51 38	15 13	25 03D	8 06	15 12	13 15	15 19	2 20	22 56	26 20	28 02	0 36	1 31	16 13	0 47	18 44
18 M	23 46 38	24 50 10	27 27	25 02	8 22	15 39	13 54	15 17	2 16	22 55	26 19	28 01	1 01	1 58	16 42	1 03	18 42
19 T	23 50 34	25 48 44	9♏51	25 03	8 47	16 08	14 34	15 14	2 12	22 54	26 17	28 00	1 26	2 26	17 10	1 18	18 39
20 W	23 54 31	26 47 20	22 28	25 05	9 21	16 38	15 13	15 11	2 08	22 53	26 15	28 00	1 50	2 53	17 39	1 33	18 37
21 Th	23 58 27	27 45 57	5♐21	25 06	10 04	17 09	15 53	15 08	2 04	22 52	26 14	27 59	2 15	3 21	18 07	1 47	18 34
22 F	0 2 24	28 44 36	18 33	25 07℞	10 55	17 42	16 32	15 05	2 00	22 50	26 12	27 59	2 40	3 48	18 36	2 01	18 32
23 Sa	0 6 21	29 43 17	2♑05	25 08	11 54	18 16	17 12	15 01	1 56	22 49	26 10	27 58	3 05	4 16	19 04	2 16	18 29
24 Su	0 10 17	0♎42 00	16 01	25 07	13 00	18 52	17 52	14 57	1 53	22 48	26 09	27 58	3 30	4 43	19 32	2 29	18 27
25 M	0 14 14	1 40 44	0♒18	25 05	14 12	19 29	18 31	14 53	1 49	22 47	26 07	27 57	3 55	5 11	20 00	2 43	18 24
26 T	0 18 10	2 39 30	14 56	25 03	15 31	20 07	19 11	14 49	1 45	22 45	26 05	27 57	4 20	5 38	20 28	2 56	18 22
27 W	0 22 7	3 38 18	29 49	25 00	16 54	20 46	19 51	14 45	1 42	22 44	26 04	27 56	4 45	6 06	20 56	3 09	18 19
28 Th	0 26 3	4 37 07	14♓49	24 57	18 22	21 27	20 31	14 40	1 38	22 43	26 02	27 56	5 10	6 33	21 23	3 22	18 17
29 F	0 30 0	5 35 58	29 49	24 55	19 54	22 09	21 10	14 36	1 35	22 41	26 01	27 56	5 35	7 00	21 51	3 35	18 14
30 Sa	0 33 56	6 34 51	14♈40	24 54D	21 30	22 51	21 50	14 31	1 32	22 40	25 59	27 55	6 00	7 28	22 18	3 47	18 11

EPHEMERIS CALCULATED FOR 12 MIDNIGHT GREENWICH MEAN TIME. ALL OTHER DATA AND FACING ASPECTARIAN PAGE IN **EASTERN TIME (BOLD)** AND PACIFIC TIME (REGULAR).

OCTOBER 2023

☽ Last Aspect day	ET / hr:mn / PT		asp	☽ Ingress sign	day	ET / hr:mn / PT	
2	9:20 pm	6:20 pm	△♇	♊	2		10:03 pm
2	9:20 pm	6:20 pm	△♇	♊	3	1:03 am	
4		11:34 pm	⚹♀	♋	5	8:32 am	5:32 am
5	2:34 am		⚹♀	♋	5	8:32 am	5:32 am
7	3:12 pm	12:12 pm	☍♇	♌	7	7:24 pm	4:24 pm
10	5:37 am	2:37 am	⚹♂	♍	10	8:02 am	5:02 am
12	4:10 pm	1:10 pm	△♇	♎	12	8:22 pm	5:22 pm
15	3:01 am	12:01 am	□♇	♏	15	7:04 am	4:04 am
17	11:44 am	8:44 am	⚹♇	♐	17	3:36 pm	12:36 pm
19	3:02 pm	12:02 pm	⚹☉	♑	19	9:55 pm	6:55 pm
21		11:00 pm	□☿	♒	21		11:06 pm
22	2:00 am		□☿	♒	22	2:06 am	
23	3:04 pm	12:04 pm	□♅	♓	24	4:33 am	1:33 am
25		11:39 pm	⚹♇	♈	26	6:02 am	3:02 am
26	2:39 am		⚹♇	♈	26	6:02 am	3:02 am
28	4:20 am	1:20 am	□♇	♉	28	7:44 am	4:44 am
30	7:36 am	4:36 am	△♇	♊	30	11:08 am	8:08 am

☽ Phases & Eclipses phase	day	ET / hr:mn / PT	
4th Quarter	6	9:48 am	6:48 am
New Moon	14	1:55 pm	10:55 am
(eclipse)	14	21° ♎ 08'	
2nd Quarter	21	11:29 pm	8:29 pm
Full Moon	28	4:24 pm	1:24 pm
(eclipse)	28	5° ♉ 09'	

Planet Ingress	day	ET / hr:mn / PT	
☿ ♎	4	8:09 pm	5:09 pm
♀ ♍	8	9:11 pm	6:11 pm
♂ ♏	11		9:04 pm
♂ ♏	12	12:04 am	
⚵ ♍	17	9:27 am	6:27 am
☿ ♏	21		11:49 pm
☿ ♏	22	2:49 am	
☉ ♏	23	12:21 pm	9:21 am

Planetary Motion	day	ET / hr:mn / PT	
♇ D	10	9:10 pm	6:10 pm

1 SUNDAY
♂ ⚻ ♅ **12:38 am**
☿ ⊻ ♀ **7:38 am** 4:38 am
☽ ⚻ ☉ **11:05 am** 8:05 am
☽ ☌ ♃ **9:37 pm** 6:37 pm

2 MONDAY
☿ ☍ ♆ **11:34 am** 8:34 am
☽ ☌ ♅ **11:57 am** 8:57 am
☽ ⚻ ♂ **1:50 pm** 10:50 am
☽ □ ♀ **4:07 pm** 1:07 pm
☽ ⚹ ♆ **5:47 pm** 2:47 pm
☽ △ ☿ **6:41 pm** 3:41 pm
☽ △ ♇ **9:20 pm** 6:20 pm

3 TUESDAY
☽ □ ♄ **3:29 am** 12:29 am
☿ △ ♇ **3:20 pm** 12:20 pm
☽ △ ☉ **8:03 pm** 5:03 pm
♀ ⚻ ♆ **8:21 pm** 5:21 pm
☽ ⊻ ♃ 11:44 pm

4 WEDNESDAY
☽ ⊻ ♃ **2:44 am**
☽ ⊻ ♅ **6:22 pm** 3:22 pm
☽ △ ♂ **11:33 pm** 8:33 pm
☽ □ ♆ 9:37 pm
☽ ⚹ ♀ 11:34 pm

5 THURSDAY
☽ □ ♆ **12:37 am**
☽ ⚹ ♀ **2:34 am**
☽ ⚻ ♇ **4:31 am** 1:31 am

☽ □ ☿ **10:33 am** 7:33 am
☽ △ ♄ **10:55 am** 7:55 am
☿ ⚻ ♄ **1:03 pm** 10:03 am
♂ ⚻ ♆ **7:09 pm** 4:09 pm

6 FRIDAY
♀ ⚻ ♇ **8:50 am** 5:50 am
☽ □ ☉ **9:48 am** 6:48 am
☽ ⚹ ♃ **11:30 am** 8:30 am

7 SATURDAY
☽ ⚹ ♅ **4:22 am** 1:22 am
☉ ⚻ ♃ **5:04 am** 2:04 am
☽ △ ♆ **10:58 am** 7:58 am
☽ □ ♂ **1:25 pm** 10:25 am
☽ ☍ ♇ **3:12 pm** 12:12 pm
☽ ⊻ ♀ **5:27 pm** 2:27 pm
☽ ⚻ ♄ **9:41 pm** 6:41 pm

8 SUNDAY
☽ ⚹ ☿ **7:47 am** 4:47 am
♂ □ ♇ **9:05 pm** 6:05 pm
☽ □ ♃ **10:55 pm** 7:55 pm

9 MONDAY
☽ ⚹ ☉ **3:07 am** 12:07 am
☽ □ ♅ **4:36 pm** 1:36 pm
☽ ⚻ ♆ **11:21 pm** 8:21 pm
♀ ☍ ♄ 11:11 pm

10 TUESDAY
♀ ☍ ♄ **2:11 am**
☽ ⚻ ♇ **3:45 am** 12:45 am
☽ ⚹ ♂ **5:37 am** 2:37 am

☽ ☍ ♄ **10:06 am** 7:06 am
☽ ☌ ♀ **10:46 am** 7:46 am

11 WEDNESDAY
☽ ⊻ ☿ **7:08 am** 4:08 am
☽ △ ♃ **11:06 am** 8:06 am
☽ ⊻ ☉ **9:18 pm** 6:18 pm

12 THURSDAY
☽ △ ♅ **5:01 am** 2:01 am
☿ ⚻ ♃ **8:32 am** 5:32 am
☽ ☍ ♆ **11:42 am** 8:42 am
☽ △ ♇ **4:10 pm** 1:10 pm
☽ ⊻ ♂ **9:34 pm** 6:34 pm
☽ ⚻ ♄ **10:13 pm** 7:13 pm

13 FRIDAY
☽ ⊻ ♀ **3:49 am** 12:49 am
♂ △ ♄ **8:29 am** 5:29 am
☽ ⚻ ♃ **10:16 pm** 7:16 pm

14 SATURDAY
☽ ☌ ☿ **4:58 am** 1:58 am
☽ ☌ ☉ **1:55 pm** 10:55 am
☽ ⚻ ♅ **4:03 pm** 1:03 p
☽ ⚻ ♆ **10:34 pm** 7:34 pm

15 SUNDAY
☽ □ ♇ **3:01 am** 12:01 am
☽ △ ♄ **8:41 am** 5:41 am
☽ ☌ ♂ **11:35 am** 8:35 am
☉ ⚻ ♅ **3:44 pm** 12:44 pm
☽ ⚹ ♀ **6:51 pm** 3:51 pm

16 MONDAY
☽ ☍ ♃ **7:31 am** 4:31 am
☽ ⊻ ☿ **11:29 pm** 8:29 pm
☽ ☍ ♅ 10:01 pm

17 TUESDAY
☽ ☍ ♅ **1:01 am**
☽ ⊻ ☉ **3:54 am** 12:54 am
☽ △ ♆ **7:20 am** 4:20 am
☿ ⚻ ♅ **10:48 am** 7:48 am
☽ ⚹ ♇ **11:44 am** 8:44 am
☽ □ ♄ **5:02 pm** 2:02 pm
☽ ⊻ ♂ **11:03 pm** 8:03 pm

18 WEDNESDAY
☽ □ ♀ **7:15 am** 4:15 am
☽ ⚻ ♃ **2:35 pm** 11:35 am
☉ ⚻ ♆ **11:40 pm** 8:40 pm

19 THURSDAY
☽ ⚻ ♅ **7:45 am** 4:45 am
☿ ⚻ ♆ **10:12 am** 7:12 am
☽ □ ♆ **1:53 pm** 10:53 am
☽ ⚹ ☿ **2:25 pm** 11:25 am
☽ ⚹ ☉ **3:02 pm** 12:02 pm
☽ ⊻ ♇ **6:12 pm** 3:12 pm
☽ ⚹ ♄ **11:10 pm** 8:10 pm
☉ ☌ ☿ 10:38 pm

20 FRIDAY
☉ ☌ ☿ **1:38 am**
☽ ⚹ ♂ **7:54 am** 4:54 am
☽ △ ♀ **4:59 pm** 1:59 pm
☽ △ ♃ **7:30 pm** 4:30 pm
☿ □ ♇ **8:51 pm** 5:51 pm

21 SATURDAY
☉ □ ♇ **10:09 am** 7:09 am
☽ △ ♅ **12:21 pm** 9:21 am
☽ ⚹ ♆ **6:17 pm** 3:17 pm
☽ ☌ ♇ **10:33 pm** 7:33 pm
☽ □ ☉ **11:29 pm** 8:29 pm
♀ △ ♃ 9:32 pm
☽ □ ☿ 11:00 pm

22 SUNDAY
♀ △ ♃ **12:32 am**
☽ □ ☿ **2:00 am**
☽ ⊻ ♄ **3:13 am** 12:13 am
☿ △ ♄ **12:12 pm** 9:12 am
☽ □ ♂ **2:21 pm** 11:21 am
☽ □ ♃ **10:27 pm** 7:27 pm
☽ ⚻ ♀ 9:17 pm

23 MONDAY
☽ ⚻ ♀ **12:17 am**
☽ □ ♅ **3:04 pm** 12:04 pm
☽ ⊻ ♆ **8:53 pm** 5:53 pm
☽ ⊻ ♇ 10:07 pm

24 TUESDAY
☽ ⊻ ♇ **1:07 am**
☉ △ ♄ **3:14 am** 12:14 am
☽ ☌ ♄ **5:34 am** 2:34 am
☽ △ ☉ **5:45 am** 2:45 am
☽ △ ☿ **10:57 am** 7:57 am
☽ △ ♂ **6:58 pm** 3:58 pm
☽ ⚹ ♃ **11:57 pm** 8:57 pm

25 WEDNESDAY
☽ ☍ ♀ **5:52 am** 2:52 am
☽ ⚹ ♅ **4:35 pm** 1:35 pm
☽ ☌ ♆ **10:22 pm** 7:22 pm
☽ ⚹ ♇ 11:39 pm

26 THURSDAY
☽ ⚹ ♇ **2:39 am**
☽ ⊻ ♄ **6:59 am** 3:59 am
☽ ⚻ ☉ **10:50 am** 7:50 am
☽ ⚻ ☿ **6:36 pm** 3:36 pm
☽ ⚻ ♂ **10:49 pm** 7:49 pm
☽ ⊻ ♃ 9:54 pm

27 FRIDAY
☽ ⊻ ♃ **12:54 am**
☽ ⚻ ♀ **11:00 am** 8:00 am
☽ ⊻ ♅ **5:57 pm** 2:57 pm
☽ ⊻ ♆ **11:53 pm** 8:53 pm

28 SATURDAY
☽ □ ♇ **4:20 am** 1:20 am
☽ ⚹ ♄ **8:40 am** 5:40 am
♂ ☍ ♃ **12:03 pm** 9:03 am
☽ ☍ ☉ **4:24 pm** 1:24 pm
☿ ☍ ♃ **11:44 pm** 8:44 pm
☽ ☌ ♃ 11:37 pm

29 SUNDAY
☽ ☌ ♃ **2:37 am**
☽ ☍ ☿ **3:00 am** 12:00 am
☽ ☍ ♂ **3:30 am** 12:30 am
☿ ☌ ♂ **10:22 am** 7:22 am

☽ △ ♀ **5:33 pm** 2:33 pm
☽ ☌ ♅ **8:36 pm** 5:36 pm
☽ ⚹ ♆ 11:51 pm

30 MONDAY
☽ ⚹ ♆ **2:51 am**
☽ △ ♇ **7:36 am** 4:36 am
☽ □ ♄ **12:04 pm** 9:04 am
☽ ⚻ ☉ 9:22 pm

31 TUESDAY
☽ ⚻ ☉ **12:22 am**
☽ ⊻ ♃ **6:28 am** 3:28 am
♀ △ ♅ **8:51 am** 5:51 am
☽ ⚻ ♂ **10:48 am** 7:48 am
☽ ⚻ ☿ **2:31 pm** 11:31 am
☽ ⊻ ♅ 10:53 pm

Eastern time in bold type
Pacific time in medium type

OCTOBER 2023

DATE	SID.TIME	SUN	MOON	NODE	MERCURY	VENUS	MARS	JUPITER	SATURN	URANUS	NEPTUNE	PLUTO	CERES	PALLAS	JUNO	VESTA	CHIRON
1 Su	0 37 53	7♎33 47	29♈13	24♈54	23♍08	23♌35	22♎30	14♉26℞	1♓29℞	22♉38℞	25♓57℞	27♑55℞	6♏25	7♎55	22♌46	3♋59	18♈09℞
2 M	0 41 50	8 32 44	13♉24	24 54	24 48	24 20	23 10	14 21	1 25	22 37	25 56	27 55	6 50	8 22	23 13	4 11	18 06
3 T	0 45 46	9 31 44	27 10	24 55	26 31	25 05	23 50	14 16	1 22	22 35	25 54	27 54	7 16	8 50	23 40	4 22	18 03
4 W	0 49 43	10 30 46	10♊29	24 57	28 15	25 52	24 30	14 10	1 19	22 34	25 53	27 54	7 41	9 17	24 07	4 34	18 01
5 Th	0 53 39	11 29 50	23 24	24 58	29 59	26 39	25 11	14 04	1 16	22 32	25 51	27 54	8 06	9 44	24 34	4 45	17 58
6 F	0 57 36	12 28 57	5♋58	24 58℞	1♎45	27 28	25 51	13 59	1 14	22 30	25 49	27 54	8 32	10 12	25 01	4 55	17 55
7 Sa	1 1 32	13 28 06	18 14	24 58	3 31	28 17	26 31	13 53	1 11	22 28	25 48	27 54	8 57	10 39	25 27	5 05	17 52
8 Su	1 5 29	14 27 17	0♌18	24 58	5 17	29 07	27 11	13 47	1 08	22 27	25 46	27 54	9 22	11 06	25 54	5 15	17 50
9 M	1 9 25	15 26 31	12 13	24 57	7 04	29 57	27 52	13 40	1 05	22 25	25 45	27 54	9 48	11 33	26 20	5 25	17 47
10 T	1 13 22	16 25 46	24 04	24 56	8 50	0♍49	28 32	13 34	1 03	22 23	25 43	27 54	10 13	12 01	26 46	5 34	17 44
11 W	1 17 19	17 25 04	5♍55	24 55	10 36	1 41	29 13	13 28	1 01	22 21	25 42	27 54D	10 38	12 28	27 12	5 43	17 41
12 Th	1 21 15	18 24 24	17 49	24 54	12 22	2 34	29 53	13 21	0 58	22 19	25 40	27 54	11 04	12 55	27 38	5 52	17 39
13 F	1 25 12	19 23 47	29 49	24 53	14 08	3 28	0♏34	13 14	0 56	22 17	25 39	27 54	11 29	13 22	28 04	6 00	17 36
14 Sa	1 29 8	20 23 11	11♎57	24 52	15 53	4 22	1 14	13 07	0 54	22 15	25 37	27 54	11 55	13 49	28 30	6 09	17 33
15 Su	1 33 5	21 22 38	24 16	24 52D	17 37	5 17	1 55	13 00	0 52	22 13	25 36	27 54	12 20	14 17	28 55	6 16	17 31
16 M	1 37 1	22 22 06	6♏45	24 52	19 21	6 12	2 36	12 53	0 50	22 11	25 34	27 54	12 46	14 44	29 21	6 24	17 28
17 T	1 40 58	23 21 37	19 28	24 53	21 04	7 08	3 16	12 46	0 48	22 09	25 33	27 54	13 12	15 11	29 46	6 30	17 25
18 W	1 44 54	24 21 10	2♐23	24 53℞	22 47	8 04	3 57	12 39	0 46	22 07	25 31	27 54	13 37	15 38	0♍11	6 37	17 22
19 Th	1 48 51	25 20 44	15 32	24 53	24 29	9 01	4 38	12 31	0 44	22 05	25 30	27 54	14 03	16 05	0 36	6 43	17 20
20 F	1 52 47	26 20 20	28 55	24 53	26 11	9 59	5 19	12 24	0 43	22 03	25 29	27 55	14 28	16 32	1 01	6 49	17 17
21 Sa	1 56 44	27 19 58	12♑33	24 52	27 51	10 57	6 00	12 16	0 41	22 01	25 27	27 55	14 54	16 59	1 25	6 55	17 14
22 Su	2 0 41	28 19 38	26 26	24 52D	29 32	11 56	6 41	12 08	0 40	21 58	25 26	27 55	15 20	17 26	1 50	7 00	17 12
23 M	2 4 37	29 19 20	10♒33	24 52	1♏11	12 55	7 22	12 01	0 39	21 56	25 25	27 56	15 45	17 53	2 14	7 05	17 09
24 T	2 8 34	0♏19 03	24 52	24 53	2 50	13 54	8 03	11 53	0 37	21 54	25 23	27 56	16 11	18 20	2 39	7 09	17 06
25 W	2 12 30	1 18 47	9♓20	24 53	4 29	14 54	8 44	11 45	0 36	21 52	25 22	27 56	16 37	18 47	3 03	7 13	17 04
26 Th	2 16 27	2 18 34	23 54	24 54	6 06	15 55	9 25	11 37	0 35	21 49	25 21	27 57	17 02	19 14	3 26	7 16	17 01
27 F	2 20 23	3 18 22	8♈29	24 54	7 44	16 55	10 07	11 29	0 34	21 47	25 20	27 57	17 28	19 41	3 50	7 20	16 59
28 Sa	2 24 20	4 18 12	22 59	24 55℞	9 20	17 57	10 48	11 21	0 34	21 45	25 18	27 58	17 54	20 07	4 14	7 22	16 56
29 Su	2 28 16	5 18 03	7♉17	24 54	10 57	18 58	11 29	11 13	0 33	21 42	25 17	27 58	18 19	20 34	4 37	7 25	16 53
30 M	2 32 13	6 17 57	21 19	24 54	12 32	20 00	12 11	11 05	0 32	21 40	25 16	27 59	18 45	21 01	5 00	7 27	16 51
31 T	2 36 10	7 17 53	5♊01	24 52	14 08	21 03	12 52	10 57	0 32	21 38	25 15	27 59	19 11	21 28	5 23	7 28	16 48

EPHEMERIS CALCULATED FOR 12 MIDNIGHT GREENWICH MEAN TIME. ALL OTHER DATA AND FACING ASPECTARIAN PAGE IN **EASTERN TIME (BOLD)** AND PACIFIC TIME (REGULAR).

NOVEMBER 2023

☽ Last Aspect day	ET / hr:mn / PT		asp	☽ Ingress sign	day	ET / hr:mn / PT	
1	**8:36 am**	5:36 am	☐♆	♋	1	**5:30 pm**	2:30 pm
3	**11:28 pm**	8:28 pm	☍♇	♌	4	**3:21 am**	12:21 am
5		11:25 pm	☐☿	♍	6	**2:39 pm**	11:39 am
6	**2:25 am**		☐☿	♍	6	**2:39 pm**	11:39 am
8	**11:55 pm**	8:55 pm	✶☿	♎	9	**3:08 am**	12:08 am
11	**10:05 am**	7:05 am	☐♇	♏	11	**1:39 pm**	10:39 am
13	**6:03 pm**	3:03 pm	✶♇	♐	13	**9:23 pm**	6:23 pm
15	**5:57 pm**	2:57 pm	☐♆	♑	15		11:41 pm
15	**5:57 pm**	2:57 pm	☐♆	♑	16	**2:41 am**	
18	**3:27 am**	12:27 am	☌♇	♒	18	**6:28 am**	3:28 am

☽ Last Aspect day	ET / hr:mn / PT		asp	☽ Ingress sign	day	ET / hr:mn / PT	
20	**5:50 am**	2:50 am	☐☉	♓	20	**9:29 am**	6:29 am
22	**10:10 am**	7:10 am	△♂	♈	22	**12:19 pm**	9:19 am
24	**12:40 pm**	9:40 am	☐♇	♉	24	**3:29 pm**	12:29 pm
26	**4:52 pm**	1:52 pm	△♇	♊	26	**7:40 pm**	4:40 pm
28	**8:03 pm**	5:03 pm	☍☿	♋	28		10:54 pm
28	**8:03 pm**	5:03 pm	☍☿	♋	29	**1:54 am**	

☽ Phases & Eclipses phase	day	ET / hr:mn / PT	
4th Quarter	5	**3:37 am**	1:37 am
New Moon	13	**4:27 am**	1:27 am
2nd Quarter	20	**5:50 am**	2:50 am
Full Moon	27	**4:16 am**	1:16 am

Planet Ingress		day	ET / hr:mn / PT	
♀	♎	8	**4:30 am**	1:30 am
☿	♐	9		10:25 pm
☿	♐	10	**1:25 am**	
♀	♏	19	**4:03 am**	1:03 am
☉	♐	22	**9:03 am**	6:03 am
♂	♐	24	**5:15 am**	2:15 am
⚳	♐	24		9:14 pm
⚳	♐	25	**12:14 am**	

Planetary Motion		day	ET / hr:mn / PT	
⚶	R	2	**9:50 pm**	6:50 pm
♄	D	4	**3:03 am**	12:03 am

1 WEDNESDAY
☽ ⊻ ♅ **1:53 am**
☽ ☐ ♀ **3:26 am** 12:26 am
☽ ☐ ♆ **8:36 am** 5:36 am
☽ ⊼ ♇ **1:47 pm** 10:47 am
☽ △ ♄ **6:29 pm** 3:29 pm

2 THURSDAY
☽ △ ☉ **12:23 pm** 9:23 am
☽ ✶ ♃ **1:31 pm** 10:31 am
☽ △ ♂ **10:01 pm** 7:01 pm
☉ ☍ ♃ 10:02 pm

3 FRIDAY
☉ ☍ ♃ **1:02 am**
☽ △ ☿ **6:49 am** 3:49 am
☽ ✶ ♅ **10:36 am** 7:36 am
☽ ✶ ♀ **5:49 pm** 2:49 pm
☽ △ ♆ **5:50 pm** 2:50 pm
♀ ☍ ♆ **6:06 pm** 3:06 pm
☽ ☍ ♇ **11:28 pm** 8:28 pm

4 SATURDAY
☽ ⊼ ♄ **4:22 am** 1:22 am
☿ ☍ ♅ **12:07 pm** 9:07 am
☽ ☐ ♃ **11:46 pm** 8:46 pm

5 SUNDAY
☽ ☐ ☉ **3:37 am** 1:37 am
☽ ☐ ♂ **12:00 pm** 9:00 am
☽ ☐ ♅ **9:11 pm** 6:11 pm
☽ ☐ ☿ 11:25 pm

6 MONDAY
☽ ☐ ☿ **2:25 am**
☽ ⊼ ♆ **4:48 am** 1:48 am
♀ △ ♇ **9:38 am** 6:38 am
☽ ⊼ ♇ **10:44 am** 7:44 am
☽ ⊻ ♀ **10:50 am** 7:50 am
☽ ☍ ♄ **3:42 pm** 12:42 pm
☿ △ ♆ **8:37 pm** 5:37 pm

7 TUESDAY
☽ △ ♃ **10:43 am** 7:43 am
☽ ✶ ☉ **9:54 pm** 6:54 pm

8 WEDNESDAY
☽ ✶ ♂ **4:29 am** 1:29 am
☽ △ ♅ **9:40 am** 6:40 am
♀ ⊼ ♄ **4:13 pm** 1:13 pm
☽ ☍ ♆ **5:20 pm** 2:20 pm
☿ ✶ ♇ **7:17 pm** 4:17 pm
☽ △ ♇ **11:20 pm** 8:20 pm
☽ ✶ ☿ **11:55 pm** 8:55 pm

9 THURSDAY
☽ ⊼ ♄ **4:12 am** 1:12 am
☽ ☌ ♀ **5:23 am** 2:23 am
☽ ⊼ ♃ **10:05 pm** 7:05 pm

10 FRIDAY
☿ ☐ ♄ **10:07 am** 7:07 am
☽ ⊻ ☉ **2:51 pm** 11:51 am
☽ ⊻ ♂ **7:29 pm** 4:29 pm
☽ ⊼ ♅ **8:43 pm** 5:43 pm

11 SATURDAY
☽ ⊼ ♆ **4:13 am** 1:13 am
☽ ☐ ♇ **10:05 am** 7:05 am
☽ △ ♄ **2:43 pm** 11:43 am
♂ ☍ ♅ **4:11 pm** 1:11 pm
☽ ⊻ ☿ **6:34 pm** 3:34 pm
☽ ⊻ ♀ **9:22 pm** 6:22 pm

12 SUNDAY
☽ ☍ ♃ **7:09 am** 4:09 am

13 MONDAY
☽ ☌ ☉ **4:27 am** 1:27 am
☽ ☍ ♅ **5:05 am** 2:05 am
☽ ☌ ♂ **7:18 am** 4:18 am
☽ △ ♆ **12:20 pm** 9:20 am
☉ ☍ ♅ **12:21 pm** 9:21 am
☽ ✶ ♇ **6:03 pm** 3:03 pm
☽ ☐ ♄ **10:28 pm** 7:28 pm

14 TUESDAY
☽ ☌ ☿ **9:04 am** 6:04 am
☽ ✶ ♀ **9:44 am** 6:44 am
☽ ⊼ ♃ **1:32 pm** 10:32 am

15 WEDNESDAY
☿ ✶ ♀ **7:48 am** 4:48 am
☽ ⊼ ♅ **10:52 am** 7:52 am
☽ ⊻ ☉ **2:44 pm** 11:44 am
☽ ⊻ ♂ **4:05 pm** 1:05 pm
☽ ☐ ♆ **5:57 pm** 2:57 pm
☿ ⊼ ♃ **10:35 pm** 7:35 pm
☽ ⊻ ♇ **11:33 pm** 8:33 pm
♀ ⊼ ♃ 11:48 pm

16 THURSDAY
♀ ⊼ ♃ **2:48 am**
☽ ✶ ♄ **3:49 am** 12:49 am
☽ △ ♃ **5:48 pm** 2:48 pm
☽ ☐ ♀ **7:16 pm** 4:16 pm
☽ ⊻ ☿ **8:17 pm** 5:17 pm

17 FRIDAY
♂ △ ♆ **3:36 am** 12:36 am
☉ △ ♆ **9:52 am** 6:52 am
☽ △ ♅ **2:51 pm** 11:51 am
☽ ✶ ♆ **9:52 pm** 6:52 pm
☽ ✶ ☉ **10:49 pm** 7:49 pm
☽ ✶ ♂ **10:51 pm** 7:51 pm
☉ ☌ ♂ 9:42 pm

18 SATURDAY
☉ ☌ ♂ **12:42 am**
☽ ☌ ♇ **3:27 am** 12:27 am
☽ ⊻ ♄ **7:38 am** 4:38 am
☽ ☐ ♃ **8:50 pm** 5:50 pm

19 SUNDAY
☽ △ ♀ **3:12 am** 12:12 am
☽ ✶ ☿ **5:39 am** 2:39 am
☽ ☐ ♅ **5:53 pm** 2:53 pm
☽ ⊻ ♆ 9:57 pm

20 MONDAY
☽ ⊻ ♆ **12:57 am**
☽ ☐ ♂ **4:38 am** 1:38 am
☽ ☐ ☉ **5:50 am** 2:50 am
☽ ⊻ ♇ **6:34 am** 3:34 am

☽ ☌ ♄ **10:45 am** 7:45 am
☉ ✶ ♇ **4:26 pm** 1:26 pm
☽ ✶ ♃ **11:20 pm** 8:20 pm

21 TUESDAY
☽ ⊼ ♀ **10:32 am** 7:32 am
☽ ☐ ☿ **2:16 pm** 11:16 am
♂ ✶ ♇ **8:18 pm** 5:18 pm
☽ ✶ ♅ **8:35 pm** 5:35 pm

22 WEDNESDAY
☽ ☌ ♆ **3:45 am** 12:45 am
☽ ✶ ♇ **9:29 am** 6:29 am
☽ △ ♂ **10:10 am** 7:10 am
☽ △ ☉ **12:35 pm** 9:35 am
☽ ⊻ ♄ **1:42 pm** 10:42 am
☽ ⊻ ♃ 10:47 pm

23 THURSDAY
☽ ⊻ ♃ **1:47 am**
☉ ☐ ♄ **4:47 am** 1:47 am
☽ ☍ ♀ **5:57 pm** 2:57 pm
☽ △ ☿ **10:52 pm** 7:52 pm
☽ ⊻ ♅ **11:26 pm** 8:26 pm

24 FRIDAY
☿ ⊼ ♅ **4:27 am** 1:27 am
☽ ⊻ ♆ **6:47 am** 3:47 am
☽ ☐ ♇ **12:40 pm** 9:40 am
☽ ⊼ ♂ **4:02 pm** 1:02 pm
☽ ✶ ♄ **5:00 pm** 2:00 pm
☽ ⊼ ☉ **7:43 pm** 4:43 pm

25 SATURDAY
☽ ☌ ♃ **4:43 am** 1:43 am
♂ ☐ ♄ **11:57 am** 8:57 am
☽ ⊼ ♀ 11:19 pm

26 SUNDAY
☽ ⊼ ♀ **2:19 am**
☽ ☌ ♅ **3:03 am** 12:03 am
☽ ⊼ ☿ **8:21 am** 5:21 am
☽ ✶ ♆ **10:42 am** 7:42 am
♀ ⊼ ♅ **10:49 am** 7:49 am
☽ △ ♇ **4:52 pm** 1:52 pm
☽ ☐ ♄ **9:22 pm** 6:22 pm
☽ ☍ ♂ **11:08 pm** 8:08 pm

27 MONDAY
☽ ☍ ☉ **4:16 am** 1:16 am
☿ ☐ ♆ **8:27 am** 5:27 am
☽ ⊻ ♃ **8:54 am** 5:54 am

28 TUESDAY
☽ ⊻ ♅ **8:22 am** 5:22 am
☽ △ ♀ **12:54 pm** 9:54 am
☽ ☐ ♆ **4:30 pm** 1:30 pm
☽ ☍ ☿ **8:03 pm** 5:03 pm
☽ ⊼ ♇ **11:03 pm** 8:03 pm

29 WEDNESDAY
☽ △ ♄ **3:51 am** 12:51 am
☽ ⊼ ♂ **8:43 am** 5:43 am
☉ ⊼ ♃ **12:38 pm** 9:38 am
☽ ✶ ♃ **3:21 pm** 12:21 pm
☽ ⊼ ☉ **3:37 pm** 12:37 pm

30 THURSDAY
☿ ⊻ ♇ **3:34 am** 12:34 am
♀ ⊼ ♆ **5:13 am** 2:13 am
☽ ✶ ♅ **4:20 pm** 1:20 pm
☽ △ ♆ 10:05 pm

Eastern time in bold type
Pacific time in medium type

NOVEMBER 2023

DATE	SID.TIME	SUN	MOON	NODE	MERCURY	VENUS	MARS	JUPITER	SATURN	URANUS	NEPTUNE	PLUTO	CERES	PALLAS	JUNO	VESTA	CHIRON
1 W	2 40 6	8♏17 51	18♊22	24♈51℞	15♏42	22♍05	13♏34	10♉49℞	0♓31℞	21♉35℞	25♓14℞	28♑00	19♏37	21♎55	5♍46	7♋29	16♈46℞
2 Th	2 44 3	9 17 51	1♋20	24 49	17 17	23 09	14 15	10 40	0 31	21 33	25 13	28 01	20 02	22 21	6 09	7 30	16 43
3 F	2 47 59	10 17 53	13 57	24 47	18 50	24 12	14 57	10 32	0 31	21 30	25 12	28 01	20 28	22 48	6 31	7 30℞	16 41
4 Sa	2 51 56	11 17 58	26 17	24 45	20 24	25 16	15 38	10 24	0 31D	21 28	25 11	28 02	20 54	23 15	6 54	7 30	16 38
5 Su	2 55 52	12 18 04	8♌22	24 45D	21 57	26 20	16 20	10 16	0 31	21 25	25 10	28 03	21 20	23 41	7 16	7 29	16 36
6 M	2 59 49	13 18 12	20 18	24 45	23 29	27 24	17 02	10 08	0 31	21 23	25 09	28 03	21 45	24 08	7 38	7 28	16 34
7 T	3 3 45	14 18 23	2♍09	24 46	25 01	28 29	17 44	10 00	0 31	21 20	25 08	28 04	22 11	24 34	8 00	7 27	16 31
8 W	3 7 42	15 18 35	14 00	24 47	26 33	29 34	18 25	9 52	0 32	21 18	25 07	28 05	22 37	25 01	8 21	7 25	16 29
9 Th	3 11 39	16 18 50	25 56	24 49	28 05	0♎39	19 07	9 43	0 32	21 16	25 06	28 06	23 03	25 27	8 42	7 22	16 27
10 F	3 15 35	17 19 06	8♎00	24 50	29 36	1 45	19 49	9 35	0 33	21 13	25 05	28 07	23 29	25 54	9 04	7 20	16 24
11 Sa	3 19 32	18 19 24	20 17	24 51℞	1♐06	2 51	20 31	9 27	0 33	21 11	25 04	28 07	23 54	26 20	9 25	7 16	16 22
12 Su	3 23 28	19 19 44	2♏49	24 51	2 37	3 57	21 13	9 20	0 34	21 08	25 03	28 08	24 20	26 47	9 45	7 13	16 20
13 M	3 27 25	20 20 06	15 37	24 50	4 07	5 03	21 55	9 12	0 35	21 06	25 03	28 09	24 46	27 13	10 06	7 08	16 18
14 T	3 31 21	21 20 30	28 41	24 47	5 36	6 10	22 38	9 04	0 36	21 03	25 02	28 10	25 12	27 39	10 26	7 04	16 16
15 W	3 35 18	22 20 56	12♐02	24 43	7 05	7 17	23 20	8 56	0 37	21 01	25 01	28 11	25 37	28 06	10 46	6 59	16 14
16 Th	3 39 14	23 21 23	25 36	24 38	8 34	8 24	24 02	8 48	0 38	20 58	25 00	28 12	26 03	28 32	11 06	6 53	16 12
17 F	3 43 11	24 21 51	9♑23	24 34	10 02	9 31	24 44	8 41	0 39	20 56	25 00	28 13	26 29	28 58	11 26	6 47	16 10
18 Sa	3 47 8	25 22 21	23 19	24 30	11 30	10 39	25 27	8 33	0 41	20 53	24 59	28 14	26 55	29 24	11 45	6 41	16 08
19 Su	3 51 4	26 22 52	7♒21	24 27	12 58	11 47	26 09	8 26	0 42	20 51	24 58	28 15	27 20	29 50	12 05	6 34	16 06
20 M	3 55 1	27 23 25	21 28	24 25D	14 24	12 55	26 51	8 19	0 44	20 48	24 58	28 16	27 46	0♏16	12 24	6 27	16 04
21 T	3 58 57	28 23 58	5♓37	24 25	15 50	14 03	27 34	8 11	0 45	20 46	24 57	28 18	28 12	0 42	12 42	6 19	16 02
22 W	4 2 54	29 24 33	19 47	24 27	17 16	15 11	28 17	8 04	0 47	20 43	24 57	28 19	28 37	1 08	13 01	6 11	16 00
23 Th	4 6 50	0♐25 08	3♈56	24 28	18 41	16 20	28 59	7 57	0 49	20 41	24 56	28 20	29 03	1 34	13 19	6 02	15 58
24 F	4 10 47	1 25 45	18 02	24 29℞	20 05	17 28	29 42	7 51	0 51	20 38	24 56	28 21	29 29	2 00	13 37	5 53	15 57
25 Sa	4 14 44	2 26 23	2♉03	24 29	21 28	18 37	0♐24	7 44	0 53	20 36	24 56	28 22	29 54	2 26	13 55	5 44	15 55
26 Su	4 18 40	3 27 03	15 56	24 27	22 49	19 46	1 07	7 37	0 55	20 33	24 55	28 24	0♐20	2 51	14 12	5 34	15 53
27 M	4 22 37	4 27 43	29 37	24 23	24 10	20 55	1 50	7 31	0 58	20 31	24 55	28 25	0 46	3 17	14 30	5 24	15 52
28 T	4 26 33	5 28 26	13♊05	24 18	25 29	22 05	2 33	7 24	1 00	20 29	24 55	28 26	1 11	3 43	14 47	5 13	15 50
29 W	4 30 30	6 29 09	26 16	24 10	26 47	23 14	3 16	7 18	1 02	20 26	24 54	28 28	1 37	4 08	15 03	5 02	15 49
30 Th	4 34 26	7 29 54	9♋09	24 02	28 03	24 24	3 59	7 12	1 05	20 24	24 54	28 29	2 02	4 34	15 20	4 51	15 47

EPHEMERIS CALCULATED FOR 12 MIDNIGHT GREENWICH MEAN TIME. ALL OTHER DATA AND FACING ASPECTARIAN PAGE IN **EASTERN TIME (BOLD)** AND PACIFIC TIME (REGULAR).

DECEMBER 2023

☽ Last Aspect day	ET / hr:mn / PT		asp	☽ Ingress sign	day	ET / hr:mn / PT	
1	**8:07 am**	5:07 am	☍♇	♌	1	**11:00 am**	8:00 am
3	**9:11 pm**	6:11 pm	⚹♀	♍	3	**10:50 pm**	7:50 pm
6	**8:50 am**	5:50 am	△♇	♎	6	**11:35 am**	8:35 am
8	**8:05 pm**	5:05 pm	□♇	♏	8	**10:35 pm**	7:35 pm
11	**3:57 am**	12:57 am	⚹♇	♐	11	**6:11 am**	3:11 am
12		10:48 pm	□♆	♑	13	**10:31 am**	7:31 am
13	**1:48 am**		□♆	♑	13	**10:31 am**	7:31 am
15	**11:04 am**	8:04 am	☌♇	♒	15	**12:56 pm**	9:56 am
17	**7:04 am**	4:04 am	⚹☉	♓	17	**2:58 pm**	11:58 am
19	**4:03 pm**	1:03 pm	⚹♇	♈	19	**5:47 pm**	2:47 pm

☽ Last Aspect day	ET / hr:mn / PT		asp	☽ Ingress sign	day	ET / hr:mn / PT	
21	**9:47 pm**	6:47 pm	△☉	♉	21	**9:50 pm**	6:50 pm
23		10:40 pm	△♇	♊	24	**3:15 am**	12:15 am
24	**1:40 am**		△♇	♊	24	**3:15 am**	12:15 am
25		11:55 pm	☍☿	♋	26	**10:15 am**	7:15 am
26	**2:55 am**		☍☿	♋	26	**10:15 am**	7:15 am
28	**5:57 pm**	2:57 pm	☍♇	♌	28	**7:23 pm**	4:23 pm
30		9:18 pm	△♂	♍	31	**6:53 am**	3:53 am
31	**12:18 am**		△♂	♍	31	**6:53 am**	3:53 am

☽ Phases & Eclipses phase	day	ET / hr:mn / PT	
4th Quarter	4		9:49 pm
4th Quarter	5	**12:49 am**	
New Moon	12	**6:32 pm**	3:32 pm
2nd Quarter	19	**1:39 pm**	10:39 am
Full Moon	26	**7:33 pm**	4:33 pm

Planet Ingress		day	ET / hr:mn / PT	
☿	♑	1	**9:31 am**	6:31 am
♀	♏	4	**1:51 pm**	10:51 am
⚶	♊	20	**4:56 am**	1:56 am
☉	♑	21	**10:27 pm**	7:27 pm
☿	♐	22		10:18 pm
☿	♐	23	**1:18 am**	
♀	♐	29	**3:24 pm**	12:24 pm

Planetary Motion		day	ET / hr:mn / PT	
♆	D	6	**8:20 am**	5:20 am
☿	℞	12		11:09 pm
☿	℞	13	**2:09 am**	
⚷	D	26	**10:10 pm**	7:10 pm
♃	D	30	**9:40 pm**	6:40 pm

1 FRIDAY

☽△♆	**1:05 am**	
☽□♀	**3:09 am**	12:09 am
☽☍♇	**8:07 am**	5:07 am
☽⚻☿	**11:10 am**	8:10 am
☽⚻♄	**1:17 pm**	10:17 am
☽△♂	**9:48 pm**	6:48 pm
☽□♃		9:44 pm

2 SATURDAY

☽□♃	**12:44 am**	
☽△☉	**6:45 am**	3:45 am
☿⚹♄	**10:27 am**	7:27 am

3 SUNDAY

☽□♅	**3:13 am**	12:13 am
♀□♇	**8:29 am**	5:29 am
☽⚻♆	**12:31 pm**	9:31 am
♂⚻♃	**6:20 pm**	3:20 pm
☽⚻♇	**7:57 pm**	4:57 pm
☽⚹♀	**9:11 pm**	6:11 pm
☽☍♄		10:26 pm

4 MONDAY

☽☍♄	**1:26 am**	
☽△☿	**5:12 am**	2:12 am
☽△♃	**12:33 pm**	9:33 am
☽□♂	**1:52 pm**	10:52 am
☽□☉		9:49 pm

5 TUESDAY

☽□☉	**12:49 am**	
☽△♅	**3:45 pm**	12:45 pm
♀△♄	**5:51 pm**	2:51 pm
☽☍♆		10:17 pm

6 WEDNESDAY

☽☍♆	**1:17 am**	
☽△♇	**8:50 am**	5:50 am
☽⚻♄	**2:26 pm**	11:26 am
☽⚺♀	**4:34 pm**	1:34 pm
☽□☿	**11:00 pm**	8:00 pm
☽⚻♃		9:42 pm

7 THURSDAY

☽⚻♃	**12:42 am**	
☽⚹♂	**6:16 am**	3:16 am
☽⚹☉	**6:37 pm**	3:37 pm
☿△♃	**11:09 pm**	8:09 pm

8 FRIDAY

☽⚻♅	**3:24 am**	12:24 am
☽⚻♆	**12:45 pm**	9:45 am
☽□♇	**8:05 pm**	5:05 pm
☽△♄		10:33 pm

9 SATURDAY

☽△♄	**1:33 am**	
☽☌♀	**9:24 am**	6:24 am
☽☍♃	**10:41 am**	7:41 am
☽⚹☿	**12:46 pm**	9:46 am
☽⚺♂	**7:46 pm**	4:46 pm
♀☍♃	**10:35 pm**	7:35 pm

10 SUNDAY

☽⚺☉	**8:48 am**	5:48 am
☽☍♅	**12:03 pm**	9:03 am
☽△♆	**8:58 pm**	5:58 pm

11 MONDAY

☽⚹♇	**3:57 am**	12:57 am
☽□♄	**9:13 am**	6:13 am
☿⚹♀	**2:17 pm**	11:17 am
☽⚻♃	**5:15 pm**	2:15 pm
☽⚺☿	**9:03 pm**	6:03 pm
☽⚺♀	**9:35 pm**	6:35 pm
☉⚻♅		10:21 pm

12 TUESDAY

☉⚻♅	**1:21 am**	
☽☌♂	**5:05 am**	2:05 am
☽⚻♅	**5:14 pm**	2:14 pm
☽☌☉	**6:32 pm**	3:32 pm
☽□♆		10:48 pm

13 WEDNESDAY

☽□♆	**1:48 am**	
☽⚺♇	**8:31 am**	5:31 am
☽⚹♄	**1:39 pm**	10:39 am
☽△♃	**8:51 pm**	5:51 pm
☽☌☿		9:47 pm

14 THURSDAY

☽☌☿	**12:47 am**	
☽⚹♀	**5:55 am**	2:55 am
☽⚺♂	**11:09 am**	8:09 am
☽△♅	**8:00 pm**	5:00 pm
☽⚺☉		10:15 pm

15 FRIDAY

☽⚺☉	**1:15 am**	
☽⚹♆	**4:27 am**	1:27 am
☽☌♇	**11:04 am**	8:04 am
☽⚺♄	**4:13 pm**	1:13 pm
☽□♃	**10:52 pm**	7:52 pm
☽⚺☿		10:42 pm

16 SATURDAY

☽⚺☿	**1:42 am**	
☽□♀	**12:33 pm**	9:33 am
☽⚹♂	**3:52 pm**	12:52 pm
☽□♅	**9:53 pm**	6:53 pm
☉□♆	**10:43 pm**	7:43 pm

17 SUNDAY

☽⚺♆	**6:28 am**	3:28 am
☽⚹☉	**7:04 am**	4:04 am
☽⚺♇	**1:11 pm**	10:11 am
☽☌♄	**6:32 pm**	3:32 pm
☽⚹♃		9:49 pm
☽⚹☿		10:21 pm

18 MONDAY

☽⚹♃	**12:49 am**	
☽⚹☿	**1:21 am**	
☿△♃	**9:28 am**	6:28 am
☽△♀	**7:30 pm**	4:30 pm
☽□♂	**8:58 pm**	5:58 pm
☽⚹♅		9:14 pm

19 TUESDAY

☽⚹♅	**12:14 am**	
☽☌♆	**9:07 am**	6:07 am
☽□☉	**1:39 pm**	10:39 am
☽⚹♇	**4:03 pm**	1:03 pm
☽⚺♄	**9:41 pm**	6:41 pm
☽□☿		9:42 pm

20 WEDNESDAY

☽□☿	**12:42 am**	
☽⚺♃	**3:42 am**	12:42 am
♀⚺♂	**1:38 pm**	10:38 am
☉⚺♇	**11:39 pm**	8:39 pm
♀☍♅		11:04 pm

21 THURSDAY

♀☍♅	**2:04 am**	
☽△♂	**3:23 am**	12:23 am
☽⚺♅	**3:44 am**	12:44 am
☽⚻♀	**3:54 am**	12:54 am
☿⚹♄	**7:33 am**	4:33 am
♂⚻♅	**9:44 am**	6:44 am
☽⚺♆	**12:59 pm**	9:59 am
☽□♇	**8:11 pm**	5:11 pm
☽△☉	**9:47 pm**	6:47 pm
☽△☿		9:21 pm
☽⚹♄		11:08 pm

22 FRIDAY

☽△☿	**12:21 am**	
☽⚹♄	**2:08 am**	
☽☌♃	**7:53 am**	4:53 am
☉☌☿	**1:54 pm**	10:54 am

23 SATURDAY

☽☌♅	**8:33 am**	5:33 am
☽⚻♂	**11:22 am**	8:22 am
☽☍♀	**2:04 pm**	11:04 am
☿⚺♇	**4:51 pm**	1:51 pm
☽⚹♆	**6:12 pm**	3:12 pm
☽⚻☿		9:50 pm
☽△♇		10:40 pm

24 SUNDAY

☽⚻☿	**12:50 am**	
☽△♇	**1:40 am**	
☽⚻☉	**7:38 am**	4:38 am
☽□♄	**7:58 am**	4:58 am
☉⚹♄	**12:28 pm**	9:28 am
☽⚺♃	**1:28 pm**	10:28 am

25 MONDAY

♀△♆	**12:15 pm**	9:15 am
☽⚺♅	**2:51 pm**	11:51 am
☽☍♂	**9:08 pm**	6:08 pm
☽□♆		9:57 pm
☽⚻♀		11:15 pm
☽☍☿		11:55 pm

26 TUESDAY

☽□♆	**12:57 am**	
☽⚻♀	**2:15 am**	
☽☍☿	**2:55 am**	
☿⚺♀	**6:18 am**	3:18 am
☽⚻♇	**8:45 am**	5:45 am
☽△♄	**3:30 pm**	12:30 pm
☽☍☉	**7:33 pm**	4:33 pm
☽⚹♃	**8:45 pm**	5:45 pm
☿□♆		11:43 pm

27 WEDNESDAY

☿□♆	**2:43 am**	
☉△♃	**10:28 am**	7:28 am
☿☌♂	**7:31 pm**	4:31 pm
☽⚹♅	**11:04 pm**	8:04 pm

28 THURSDAY

☽⚻☿	**7:40 am**	4:40 am
☽⚻♂	**9:17 am**	6:17 am
☽△♆	**9:45 am**	6:45 am
☽△♀	**5:12 pm**	2:12 pm
♂□♆	**5:16 pm**	2:16 pm
☽☍♇	**5:57 pm**	2:57 pm
♀⚹♇		10:01 pm
☽⚻♄		10:15 pm

29 FRIDAY

♀⚹♇	**1:01 am**	
☽⚻♄	**1:15 am**	
☽□♃	**6:18 am**	3:18 am
☽⚻☉	**10:19 am**	7:19 am

30 SATURDAY

☽□♅	**9:39 am**	6:39 am
☽△☿	**4:00 pm**	1:00 pm
☽⚻♆	**8:57 pm**	5:57 pm
☽△♂		9:18 pm

31 SUNDAY

☽△♂	**12:18 am**	
☽⚻♇	**5:34 am**	2:34 am
☽□♀	**11:23 am**	8:23 am
☽☍♄	**1:24 pm**	10:24 am
☽△♃	**6:10 pm**	3:10 pm

Eastern time in bold type
Pacific time in medium type

DECEMBER 2023

DATE	SID.TIME	SUN	MOON	NODE	MERCURY	VENUS	MARS	JUPITER	SATURN	URANUS	NEPTUNE	PLUTO	CERES	PALLAS	JUNO	VESTA	CHIRON
1 F	4 38 23	8♐30 40	21♋45	23♈54℞	29♐17	25♎34	4♐42	7♉06℞	1♓08	20♉22℞	24♓54℞	28♑30	2♐28	4♏59	15♍36	4♋39℞	15♈46℞
2 Sa	4 42 19	9 31 28	4♌05	23 48	0♑28	26 44	5 25	7 01	1 11	20 19	24 54	28 32	2 54	5 25	15 52	4 27	15 44
3 Su	4 46 16	10 32 17	16 10	23 42	1 36	27 54	6 08	6 55	1 13	20 17	24 54	28 33	3 19	5 50	16 08	4 15	15 43
4 M	4 50 13	11 33 07	28 06	23 39	2 42	29 05	6 51	6 50	1 16	20 15	24 53	28 34	3 45	6 15	16 23	4 02	15 42
5 T	4 54 9	12 33 59	9♍57	23 38D	3 44	0♏15	7 34	6 44	1 19	20 12	24 53	28 36	4 10	6 41	16 38	3 49	15 41
6 W	4 58 6	13 34 52	21 47	23 38	4 41	1 26	8 17	6 39	1 23	20 10	24 53D	28 37	4 36	7 06	16 53	3 36	15 39
7 Th	5 2 2	14 35 46	3♎42	23 39	5 34	2 36	9 01	6 34	1 26	20 08	24 53	28 39	5 01	7 31	17 07	3 22	15 38
8 F	5 5 59	15 36 41	15 48	23 41℞	6 21	3 47	9 44	6 30	1 29	20 06	24 53	28 40	5 26	7 56	17 22	3 08	15 37
9 Sa	5 9 55	16 37 38	28 08	23 41	7 02	4 58	10 27	6 25	1 33	20 04	24 53	28 42	5 52	8 21	17 36	2 54	15 36
10 Su	5 13 52	17 38 36	10♏47	23 39	7 37	6 09	11 11	6 21	1 36	20 01	24 53	28 43	6 17	8 46	17 49	2 40	15 35
11 M	5 17 48	18 39 35	23 48	23 35	8 03	7 21	11 54	6 17	1 40	19 59	24 54	28 45	6 42	9 11	18 02	2 25	15 34
12 T	5 21 45	19 40 36	7♐12	23 29	8 21	8 32	12 38	6 13	1 43	19 57	24 54	28 47	7 08	9 36	18 15	2 10	15 33
13 W	5 25 42	20 41 37	20 57	23 20	8 29℞	9 43	13 21	6 09	1 47	19 55	24 54	28 48	7 33	10 00	18 28	1 55	15 33
14 Th	5 29 38	21 42 39	4♑59	23 10	8 27	10 55	14 05	6 05	1 51	19 53	24 54	28 50	7 58	10 25	18 40	1 40	15 32
15 F	5 33 35	22 43 42	19 15	23 00	8 14	12 07	14 49	6 02	1 55	19 51	24 55	28 51	8 24	10 50	18 52	1 25	15 31
16 Sa	5 37 31	23 44 45	3♒39	22 51	7 49	13 18	15 33	5 59	1 59	19 49	24 55	28 53	8 49	11 14	19 04	1 09	15 31
17 Su	5 41 28	24 45 49	18 03	22 44	7 13	14 30	16 16	5 56	2 03	19 47	24 55	28 55	9 14	11 39	19 15	0 54	15 30
18 M	5 45 24	25 46 53	2♓24	22 39	6 25	15 42	17 00	5 53	2 07	19 45	24 56	28 56	9 39	12 03	19 26	0 38	15 29
19 T	5 49 21	26 47 57	16 38	22 36D	5 27	16 54	17 44	5 50	2 12	19 44	24 56	28 58	10 04	12 27	19 36	0 22	15 29
20 W	5 53 17	27 49 02	0♈43	22 36	4 19	18 06	18 28	5 48	2 16	19 42	24 56	29 00	10 29	12 51	19 46	0 07	15 29
21 Th	5 57 14	28 50 07	14 38	22 37℞	3 04	19 18	19 12	5 45	2 21	19 40	24 57	29 02	10 54	13 15	19 56	29♊51	15 28
22 F	6 1 11	29 51 12	28 23	22 37	1 44	20 30	19 56	5 43	2 25	19 38	24 57	29 03	11 19	13 39	20 06	29 35	15 28
23 Sa	6 5 7	0♑52 18	11♉59	22 35	0 22	21 43	20 40	5 42	2 30	19 37	24 58	29 05	11 44	14 03	20 15	29 19	15 28
24 Su	6 9 4	1 53 24	25 25	22 31	28♐59	22 55	21 24	5 40	2 34	19 35	24 59	29 07	12 09	14 27	20 23	29 03	15 27
25 M	6 13 0	2 54 30	8♊42	22 24	27 40	24 08	22 08	5 39	2 39	19 33	24 59	29 09	12 34	14 51	20 32	28 47	15 27
26 T	6 16 57	3 55 36	21 47	22 14	26 27	25 20	22 52	5 38	2 44	19 32	25 00	29 10	12 59	15 14	20 40	28 32	15 27
27 W	6 20 53	4 56 43	4♋40	22 01	25 20	26 33	23 37	5 37	2 49	19 30	25 01	29 12	13 23	15 38	20 47	28 16	15 27D
28 Th	6 24 50	5 57 50	17 21	21 48	24 23	27 45	24 21	5 36	2 54	19 29	25 01	29 14	13 48	16 01	20 54	28 00	15 27
29 F	6 28 47	6 58 57	29 48	21 35	23 36	28 58	25 05	5 35	2 59	19 27	25 02	29 16	14 13	16 25	21 01	27 45	15 27
30 Sa	6 32 43	8 00 04	12♌02	21 22	22 59	0♐11	25 50	5 35	3 04	19 26	25 03	29 18	14 37	16 48	21 08	27 30	15 27
31 Su	6 36 40	9 01 12	24 05	21 12	22 33	1 24	26 34	5 35D	3 09	19 24	25 04	29 20	15 02	17 11	21 14	27 15	15 28

EPHEMERIS CALCULATED FOR 12 MIDNIGHT GREENWICH MEAN TIME. ALL OTHER DATA AND FACING ASPECTARIAN PAGE IN **EASTERN TIME (BOLD)** AND PACIFIC TIME (REGULAR).

Notes